FORCED
Founders

INDIANS,

DEBTORS, SLAVES,

AND THE MAKING

OF THE AMERICAN

REVOLUTION IN

VIRGINIA

Forced
Founders

Woody Holton

Published for the
Omohundro Institute of Early
American History and Culture,
Williamsburg, Virginia, by the
University of North Carolina Press,
Chapel Hill and London

The Omohundro Institute of Early American
History and Culture is sponsored jointly by the
College of William and Mary and the Colonial
Williamsburg Foundation. On November 15, 1996,
the Institute adopted the present name in honor
of a bequest from Malvern H. Omohundro, Jr.

© 1999
The University of North Carolina Press
All rights reserved
Set in Minion type by Keystone Typesetting, Inc.
Manufactured in the United States of America
Library of Congress Cataloging-in-Publication Data
Holton, Woody.
Forced founders : Indians, debtors, slaves, and the making of the
American Revolution in Virginia / Woody Holton.
    p.   cm.
Includes bibliographical references and index.
ISBN 0-8078-2501-8 (alk. paper) —
ISBN 0-8078-4784-4 (pbk.: alk. paper)
1. United States—History—Revolution, 1775–1783—Causes.
2. United States—History—Revolution, 1775–1783—Social aspects.
3. Virginia—History—Revolution, 1775–1783.   4. Virginia—Social
conditions—18th century.   5. Gentry—Virginia—History—18th
century.   6. Social classes—Virginia—History—18th century.
I. Omohundro Institute of Early American History & Culture.
II. Title.
E210.H695   1999
973.3′11—dc21   98-51937
                CIP

The paper in this book meets the guidelines for permanence
and durability of the Committee on Production Guidelines for
Book Longevity of the Council on Library Resources.

03   02   01   00   99   5   4   3   2   1

FOR MY PARENTS

ACKNOWLEDGMENTS

I want to thank the people that made this book possible.

I am grateful to the staffs of the following institutions for their help in locating and using books and manuscripts in their care: the Special Collections Department of Alderman Library at the University of Virginia, the Alexandria, Virginia, Public Library, the Christ Church Foundation library, Clements Library at the University of Michigan (especially Rob Cox, now of the American Philosophical Society), the Glasgow County Archives, the Historical Society of Pennsylvania, Houghton Library at Harvard University, the Archives Research Room at the Library of Virginia (especially Minor T. Weisiger), the archives department of the Library of Congress (especially Jeffrey M. Flannery), the Maryland Hall of Records, the Massachusetts Historical Society, the New-York Historical Society, the John D. Rockefeller, Jr., Library at Colonial Williamsburg (especially Liz Eckert), the Southern Historical Collection at the University of North Carolina, the archives department of Swem Library at the College of William and Mary, the Virginia Baptist Historical Society, and Virginia county courthouses (Augusta, Bedford, Frederick).

I would like to thank the following individuals and institutions for advancing this project in a variety of ways: the Bloomsburg University History Department, the Boston Public Library interlibrary loan office, the Cambridge, Massachusetts, Public Library interlibrary loan office, Elisabeth and Robert Carter, Dan Clark, Greg Crider, the Duke University History Department (especially for the T. Malcolm Carroll fellowship), Brandee E. Faust, Mary K. Geiter, Susan E. Hurley, Richard F. Neel, Jr., the late Alice C. Rogers, Beverly Sensbach, Werner Sensbach, the Virginia Foundation for the Humanities and Public Policy (for the fellowship and for the useful suggestions of seminar participants), the Virginia Historical Society (for the Mellon fellowships, for the useful suggestions at a Society seminar, and for Frances Pollard's unerring guidance), and Mary Ellen Zeisloft.

The following people read portions of the manuscript and offered helpful suggestions, most of which I have used: Suzanne Adelman, David Ammerman, Sara Bearss, Staige D. Blackford, T. H. Breen, Kevin Butterfield, Barbara DeWolfe, Gregory E. Dowd, Richard Durschlag, Emory G. Evans, Paul M. Gaston, John M. Hemphill, Jr., Warren Hofstra, Francis Jennings, Tom Jordan, Staughton Lynd, Turk McCleskey, Michael N. McConnell, James Merrell, Robert Nelson, Michael Lee Nicholls, Evelyn Thomas Nolen, Sanford M. Pooler, Jr., Bruce A. Ragsdale, Julie Richter, Sharon M. Sauder, John E. Selby, Robert Shaposka, W. A. Speck, Sarah Stroud, Alan Taylor, and Anthony F. C. Wallace.

Several groups in addition to some of those already mentioned allowed me to describe certain aspects of the project and then offered useful suggestions: the American History Seminar at Cambridge University, the American Studies Department at the University of Wales, Swansea, the Bloomsburg University Social Studies Club, participants in the National Women's Studies Association Mid-Atlantic Conference (1997), the Roanoke Valley Historical Society, and the Southern History Seminar at the University of Virginia.

A small group of editors made improvements to every chapter of the manuscript. I want to thank Fred Anderson, M. Kathryn Burdette, Edward Countryman, John d'Entremont, Lawrence Goodwyn, Lisa D. Hammond, Ronald Hoffman, James Horn, Joseph Jones, Laura Jones, John M. Murrin, an anonymous outside reviewer for the Omohundro Institute of Early American History and Culture, Julius Scott, Brent Tarter, Thad W. Tate, and especially Fredrika J. Teute.

A few people made extraordinary contributions to the book, and I want to express my appreciation to them. Thank you, the Holton family, Marjoleine Kars (whose successful effort to recover the world of the North Carolina Regulators inspired me to try to do the same with various Virginians), Michael A. McDonnell (whose forthcoming book is much more than a sequel to *Forced Founders*), and Jon F. Sensbach (who is as good a friend as he is a writer). My most enthusiastic thanks go to Peter H. Wood, who put more work into this book than anyone but the author and more wisdom into it than anyone.

CONTENTS

ILLUSTRATIONS

ABBREVIATIONS

CWF
    Colonial Williamsburg Foundation library

Duke
    Manuscripts Department, Perkins Library, Duke University, Durham,
    N.C.

Houghton
    Houghton Library, Harvard University

JHB
    John Pendleton Kennedy, ed., *Journal of the House of Burgesses of*
    Virginia . . . Including the Records of the Committee of Correspondence
    (Richmond, Va., 1905–1915)

JNH
    Journal of Negro History

JSH
    Journal of Southern History

LC
    Library of Congress

LVA
    Library of Virginia, Richmond

MHM
    Maryland Historical Magazine

Revolutionary Virginia
    William J. Van Schreeven, Robert L. Scribner, and Brent Tarter, eds.,
    Revolutionary Virginia: The Road to Independence ([Charlottesville, Va.,]
    1973–1983)

SAL
   William Waller Hening, [ed.], *The Statutes at Large; Being a Collection of All the Laws of Virginia* . . . (Richmond, Va., 1819–1823)
UVA
   Special Collections Department, Alderman Library, University of Virginia, Charlottesville, Va.
VCRP
   Virginia Colonial Records Project microfilm
VG
   Virginia Gazette
VHS
   Virginia Historical Society
VMHB
   Virginia Magazine of History and Biography
William and Mary
   Archives Department, Earl Gregg Swem Library, College of William and Mary, Williamsburg, Va.
WMQ
   William and Mary Quarterly

INTRODUCTION

Americans tend to think of the Virginia gentry, the colonial elite that gave us Thomas Jefferson and George Washington, as a proud and optimistic ruling class. They do not imagine gentlemen resorting to desperate measures such as crashing down the gates of prisons or placing weapons in the hands of slaves. But, in April 1774, Jacob Hite, one of the wealthiest men in Berkeley County, Virginia, did both of those things, and more. The desperation experienced by men like Hite—and, to a surprising extent, by men like Jefferson and Washington as well—helped drive them into the American Revolution. Since they took Britain's largest American colony with them, anyone interested in the origins of the Independence movement needs to understand why they felt so desperate.

Hite was the son of a highly successful Shenandoah Valley land speculator and had hoped to replicate his father's success farther west.[1] In the late 1760s, he and his business partner Richard Pearis contrived a way to obtain a large tract of land from the Cherokee Indians. Pearis had a son, George, by a Cherokee woman. Métis like George Pearis were viewed by Cherokee headmen as useful diplomatic bridges to British America whose interests should be promoted; so, when George asked headmen for a 150,000-acre tract just west of South Carolina, they gave it to him. George Pearis then sold the land to his father and Jacob Hite. It was a clever scheme, but a British official feared that it might provoke the Cherokees to join an anti-British confedera-

---

1. Warren R. Hofstra, "Land Policy and Settlement in the Northern Shenandoah Valley," in Robert D. Mitchell, ed., *Appalachian Frontiers: Settlement, Society, and Development in the Preindustrial Era* (Lexington, Ky., 1991), 107–108.

tion that Indian diplomats were just then assembling. He persuaded a South Carolina court to void the deal.[2]

The revocation of the Cherokee deed left Jacob Hite with no way to pay a £1,600 debt to James Hunter, a Scottish trader in Fredericksburg. Hunter, who was feeling pressure from his own creditors in England, sued, won, and in 1773 demanded that Berkeley County sheriff Adam Stephen auction off enough of Hite's property to pay the debt. For Hite, Hunter's demand could not have come at a worse time. By the fall of 1773, the price of tobacco had sunk to one of its lowest levels ever. Even in the Shenandoah Valley, where Jacob Hite lived and where little tobacco was grown, the credit market collapsed, and the price of most everything farmers produced and owned plummeted.[3] During that period of cash scarcity and deflation, the liquidation of Hite's debt to Hunter would require the sale of a large portion of his property. He would be ruined. Hite managed to fend off Sheriff Stephen for a year, but, on April 12, 1774, the sheriff seized fifteen of Hite's slaves and twenty-one of his horses and took them to Martinsburg, the county seat. He locked the slaves in the county jail and the horses in the jailer's stable, and then he announced an auction.

Hite had to think fast. On Thursday morning, April 14, his son Thomas and a gang of men armed with "Guns Swords Pistols and Axes" advanced on Martinsburg. Sheriff Stephen deputized several men and directed them to guard Jacob Hite's slaves and horses. But Thomas Hite's gang surrounded the jail, overpowered the guards, broke down the doors of the jail and the stable, and seized the slaves and horses. The gang also freed Murty Handley, a smallholder that had been imprisoned for debt, and another person that had been jailed on suspicion of being a runaway servant. The group captured two of the prison guards, tied them up, and confined them, along with the slaves, at Jacob Hite's house. Later that day, Hite got word that Sheriff Stephen's posse was about to attack. If the sheriff achieved his purpose of selling Hite's horses and slaves, the worst victims would be the slaves them-

2. Pearis later managed to revive the claim. See John Richard Alden, *John Stuart and the Southern Colonial Frontier: A Study of Indian Relations, War, Trade, and Land Problems in the Southern Wilderness, 1754–1775* (Ann Arbor, Mich., 1944), 299–300; Tom Hatley, *The Dividing Paths: Cherokees and South Carolinians through the Era of Revolution* (New York, 1993), 207–208; J. Russell Snapp, *John Stuart and the Struggle for Empire on the Southern Frontier* (Baton Rouge, 1996), 41. Snapp shows that other southern elites also resented imperial obstruction of their efforts to acquire Indian land.

3. Thomas Jett to John Backhouse, July 19, 1773, to Frances Ward, July 23, 1773, Jett Letterbook, Jerdone Papers, William and Mary; R. Walter Coakley, "The Two James Hunters of Fredericksburg: Patriots among the Virginia Scotch Merchants," *VMHB*, LVI (1948), 10–13; Robert Pleasants to brother, Aug. 28, 1773, Robert Pleasants Letterbook, LC.

selves, since their families would probably be divided forever. Recognizing that he and his slaves had a common interest in preventing their sale—and desperately needing more fighters—"Hite went into the Kitchen where his Negroes were, and told them to follow up the White men and upon the first gun that was fired to rush in with what weapons they had and to do what they cou'd but to take care not to hurt their own men," one of Hite's white supporters later reported. Hite's slaves never got the chance to test their mettle against the sheriff's posse, since its attack was delayed long enough for Hite to start them south down the Great Wagon Road toward his illegal settlement in Cherokee country. Along the road, at least some of Hite's enslaved workers were captured, and later they were sold at auction.[4]

The conflict did not end there. Hite sued the men in Sheriff Stephen's posse, and the deputies feared that the jury would side with Hite, "it being too general a wish among the people to evade the payment of their Debts and render the authority of [court] Judgments . . . of none effect." The widespread wish to prevent the enforcement of court judgments against Virginia debtors became a troubling "Subject of Conversation" in Williamsburg, the provincial capital, but, as it turned out, the wish was soon to be granted.[5] In June 1774, less than two months after Hite's gang broke open the Berkeley County jail, Virginia courts began to refuse to try suits brought by creditors against debtors. The courts closed partly to protest Parliament's assault on American liberty and partly to prevent creditors from depriving debtors such as Hite and Handley of their property and freedom.

The Hite gang's assault on the Berkeley County jail raises questions about the elite Virginians that led Britain's largest North American colony into the Revolution. Jacob Hite clearly was a desperate man. Did a similar sense of desperation overcome other gentlemen on the eve of the Revolution? Our tendency is to answer, No. Men like George Washington, Thomas Jefferson,

4. Alexander [Dromgoole] and David Gilkey, depositions, Apr. 16, 1774 (photocopies), Adam Stephen Papers, LVA; Adam Stephen, letter, Dixon and Hunter's *VG*, Sept. 30, 1775. The Berkeley County court found Thomas Hite and six other men innocent of felony (a capital charge) but "Guilty of a Breach of the Peace." It required each of them to post a peace bond (May 7, 1774, Berkeley County court, minute book [microfilm, Church of Jesus Christ of Latter-day Saints Archives, Genealogical Department, Salt Lake City, Utah]).

5. John Mercer to Adam Stephen, Apr. 19, 1774, [John Mercer?] to [Adam Stephen], June 10, 1774, "The Petition," [May 1774], all in Stephen Papers, LVA. Hite's battle against Sheriff Stephen's posse "nearly brought on a minor civil war." See Freeman H. Hart, *The Valley of Virginia in the American Revolution, 1763–1789* (Chapel Hill, N.C., 1942), 24n, 56–57; Harry M. Ward, *Major General Adam Stephen and the Cause of American Liberty* (Charlottesville, Va., 1989), 104–106, 125–127.

and Patrick Henry live in the American memory as the proud exemplars of a supremely confident gentry class. Historians have long assumed it was that very confidence that emboldened Virginia gentlemen to lead their colony— and twelve of her sisters—out of the British Empire.

The gentry's self-assurance, we are told, rested on a firm foundation: gentlemen such as Washington and Jefferson "exercised almost unchallenged hegemony" over other classes in the province. They had established authority over the poorest 40 percent of Virginians by enslaving them.[6] Native Americans might slow, but they could not halt, the colony's westward advance. Even the gentry's relationship with British merchants, about which Jefferson and others frequently complained, has been presented in modern scholarship as more beneficial to gentlemen than they were willing to admit. Their British "friends"—for such they called them in their correspondence— marketed their tobacco, filled their invoices by making the rounds of the London tradesmen, and even loaned them money.

From that viewpoint, the key to the Virginia gentlemen's secure position at the top of the social pyramid was their remarkably cordial relationship with small farmers. Elsewhere in eighteenth-century America—in the Hudson Valley, with its vast landed estates, in both Carolinas, and especially in the great northern seaports—elites often seemed besieged by farmers, tenants, artisans, and sailors. But the Virginia gentleman that consorted with his lower-class neighbors was greeted with deference, historians tell us. The gentry and smallholder classes were united by their mutual interest in growing tobacco and in controlling slaves and women.[7] Altogether, with the help

6. "The blacks' cultural disorientation made them less difficult to control than the white servants." See T. H. Breen, *Puritans and Adventurers: Change and Persistence in Early America* (New York, 1980), 150; Edmund S. Morgan, *American Slavery, American Freedom: The Ordeal of Colonial Virginia* (New York, 1975), 380–381; Samuel M. Rosenblatt, "The Significance of Credit in the Tobacco Consignment Trade: A Study of John Norton and Sons, 1768–1775," *WMQ*, 3d Ser., XIX (1962), 383–399; Jacob M. Price, *Capital and Credit in British Overseas Trade: The View from the Chesapeake, 1700–1776* (Cambridge, Mass., 1980), 16–19.

7. On South Carolina, see Rachel N. Klein, *Unification of a Slave State: The Rise of the Planter Class in the South Carolina Backcountry, 1760–1808* (Chapel Hill, N.C., 1990); Joyce E. Chaplin, *An Anxious Pursuit: Agricultural Innovation and Modernity in the Lower South, 1730–1815* (Chapel Hill, N.C., 1993). On North Carolina, see Marjoleine Kars, " 'Breaking Loose Together': Religion and Rebellion in the North Carolina Piedmont, 1730– 1790" (Ph.D. diss., Duke University, 1994); Marvin L. Michael Kay, "The North Carolina Regulation, 1766–1776: A Class Conflict," in Alfred F. Young, ed., *The American Revolution: Explorations in the History of American Radicalism* (DeKalb, Ill., 1976), 71–123. On Maryland, see Ronald Hoffman, *A Spirit of Dissension: Economics, Politics, and the Revolution in Maryland* (Baltimore, 1973). On Philadelphia, see Richard Alan Ryerson, *The Revolution is*

of his junior partners among the yeomanry, the Virginia gentleman seems to have controlled the movements of Indians, merchants, slaves, and small-holders almost as if they were puppets. Little wonder, then, that gentlemen felt secure enough to take the Old Dominion into the American Revolution.

Starting in the 1960s, those two notions—that the gentry was brimming with confidence, and that it was in complete control of its relations with Indians, smallholders, slaves, and even British merchants—were challenged. Some historians found that the gentry's confidence was laced with anxiety.[8] Others have shown that, although the old image of gentlemen exerting enormous influence over those groups was not false, none of them was the gentry's puppet. In fact, each had its own ability to pull strings. One arena in which they powerfully influenced gentlemen was imperial politics. In complex ways and without intending to, Indians, merchants, and slaves helped drive gentlemen like Jacob Hite and smallholders like Murty Handley into the rebellion against Britain. In addition, small farmers exerted direct and deliberate pro-Independence pressure upon gentlemen.

That particular web of influences helping to push Virginia into the War of Independence is the subject of this work. From 1763 to 1776, Indians, mer-

---

Now Begun: The Radical Committees of Philadelphia, 1765–1776 (Philadelphia, 1978). On New York, see Edward Countryman, *A People in Revolution: The American Revolution and Political Society in New York, 1760–1790* (Baltimore, 1981); Staughton Lynd, *Anti-Federalism in Dutchess County, New York: A Study of Democracy and Class Conflict in the Revolutionary Era* (Chicago, 1962). On Boston, see Barbara Clark Smith, "Food Rioters and the American Revolution," *WMQ*, 3d Ser., LI (1994), 3–38; Dirk Hoerder, *Crowd Action in Revolutionary Massachusetts, 1765–1780* (New York, 1977). On all three northern seaports, see Gary B. Nash, *The Urban Crucible: Social Change, Political Consciousness, and the Origins of the American Revolution* (Cambridge, Mass., 1979); Morgan, *American Slavery, American Freedom*, chap. 18; Edward Countryman, *Americans: A Collision of Histories* (New York, 1996), 16; Jack P. Greene, *Pursuits of Happiness: The Social Development of Early Modern British Colonies and the Formation of American Culture* (Chapel Hill, N.C., 1988), 94; Pauline Maier, *The Old Revolutionaries: Political Lives in the Age of Samuel Adams* (New York, 1980), 182.

8. According to Bernard Bailyn, elite Americans of the eighteenth century "looked ahead with anxiety rather than with confidence" (*The Ideological Origins of the American Revolution* [Cambridge, Mass., 1967], 79). Jack P. Greene has noted the Virginia gentry's "peculiar combination of anxiety and confidence" ("Society, Ideology, and Politics: An Analysis of the Political Culture of Mid-Eighteenth-Century Virginia," in Greene, Richard L. Bushman, and Michael Kammen, *Society, Freedom, and Conscience: The American Revolution in Virginia, Massachusetts, and New York*, ed. Richard M. Jellison [New York, 1976], 76). Kathleen M. Brown notes that "Virginia's elite planters were never able to allay self-doubts about the security and legitimacy of their position" (*Good Wives, Nasty Wenches, and Anxious Patriarchs: Gender, Race, and Power in Colonial Virginia* [Chapel Hill, N.C., 1996], 319, 365). See also Gordon S. Wood, "Rhetoric and Reality in the American Revolution," *WMQ*, 3d Ser., XXIII (1966), 3–32.

chants, slaves, and debtors helped propel free Virginians into the Independence movement in three distinct ways. First, the free Virginians' efforts to influence imperial policy were contested by Native Americans, British merchants, and enslaved Virginians. The elimination of the government as an instrument or ally of merchants, Indians, and slaves was one reason for white Virginians to rebel against Britain. Second, free Virginians were attracted to the most important resistance strategy of the prewar period—the commercial boycott against Britain—because it seemed likely not only to impel Parliament to repeal laws considered oppressive by white Americans but also to reduce the Virginians' debts to British merchants. Third, the thoroughgoing boycott adopted by the First Continental Congress in October 1774 transformed Virginia's society and economy in unexpected ways. It presented opportunities to enslaved Virginians and put extraordinary pressure upon the colony's small farmers. In responding to those opportunities and pressures, slaves and farmers challenged the authority of the provincial gentry. Those challenges indirectly helped induce gentlemen to turn the protests of 1774 into the Independence movement of 1776.

Who were the members of the pre-Revolutionary gentry? And how was the gentry related to other groups within and beyond Virginia? The two questions call forth the same answer, since it was the gentry's relations with Indians, British merchants, slaves, and smallholders that defined it as a class. Satirist James Reid declared in the 1760s that a Virginian qualified as a gentleman as soon as he acquired "Money, Negroes and Land enough." Other definitions of the gentry would isolate essentially the same people. Gentlemen sat in the House of Burgesses, on the Executive Council, and on the benches of the county courts. Although nearly half of white Virginians owned one or two field slaves, almost all of the domestic slaves—along with most of the brick houses, imported luxuries like books, and the most fertile tidewater lands—were owned by members of the gentry. Gentlemen and gentlewomen were the wealthiest 10 percent of free Virginians; they owned one-half of Virginia's property.[9] Most Virginia tobacco growers sold their crops in the colony, but gentlemen consigned theirs to British merchants.

9. James Reid, in Greene, "Society, Ideology, and Politics," in Greene, Bushman, and Kammen, *Society, Freedom, and Conscience*, ed. Jellison, 15; John E. Selby, *The Revolution in Virginia, 1775–1783* (Charlottesville, Va., 1988), 24; Allan Kulikoff, *Tobacco and Slaves: The Development of Southern Cultures in the Chesapeake, 1680–1800* (Chapel Hill, N.C., 1986), 262; Herbert Sloan and Peter Onuf, "Politics, Culture, and the Revolution in Virginia: A Review of Recent Work," *VMHB*, XCI (1983), 269. Many scholars have followed Jack P. Greene in defining the gentry culturally. See Greene, "Society, Ideology, and Politics," 18; T. H. Breen, *Tobacco Culture: The Mentality of the Great Tidewater Planters on the Eve of Revolution* (Princeton, N.J., 1985), 36.

Although all of those definitions of the gentry are useful, none is as precise as James Reid's; he knew that what set elite Virginians apart was not simply the amount of property they owned but also the type. Reid's "Money, Negroes and land" were essentially the factors of production: capital, labor, and land. Gentlemen struggled for control of each factor against other groups—against British merchants over capital, against agricultural workers (both enslaved and free) over the fruits of their labor, and against Indians over their land.

Just as the gentry was defined as a class by its relations with Indians, merchants, and free and enslaved laboring-class Virginians, those other groups may be defined in relation to the gentry. Gentry-Indian relations underwent a major transformation after 1750, when free Virginians began to covet the land west of the Appalachian Mountains. That was the fruitful hunting territory of the Upper Ohio nations—principally the Mingos, Shawnees, and Delawares. The Upper Ohioans' most fertile territory beyond the mountains, Kentucky, was also the hunting land of the Cherokees. Although Cherokees and Upper Ohioans disagreed about who owned Kentucky, they agreed that Britain did not. When Virginia land speculators began staking claims to Kentucky, they courted conflicts with settlers, Indians, and British bureaucrats.

Another group that came into conflict with the gentry, and with small-holders as well, comprised the tobacco merchants of England and Scotland. By the time of the American Revolution, tobacco growers large and small owed huge debts to the British merchants; during the preceding century, Virginia's per capita debt had nearly doubled.[10] Growers blamed their debts partly on the Navigation Acts, which gave British merchants a monopoly of their trade. Although by the 1760s free Virginians had submitted to the Navigation Acts for more than a century, they deeply resented them, and they resolutely refused to endure any additional burden. When the British government tried to impose just such a new burden—taxes—the Americans were irate. The conflict between Virginia debtors and British merchant-creditors aggravated the imperial struggle in another way as well: it was partly to reduce their debts to British merchants that free Virginians participated in the patriotic nonimportation and nonexportation associations.

The eighteenth-century tobacco trade was complex, and, in order to be clear at all times about what type of merchant I am referring to, I make some

10. As a proportion of its annual imports from Britain, Virginia's debt load had nearly tripled between 1664 and 1776. See Price, *Capital and Credit*, 13–14; Robert E. Brown and B. Katherine Brown, *Virginia, 1705–1786: Democracy or Aristocracy?* (East Lansing, Mich., 1964), 97.

distinctions between the word *merchants* and its synonyms that eighteenth-century Virginians would not have recognized. The mercantile firms and transatlantic slave traders in Glasgow, London, and other British ports will be called *merchants*. The employees of those merchants that were located in the Chesapeake will be denoted *storekeepers* or *factors*. Such employees may be distinguished from a third group, independent Virginia entrepreneurs, who shall be designated *traders*.

Another relationship that changed radically in the eighteenth century was that between slaveowners and the people they owned. The enslaved portion of Virginia's population grew from less than 9 percent at the turn of the century to 40 percent in 1775, by which time an estimated 186,000 Virginians were black. Natural increase, which had begun by 1730, was good news for slaveowners not only financially but also because it allowed the House of Burgesses to exclude the workers that were considered most dangerous, newly enslaved Africans, from the province. But if Afro-Virginia demography worked in the slaveholders' favor, British politics did not. When the House of Burgesses tried to impose prohibitive duties on every African brought to Virginia, British merchants persuaded the Privy Council (Britain's executive body) to veto the duties. Where, in other cases, the power that merchants wielded over the London government hurt gentry Virginians financially, here—in combination with the threat that slaves posed—it also endangered their lives. The lure of political independence grew as a consequence.

Starting in late 1774, enslaved Virginians did even more to hasten the growth of patriotic sentiment. By drawing the last royal governor into an alliance with them, freedom-seeking Afro-Virginians helped estrange white Virginians from the royal government and prepare them for Independence.

So far, this summary of political and social relations in pre-Revolutionary Virginia has focused on gentlemen and taken note of areas, such as the conflict against enslaved Virginians, where the interests of the gentry converged with those of smallholders. Actually, one of the most important relationships in the colony was that between gentlemen and smallholders. Among an estimated 280,000 white Virginians in 1775, no more than 10 percent were gentlemen; perhaps another 10 percent were artisans, traders, and overseers of slaves. That leaves well over 200,000 people in the yeomanry. Small farmers came under tremendous pressure in 1775, when the nonexportation provisions of the Continental Association deprived them of their export income and nonimportation subjected them to severe shortages. Those pressures drew forth an agrarian response that, in complex ways, contributed to the gentry's decision to make a formal declaration of Independence.[11]

Here another descriptive distinction needs to be made. Eighteenth-century Virginians sometimes applied the term *planters* to small-scale tobacco growers; at other times it meant everyone that grew tobacco, including gentlemen. By the middle of the nineteenth century, census takers would introduce yet another definition of *planters*; they were people that owned twenty or more slaves. In order to avoid all that confusion, this book eschews the term *planters* altogether (except in quotations). Instead, *gentlemen* will be distinguished from *small farmers* (also called *smallholders*). On many of the issues discussed here, the interests of smallholders were similar to those of long-term tenants, so for brevity's sake *smallholders* must be stretched to include both groups. On occasions when the interests of tobacco-growing smallholders and gentlemen converged, I will refer to the two groups together as *tobacco growers*.

Since this work argues that nonelites powerfully influenced Revolutionary politics, the reader may well ask how it is possible to know very much about those people when the majority of them could not write and the few that could left few records. I did not find using gentry sources to study nongentlemen as difficult as I had feared, for it quickly became obvious that gentlemen were very interested in the actions of Indians, slaves, and smallholders (as well as British merchants, who left plenty of records of their own). To cite only one example, even in July 1776, Landon Carter showed less interest in imperial affairs than in recovering a group of slaves that had escaped his custody.[12] To be sure, nonelites often deceived elites, and elites' biases often distorted their reporting. But if used with care, top-down sources can in fact be effectively used for bottom-up history.

It seems wise to underscore at the outset that this book is rather narrowly focused. Although I suspect that elite patriots in other colonies were influenced by nonelites just as much as Virginia gentlemen were, this work is only about the Old Dominion. It is not a comprehensive social history of pre-Revolutionary Virginia but a study of some (not all) of the causes (not the effects) of Virginia's Revolution. The story told here reveals that, when Virginia gentlemen launched their struggle to preserve and extend their freedom, they were powerfully influenced by other freedom struggles—movements put together by Indians, debtors, merchants, slaves, and smallholders.

11. Peter H. Wood, "The Changing Population of the Colonial South: An Overview by Race and Region, 1685–1790," in Wood, Gregory A. Waselkov, and M. Thomas Hatley, eds., *Powhatan's Mantle: Indians in the Colonial Southeast* (Lincoln, Nebr., 1989), 38.

12. Jack P. Greene, ed., *The Diary of Colonel Landon Carter of Sabine Hall, 1752–1778*, II (Charlottesville, Va., 1965), 1052–1066.

PART ONE : GRIEVANCES

1763–1774

He has endeavoured to
prevent the Population of
these States; for that Purpose . . .
raising the Conditions of new
Appropriations of Lands.
—Declaration of Independence

I

LAND SPECULATORS

VERSUS INDIANS AND

THE PRIVY COUNCIL

During the winter of 1768–1769, Thomas Jefferson set about obtaining government patents for seven thousand acres of land to the west of the Appalachian Mountains. Jefferson actually had no plans to move west. About the time of his birth in 1743, however, a wave of westward expansion had breached the Blue Ridge Mountains of Virginia and joined another wave sweeping south along the Shenandoah Valley from Pennsylvania. By 1769, frontier families were already moving west of the Appalachians. Jefferson knew that, as soon as he could obtain his land patents and divide them into farmsteads of about two hundred acres each, he would find numerous customers for them.[1]

Jefferson's hunger for western wealth was shared by other Virginia gentlemen. George Washington recognized that "the greatest Estates we have in this Colony were made . . . by taking up and purchasing at very low rates the rich back Lands which were thought nothing of in those days, but are now the most valuable Lands we possess." Washington gazed with equal parts

---

1. William P. Palmer, ed., *Calendar of Virginia State Papers and Other Manuscripts*, I, *1652–1781* (Richmond, Va., 1875), 262 (hereafter cited as *CVSP*); Thomas Nelson et al. and George Rogers et al., petitions for land [1768–1769], Virginia Colonial Papers, folder 47, LVA; Feb. 18, 1769, Nov. 29, 1773, in James A. Bear, Jr., and Lucia C. Stanton, eds., *Jefferson's Memorandum Books: Accounts, with Legal Records and Miscellany, 1767–1826* (Princeton, N.J., 1997), I, 138–139, 350, *The Papers of Thomas Jefferson*, 2d Ser.

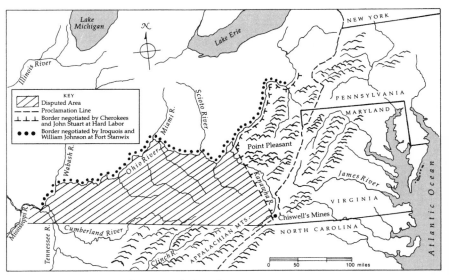

FIGURE 1. Conflicting Indian Boundaries of 1768.
Drawn by Richard Stinely (based on a map by Werner Sensbach)

envy and admiration toward the Shenandoah Valley, where "the Hite's and [other] first takers up of those Lands" had made "Fortunes."[2]

The ability of gentlemen such as Jefferson and Washington to profit from the sale of western land depended not only upon their entrepreneurial skills but also upon their political influence. In October 1768, shortly before Jefferson began applying for his western grants, the Cherokee Indians negotiated a treaty with the British government in which they retained every acre that Jefferson claimed. The agreement (known as the Treaty of Hard Labor) also interfered with Washington's land speculation, so it was evidently with some enthusiasm that the owners of Mount Vernon and Monticello joined every other member of the Virginia House of Burgesses in asking the imperial government to revoke it. The burgesses' petition, adopted in December 1769, asked London's permission for Virginia to annex Kentucky and all of the land north to the mouth of the Kanawha River.[3] The government's response

2. George Washington to John Posey, June 24, 1767, in W. W. Abbot et al., eds., *The Papers of George Washington*, Colonial Series (Charlottesville, Va., 1983–), VIII, 3; Philip Alexander Bruce, *Virginia: Rebirth of the Old Dominion*, I (Chicago, 1929), 343; David Alan Williams, "Political Alignments in Colonial Virginia Politics, 1698–1750" (Ph.D. diss., Northwestern University, 1959), 329; Turk McCleskey, "Rich Land, Poor Prospects: Real Estate and the Formation of a Social Elite in Augusta County, Virginia, 1738–1770," *VMHB*, XCVIII (1990), 449–486.

3. House of Burgesses, memorial to Botetourt, Dec. 13, 1769, *JHB, 1766–1769*, 335–336.

to the burgesses' petition would powerfully influence the financial standings of gentlemen like Jefferson and Washington. Ultimately, it would also affect their allegiance to Britain (see Figure 1).

The fate of the House of Burgesses' petition rested with British officials whose visions of the west incorporated the Indians that lived there. In the 1760s, Kentucky was the principal hunting ground both for the Cherokees (about 7,200 people) and for the Upper Ohio Valley nations: the Mingos (600), Shawnees (1,800), and Delawares (3,500). As one Cherokee put it in 1775, Indians "looked upon their Cattle or Game in [Kentucky] to be as beneficial to them as the tame Cattle were to the white People." Peltry was vital to these nations not only in itself but also as a cash crop, for they imported a higher percentage of their clothing and tools than many back-country whites. Indeed, long before Europeans arrived in North America, hunters there had known that they could rise in status by achieving success as traders. After America's commercial network was linked to Europe's, successful trading became increasingly important to Indian men's identity. One Cherokee, Old Hop, told a visiting European that a fresh supply of red cloth would enable him "to appear like a man."[4]

The reason that the Indians' desire to preserve their Kentucky hunting territory attracted the attention of imperial officials in London was not that officials felt any moral obligation to the Indians, nor even that they were determined to maintain the flow of deerskins into British ports. What did worry statesmen in the mother country was the likelihood that, if Virginians occupied Kentucky, Indians would attack them, and the British army might have to come to the rescue at great cost to the imperial treasury. The danger was not imaginary. Upon learning of the burgesses' bid for Kentucky, the British agent that had negotiated the Hard Labor treaty recalled that a 1763 Indian attack—inappropriately termed "Pontiac's Rebellion"—had proved "expensive and destructive to his Majesty's Subjects" and to his government. Because the government was so determined to prevent another uprising, the natives' effort to preserve their Kentucky hunting territory helped to produce an imperial land policy that protected their interests but at the same

---

4. Tom Hatley, *The Dividing Paths: Cherokees and South Carolinians through the Era of Revolution* (New York, 1993), 9–10; Statement to Richard Henderson, March 1775, paraphrased in deposition of John Lowry, [1777–1778], in Julian P. Boyd et al., eds., *The Papers of Thomas Jefferson* (Princeton, N.J., 1950–), II, 95 (my thanks to Richard Durschlag for this reference); Michael N. McConnell, *A Country Between: The Upper Ohio Valley and Its Peoples, 1724–1774* (Lincoln, Nebr., 1992), 262; Kathryn E. Holland Braund, *Deerskins and Duffels: The Creek Indian Trade with Anglo-America, 1685–1815* (Lincoln, Nebr., 1993), 10.

time poisoned the relationship between Virginia gentlemen and the government of Britain.[5]

I

Six and a half years before the House of Burgesses drew up its petition for Kentucky, Indians had signaled their determination to defend their land. As Virginian Peter Fontaine reported in August 1763, warriors of the Upper Ohio Valley, Wabash River, and Great Lakes nations "entered into a combination against us, resolved it seems to prevent our settling any farther than we have, viz., much about the main Blue Ridge of mountains."[6] Thus participants in Pontiac's Rebellion raided twelve British forts and numerous settlements as far east as Winchester, Virginia. At the time of the uprising, royal officials in London were already studying a proposal to confine Britain's North American colonies behind a western boundary. They had two principal goals: one was to keep the colonists within Britain's economic and political orbit, the other to halt colonial encroachments on Indian land in order to prevent a costly Anglo-Indian war. The boundary idea came too late to prevent the uprising but carried the day when news of Pontiac's Rebellion

5. Stuart to Botetourt, Jan. 13, 1770, in K. G. Davies, ed., *Documents of the American Revolution, 1770–1783*, Colonial Office Series (Shannon, Ireland, 1972–1981), II, 27. The most accurate information on this subject is in Jack M. Sosin, *Whitehall and the Wilderness: The Middle West in British Colonial Policy, 1760–1775* (Lincoln, Nebr., 1961), 193–195; Randolph C. Downes, *Council Fires on the Upper Ohio: A Narrative of Indian Affairs in the Upper Ohio Valley until 1795* (Pittsburgh, 1940), 144–145; Richard White, *The Middle Ground: Indians, Empires, and Republics in the Great Lakes Region, 1650–1815* (Cambridge, 1991), 354; Gregory Evans Dowd, *A Spirited Resistance: The North American Indian Struggle for Unity, 1745–1815* (Baltimore, 1992), 42–45; McConnell, *Country Between*, 248–268; Eric Hinderaker, *Elusive Empires: Constructing Colonialism in the Ohio Valley, 1673–1800* (Cambridge, 1997), 169. However, none of those scholars focuses on the narrow question of whether Indian coalition-building and consequent British limits on land speculation helped induce colonial Americans to rebel against Britain. The most extensive discussion of the topic is Dorothy V. Jones, *License for Empire: Colonialism by Treaty in Early America* (Chicago, 1982), 101–104.

6. Peter Fontaine to Moses and John Fontaine and Daniel Torin, Aug. 7, 1763, in Ann Maury, trans. and comp., *Memoirs of a Huguenot Family* (New York, 1853), 372. In assessing the causes of Pontiac's Rebellion, Howard H. Peckham focuses on the cutoff of British subsidies to the Indians (*Pontiac and the Indian Uprising* [Princeton, N.J., 1947], 101). That might have been the paramount concern around Detroit, where Peckham focuses his attention, but, on the Virginia and Pennsylvania frontiers, "The Chief cause of all the late Wars was about Lands," as an Onondaga speaker told William Johnson in 1765. See Congress between William Johnson, the Six Nations, and the Delawares, May 4, 1765, in E. B. O'Callaghan and B. Fernow, eds., *Documents relative to the Colonial History of the State of New-York . . .* (Albany, 1856–1887), VII, 726 (hereafter cited as *DRCH*); Dowd, *Spirited Resistance*, 33–36; White, *Middle Ground*, 269–314; McConnell, *Country Between*, 181–206.

reached London. On October 7, 1763, British officials drew a line along the watershed between rivers flowing east into the Atlantic and those flowing west into the Mississippi. American governors were prohibited from issuing any land grants beyond this line.[7]

Most historians deny that the so-called Proclamation of 1763 was a cause of the American Revolution. They ask how the proclamation could have angered colonists when it was only a "paper blockade" that failed to prevent settlers from simply crossing the Appalachian Mountains and establishing farms. Indeed, as a *Virginia Gazette* essayist pointed out in 1773, "not even a second Chinese wall, unless guarded by a million of soldiers, could prevent the settlement of the lands on Ohio and its dependencies." The ease with which yeomen families slipped across the imaginary Proclamation Line has led scholars, particularly "pro-Indian" historians, to assume that the barrier was also ineffective against speculators.[8]

That assumption is wrong. Speculators must be distinguished from settlers as a separate class with very different interests. Speculators could not sell land until they secured clear title to it. Starting back in 1745, the gentry-dominated Executive Council of Virginia gave gentry-owned land companies preliminary grants to millions of acres west of the Appalachian Mountains. Then the land firms' effort to acquire and sell this land was interrupted, first by the start of the Seven Years' War in 1754, and then by the

7. Royle's *VG*, Nov. 4, 1763; "Proclamation of 1763," in *SAL*, VII, 663–669. "By a happy coincidence of circumstances," the government's economic and political goals met "together in the same point"—the Proclamation of 1763 ("Mr. Pownall's Sketch of a Report," in R. A. Humphreys, "Lord Shelburne and the Proclamation of 1763," *English Historical Review*, XLIX [1934], 259). See also Peter D. G. Thomas, "The Grenville Program, 1763–1765," in Jack P. Greene and J. R. Pole, eds., *The Blackwell Encyclopedia of the American Revolution* (Cambridge, Mass., 1991), 107; John Mack Faragher, ed., *The Encyclopedia of Colonial and Revolutionary America* (New York, 1990), 334–335.

8. Theda Perdue and Michael D. Green, eds., *The Cherokee Removal: A Brief History with Documents* (Boston, 1995), 6; "A Friend to the True Interest of Britain in America," Rind's *VG*, Jan. 14, 1773; Herbert Sloan and Peter Onuf, "Politics, Culture, and the Revolution in Virginia: A Review of Recent Work," *VMHB*, XCI (1983), 265; Freeman Hansford Hart, *The Valley of Virginia in the American Revolution, 1763–1789* (Chapel Hill, N.C., 1942), 69–70; Thad W. Tate, "The Coming of the Revolution in Virginia: Britain's Challenge to Virginia's Ruling Class, 1763–1776," *WMQ*, 3d Ser., XIX (1962), 338; Norman K. Risjord, *Jefferson's America, 1760–1815* (Madison, Wis., 1991), 79; James A. Clifton, *The Prairie People: Continuity and Change in Potawatomi Indian Culture, 1665–1965* (Lawrence, Kan., 1977), 135; Georgiana C. Nammack, *Fraud, Politics, and the Dispossession of the Indians: The Iroquois Land Frontier in the Colonial Period* (Norman, Okla., 1969), 93; McConnell, *Country Between*, 243–244; Daniel M. Friedenberg, *Life, Liberty, and the Pursuit of Land: The Plunder of Early America* (Buffalo, 1992), chap. 12.

1758 Treaty of Easton, which reserved the area west of the Appalachian Mountains for the Indians. During this time, the Virginia land firms' preliminary grants expired, which prevented most of them from securing title to the land they claimed. The companies were barred from renewing their preliminary grants by the Proclamation of 1763. Many years later, a lawyer for two land firms pronounced the proclamation a species of "tyranny" that was "sufficient to prevent the operations of the companies."[9]

The Proclamation of 1763 infuriated Virginia land speculators. "I shall call upon you some Time next Week and condole with you in your late Misfortune," Virginian David Robinson wrote fellow speculator William Thompson when he learned of the new boundary. "Colo. Buchanan is going to London to redress his Grievances." Robinson found widespread opposition to the British government's policy of giving the Indians land—*their* land—for peace. "Capt. Sayers has been damning this Month about the Loss of the Dunkard's Bottom and is not yet reconciled," he told Thompson. " 'Tis a great Mercy that Roanoak [River] has not in like Manner been given as a Compliment to our good Friends and faithfull Allies, the Shanee Indians." Anglican minister Jonathan Boucher reported that a friend had planned to settle west of the Appalachian Mountains, "But This is put a Stop to by a very impolitic, as well as unjust Proclama'n, forbidding any of the King's Subjects to settle Lands so far back." Arthur Lee spent much of the 1760s searching

9. Apr. 26, 1745, July 12, 1749, in H. R. McIlwaine, Wilmer L. Hall, and Benjamin J. Hillman, eds., *Executive Journals of the Council of Colonial Virginia* (Richmond, Va., 1925–1966), V, 172–173, 296–297 (hereafter cited as *Executive Journals of the Council*); Warren M. Billings, John E. Selby, and Thad W. Tate, *Colonial Virginia: A History* (White Plains, N.Y., 1986), 252. Like the Proclamation of 1763, the 1758 Treaty of Easton was intended to halt an Indian war—in this case, a wave of attacks that had begun in 1755. The Treaty of Easton inaugurated an anti-expansionist imperial policy that prevented Ohio Valley Indians from attacking the British colonies until 1763, when illegal settler encroachments provoked Pontiac's Rebellion (Woody Holton, "The Revolt of the Ruling Class: The Influence of Indians, Merchants, and Laborers on the Virginia Gentry's Break with England" [Ph.D. diss., Duke University, 1990], 34–50). On the Proclamation of 1763 and its effect on the Virginia land firms, see John Taylor, plea, "Case of the Loyal and Greenbrier Companies," May 1783, in Daniel Call, reporter, *Reports of Cases Argued and Decided in the Court of Appeals of Virginia*, IV (Richmond, Va., 1833), 29; Isaac Samuel Harrell, *Loyalism in Virginia: Chapters in the Economic History of the Revolution* (Durham, N.C., 1926), 16–18. Although most modern historians play down the importance of the Proclamation of 1763 to the American Revolutionaries, the Revolutionaries that wrote their own histories considered it a crucial document. See Thomas Jefferson, *Notes on the State of Virginia*, ed. William Peden (Chapel Hill, N.C., 1954), 195; Edmund Randolph, *History of Virginia*, ed. Arthur H. Shaffer, VHS Documents, IX (Charlottesville, Va., 1970), 166. Cf. "Jno. Heavin's Bond," July 8, 1776, Campbell-Preston-Floyd Family Papers, 1741–1925, I, Manuscripts Division, LC.

Westminster for a British official willing to approve a 2,500,000-acre, trans-Appalachian grant to the Mississippi Land Company, which he had formed along with four of his brothers and thirty-eight other Virginia gentlemen. Lee's lobbying proved unsuccessful, and by 1768 he had decided that "the present Ministry, is truly antiamerican; and very averse to making Grants, except . . . in small portions."[10]

One of Lee's Mississippi Company partners, George Washington, was more optimistic. In September 1767, he assured a friend that the Proclamation of 1763 would prove to be nothing more than "a temporary expedien[t] to quiet the Minds of the Indians." Scarcely a year later, however, Cherokee headmen and British Indian agent John Stuart negotiated the Treaty of Hard Labor, leaving the region that is now Kentucky, southwest Virginia, and southern West Virginia in Cherokee country. The Hard Labor treaty was no more popular among Virginia land speculators than the Proclamation of 1763. "Both Intendant and Indians are on a wrong s[c]ent, at least one very Dif[fer]ent from what we Intend," Thomas Lewis, the chief government surveyor for Augusta County on the Virginia frontier, told his deputy and fellow land jobber, William Preston, in January 1769.[11]

10. David Robinson to William Thompson, Feb. 18, 1764, Draper Manuscripts, document 2QQ44 (microfilm), State Historical Society of Wisconsin, Madison, 1980 (hereafter cited as Draper Mss.); Jonathan Boucher to Rev. James, Mar. 9, 1767, "Letters of Rev. Jonathan Boucher," *MHM*, VII (1912), 344; Arthur Lee to Richard Parker and Richard Henry Lee, Dec. 23, 1768, in Paul P. Hoffman, ed., *The Lee Family Papers, 1742–1795* (microfilm, Charlottesville, Va., 1966); Mississippi Land Company, petition to Privy Council, [December 1768], in Abbot et al., eds., *Papers of Washington*, Colonial Series, VIII, 149–153; Francis Fauquier to Board of Trade, Feb. 13, 1764, Board of Trade to Fauquier, July 13, 1764, in George Reese, ed., *The Official Papers of Francis Fauquier, Lieutenant Governor of Virginia, 1758–1768* (Charlottesville, Va., 1980–1983), III, 1076–1079, 1125; John Blair to Hillsborough, Sept. 27, 1768, C.O. 5/1346, 191, P.R.O., VCRP; William Herbert to William Byrd III, Mar. 6, 1764, in Marion Tinling, ed., *The Correspondence of the Three William Byrds of Westover, Virginia, 1684–1776* (Charlottesville, Va., 1977), II, 768; John Mercer to Charlton Palmer, Apr. 17, 1764, in Lois Mulkearn, ed., *George Mercer Papers Relating to the Ohio Company of Virginia* ([Pittsburgh], 1954), 184–185; Augusta County freeholders, petition, Nov. 24, 1766, House of Burgesses, resolution, Dec. 13, 1766, *JHB, 1766–1769*, 37, 69; Patricia Givens Johnson, *William Preston and the Allegheny Patriots* (Pulaski, Va., 1976), 81, 89; Alfred Procter James, *George Mercer of the Ohio Company: A Study in Frustration* ([Pittsburgh], 1963), 59; Williams, "Political Alignments," 337; Feb. 10, 1764, in Adelaide L. Fries et al., eds., *Records of the Moravians in North Carolina*, I, 1752–1771 (Raleigh, 1922), 285. The chorus of complaints from Virginia land speculators against the Proclamation of 1763 belies the statement in the standard survey of colonial Virginia that "no one seemed disposed to fight" the proclamation (Billings, Selby, and Tate, *Colonial Virginia*, 291).

11. Washington to William Crawford, Sept. [17], 1767, in Abbot et al., eds., *Papers of*

The Hard Labor treaty did not drive Virginia land speculators to despair and resignation. In fact, one of them, Patrick Henry, chose this very time to invest in the disputed area. Henry bought 3,334 acres of land on the Holston and Clinch Rivers from his insolvent father-in-law. He recalled later that the boundary the Cherokee headmen had negotiated with Stuart "would have cut off the said lands on Hols[t]on and Clinch, and under that risque I purchased it, hoping that line would be altered." Many Virginia land speculators did more than hope. They launched a campaign to persuade the Privy Council to let them have Kentucky and the area north to the forks of the Ohio. The speculators had some powerful allies: northern Indian agent William Johnson and Johnson's own allies and adoptive kinsmen, the headmen of the Six Nations of the Iroquois. Less than a month after John Stuart and the Cherokees negotiated the Hard Labor treaty, the Iroquois met Johnson at Fort Stanwix, New York, and sold the same area to Virginia. The Iroquois almost never hunted in Kentucky. Thus their claim to it, which was based upon their status as the diplomatic "elder Brethren" of some of the nations that did hunt there, was not very sound. Iroquois leaders nonetheless insisted (at the covert request of Johnson, one suspects) that Britain accept the vast territory described in the Treaty of Fort Stanwix. Since the Iroquois confederacy had long been the British Empire's most important Indian ally, Johnson and the Virginia land speculators felt confident that imperial officials would have no choice but to accept the Fort Stanwix cession, void the Hard Labor treaty, and let Virginia have Kentucky. For their part, the Iroquois left the November 1768 Stanwix congress with a promise of goods worth ten thousand pounds—the largest amount Britain had ever paid Indians for land. They also hoped that the Stanwix cession would divert the flow of European and African colonists from their own land.[12]

Washington, Colonial Series, VIII, 28; Thomas Lewis to William Preston, Jan. 14, 1769, Draper Mss., 2QQ106.

12. Patrick Henry, fee book, in William Wirt Henry, *Patrick Henry: Life, Correspondence, and Speeches* (New York, 1891), I, 121; Thomas Gage to William Johnson, Apr. 3, 1769, John Stuart to William Johnson, [Apr. 14, 1769], Red Hawk, speech, all enclosed in McKee to Croghan, Feb. 20, 1770, *The Papers of Sir William Johnson* (Albany, 1921–1965), VI, 694, VII, 407, XII, 709; Patricia Givens Johnson, *General Andrew Lewis of Roanoke and Greenbrier* (Christiansburg, Va., 1980), 141–153; Congress between William Johnson, the Six Nations, and other nations, Fort Stanwix, Oct. 24–Nov. 6, 1768, *DRCH*, VIII, 111–134; Peter Marshall, "Sir William Johnson and the Treaty of Fort Stanwix, 1768," *Journal of American Studies*, I (October 1967), 149–179; Sosin, *Whitehall and the Wilderness*, 171–177; McConnell, *Country Between*, 248–253. By the time of Fort Stanwix, the Iroquois had several decades' worth of experience at selling Britain land they did not own—both to obtain British manufactured

FIGURE 2. Sir William Johnson's Indian Testimonial, c. 1770, detail.
© *Collection of The New-York Historical Society*

Many British colonists believed that the British government would not only ratify the Fort Stanwix cession but also repeal the Proclamation of 1763. Stanwix thus set off a land rush. Veterans of the Seven Years' War, led by George Washington, asked the Executive Council for land bounties that the government had promised them after the war. Colonel Washington also began buying up his fellow veterans' bounty rights. He advised his brother Charles to approach veterans "in a joking way, rather than in earnest at first" in order to "see what value they seem to set upon their Lands." If Charles Washington could obtain the veterans' grants for seven pounds or less per thousand acres, he was directed to do so. Thomas Walker of Albemarle County—whose great-grandson considered him "as great a land-monger as Genl. Washington"—reactivated the dormant Loyal Land Company. Between November 1768 and April 1769, he persuaded government surveyors

---

goods and to divert colonial settlement from the areas where they themselves lived and hunted (Francis Jennings, *The Ambiguous Iroquois Empire: The Covenant Chain Confederation of Indian Tribes with English Colonies from Its Beginnings to the Lancaster Treaty of 1744* (New York, 1984), 325–346, 388–397).

to mark off hundreds of homesteads within the Loyal Company's ill-defined preliminary grant.[13] In February 1769, Walker's neighbor Thomas Jefferson, whose late father had been a Loyal Company member, asked the company for five thousand acres. Jefferson also joined two new syndicates seeking land; his share in each was to be one thousand acres. In joining two different land companies (something that few if any other Virginians did at this time), Jefferson hoped to evade an instruction adopted in 1754 by the Privy Council that prohibited any person from taking more than one thousand acres of Indian land.[14]

13. George Washington to Charles Washington, Jan. 31, 1770, in Abbot et al., eds., *Papers of Washington*, Colonial Series, VIII, 301; Francis Jennings, *Empire of Fortune: Crowns, Colonies and Tribes in the Seven Years War in America* (New York, 1988), 62–63 n. 48; "Proclamation of 1763," in *SAL*, VII, 666; William Byrd to Virginia Executive Council, Dec. 15, 1768, summarized Dec. 19, 1768, executive order, Apr. 25, 1769, both in *Executive Journals of the Council*, VI, 310, 314; David Robinson to William Preston, May 1, 1769, Draper Mss., 2QQ109; David Ross to John Cameron, Dec. 20, 1768, enclosed in John Stuart Hillsborough, Jan. 20, 1770, C.O. 5/71, 129–131; Lewis Preston Summers, *History of Southwest Virginia, 1746–1786, Washington County, 1777–1870* (Richmond, Va., 1903; reprint, Baltimore, 1966), 93; McConnell, *Country Between*, 257. Stanwix also set off land rushes in New York and Pennsylvania. See July 18, 1769, New York Council Minutes, XXVI, 153–154, New York State Archives, in Francis Jennings, ed., *Iroquois Indians: A Documentary History of the Diplomacy of the Six Nations and Their League* (microfilm, Woodbridge, Conn., 1984); Henry Moore to Hillsborough, Jan. 27, 1769, *DRCH*, VIII, 149. On Thomas Walker and the Loyal Land Company, see Franklin Minor to Lyman Draper, Mar. 23, 1852, Draper Mss., 13ZZ.; Loyal Company and Greenbrier Company surveys in Augusta County, [November 1768–May 1769], Virginia Land Office Records, LVA; [William Preston], survey for Anne Grayson, Mar. 20, 1769, William Preston, survey book, [1768–1769], Preston Family Papers (1727–1896), folders 581, 589, VHS; William Preston, receipt to Josiah Ramsay, Apr. 13, 1769, Wyndham Robertson Papers (Manuscripts Department, University of Chicago library; microfilm at LVA), folder 5; John Norton to Thomas Walker, July 8, 1769, Thomas Walker Papers (part of the William Cabell Rives Papers), container 162, LC.

14. Jefferson's activities disprove his later claim that he did not speculate in western land before 1776. See Jefferson to James Madison, Nov. 11, 1784, Jan. 30, 1787, in Boyd et al., eds., *Papers of Jefferson*, VII, 503–504, XI, 93; *CVSP*, I, 262; Thomas Nelson et al. and George Rogers et al., petitions for land, [1768–1769], Virginia Colonial Papers, folder 47, LVA; entries, Feb. 18, 1769, Nov. 29, 1773, in Bear and Stanton, eds., *Jefferson's Memorandum Books*, I, 138–139, 350; Miscellaneous Accounts, 1764–1779 [#5572], Jefferson Papers, Henry E. Huntington Library.

In his role as an attorney, Jefferson agreed to seek several hundred acres of trans-Appalachian land for George Davidson. Under their agreement, if Jefferson managed to acquire up to sixteen hundred acres, he was to receive half of the land. If he could obtain more than sixteen hundred acres, all of the additional land would be his ("Lands claimed by Andr. Lewis," [1772], in *Jefferson's Memorandum Books*, 279–281). Nothing came of the

Early in 1769, at the height of the land rush that followed the Stanwix congress, the British government signaled its intention to keep its promise to leave Kentucky on the western side of the Anglo-Cherokee border. By April 1769, the Virginia Executive Council had no choice but to void the hundreds of surveys that had been done for Virginia speculators and to put a halt to further surveying. This setback only intensified the speculators' effort to persuade the government to let them have Kentucky and the adjacent region. The same Executive Council that reluctantly voided the trans-Appalachian surveys declared at the same time that the Hard Labor boundary "would be highly injurious to this Colony, and to the Crown of Great Britain, by giving to the Indians, an extensive tract of Land." In December, the House of Burgesses adopted the petition for Kentucky mentioned above. In the region west of the Hard Labor boundary, Virginia land speculators had received preliminary grants totaling six to seven million acres. The disputed area also contained nearly fifty thousand square miles of additional land that would be available to speculators to sell in the future. Virginia would, if the Privy Council honored the petition, nearly double its land area.[15]

II

The fate of the assembly's petition for Kentucky hinged upon the Privy Council's acceptance of its contention that, with the relinquishment by the Iroquois of their claim to Kentucky and the adjacent region, "no Tribe of *Indians*, at present, sets up any Pretensions" to the area.[16] Actually, the

---

scheme, most likely because the land in question was west of the Proclamation Line. My thanks to Anthony F. C. Wallace for sharing his research on this topic with me.

15. Hillsborough to Johnson, Jan. 4, 1769, *DRCH*, VIII, 145; Dec. 16, 1768, Apr. 25, 1769, *Executive Journals of the Council*, VI, 309, 314–315. The council also began, at that time, to refuse to issue trans-Appalachian patents to people suing original patentees to obtain grants that they had forfeited by not fulfilling the conditions. The council had stopped making new patents in 1759 (in compliance with the Treaty of Easton) but had repatented six forfeited tracts between 1762 and 1769 (Patent Books XXXIV, 335, XXXVIII, 623, Virginia Colonial Land Office Records). With the exception of bounty grants to Seven Years' War veterans, Virginia issued only two more trans-Appalachian patents before Independence (Patent Book XLI, 325, 438–439). On the speculators' plans to obtain the region west of the Hard Labor boundary, see George Washington to Charles Washington, Jan. 31, 1770, in Abbot et al., eds., *Papers of Washington*, Colonial Series, VIII, 300–301; Jefferson, *Notes on Virginia*, ed. Peden, 4.

16. House of Burgesses, memorial to Botetourt, Dec. 13, 1769, *JHB, 1766–1769*, 335. The burgesses persuaded Governor Botetourt to lobby his government colleagues to give Kentucky to Virginia (Botetourt to Hillsborough, Botetourt to Stuart, Dec. 18, 1769, C.O. 5/1348, 63, 87). See also Thomas Walker and Andrew Lewis to Botetourt, Dec. 14, 1768, Botetourt to

nations that hunted in Kentucky denied the right of the Iroquois to sell it. The Shawnees acknowledged the "Six Nations as our elder Brethren and as such have listened to them while we found their advice good," Shawnee headman Red Hawk told British officials, "but their power extends no further with us." Alexander McKee, whose mother was Shawnee, was a British agent charged with monitoring the Upper Ohio Valley Indians. McKee wrote that the "numbers of White people and Surveyors that come out" to the Ohio River in the spring of 1769 "to Settle and Survey the Country about Fort Pitt [Pittsburgh] and down [the] Ohio has set all their Warriors in a rage."[17]

No Indian nation acting alone could do the British much damage. The natives' power depended upon their ability to unify across national borders. In June 1765, warriors from two of the nations that had participated in Pontiac's Rebellion, the Mascoutens and Kickapoos, killed three diplomats representing a third, the Shawnees. "The killing those three Shanna Deputys has Intirely broake up [the anti-British] Confedrecie," Indian agent George Croghan reported the following month. The attack placed the Shawnees and their Upper Ohio allies the Delawares in a virtual state of war with the Mascoutens, Kickapoos, and their allies on the Wabash River, the Miamis, Piankashaws, and Weas.[18]

Stuart, Botetourt to Walker and Lewis, Dec. 20, 1768, all enclosed in Botetourt to Hillsborough, Dec. 24, 1768, C.O. 5/1347, 63–65, 91–92, 95–97; Thomas Lewis to William Preston, Jan. 14, 1769, Draper Mss., 2QQ106; Gage to Hillsborough, Apr. 1, 1769, in Clarence Edwin Carter, ed., *The Correspondence of General Thomas Gage with the Secretaries of State, 1763–1775* (New Haven, Conn., 1931–1933), I, 222.

17. McKee journal, [summer 1769], enclosed in McKee to William Johnson, Sept. 18, 1769, Red Hawk, speech, enclosed in McKee to Croghan, Feb. 20, 1770, *Papers of William Johnson*, VII, 185, 407. The Upper Ohio Valley nations viewed the Iroquois in the same way that the British colonists viewed the British government—they were willing to acknowledge the sovereignty of the Iroquois, but only so long as the Iroquois did not try to exercise it (Gage to Hillsborough, Jan. 6, 1770, *Papers of William Johnson*, VII, 332).

18. Croghan to Johnson, July 12, 1765, *Papers of William Johnson*, XI, 838; John Reid to George Croghan, Alexander McKee to Croghan, Sept. 1, 1765, Cadwalader Family Collection, George Croghan section, boxes 6 (file labeled "McKee"), 7 (file labeled "Reid"), Historical Society of Pennsylvania (hereafter cited as HSP); Dorothy Libby, "An Anthropological Report on the Piankashaw Indians," in Libby and David B. Stout, *Piankashaw and Kaskaskia Indians* (New York, 1974), 102. The three Shawnees that were killed were part of a delegation of Upper Ohio diplomats that accompanied British Indian agent George Croghan when he went down the Ohio River in 1765 to try to negotiate an end to Pontiac's Rebellion. Three Britons were also killed in the attack. Although the Kickapoo and Mascouten warriors claimed they had mistaken the Indians in the party for their Cherokee enemies, it is possible that they deliberately killed the Shawnees to punish them for an earlier Shawnee decision to

In 1769, on the heels of the Stanwix land deal and in the midst of the ensuing Virginia land rush, the Wabash River and Upper Ohio confederacies launched an effort to settle their differences. As a Shawnee headman later recalled, Wabash headmen metaphorically approached him and his colleagues "with Tears . . . asking pardon, Acknowledging the fault they had Committed against the Shawnese—the wives of their Chiefs have likewise askt pardon, of Ours." Although the Wabash headmen's peace message apparently elicited no reply, when the headwomen's message arrived in Shawnee country, a male sachem later reported, "our Wives heard it with pleasure, and they pass'd it to the Delawares, where all the Wives of Chiefs Received it in the same manner, and [it] was pass'd to all the Different Villages." Later the Shawnees would make a large wampum belt and state that "all the Wives of as many Tribes as there is Marks upon the Belt Received" the Wabash women's peace initiative "with pleasure."[19]

Among the Upper Ohio nations, when a female village sachem (known as a "peace woman") asked a male war sachem to break off a planned attack, "she seldom fail[ed] to dissuade him," American Indian agent C. C. Trowbridge reported in 1824. The headwomen on the Upper Ohio persuaded their male counterparts "to listen to the Speech of the Wives of the Ouabach [Wabash], and to forget all the Insults given them by these Nations," a Shawnee headman later reported. This Shawnee speaker made a compelling appeal to the diverse Indian nations threatened by "the Cession of Lands made to the English by the Six Nations," British general Thomas Gage learned. "Be always united," the Shawnee diplomat said.[20] Heeding this ad-

---

abandon the rebel coalition. It is also possible that a second source of friction between the Wabash River and Upper Ohio nations was created in 1768, when the Upper Ohio nations made peace with the Cherokees, who were until that time the enemies of both the Wabash River and Upper Ohio nations. After 1768, the Cherokees continued to attack the Wabash River nations. The killings might have been the reason that, in 1767, when several headmen tried to reassemble the old league, the plan fizzled like a damp fuse. See Peckham, *Pontiac and the Indian Uprising*, 279–281; Dowd, *Spirited Resistance*, 42; Nicholas B. Wainwright, *George Croghan, Wilderness Diplomat* (Chapel Hill, N.C., 1959), 220–221, 244–247.

19. The Wabash River messages were conveyed through the Hurons, who were the diplomatic "grandfathers" of all the nations in modern-day Ohio, and their allies the Chippewas, Ottawas, and Potawatomis. See unnamed Shawnee chief, council with Great Lakes nations and George Turnbull, Sept. 25, 1769, enclosed in Turnbull to Gage, Sept. 30, 1769, Thomas Gage Papers, William L. Clements Library, University of Michigan, Ann Arbor; Martin W. Walsh, "The 'Heathen Party': Methodist Observation of the Ohio Wyandot," *American Indian Quarterly*, XVI (Spring 1992), 190.

20. Trowbridge referred specifically to the Shawnees. See *Shawnese Traditions*, ed. Vernon Kinietz and Ermine W. Voegelin [Ann Arbor, Mich., 1939], 13; unnamed Shawnee chief,

vice, the Upper Ohio and Wabash nations revived the coalition that had rebelled against the British in 1763.

At the same time that the Shawnee and Delaware headmen made peace with the Wabash nations, they began to seek members for the anti-British league among the nations south of the Ohio River. This was a momentous step, for the southern nations were quite numerous. As of 1760, in addition to 7,000 Cherokees, there were about 13,000 Creeks, and the Chickasaws and Choctaws had a combined population of about 15,000. None of these power-ful southern nations had participated in Pontiac's Rebellion. If any of them now joined the anti-British coalition—and if all of the nations that had taken up arms in 1763–1764 agreed to fight again—the new league would be more powerful than any that Anglo-Americans had ever faced.[21] Yet the insur-gents' chances of recruiting any southern nations for the league seemed slim indeed. Any effort to bring them into the league would be hampered by long-standing animosities among them. Nor was this the only obstacle. The hostility between the white northerners and southerners that would face each other across the Ohio River exactly a century later would scarcely surpass the mutual animosity of the Indian nations that inhabited the op-posite banks of the same river in the 1760s. In one of the more bitter and

---

council with Great Lakes nations and George Turnbull, Sept. 25, 1769, enclosed in Turnbull to Gage, Sept. 30, 1769, Gage Papers; Gage to Hillsborough, Jan. 6, 1770, *Papers of William Johnson*, VII, 332. The Wabash River (Miami, Wea, Kickapoo, Mascouten, and Piankashaw) and Upper Ohio Valley (Shawnee, Delaware, and Mingo) confederacies had attempted reconciliation three times before, in 1766, in 1767, and in May 1769. But it was not until the Wabash female sachems' peace initiative of mid-1769 that the "Wabash Confed[eracy]" was "reconcilled [to] the Shawanese." See Alexander McKee to George Croghan, Feb. 20, 1770, McKee journal, enclosed in McKee to Johnson, Sept. 18, 1769, in *Shawnese Traditions*, 184, 405; William Johnson, "State of the Trade, Politicks, and Proceedings of the Indians in the Northern District," [Sept. 22, 1767], in Clarence Walworth Alvord and Clarence Edwin Carter, eds., *Trade and Politics, 1767–1769* (Springfield, Ill., 1921), 46; Croghan to Johnson, Aug. 8, 1769, *Papers of William Johnson*, VII, 78. For additional details of the Wabash–Upper Ohio negotiations, see Woody Holton, "The Ohio Indians and the Coming of the American Revolution in Virginia," *JSH*, LX (1994), 462–463.

21. Peter H. Wood, "The Changing Population of the Colonial South: An Overview by Race and Region, 1685–1790," in Wood, Gregory A. Waselkov, and M. Thomas Hatley, eds., *Powhatan's Mantle: Indians in the Colonial Southeast* (Lincoln, Nebr., 1989), 38; Clar-ence E. Carter, "British Policy towards the American Indians in the South, 1763–8," *English Historical Review*, XXXIII (1918), 37–56. Although historians of the American Revolu-tion that mention Indians tend to focus upon the Iroquois, by the late 1780s British offi-cials recognized that they needed to devote at least as much attention to the Indians of the South.

enduring trans-Ohio conflicts, the Shawnees, Delawares, and Mingos battled the Cherokees.[22]

Then the Cherokee–Upper Ohio war took an unexpected turn. In April 1765, Nocoknowa, a headman of the Overhill branch of the Cherokees, decided to lead a war party against the Upper Ohio nations. Nocoknowa and nine other Overhills followed the "warrior's path" in a generally northeastward direction through the valley between the Blue Ridge and Allegheny Mountains. This route took them through Augusta County, Virginia, but they easily obtained a safe-conduct pass, for Virginia and the Cherokees were at peace. At dawn on May 8, as the Overhills slept in a barn near Staunton, they were attacked by a group of twenty to thirty Virginians. Five members of the Overhill party, including Nocoknowa, were killed instantly. The other five escaped, but two were injured, and one of these died.

The unprovoked attack against the Overhills horrified leading Virginians, who were certain that the Cherokees would launch revenge raids. Instead, Cherokee headmen informed Virginia lieutenant governor Francis Fauquier

22. For instance, the Creeks battled the Choctaws in a war that claimed at least six hundred lives between 1765 and 1771. See Richard White, *The Roots of Dependency: Subsistence, Environment, and Social Change among the Choctaws, Pawnees, and Navajos* (Lincoln, Nebr., 1983), 76–78; Braund, *Deerskins and Duffels*, 133–135; John Richard Alden, *General Gage in America: Being Principally a History of His Role in the American Revolution* (Baton Rouge, Louis., 1948), 136–137.

The Cherokees were involved in a struggle against the Iroquois that was similar to the 1760s trans-Ohio conflict. See Johnson to Board of Trade, Nov. 16, 1765, *DRCH*, VII, 777–778; Theda Perdue, "Cherokee Relations with the Iroquois in the Eighteenth Century," in Daniel K. Richter and James H. Merrell, eds., *Beyond the Covenant Chain: The Iroquois and Their Neighbors in Indian North America, 1600–1800* (Syracuse, N.Y., 1987), 137; Daniel K. Richter, *The Ordeal of the Longhouse: The Peoples of the Iroquois League in the Era of European Colonization* (Chapel Hill, N.C., 1992), 237–238; R. David Edmunds, *The Potawatomis, Keepers of the Fire* (Norman, Okla., 1978), 97; Arrell M. Gibson, *The Chickasaws* (Norman, Okla., 1971), 48, 51; Peckham, *Pontiac and the Indian Uprising*, 279–281. British colonists recognized that the raids and counterraids Indian nations directed at each other back and forth across the Ohio River were their best protection against a devastating general Indian attack. See John Wilkins to Gage, Jan. 2, 1769, in Alvord and Carter, eds., *Trade and Politics*, 483; Johnson to Gage, Sept. 12, 1769, Croghan to Johnson, May 10, 1770, *Papers of William Johnson*, VII, 163, 652. John Stuart acknowledged privately that the British were "the incendiaries who kindled" the Choctaw-Creek war (to Hillsborough, Dec. 2, 1770, in Davies, ed., *Documents of the American Revolution*, II, 281). See also Johnson to Gage, Nov. 8, 1770, Gage to Johnson, Nov. 19, 1770, in *Papers of William Johnson*, VII, 993, 1016; Alden, *General Gage*, 136–137. One ray of hope for Indian coalition-builders was that a band of Shawnees lived with a southern nation, the Creeks. Perhaps they could be persuaded to serve as the crucial link in a Shawnee-Creek alliance. See Dowd, *Spirited Resistance*, 24, 51; McConnell, *Country Between*, 209, 238.

that they would send one of their most gifted diplomats, Attakullakulla, or Little Carpenter, to Williamsburg "to see what Justice the Government here were disposed to give them," as Fauquier reported.[23] Attakullakulla informed Fauquier that the British government could compensate the Cherokees for their losses by using its enormous political and economic influence to help them make peace with the Shawnees—the very people their war party had been planning to attack when it had itself been set upon by the Virginians. The Cherokees also wanted to reach an accommodation with another of the Upper Ohio Valley nations, the Delawares, and even with the Iroquois. Fauquier assented to the Cherokees' request and hoped that "by thus studying their interests, we may prevent their taking Revenge on the White People." By the end of 1768, with the sometimes-grudging assistance of British officials, the Cherokees achieved their goal of peace with the Shawnees, Delawares, and Six Nations.[24]

After the unexpected "Charroky paice," the Shawnee promoters of an anti-British confederacy "inlarged thire plan" by recruiting the Cherokees and other southern nations, Indian agent George Croghan learned. The coalition builders' appeal could be summarized in one word: Kentucky. Formerly this "bloody Ground" (as Cherokee leader Dragging Canoe called Kentucky) had been a source, as well as a scene, of contention between Indian nations north and south of the Ohio River.[25] Now that it was in danger

23. Andrew Lewis to Fauquier, May 9, 1765, Francis Fauquier to Board of Trade, Aug. 1, 1765, in Reese, ed., *Papers of Francis Fauquier*, III, 1234–1236, 1265–1266. Many Augusta County whites did not share Fauquier's interest in making peace with the Cherokees, and, in fact, they rescued the killers from the sheriff and plotted to assassinate Attakullakulla (Albert H. Tillson, Jr., *Gentry and Common Folk: Political Culture on a Virginia Frontier, 1740–1789* [Lexington, Ky., 1991], 49).

24. Fauquier to Johnson, July 22, 1765, in Reese, ed., *Papers of Francis Fauquier*, III, 1262. In addition to helping the Cherokees make peace with the Iroquois and with the Upper Ohio Valley nations, Fauquier promised to bring the killers to justice and to give condolence presents to the victims' families. When news of the Augusta County massacre reached London, the Privy Council ordered Fauquier to step up enforcement of the Proclamation of 1763, which he promptly did. See Privy Council, additional instruction, Oct. 24, 1765, Fauquier, proclamation, Apr. 10, 1766, in Reese, ed., *Papers of Francis Fauquier*, III, 1287–1288, 1355–1356; Alden, *John Stuart*, 222–224; Hatley, *Dividing Paths*, 184–185. For a different interpretation of British motives for helping the Cherokees make peace with their native enemies, see Perdue, "Cherokee Relations with the Iroquois," in Richter and Merrell, eds., *Beyond the Covenant Chain*, 144.

25. Thomas Gage to Johnson, Apr. 23, 1769, McKee journal, [summer 1769], Croghan to Johnson, May 10, 1770, all in *Papers of William Johnson*, VI, 708–709, VII, 184, 652; Dragging Canoe, in *CVSP*, I, 283.

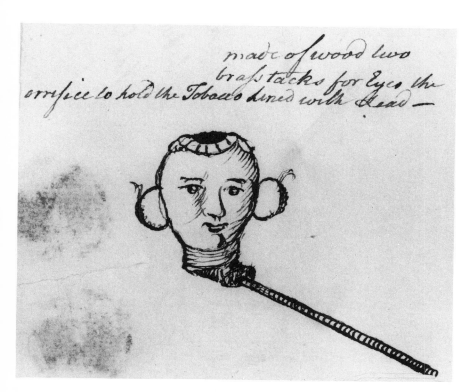

made of wood two brass tacks for Eyes the orrifice to hold the Tobacco lined with Lead —

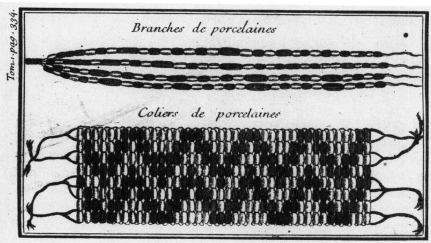

Tom. I, pag. 334.

Branches de porcelaines

Coliers de porcelaines

FIGURE 3. Drawing of a Pipe; A Belt and Strings of Wampum. *Although Native American leaders most often communicated with each other using belts and strings made out of wampum, tobacco pipes such as this one were also used as diplomatic gifts. Pipe drawing enclosed in Thomas Gage to William Johnson, Mar. 18, 1770, Thomas Gage Papers, used by permission of the Houghton Library, Harvard University; wampum belt from [Claude Charles Le Roy] Bacqueville de La Potherie,* Histoire de l'Amérique septentrionale . . . *(Paris, 1772), courtesy of the Robert Dechert Collection, Department of Special Collections, Van Pelt/Dietrich Library Center, University of Pennsylvania, Philadelphia*

of being lost to the Anglo-Americans, Kentucky had become—potentially, at least—a bond of union.

The Upper Ohioans' recruitment of the Cherokees began in the spring of 1769, when they persuaded six visiting Cherokees to send "a vast number of long Speeches" as well as "two Belts, and Several Strings of Wampum" to the nations north of the Ohio River. The gist of these speeches, belts, and strings was that the Cherokees were ready to make peace with "all the other nations of Indians, upon this Continent." Actually, the six Cherokees that sent all this wampum did not really represent their whole nation, and the north bank Indians that received it probably knew this. They were nonetheless urged to accept it by Shawnee diplomats, who argued that Indians should stick together because they were all members of the same race. "Have only the same mind, all of you who Inhabit the same Continent, and are of the same Colour," a Shawnee headman counseled natives north and south of the Ohio. Although European settlers and their descendants had long viewed the American Indian population as a single race, the notion of a common racial identity had been embraced by precious few of the Native Americans themselves. The Shawnee diplomat that urged Indians to unite with those "of the same Colour" was promoting a transformation from tribal to racial self-identity as a foundation for political unity. The Great Lakes nations—the Chippewas (or Ojibwas), Hurons, Ottawas, and Potawatomis—"agreed to Confirm a Peace with the Cherokees" as soon as a congress could be arranged.[26]

26. Unnamed Shawnee chief, council with Great Lakes nations and John Turnbull, Sept. 25, 1769, enclosed in Turnbull to Gage, Sept. 30, 1769, Gage Papers. The Shawnee diplomat claimed that those words had first been spoken by Indian agent William Johnson (Johnson to Gage, Jan. 5, 1770, in *Papers of William Johnson*, XII, 769).

The new solidarity was accompanied by growing racial separatism. "God . . . allowed the white people to live one way, and Indians another way," Shawnee chief Red Hawk told a Baptist missionary in the early 1770s as he banished him from Shawnee country (Dowd, *Spirited Resistance*, 41–45). See also Red Hawk, speech to Alexander McKee, enclosed in McKee to Croghan, Feb. 20, 1770, in *Papers of William Johnson*, VII, 407; White, *Middle Ground*, 441–442. Scholars, notably David Brion Davis and Barbara Jeanne Fields, have shown that the American Revolution accelerated the process by which European Americans invented the concept of race and defined Native Americans and Africans as separate and inferior races. See Davis, *The Problem of Slavery in the Age of Revolution, 1770–1823* (Ithaca, N.Y., 1975), 303; Fields, "Ideology and Race in American History," in J. Morgan Kousser and James M. McPherson, eds., *Region, Race, and Reconstruction: Essays in Honor of C. Vann Woodward* (New York, 1982), 143–177, and "Slavery, Race and Ideology in the United States of America," *New Left Review*, 181 (1990), 95–118. What has not always been recognized is that many Native Americans and Africans, for their own purposes, participated in the

Near the end of 1769, a deputation of Shawnee and Delaware headmen carried the organizing effort south of the Ohio River. At meetings in Cherokee country, they "complained much of encroachments upon their Lands and of the Extensive cession obtained by Sir William Johnson from the Six Nations, which they told the Cherokees included all their Hunting Ground," southern Indian agent John Stuart learned. Then the Shawnee and Delaware diplomats gave the Cherokees a set of "peace talks from the Western Tribes."[27] Oconostota, a Cherokee headman that had recently accepted the necessity of accommodating the British, told British officials that the Shawnee and Delaware ambassadors that arrived in Cherokee country at the end of 1769 were rebuffed by most Cherokees. But he acknowledged that one Overhill town, Chilhowee, "listened a Good deal to the proposals of the Shawnee and wanted to Convene a meeting of" all the Cherokee headmen "to confer with them." When some of the Shawnee deputies in the Cherokee country headed south to carry the north-south coalition proposal to the Creeks, who were longstanding enemies of the Cherokees, they were "accompanied by some Cherokees."[28]

---

invention of the concept of race (White, *Middle Ground*, 507). On the Great Lakes nations' interest in the Native American congress, see Croghan to Johnson, Dec. 22, 1769, in *Papers of William Johnson*, VII, 316. By May 1770, the idea of making peace with the Cherokees would also be endorsed by the Wabash River nations (McKee to Croghan, Feb. 20, 1770, Croghan to Johnson, May 10, 1770, in *Papers of William Johnson*, 404–405, 652).

27. Stuart to Gage, Dec. 12, 1770, Gage Papers. The Shawnee members of the legation took the leading role, just as they had in the negotiations north of the Ohio (Gage to Stuart, Oct. 16, 1770). It is possible that the Shawnee and Delaware diplomats did not mention the proposed congress until a second meeting with the Cherokees later in 1770. In January, Stuart had stated only that their goal was to "sound the disposition of those Indians" (to Gage, Jan. 27, 1770).

28. Stuart to Gage, Apr. 24, 1770, Gage Papers. One reason the people of Chilhowee were so willing to join the anti-British league was that they were still angry about the unavenged killings of the Chilhowee warriors near Staunton, Virginia, four and a half years earlier. Chilhowee, one of the westernmost Cherokee towns, might also have been influenced by its near neighbors, the anti-British Creeks. A Creek chief named "The Mortar," who had ties to the Cherokees, had frequently visited them to propose a joint attack against the British. See Alden, *John Stuart*, 217–218; Hatley, *Dividing Paths*, 158–159. Chilhowee was built on former Creek territory; the name "Chilhowee" appears to be the Cherokee pronunciation of a Creek name. In 1775, when accommodationist Cherokee headmen sold a vast tract of Cherokee land to a group of Anglo-Americans, the people of Chilhowee were prominent among the Cherokees that rebelled against the accommodationists and moved farther down the Tennessee River, where they joined with a group of Shawnees to resist Anglo-American encroachment. See Hatley, *Dividing Paths*, 6, 223; Dowd, *Spirited Resistance*, 47–49, 54;

The promoters of an anti-British confederacy achieved the same mixed results in the Creek country. When Indian agent Charles Stuart later questioned the avowedly pro-British Creek headman Emistisiguo "very particularly about the Business of the Shawnese in their Nation[,] he was rather reserved upon the Subject; but said, that their Talks were not good," John Stuart reported. Emistisiguo told Charles Stuart that the legation's only goal was to ask the Creeks to join them in a raid against the Choctaws, but British general Frederick Haldimand learned that the proposed raid was only a "pretext." The diplomats' real goal was to recruit the Creeks for an anti-British "confederation." The Shawnees' southern mission also made a side trip to the Chickasaws' country and sent peace talks to the only other important southern tribe, the Choctaws.[29]

The Shawnees and Cherokees that visited the Creeks in early 1770 planned to return during the "Green corn Dance" the following August. Their choice of timing carried great significance. The Green Corn Ceremony, or busk, was the most important event in the Creek calendar—not only a celebration of the ripening of the year's second corn crop but a time of purification and renewal, during which Creek towns often settled disputes with long-standing enemies. Thus the busk was the perfect time for the Shawnee diplomats to appeal to the Creeks to make peace with the Cherokees and

---

Peter H. Wood, "North America in the Era of Captain Cook: Three Glimpses of Indian-European Contact in the Age of the American Revolution," in Stuart B. Schwartz, ed., *Implicit Understandings: Observing, Reporting, and Reflecting on the Encounters between Europeans and Other Peoples in the Early Modern Era* (Cambridge, 1994), 494–495. On the Shawnees' trip south to propose their idea to the Creeks, see Stuart to Botetourt, Jan. 13, 1770, in Davies, ed., *Documents of the American Revolution*, II, 28; Gage to Johnson, Nov. 19, 1770, in *Papers of William Johnson*, VII, 1016. Despite the official hostility between the Creeks and Cherokees, some Cherokees had, for years, "kept on a secret Correspondence with the disaffected Creeks." See Stuart to Fauquier, Nov. 24, 1766, in Reese, ed., *Papers of Francis Fauquier*, III, 1398; Alden, *John Stuart*, 217; David H. Corkran, *The Creek Frontier, 1540–1783* (Norman, Okla., 1967), 199, 255, 273, 275–276; Braund, *Deerskins and Duffels*, 149–150.

29. John Stuart to Gage, Aug. 6, 1770, Gage Papers; Corkran, *Creek Frontier*, 273. When Charles Stuart learned that the Shawnees had been in Creek country, he told John Stuart, "We should be very watchful of their motions" (June 12, 1770, in Davies, ed., *Documents of the American Revolution*, II, 105). On the Shawnees' negotiations with Chickasaws and Choctaws, see Frederick Haldimand to Gage, May 31, 1770, Haldimand Papers, British Museum, Additional Manuscripts (Library of Congress photocopy). The trip to Chickasaw country might actually have been made somewhat earlier. See McKee to Croghan, Feb. 20, 1770, *Papers of William Johnson*, VII, 404; Charles Stuart to John Stuart, June 17, 1770, in Davies, ed., *Documents of the American Revolution*, II, 108–110. Presumably, the diplomats also met with the southern band of the Shawnees, who lived along the Coosa River in Creek country (Dowd, *Spirited Resistance*, 109).

other potential members of the anti-British coalition. Although the Shaw-nees' first visit to the Creeks was not official, British leaders learned that the delegation that would return during the busk would be. Its members were to bring "long strings" or even "belts."[30]

During the same months that the Upper Ohio nations worked to build the anti-British coalition, they also stockpiled gunpowder and shot. Throughout the fall of 1769, Indian traders in Pittsburgh, Detroit, and "the Indian Coun-try" informed Indian agent George Croghan that native hunters bought "no Goods from any of the Traders but Amunition of which they are laying up great Quantitys." Indians not only obtained munitions "for their Peltry" but were "likewise offering their Horses for Amunition which is very uncom-mon," Croghan told Gage on New Year's Day 1770. Two months later, Alex-ander McKee reported that the Shawnees were "still laying up and have now a greater Quantity of Amunition than they ever had before." By May 1770, Croghan was so sure that an Indian confederacy was about to attack the British settlements, he traveled to Pittsburgh to try to sell the buildings and merchandise he owned there to someone that did not know they were in imminent danger of being set ablaze by Indian warriors.[31]

Actually, the prospects for an anti-British confederacy would remain uncertain until at least August 1770, when the Shawnees intended to host a "Great Meeting . . . of the Western and Southren Indians," as Croghan reported. "They talk of between 2 and 3000 Men being to assemble att this Meeting," Croghan told General Gage. "There is Greatt preparations mak-ing . . . by a Number of those Nations being imployd hunting to Dry Mate for the suport of the Distant Nations that is Expected." Croghan was skepti-cal about the Upper Ohio hosts' claim that thousands of warriors would attend the congress. "I Dont thin[k] there will be so many," he told General Gage. Croghan also doubted that the Shawnees would achieve their diplo-matic objectives at the meeting. He believed that their design of a "Gineral Confederacy" was "two Great an undertaking for them Ever to bring about." Croghan sent two spies to the August 1770 Scioto congress, then retired to his estate near Pittsburgh to await the results. When the news finally reached

30. Charles Stuart to John Stuart, June 17, July 17, 1770, in Davies, ed., *Documents of the American Revolution*, II, 110; John Stuart to Gage, Aug. 6, 1770, Gage Papers; Haldimand to Gage, May 31, 1770, Haldimand Papers; Joel W. Martin, *Sacred Revolt: The Creeks' Struggle for a New World* (Boston, 1991), 34–42. The Green Corn Ceremony was also important to later generations of Native American insurgents (Dowd, *Spirited Resistance*, 8–9).

31. Croghan to Gage, January 1, 1770, Gage Papers; McKee to Croghan, Feb. 20, 1770, *Papers of William Johnson*, VII, 405; Tyorhansera, Iroquois congress with William Johnson, July 16, 1771, *DRCH*, VIII, 283; Croghan to Johnson, Dec. 22, 1769, May 10, 1770, *Papers of William Johnson*, VII, 315, 653.

him in mid-September, he was stunned. At the congress, every major nation north of the Ohio River agreed to make peace with every nation south of the river. This was an outcome "which I must confess I thought impossible to bring about," he told General Gage. Gage called the Shawnees' diplomatic success "a notable Piece of Policy."[32]

British officials such as Croghan and Gage came to admire the expertise of the forest diplomats, but they still believed that one of the Indians' strategies was a failure. Officials assumed that their native counterparts intended to keep their "secret councils . . . in the woods" hidden from the British until they could finish assembling the league and launch surprise attacks against the British forts and settlements. Secrecy was impossible, however, because the links between Indian and Anglo-American communities were just too numerous. In addition to accommodationist headmen, there were Indians that had become Christians, and settlers (mostly traders and former captives) that had become Indians. Substantial intermarriage produced children with one foot in each world. For instance, Alexander McKee, apparently the son of a British trader and a Shawnee matron, was the British government's principal informant on the Upper Ohio nations.[33]

Although British officials might indeed have been correct in their surmise that the organizers of the pan-Indian league regretted their inability to keep

32. Croghan to Gage, July 13, Aug. 8, 1770, Gage Papers. Like the Shawnee diplomats' second trip to Creek country, the "Great Meeting" on the Scioto River was scheduled to take place during the Green Corn Ceremony. Evidently, one reason Shawnee leaders chose that time for the grand congress was that the Green Corn Ceremony was practiced in some form by all of the nations invited to the congress; participating in the ceremony together would help unite them. See Elisabeth Tooker, "Iroquois since 1820," in Bruce G. Trigger, ed., *Northeast* (Washington, D.C., 1978), 462, vol. XV of William C. Sturtevant, ed., *Handbook of North American Indians;* Charles Hudson, *The Southeastern Indians* (Knoxville, Tenn., 1976), 365–375; William N. Fenton, "The Iroquois in History," in Eleanor Burke Leacock and Nancy Oestreich Lurie, eds., *North American Indians in Historical Perspective* (New York, 1971), 135. On Croghan and Gage's reaction to the turnout for the Indian congress, see Croghan to Gage, Sept. 20, 1770, Gage to Stuart, Oct. 16, 1770, Gage Papers. Although there is no evidence that any Cherokees or other southern Indians attended the congress, Cherokee headmen later admitted to John Stuart "that some of their young men may possibly have been at the Congress at Sciota" (Stuart to Gage, Dec. 12, 1770).

33. Board of Trade to Shelburne, Dec. 23, 1767, *DRCH*, VII, 1004. Croghan noted that, although the Shawnees were "very reserved to thier most Intimate Friends amongst the Traders," they would tell McKee "any thing they Knew as they Consider him as one of thire own pople his Mother being one of thire Nation" (Croghan to Johnson, Sept. 18, Dec. 22, 1769, *Papers of William Johnson*, VII, 182, 315). "McKee's mother was probably an adopted white Shawnee captive, and his wife was Shawnee" (White, *Middle Ground*, 455). On the multiple links among individuals that subverted categories such as "Indians" and "settlers," see *Middle Ground*, esp. 324.

their "private Councils" secret, it is also possible that the Indians actually *wanted* the British to know what they were up to. If imperial officials learned enough about the growing anti-British league to fear that they were about to be drawn into a costly Indian war, they might try to thwart the coalition by redressing the mutual grievances that held it together. In particular, they might try to keep the Cherokees out of the league by keeping Virginians out of Kentucky. Thus Shawnee diplomats could accomplish their designs without having to subject their fragile coalition to a trial of strength.

Indeed, native diplomats quite often used the threat of an anti-British league to intimidate their British counterparts. In 1769, Seneca leaders told northern Indian agent William Johnson that a proposal to attack the British "might probably be agreed to by too many of the warriors if those affairs which gave them so much uneasiness were not adjusted."[34] Early in 1770, when Shawnee headman Red Hawk learned that George Croghan planned to visit Fort Pitt that spring to hear the Upper Ohio villagers' grievances, Red Hawk protested the Stanwix land deal and pointedly informed Croghan that there would be "Chiefs from the Southren Indians as well as from all the Western Nations to speak to him at that time." "I observe," said Croghan when he received Red Hawk's speech, that the Shawnees "seem to gaskinade or T[h]reaten."[35]

Although the Shawnees proved unable to produce any Cherokee representatives at their summer 1770 meetings with Croghan at Fort Pitt, they did use these meetings to emphasize again the link between British encroachments and Indian unity. On August 1, just before heading down the Ohio to the grand congress on the Scioto, a Shawnee representative told Croghan he feared that the British "designed to take all our Country and then destroy us." The ambassador "pulled out of his Council Bag Sixteen belts of Wampum mostly black and said look at these belts." He claimed they came from the Cherokees, "the French," and numerous western nations and that they urged

34. Croghan to Gage, Jan. 1, 1770, Gage Papers; Johnson to Hillsborough, Aug. 26, 1769, *DRCH*, VIII, 184. Alexander McKee played a prominent role in reporting on the pan-Indian league to British higher-ups. On at least one occasion (in 1769, when he said the Shawnee and the Wabash River nations had "Settled all . . . former Disputes"), McKee overestimated the success of the coalition. It is possible that McKee deliberately exaggerated the coalition's strength in order to frighten his fellow British officers into opposing Virginia's petition for Kentucky. Thus McKee, Britain's half-Shawnee agent in the Ohio country, might have been an agent not only of the British but of the Shawnees as well (McKee journal, [summer 1769], enclosed in McKee to Croghan, Sept. 18, 1769, *Papers of William Johnson*, VII, 184).

35. Red Hawk, speech to George Croghan, McKee journal, Cadwalader Family Collection, Croghan section, box 6, folder 30, HSP; Croghan to Johnson, Apr. 28, 1770, *Papers of William Johnson*, VII, 609.

the Ohio nations to "watch what you [the British] were about." The implication was that, if the British continued to encroach upon Indian land, the Cherokees and the various western nations would unite to oppose them.[36]

The link that Native Americans such as this Shawnee representative drew between their anger at British territorial infringements and their effort to build an anti-British confederacy was immediately clear to British officials in America. The "large Cession of Lands made by the Six Nations" at Stanwix, General Thomas Gage asserted in March 1770, "is the cause of jealousy, and the origin of their present discontent, from whence is derived all the Meetings, and Cabals of the Ohio Seneccas [Mingos], Shawnese, Delawares etc." Any inclination of imperial officials to approve the Stanwix land purchase and Virginia's petition for Kentucky had to contend with their desperate need to avoid a conflict against a pan-Indian league. It was not that they harbored any sentimental aversion to war. The issue was the expense. As John Stuart reminded Gage early in 1770, previous Indian wars had been "expensive" to the imperial treasury, and the cost of fighting a league that united nations north and south of the Ohio River would be even greater. By the early 1770s, Hillsborough worried that the British government would soon be drawn into a "general Indian War, the expense whereof will fall on this Kingdom."[37]

The king's American expenses had already caused him trouble. In order to prevent a costly Indian war, British officials decided not to approve the House of Burgesses' December 1769 petition for Kentucky. In the same packet of letters that revealed the burgesses' territorial ambitions, Hills-

---

36. Shawnee headman, Croghan journal, Aug. 1, 1770, enclosed in Croghan to Gage, Aug. 8, 1770, Gage Papers, in Jennings, ed., *Iroquois Indians*. If the Shawnees really had received encouraging messages from "the French," this deliberately ambiguous term probably referred only to the French-speaking habitants in Indian country.

37. Gage to Carleton, Mar. 26, 1770, Gage Papers. Stanwix was "the Cause of all the Commotions that have lately happened, among the Indians" (Gage to Hillsborough, Jan. 6, 1770, *Papers of William Johnson*, VII, 332). George Croghan and William Johnson, who had personal stakes in the Stanwix land deal, tried unsuccessfully to keep other British officials from discovering that it was the basis of the anti-British Indian league. When Johnson suggested to Gage that the Indians had formed their league because colonists had stolen their horses and committed other crimes against individual Indians, however, Gage quickly replied that the Indians had "other Grievances at Heart, besides Horse stealing or other Trifles of the kind" (Johnson to Gage, May 10, 1770, Gage to Johnson, May 20, 1770, *Papers of William Johnson*, VII, 654, 822). On Hillsborough's fears about the financial consequences of an Indian war, see Stuart to Gage, Jan. 27, 1770, Gage Papers; Hillsborough to Johnson, July 1, 1772, *DRCH*, VIII, 302.

borough found John Stuart's letter warning that the British occupation of Kentucky "would be productive of a general rupture with and coalition of all the tribes on the continent." Hillsborough had other fears as well. He owned substantial rental property in Ireland, whence droves of tenants had already emigrated to America. He was, as Benjamin Franklin said, "terribly afraid of dispeopling Ireland." Thus Hillsborough the landholder joined Hillsborough the imperial official in opposing further colonial encroachment on Indian land. He denounced the burgesses' plan and cited Stuart's warning as the reason.[38] Later, on June 12, 1770, the very day he learned that some Cherokees had welcomed the Shawnee and Delaware advocates of an anti-British coalition, he wrote Stuart, assuring him that he understood the vital need to allow the Cherokees to keep Kentucky. The colonial secretary conveyed to his Cherokee counterparts his pleasure at the "disregard" that they (or, rather, most of them) had shown to "the Emissaries from the Shawanese and Delawares." In an implicit quid pro quo, Hillsborough at the same time promised Cherokee headmen that he would "give every Facility and Dispatch in my Power to the final Settlement of [a] Boundary between them and Virginia"— a boundary that would leave Kentucky in Cherokee country.[39]

Faced with Hillsborough's insistence, the Virginia House of Burgesses voted on June 15, 1770, to accept defeat on the Kentucky question. The

38. Stuart to Botetourt, Jan. 13, 1770, in Davies, ed., *Documents of the American Revolution*, II, 28; Hillsborough to Stuart, Apr. 14, 1770, C.O. 5/71, 149–151; Benjamin Franklin to William Franklin, Sept. 12, 1766, in Leonard W. Labaree et al., eds., *The Papers of Benjamin Franklin* (New Haven, 1959–), XIII, 414. Bernard Bailyn suggests that the anxiety of British landlords like Hillsborough about emigration from Britain to America was the only major reason they tried to brake colonists' westward expansion (Bailyn, *Voyagers to the West: A Passage in the Peopling of America on the Eve of the Revolution* [New York, 1986], 49–66). Actually, Hillsborough's anti-expansionism was shared by his successor as American secretary, Lord Dartmouth, and one of Dartmouth's chief concerns was to avert an Indian war. He told William Johnson he feared that colonists that settled west of the Proclamation Line would "hasten that union of interest among the Savages which you have . . . endeavoured to prevent." See Dec. 1, 1773, *DRCH*, VIII, 404; Hinderaker, *Elusive Empires*, 169; Stephen Aron, *How the West Was Lost: The Transformation of Kentucky from Daniel Boone to Henry Clay* (Baltimore, 1996), 17–18; John Shy, "The Spectrum of Imperial Possibilities: Henry Ellis and Thomas Pownall, 1763–1775," in Shy, *A People Numerous and Armed: Reflections on the Military Struggle for American Independence* (New York, 1976), 42; J. Russell Snapp, *John Stuart and the Struggle for Empire on the Southern Frontier* (Baton Rouge, 1996).

39. Hillsborough to Stuart, June 12, 1770, C.O. 5/71, 253. The letter from Stuart to which Hillsborough responded had been sent on May 2. In it, Stuart reported, "Some emissaries from the Shawnese and Delawares were sometime ago amongst the Cherokees and are now in the Creek nation to sound the dispostion of said Indians towards a confederacy with them and the Western Indians, upon the principle of defending their lands from our encroachments" (Davies, ed., *Documents of the American Revolution*, II, 87).

following October, Acting Governor William Nelson promised Hillsborough that the government of Virginia would grant no trans-Appalachian land until "set at liberty to do it."[40]

IV

Because of the British government's denial of Virginia's bid for Kentucky, its refusal to revoke the Proclamation of 1763, and the Indian coalition-building that had helped to bring about these imperial policies, the total yield of the Virginia land rush set off by the Fort Stanwix treaty was a pile of rejected land petitions and worthless surveys. Virginia speculators had been denied title to millions of acres of land to which they had already received preliminary grants. They had also lost (temporarily, they still hoped) the opportunity to sell all of Kentucky and the adjoining areas—nearly as much land as they and their forebears had sold in the entire history of the Virginia colony.[41] The speculators' failure is inscribed in the colonial land patent

40. June 15, 1770, *JHB, 1770–1772,* 74; Nelson to Hillsborough, Oct. 18, 1770, in John C. Van Horne, ed., *The Correspondence of William Nelson as Acting Governor of Virginia, 1770–1771,* VHS Documents, II (Charlottesville, Va., 1975), 42; Thomas Walker to [William Preston], May 27, 1771, Draper Mss., 2QQ125. Hillsborough pressured northern Indian agent William Johnson to tell Iroquois, Shawnee, and Cherokee diplomats that the British government would not allow colonists to settle in the portion of the Stanwix cession that lay south of the mouth of the Kanawha River. By bowing both to the Iroquois demand that Britain accept the Stanwix cession *and* to the Cherokee demand that no British subjects occupy Kentucky, the imperial government mananged to reconcile the seemingly irreconcilable treaties that its agents had negotiated with those two nations in the fall of 1768 (Downes, *Council Fires,* 148). Thomas Gage emphasized to William Johnson that "the Fear of a Rupture with" the Indians had "no doubt occasioned Virginia to be bounded by" the Kanawha–New River (Sept. 10, 1769, *Papers of William Johnson,* VII, 160).

Preventing a costly war against the Indians was not the Privy Council's only reason for maintaining the Proclamation Line. British imperialists also hoped the line would confine American colonists within Britain's economic and political orbit (Charles R. Ritcheson, *British Politics and the American Revolution* [Norman, Okla., 1954], 63–64). For about four years, there was an additional reason for the government to prohibit Virginia governors from giving away land in what is now West Virginia and western Pennsylvania: a proposal to grant ten million acres to a syndicate headed by Thomas Walpole. See Hillsborough to Botetourt, July 31, 1770, in Davies, ed., *Documents of the American Revolution,* II, 156; Sosin, *Whitehall and the Wilderness,* 181–210.

41. Unpatented Loyal Company surveys in Augusta County, [Nov. 1768–Apr. 1769], unpatented Greenbrier Company surveys in Augusta County, [Apr.–May 1769], Virginia Colonial Land Office Records; Thomas Lewis to William Preston, Mar. 15, 1774, Draper Mss., 3QQ13; "Copy of Grants of Lands Made from April 1745," Etting Collection, Ohio Company Papers, box 40, file 80, HSP; Loyal Company contract, n.d., Page-Walker Papers

books. The patented land area of Virginia had nearly doubled between 1727 and 1749; from 1749 to 1773, it grew by less than one-third.[42]

Although the Proclamation of 1763 was aimed at both settlers and speculators, it was much more successful in denying legal title to speculators than in keeping farm families from simply moving west. Since the whole purpose of speculating in Native American land was to sell it to settlers, the proclamation was far more harmful to speculators than if it had hindered them and settlers equally. Although hundreds of families settled inside the vast tracts claimed by land firms like the Loyal Company, none would "think of paying, until the company could perfect his title; and this they never could do" until after Independence, a Virginia judge explained a generation later. Squatters also vexed Patrick Henry and George Washington. Washington lamented in 1772 that squatters took advantage of the Privy Council's ban on legal west-

---

(#3098), box 1, UVA; Fincastle County surveys, abstracted in Lewis Preston Summers, ed., *Annals of Southwest Virginia, 1769–1800* (Abingdon, Va., 1929), 652–665; Jefferson, *Notes on Virginia*, ed. Peden, 4. One group of speculators did get patents. That was the small group of Seven Years' War veterans that were able to claim land under a bounty offer Governor Robert Dinwiddie had made in 1754. But the Dinwiddie claimants' good fortune was not shared by the much larger group of veterans claiming land under the Privy Council's postwar bounty offer, whose claim the Executive Council refused even to consider. Those veterans, and every other Virginia land speculator except the Dinwiddie claimants and four other minor exceptions, got nothing.

42. John M. Hemphill II, "Prerogative, Patronage, and Power: The Political Process and the Decline of Royal Authority in Virginia, 1696–1775" (paper delivered at the annual meeting of the Southern Historical Association, Memphis, Nov. 4, 1982); Peter V. Bergstrom, *Markets and Merchants: Economic Diversification in Colonial Virginia, 1700–1775* (New York, 1985), 49. Numerous historians have wrongly stated that the 1768 Fort Stanwix treaty superseded and voided the Proclamation of 1763. See Bailyn, *Voyagers to the West*, 537; Eugene M. Del Papa, "The Royal Proclamation of 1763: Its Effect upon Virginia Land Companies," *VMHB*, LXXXIII (1975), 406–407; John Richard Alden, *The South in the Revolution, 1763–1789* ([Baton Rouge, La.], 1957), 134; Bil Gilbert, *God Gave Us This Country: Tekamthi and the First American Civil War* (New York, 1989), 56–61; Wilbur R. Jacobs, "British Indian Policies to 1783," in Wilcomb E. Washburn, ed., *History of Indian-White Relations* (Washington, D.C., 1988), 11, vol. IV of *Handbook of North American Indians*, ed. Sturtevant; Norman K. Risjord, *Jefferson's America, 1760–1815* (Madison, Wis., 1991), 79–80. Virginia land speculators persuaded the British government to obtain a small additional slice of Kentucky from the Cherokees in 1770, and it was enlarged by means of creative surveying the following year. See Andrew Lewis and John Donelson, depositions, [1777–1778], in Boyd et al., eds., *Papers of Jefferson*, II, 78–80; John Richard Alden, *John Stuart and the Southern Colonial Frontier: A Study of Indian Relations, War, Trade, and Land Problems in the Southern Wilderness, 1754–1775* (Ann Arbor, Mich., 1944), 279–281. But it did not matter where the boundary ran so long as the Proclamation of 1763, which banned all trans-Appalachian patents, remained in force.

ern expansion to set up housekeeping in the forbidden zone. If the ban were lifted, they planned to bypass gentry middlemen and "sollicit legal Titles" directly from the British government "on the ground of preoccupancy."[43]

The Proclamation of 1763 was anathema to every Virginia land speculator, but settlers were ambivalent about it. On the one hand, since no land titles could be procured, farm families were able (as Lord Dunmore, the last royal governor, complained) to "Settle without any." Relieved of the burden of supporting gentry surveyors, speculators, and landlords, settlers were, according to one, "as free as any buck a-goin." In addition to inadvertently shielding squatters, the imperial government's anti-expansionist policy inhibited the establishment of government institutions in the backcountry, making the region safer than ever for absconding debtors. In 1774, a Fincastle County justice instructed Sheriff James Thompson to seize property from one of trader Alexander Baine's debtors, Daniel Boone. Thompson brought the writ back, marked "Not Ex[ecute]d gone to Kentucky."

The protection that the Proclamation of 1763 afforded to squatters and debtors might even have led some of them to support it. But most farmers in the backcountry probably opposed the proclamation, for it prevented them from securing clear title to the land they claimed. Farmers that settled west of the Appalachians worried that they would improve a homestead—clear

43. Dabney Carr, opinion, *David French v. Successors of the Loyal Company* (1834), in Benjamin Watkins Leigh, reporter, *Reports of Cases Argued and Determined in the Court of Appeals, and in the General Court of Virginia*, V (Richmond, Va., 1836), 637; Washington to Dunmore, June 15, 1772, William Crawford to Washington, Aug. 2, 1771, Mar. 15, 1772, May 1, 1772, Dec. 29, 1773, all in Abbot et al., eds., *Papers of Washington*, Colonial Series, VIII, 513, IX, 25–26, 37, 55, 418–420; May 5, 1772, *Executive Journals of the Council*, VI, 458; Mississippi Company to Thomas Cumming, Mar. 1, 1767, in Clarence E. Carter, ed., "Documents Relating to the Mississippi Land Company, 1763–1769," *American Historical Review*, XVI (1910–1911), 316 (hereafter cited as *AHR*); "A Copy from the Register of the Proceedings of the Loyal Company Now in the Possession of Edm. Pendleton, January 7th. 1815," Walker Papers, container 165; Thomas Walker to William Preston, May 27, 1771, in Archibald Henderson, ed., *Dr. Thomas Walker and the Loyal Company of Virginia* (Worcester, Mass., 1931), 69; Walker to Reece Bowen et al., Mar. 28, 1774, William Fleming Papers (Cyrus Hall McCormick Library, Washington and Lee University, Lexington, Va.; photostat at LVA); Samuel Pepper, William Preston, and William Thompson, "Articles of Agreement . . . ," Jan. 3, 1775, Preston Family Papers, folder 860; Preston to Robert Doack, Oct. 1, 1771, William Campbell to Margaret Campbell, May 1, 1772, Campbell-Preston-Floyd Family Papers, I, LC; Loyal Company contract, n.d., Page-Walker Papers, box 1; Fincastle County surveys, abstracted in Summers, ed., *Annals of Southwest Virginia*, 652–665; Committee of Propositions and Grievances, report, Nov. 11, 1778, *Journal of the House of Delegates of the Commonwealth of Virginia; Begun . . . on Monday, the Fifth Day of October, in the Year of Our Lord One Thousand Seven Hundred and Seventy-Eight* (Richmond, 1827), 54.

and fence fields, erect buildings, and so forth—only to be evicted by someone that secured title to the tract after the expected repeal of the Proclamation of 1763. Many of these farmers engaged in small-scale land speculation, which suffered the same fate as the grander ventures of the gentry.[44]

The Indian congress that had met in Lower Shawnee Town in August 1770 continued to convene annually for the next few years, but few southern Indian diplomats ever attended it. The warfare between the southern Indians and the nations of the Wabash River continued. Still, even as the anti-British league became more and more a phantom, imperial officials became increasingly frightened of it, and their determination to prevent British colonists from provoking an Indian war continued to grow.[45]

Optimistic Virginia land dealers nonetheless held out hope that the Proclamation of 1763 would soon be repealed. There were straws enough at which to grasp. John Murray, the fourth earl of Dunmore, became governor late in 1771 and began issuing bounty patents to veterans of the Seven Years' War. Although he issued no patents to Loyal Company customers, he did provide sufficient encouragement that, at the end of 1773, the firm "recommenced," as post-Revolutionary suit papers attest, "and continued thenceforth until the revolution, making surveys . . . of such lands as they had contracted to sell." Dunmore's expansionism encouraged other speculators. In 1772, George Mason revived the Ohio Company. The following year,

44. Dunmore to Dartmouth, Apr. 2, 1774, C.O. 5/1352, 99; Adam O'Brien, in Faye Bartlett Reeder, "The Evolution of the Virginia Land Grant System in the Eighteenth Century" (Ph.D. diss., Ohio State University, 1937), 128; Thomas D. Curtis, "Land Policy: Pre-condition for the Success of the American Revolution," *American Journal of Economics and Sociology*, XXXI (1972), 209–224; John Byrd, writ, Aug. 4, 1775, Fincastle County Court Papers (photocopy), LVA; Fauquier to Board of Trade, May 22, 1766, in Reese, ed., *Papers of Francis Fauquier*, III, 1362. On small-scale land speculation, see Robert D. Mitchell, *Commercialism and Frontier: Perspectives on the Early Shenandoah Valley* (Charlottesville, Va., 1977), chap. 3.

45. In fact, there were nearly continuous contacts between insurgent Shawnees and rebels from southern nations. Those culminated in the discussions that Tecumseh had with the Creeks in 1811. See Colin G. Calloway, " 'We Have Always Been the Frontier': The American Revolution in Shawnee Country," *American Indian Quarterly*, XVI (1992), 42; Wood, "North America in the Era of Captain Cook," in Schwartz, ed., *Implicit Understandings*, 495; Martin, *Sacred Revolt*; Dowd, *Spirited Resistance*, 44–52; White, *Middle Ground*, 354–356; McConnell, *Country Between*, 266–268; Hillsborough to Johnson, July 1, 1772, *DRCH*, VIII, 302. Largely because British officials continued to fear the Indian coalition, the "senseless prohibiting proclamation" of 1763 remained in force ("A Virginian," Rind's *VG*, Mar. 3, 1774).

Patrick Henry bought up veterans' bounty rights, and Thomas Jefferson joined in a land scheme that promised him at least ten thousand acres.[46]

Henry and Jefferson's optimism was not shared by George Washington. "I am not without my fears that we may yet meet with some rubs before this matter is finished," Washington wrote on February 28, 1774. The cause of Washington's anxiety was that Lord Hillsborough, who had resigned as colonial secretary in 1772 but retained influence in British politics, had declared that American veterans had no right to bounty land. Hillsborough's stance fueled Washington's patriotism. "I consider it in no other light than as one, among many proofs, of that Nobleman's Malignant disposition to American's," wrote Washington. All officers should share equally in the king's bounty, he said; "I can see no cause why Americans . . . should be stigmatiz'd."[47]

Washington was right to worry. The new colonial secretary, Lord Dartmouth, wrote in a letter of April 6, 1774, to Governor Dunmore that Virginia veterans were not entitled to claim bounty land, even east of the Proclamation Line. Only ten veterans received bounty patents before Dunmore implemented Dartmouth's order. Although the April 1774 order affected only veterans, the Privy Council had voted earlier to abolish all free land grants. On February 3, 1774, the council decided that, henceforth, American land would be sold at auction to the highest bidder.[48]

Would the Privy Council's abolition of land grants actually be enforced in Virginia? George Mason meant to find out. Mason had bought up head-

46. *French v. The Successors of the Loyal Company*, in Leigh, reporter, *Reports of Cases*, V, 629; Patent Book XLII, Virginia Land Office Records, 505–524; Mason to Carter, Mar. 12, 1776, in Robert A. Rutland, ed., *The Papers of George Mason, 1725–1792* (Chapel Hill, N.C., 1970), I, 263; [Patrick Henry] to [William Fleming?], Nov. 22, 1773, Fleming Papers; entry, Nov. 29, 1773, in Bear and Stanton, eds., *Jefferson's Memorandum Books*, I, 350; John Hisox et al., petition for land, Mar. 11, 1773, *Executive Journals of the Council*, VI, 521.

47. Washington to William Preston, Feb. 28, 1774, Peter Hog to Washington, Dec. 11, 1773, John Armstrong to Washington, Dec. 24, 1773, in Abbot et al., eds., *Papers of Washington*, Colonial Series, IX, 404, 415–416, 500–501. Washington had received several bounty patents and hoped to receive many more.

48. Apr. 6, 1774, C.O. 5/1352, 1–2; Patent Book XLII, 505–524, Virginia Land Office Records. Hoping to choke off British emigration and colonial expansion—and to take a bigger share of the profits arising from land sales—the ministry not only established real estate auctions but also set a minimum price of six pence per acre, five times the nominal fee grantees had paid. Land granted in the future would also pay double the existing quitrents. See Dartmouth to nine American governors, Feb. 5, 1774, in Davies, ed., *Documents of the American Revolution*, VIII, 42–45; "Mr. [William] Knox on the proposed mode of granting lands in America . . . ," [1773?], Dartmouth Manuscripts (Staffordshire Record Office, Stafford, Eng.); Bailyn, *Voyagers to the West*, 49–66.

rights worth fifty thousand acres of land. On May 27, 1774, Mason, probably with help from Thomas Jefferson, petitioned the Executive Council of Virginia to grant him fifty thousand acres west of the Appalachian Mountains.[49] Although Mason claimed he had a "strict Right" to the land, the Executive Council, citing the Proclamation of 1763, refused to give it to him. Across the Atlantic at the same time, ministers devised a new way to thwart colonial attempts to settle beyond the western branches of the Ohio River. Dartmouth believed that "nothing can more effectively tend to discourage such attempts" than giving all the land west of the Ohio to the province of Quebec, and his recommendation was incorporated into the Quebec Act, passed in Parliament in June 1774.[50] Thus the Ohio, the river that the Virginia gentry had once viewed as a sure route to wealth, became a barrier instead.

In the fall of 1774, Virginia land dealers made one last effort to obtain Kentucky. They knew that a principal reason the Privy Council denied them title to the land west of the Appalachians was that the Cherokee and Upper Ohio nations would not give it up. The Virginians believed that if they could secure from the Shawnees and Mingos what they had already received from the Iroquois—deeds to Kentucky—they could persuade the Privy Council that the Proclamation of 1763 was no longer needed. Since the Shawnees and Mingos were unwilling to give up their hunting territory peacefully, the Virginians decided to secure the deeds by force.

But first the speculators needed what land dealer Edmund Pendleton called a "pretence" for attacking the Indians. They found one in the spring of 1774, when a half-French Mingo named John Logan raided Virginia and

49. There is a copy of Mason's petition, corrected by Jefferson, in the Jefferson Papers at the Library of Congress. That version of the petition with an assigned date of June 1774 is printed in Boyd et al., eds., *Papers of Jefferson*, I, 112–116. The government of Virginia rewarded anyone that imported a slave or servant into the province with fifty acres (Billings, Selby, and Tate, *Colonial Virginia*, 41).

50. May 27, June 17, 1774, *Executive Journals of the Council*, VI, 562, 578; "Inventory of Mason's Headright Certificates," in Rutland, ed., *Papers of George Mason*, II, 532. Speculators willing to participate in the new auction system could still obtain land east of the Proclamation Line, but few believed that very much fertile eastern land remained unpatented (Mitchell, *Commercialism and Frontier*, 74, 93). On Parliament's decision to give the region west of the Ohio to Quebec, see Dartmouth to Hillsborough, May 1, 1774, in B. D. Bargar, *Lord Dartmouth and the American Revolution* (Columbia, S.C., 1965), 124. William Knox, Dartmouth's secretary, said that Parliament annexed the region between the Ohio and Mississippi Rivers to Quebec "with the avowed purpose of excluding all further settlement therein." See [William Knox], *The Justice and Policy of the Late Act of Parliament, for Making More Effectual Provision for the Government of the Province of Quebec . . .* (London, 1774), 43; Justin Winsor, "Virginia and the Quebec Bill," *AHR*, I (1895–1896), 439–440.

Pennsylvania settlements in retaliation for the murder of his family by a group of Virginians. Logan's kinspeople had been killed soon after John Connolly, Governor Dunmore's representative at Pittsburgh, issued a circular letter that essentially declared war on the Indians.[51] It seems likely that Connolly's circular and the murder of Logan's family were part of a deliberate effort by leading Virginians to provoke a revenge raid that would justify an invasion of the Ohio country. Logan's raid was actually quite limited. It was nevertheless well publicized—and exaggerated—by Virginia leaders. "The Oppertunty we hav So long wished for, is now before us," declared William Preston. Preston was militia lieutenant and government land surveyor for Fincastle County, every acre of which was west of the Proclamation Line. During October 1774, in what came to be known as Dunmore's War, an army of two thousand Virginians attacked the Shawnee and Mingo towns on the Muskingum River, a northern tributary of the Ohio, and forced headmen to deed all the land east of the Ohio River, including all of Kentucky, to Virginia.[52]

51. Pendleton to Joseph Chew, June 20, 1774, in David John Mays, ed., *The Letters and Papers of Edmund Pendleton, 1734–1803* (Charlottesville, Va., 1967), I, 94; White, *Middle Ground*, 362; Jack M. Sosin, *The Revolutionary Frontier, 1763–1783* (New York, 1967), 85; John Campbell to William Sinclair, July 26, 177[4], in Barbara DeWolfe, ed., *Discoveries of America: Personal Accounts of British Emigrants to North America during the Revolutionary Era* (Cambridge, 1997), 155. "The reception of [Connolly's circular] letter was the epoch of open hostilities with the Indians," George Rogers Clark later recalled (Downes, *Council Fires*, 161). Michael Cresap declared that "it was in consequence of a circular letter from said *Conolly*, directed to the inhabitants on the *Ohio*, that he murdered the *Indians*" (["Remarks on the Proceedings of Dr. Conolly, Pittsburgh, June 25, 1774,"] in Peter Force, comp., *American Archives: Consisting of a Collection of Authentick Records, State Papers, Debates, and Letters and Other Notices of Publick Affairs*, 4th Ser. [Washington, D.C., 1837–1846], I, 484). See also Reuben Gold Thwaites and Louise Phelps Kellogg, eds., *Documentary History of Dunmore's War, 1774* (Madison, Wis., 1905), xiii–xiv, 12n; White, *Middle Ground*, 357; McConnell, *Country Between*, 275.

52. Preston, circular letter, July 20, 1774, William Christian to William Preston, Nov. 8, 1774, in Thwaites and Kellogg, eds., *Dunmore's War*, 92–93; "Virginius," Rind's *VG*, Mar. 24, 1774; White, *Middle Ground*, 361; McConnell, *Country Between*, 275–276. Some historians continue to discuss the 1774 Indian raids without reporting the massacre of John Logan's relatives that prompted them (Billings, Selby, and Tate, *Colonial Virginia*, 337). For evidence that retaliation for Logan's raid was only the "pretence" for an invasion whose actual purpose was to acquire Indian land, see Holton, "Revolt of the Ruling Class," 431–437. On Dunmore's War, see William Christian to William Preston, Nov. 8, 1774, in Thwaites and Kellogg, eds., *Dunmore's War*, 301–304.

The other principal reason for Dunmore's War was that the Shawnees had (nonviolently) stopped participants in the 1773–1774 Virginia land rush from surveying their hunt-

Unfortunately for the Virginia militia officers that had obtained the Kentucky deed, it had little effect on imperial land policy. The Privy Council knew that the Shawnees and Mingos would not feel bound to a document that had been forced upon them. Besides, by this time Virginia was in open revolt against Britain, and British officials—even Governor Dunmore—were in no mood to accommodate the rebels.[53]

Until 1774, Virginia land speculators had held out hope that the Proclamation of 1763 would turn out to be what George Washington had once called it: "a temporary expedien[t]" likely to be repealed soon. That hope disappeared in 1774, when speculators learned in quick succession about the Privy Council's February abolition of land grants, Dartmouth's April ban on grants to American veterans, the Executive Council's June decision to continue enforcement of the Proclamation of 1763, and Parliament's June passage of the Quebec Act (see Figure 4). This multifaceted assault on land speculation angered Virginia gentlemen. Veterans of the Seven Years' War castigated "the present faithless and venal Ministry" (as William Peachey called it) for denying them the bounty to which they felt entitled. Edmund Pendleton, a Loyal Company member, wrote that, when gentry land peddlers learned of the new system of government land auctions, they "were very angry with the Ministry for degrading Royaltie into the Pedlar hawking Lands for sale." Drawing on his legal training, Pendleton argued that the ministry had probably violated the British constitution by trying to "alter the terms" on which Virginians acquired Indian land. The Privy Council's land grant ban was also protested by another lawyer, Thomas Jefferson, who declared that George III "has no right to grant lands of himself."[54] As dele-

ing land ("Speech of Six Shawanese Indians," June 28, 1773, in *Papers of William Johnson*, VIII, 834).

53. Francis Jennings, "The Indians' Revolution," in Alfred F. Young, ed., *The American Revolution: Explorations in the History of American Radicalism* (DeKalb, Ill., 1976), 343; Downes, *Council Fires*, chap. 7; Jack M. Sosin, "The British Indian Department and Dunmore's War," *VMHB*, LXXIV (1966), 34–50; Turk McClesk[e]y, "Dunmore's War," in Richard L. Blanco, ed., *The American Revolution, 1775–1783: An Encyclopedia* (New York, 1993), I, 492–497; McConnell, *Country Between*, 268–279; Holton, "Ohio Indians," *JSH*, LX (1994), 473–474; White, *Middle Ground*, 365. None of the land dealers openly stated that persuading the Privy Council to repeal the Proclamation of 1763 was a key reason they had obtained the deed to Kentucky. But the speculators surely knew that the deed would be worthless to them unless the Privy Council allowed them to take title to it. See Jennings, "Indians' Revolution," in Young, ed., *American Revolution*, 338.

54. Washington to William Crawford, Sept. [17], 1767, in Abbot et al., eds., *Papers of Washington*, Colonial Series, VIII, 28; William Peachey to William Preston, Jan. 24, 1775,

gates attending the First Continental Congress compiled a list of their grievances against the British government, Richard Henry Lee told them the
Quebec Act was "the worst grievance" of all.[55]

Lee exaggerated. It is clear that the British government's decision to abolish Virginia land speculation west of the Alleghenies was not the Virginia
patriots' paramount concern. After all, some speculators did not become
patriots, and many patriots had never speculated. But the abolition of land
grants was surely a major complaint for Virginia's leading revolutionaries,
because it hurt almost all of them. George Mason, who would write the
constitution for the new Commonwealth of Virginia, had watched the Proclamation of 1763 destroy first his beloved Ohio Company and then his hopes
of obtaining fifty thousand acres of Kentucky land using headrights. Richard

Preston Family Papers, folder 863; Edmund Pendleton to Joseph Chew, June 20, 1774, in
Mays, ed., *Letters and Papers of Edmund Pendleton*, I, 92; "A Native, and Member of the
House of Burgesses" [Jefferson], "A Summary View of the Rights of British America," in
Boyd et al., eds., *Papers of Jefferson*, I, 133; Dunmore to Dartmouth, June 9, 1774, in Davies,
ed., *Documents of the American Revolution*, VIII, 130–131; Thomas Lewis to William Preston,
June 8, 1774, Draper Mss., 3QQ38; Clarence Walworth Alvord, *The Mississippi Valley in
British Politics: A Study of the Trade, Land Speculation, and Experiments in Imperialism
Culminating in the American Revolution* (Cleveland, Ohio, 1917), II, 215–216; Johnson, *Wil-
liam Preston*, 114; Isaac S. Harrell, "Some Neglected Phases of the Revolution in Virginia,"
WMQ, 2d Ser., V (1925), 160. On paper, the Privy Council had only switched from giving
away land to selling it, but many land speculators chose to interpret the council's order as an
absolute barrier to acquiring Indian land.

55. Richard Henry Lee, Patrick Henry, speeches in Continental Congress, Oct. 14, 17,
1774, James Duane's notes, in Bernhard Knollenberg, *Growth of the American Revolution,
1766–1775* (New York, 1975), 124, 383n. William Lee declared that "every tie of allegiance is
broken by the Quebec act" (William Lee to Richard Henry Lee, Sept. 10, 1774, July 13, 1775, in
Worthington Chauncey Ford, ed., *Letters of William Lee . . . , 1766–1783* [1891], [New York,
1968], I, 89, 163–164). See also Samuel W. Jones, "Memoir of the Hon. James Duane," in
Jennings, "Indians' Revolution," in Young, ed., *American Revolution*, 340; George Mason to
Richard Henry Lee, Apr. 12, 1779, in Rutland, ed., *Papers of George Mason*, II, 499; Thomas
Hill to Thomas Adams, Aug. 20, 1774, Adams Family Papers (1672–1792), section 6 (micro-
film, VHS); Continental Association, Oct. 20, 1774, in Boyd et al., eds., *Papers of Jefferson*, I,
150; "Americanus," Purdie's *VG*, [Apr. 8, 1775], in *Revolutionary Virginia*, II, 352; Rind's *VG*,
Sept. 1, 1774; Adam Stephen to William Fleming, May 31, 1775, in Harry M. Ward, *Major
General Adam Stephen and the Cause of American Liberty* (Charlottesville, Va., 1989), 123;
Oct. 26, 1774, in William Eddis, *Letters from America*, ed. Aubrey C. Land (Cambridge,
Mass., 1969), 90; Hilda Neatby, *Quebec: The Revolutionary Age, 1760–1791* (Toronto, 1966),
134; Curtis P. Nettels, *The Roots of American Civilization: A History of American Colonial Life*
(New York, 1938), 612, 644; Winsor, "Virginia and the Quebec Bill," *AHR*, I (1895–1896), 439,
442; ["Richard Henry Lee's Draft Address to the King,"] [Oct. 21? 1774], in Paul H. Smith et
al., eds., *Letters of Delegates to Congress*, I (Washington, D.C., 1976), 226.

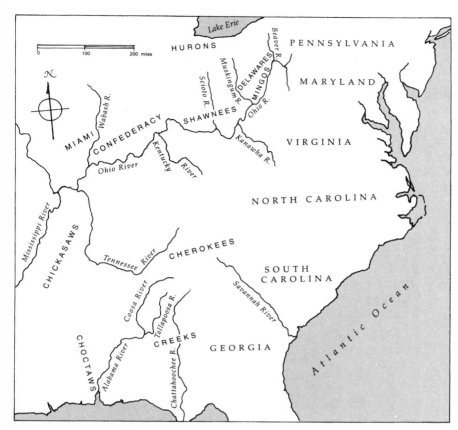

FIGURE 4. Virginia and Its Neighbors, 1776.
Drawn by Richard Stinely

Henry Lee, who would introduce the motion for Independence at the Continental Congress, had seen his Mississippi Land Company's hope of obtaining 2,500,000 acres of Indian land disappear behind a double barrier: the Proclamation of 1763 and the Quebec Act of 1774. Another Mississippi Company member, George Washington, had bought up thousands of acres in veterans' claims to bounty land, only to have Lord Dartmouth deny these claims. Thomas Jefferson was a partner in three land firms that would have yielded him a total of seventeen thousand acres of Indian land, were it not for the Privy Council's land restrictions. Patrick Henry had participated in at least five land ventures between 1767 and 1773. He knew that he had wasted his money acquiring worthless claims—that is, if the ministry had its way.[56]

56. July 12, 1749, May 27, June 17, 1774, *Executive Journals of the Council*, V, 295–296, VI, 562, 578; Carter, ed., "Documents Relating to the Mississippi Land Company," *AHR*, XVI

The ministry did not have its way, of course. Led by land speculators, white Virginians declared Independence from Britain in 1776 and adopted a state constitution that nullified the Proclamation of 1763 and the Quebec Act.[57] Thus it is clear that in Virginia, the decision for Independence was partly the result of a complex struggle involving the British government and three groups of Americans: land speculators, backcountry settlers, and Ohio Valley Indians. Often in American history, Indians are seen as the passive victims of white decisions. In this case, the lines of force also ran in the opposite direction. Delaware and Shawnee diplomats powerfully influenced the most important decision white Americans ever made.

(1910–1911), 311–319; Bartholomew Dandridge to Washington, Feb. 16, 1774, John David Wilper to Washington, Mar. 23, 1774, in Abbot et al., eds., *Papers of Washington*, Colonial Series, IX, 479–480, X, 3–4. On Henry's speculations, see Henry to William Fleming, June 10, 1767, Draper Mss., 15ZZ3; Patrick Henry, fee book, cited in William Wirt Henry, *Patrick Henry*, I, 121; [Patrick Henry] to [William Fleming?], Nov. 22, 1773, Fleming Papers; depositions, William Christian, June 3, 1777, Patrick Henry, June 4, 1777, in *CVSP*, I, 262, 288–290.

57. Virginia Constitution, in Rutland, ed., *Papers of George Mason*, I, 309; Harrell, *Loyalism in Virginia*, 22.

2

TOBACCO GROWERS

VERSUS MERCHANTS

AND PARLIAMENT

Robert Routledge spent the morning of Tuesday, June 3, 1766, getting drunk. Routledge had greeted life in Cumberland in northern England, but he now lived in Virginia, where he sold foreign merchandise— everything from British textiles to Jamaican rum—to tobacco farmers. June 3 found him in Cumberland County, Virginia, at Benjamin Mosby's tavern. It is likely that Routledge was celebrating that morning. Word had just arrived that Parliament had repealed the Stamp Act, partly because Virginia's gentlemen justices had refused to hear any cases while it remained in force. The gentry's tactic had enlisted British creditors in the campaign to repeal the Stamp Act. If Robert Routledge really was celebrating that morning, it was not only because the stamp tax had been abolished but because courthouses, like the one near Mosby's tavern, would soon reopen their doors. Now he could resume legal action against his numerous debtors in the colony.

John Chiswell was also in Benjamin Mosby's tavern that Tuesday morning, but it is unlikely that he was celebrating. Chiswell was thousands of pounds in debt, and for him the reopening of the courts would be a disaster— especially at this time, because Chiswell's son-in-law, the speaker of the House of Burgesses, John Robinson, had just died. Robinson had taken more than £100,000 out of the provincial treasury and lent it to himself and numerous friends, including John Chiswell. Now that he was dead, the administrators of his estate (court-appointed executors) would open his books, discover the loans, and demand that Robinson's debtors immediately

FIGURE 5. John Robinson, Speaker of the House of Burgesses.
Courtesy, Virginia Historical Society

repay the funds that he had misappropriated. The problem was that Chiswell did not have the money.

Chiswell, Robinson, and William Byrd of Westover (another of Robinson's debtors) had formed a company to mine for lead near the New River on the Virginia frontier. By 1766, however, the mine had failed, partly because it was west of the Anglo-Indian boundary established by the Proclamation of 1763. The proclamation had prevented the mine partners from taking title to their diggings, and it had also discouraged colonists—whose very presence would have boosted the value of the land around the mine—from settling in the area. The failure of the mining venture accelerated the process by which Chiswell, Robinson, and other Virginia gentlemen fell deep into debt.

Chiswell's and Routledge's conflicting attitudes about the reopening of the courts were probably among the reasons that the two men got into an argument that Tuesday. Things quickly got out of hand. Chiswell called the trader "a villain who came to Virginia to cheat and defraud men of their property" and a "Scotch rebel." This last insult linked Routledge to the Jacobite rebellion of 1745, an attempt, led by James II's grandson "Bonnie Prince Charlie" and centered in Scotland, to restore the Stuart monarchy.

No one in pre-Revolutionary Virginia would have been surprised to hear one of the colony's numerous Scottish storekeepers tarred with the Jacobite brush. Virginia farmers hated the Scots for the same reasons that farmers always hate merchants. The gentry hated them for these reasons and also for supplanting the gentlemen themselves as Virginia's commercial middlemen. Thus the last insult that Chiswell hurled against Routledge would have been entirely conventional—if Routledge had been Scottish. But Routledge was from Cumbria, in England. By 1766, Virginians no longer used the term *Scottish* exclusively in reference to a national identity. *Scottish* also evoked an economic class, the men that came to the colony for a few years to seek their fortunes selling British manufactures and buying tobacco. As further evidence of the transformation in the meaning of *Scottish*, it should be noted that John Chiswell, the man that attacked an Englishman for being "Scotch," was himself the son of a Scottish immigrant.

No one at the time paused to consider the irony of Chiswell's words, for he now ordered his young slave to bring him a weapon that symbolized his status as a Virginia gentleman: his sword. The young man refused. Chiswell, incensed at being defied by a black person as well as a "Scotch rebel," threatened to kill the slave, and the sword was soon produced. The emboldened Chiswell now advanced on Routledge. With a final shout of "Presbyterian fellow," he thrust his sword. "He is dead, and I killed him," he said.[1]

---

1. Jesse Thomas, deposition, Purdie and Dixon's *VG*, Sept. 12, 1766; Carl Bridenbaugh, "Violence and Virtue in Virginia, 1766: or, The Importance of the Trivial," Massachusetts Historical Society, *Proceedings*, LXXVI (Boston, 1964), 3–29. Virginia lieutenant governor Francis Fauquier was a founding member of the mine partnership but soon dropped out (Vera Lee Austin, "The Southwest Virginia Lead Works, 1756–1802" [M.A. thesis, Virginia Polytechnic Institute and State University, 1977]. On the impact of the Proclamation of 1763

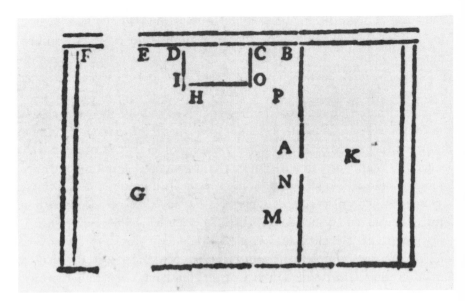

FIGURE 6. *Purdie and Dixon's* Virginia Gazette, *July 18, 1766. Detail of the crime scene at Mosby's tavern. The right-hand side of the picture traces Chiswell's activity, the left-hand side Routledge's. The box at the top represents a table. At K, Chiswell was given his sword by his slave; on coming back into the room, he proceeded from M to B, insulting Routledge while keeping his back to the wall (lest someone attempt to disarm him). Meanwhile, Routledge was guided from G to the door at EF by Joseph Carrington, a concerned bystander. When Chiswell, now at P, called out "Presbyterian fellow," Routledge stepped over to D, at which point Chiswell moved to O and "stabbed him through the heart across the table." Routledge sank into the arms of Carrington at E "and instantly expired." Courtesy, Virginia Historical Society*

For the modern reader, the Routledge murder and the insults that accompanied it help to define two classes that were just then becoming distinct in Virginia. A generation earlier, many of the men at the apex of the colony's pyramid of wealth and power could not easily be identified as "gentlemen" or "merchants." Many were Britons that had come to Virginia as traders and then either bought or married their way into the gentry class. Other elites derived part of their income from tobacco growing, part from selling Indian land, and part from trade. But by 1766 these trader-growers were dissolving into two new classes: gentlemen tobacco growers like John Chiswell and British traders like Robert Routledge. Chiswell's murder of Routledge was part of an emerging class conflict between these growers and merchants, and

upon the mine, see William Herbert to William Byrd III, Mar. 6, 1764, in Marion Tinling, ed., *The Correspondence of the Three William Byrds of Westover, Virginia, 1684–1776* (Charlottesville, Va., 1977), II, 768.

it was not the last time that the conflict turned violent. The struggle between Virginia tobacco growers and British merchants helped to spark the American Revolution.

If John Chiswell's killing of Robert Routledge highlighted the extent to which gentlemen like Chiswell were influenced by their mounting debts, so did another fatality that involved Chiswell. On Wednesday, October 15, the day before he was to be tried for his life, Chiswell killed himself. When Chiswell's son-in-law died four months earlier, he had carried to his grave the distinction of owing more money than almost anyone in Virginia history; John Burk, who interviewed members of the Revolutionary generation for his *History of Virginia*, hinted that Robinson, like Chiswell, might have died at his own hands.[2] Chiswell and Robinson's friend William Byrd was also a major debtor. Byrd was the son and grandson of trader-growers that bequeathed to him a huge estate. He eschewed commerce, squandered his patrimony, and fell hopelessly in debt to British merchants. On New Year's Eve 1776, he shot himself. If Speaker Robinson's death really was a suicide (it is certain that Chiswell's and Byrd's were), we are faced with the extraordinary fact that all three partners in the New River lead mine—a venture that failed partly because it ended up on the Indian side of the Proclamation Line—killed themselves.

Several other Virginia gentlemen took their own lives during the era of the American Revolution as well. Many of these suicides, like those of the mine partners, had something to do with debt.[3] Debt also killed in less direct

2. John Burk et al., *The History of Virginia from Its First Settlement to the Present Day* (Petersburg, Va., 1804–1816), III, 332; Charles Campbell, *History of the Colony and Ancient Dominion of Virginia*, II (Philadelphia, 1860), 547. There is strong evidence both for and against Burk's suggestion that Robinson might have killed himself. On May 16, 1766, less than a week after Robinson's death, Rind's *VG* reported that the sixty-two-year-old Robinson had died from the "Torments of the [kidney] Stone" (Joseph Albert Ernst, *Money and Politics in America, 1755–1775: A Study in the Currency Act of 1764 and the Political Economy of Revolution* [Chapel Hill, N.C., 1973], 174). But Burk stated that, less than a month before Robinson died, on Apr. 12, 1766, a report revealed that he had stolen more than £100,000 of public funds (*History of Virginia*, III, 332). The report had disappeared by the time twentieth-century historians tackled the subject (Francis Fauquier to Board of Trade, May 11, 1766, in George Reese, ed., *The Official Papers of Francis Fauquier, Lieutenant Governor of Virginia, 1758–1768* [Charlottesville, Va., 1980–1983], III, 1359).

3. The deeply indebted William Daingerfield made out his will on Jan. 4, 1783, and then, a few days later, slit his own throat. See Edward Miles Riley, ed., *The Journal of John Harrower: An Indentured Servant in the Colony of Virginia, 1773–1776* (Williamsburg, Va., 1963), xix–xx; William W. Hening, credit report on William Houston, "British Mercantile Claims, 1775–1803," *Virginia Genealogist*, XXVIII (1984), 50. A Colonel Tucker, who failed in trade and lost

ways. It will be recalled that Jacob Hite's debt to Scottish merchant James Hunter drove him to attack the Berkeley County jail and arm his slaves against a sheriff's posse. Seeking financial redemption, Hite later moved from Berkeley County to Cherokee country to trade for deerskins and land. He angered the Cherokees, and on July 1, 1776, a band of warriors killed him.[4] It is not known whether a proportionate number of smallholders were driven to early graves by their debts, but clearly debt harmed them even more than gentlemen. Thomas Swetnam fell so deep into debt that "his property was quite exhausted and his children [were] all passed out among his neighbors."[5]

Debt destroyed not only lives and families but the personal independence that free Virginians cherished. As these men and women that loathed debt fell deeper and deeper into it, they sought to explain what had happened.[6]

£2,500 worth of merchandise in a fire, "never could recover his Spirits" and presently died, leaving "his affairs in a desperate situation." See William Nelson to John Norton, Sept. 12, 1766, John Norton to John Hatley Norton, July 31, 1767, William Nelson to John Norton, Aug. 14, 1767, all in Frances Norton Mason, ed., *John Norton and Sons, Merchants of London and Virginia: Being the Papers from Their Counting-House for the Years 1750 to 1795* (Richmond, Va., 1937), 17, 30, 32; William Nelson to Samuel Martin, July 2, 1772, "Nelson Letter Book," *WMQ*, 1st Ser., VII (1898), 29; Robert Pleasants to William Fisher, Mar. 23, 1772, Pleasants Letterbook, LC. John Gilchrist, who killed himself during the worst of the depression of 1772–1774, might have had money problems (Rind's *VG*, Oct. 21, 1773).

The suicides that are acknowledged in surviving sources may be only a small portion of the total, since the property of a suicide escheated to the government, and would-be heirs (as well as sympathetic and embarrassed friends) covered them up. A newspaper account declared that John Chiswell died "after a short illness" that it attributed to "nervous fits, owing to a constant uneasiness of the mind" (Purdie and Dixon's *VG*, Oct. 17, 1766). The marquis de Chastellux mentioned Byrd's death but not his suicide (Howard C. Rice, Jr., trans. and ed., *Travels in North America in the Years 1780, 1781, and 1782* [Chapel Hill, N.C., 1963], II, 430).

4. Mildred Edwards Whitmire, "A Man and His Land: The Story of Jacob and Frances Madison Hite and the Cherokees," *Magazine of the Jefferson County Historical Society*, XLIV (1978), 37–58. Debt also is said to have contributed to the illness that killed Thomas Nelson, Virginia's third governor after Independence (Emory G. Evans, "The Rise and Decline of the Virginia Aristocracy in the Eighteenth Century: The Nelsons," in Darrett B. Rutman, ed., *The Old Dominion: Essays for Thomas Perkins Abernethy* [Charlottesville, Va., 1964], 77–78).

5. Robert Hening, credit report on Thomas Swetnam, "British Mercantile Claims, 1775–1803," *Virginia Genealogist*, XV (1971), 57.

6. T. H. Breen, *Tobacco Culture: The Mentality of the Great Tidewater Planters on the Eve of Revolution* (Princeton, N.J., 1985); Bernard Bailyn, *The Ideological Origins of the American Revolution* (Cambridge, Mass., 1967). Jacob M. Price argues that the free Virginians' growing debts to British merchants need not be viewed negatively. They were tangible evidence of British merchants' confidence in the colony's potential for growth and an essential

The wealthiest debtors, gentlemen, attributed their financial difficulties to their loss of middleman income from selling Indian land to settlers and from selling foreign goods to Virginia farmers in return for their tobacco (a sector in which gentlemen had been largely replaced by English and Scottish traders). Gentlemen also believed that both they and their less wealthy debtors could blame their money problems on their own extravagance. Another reason for the colonists' debts was political. Many of them were convinced that the British merchant class had persuaded Parliament to adopt commercial, monetary, and immigration policies that favored the mercantile interest at their expense. They believed that Parliament's commitment to mercantilism cost them hundreds of thousands of pounds sterling every year and trapped them in debt to the merchants.[7]

Virginians felt that the most important result of the British merchants' influence on Parliament was the Navigation Acts, the parliamentary legislation that gave Britain a monopoly of their trade, restricted their manufacturing, and shaped the Virginians' bitter response to taxes imposed by British ministers in the 1760s. Conflict between Virginia colonists and British mercantilism was also fueled by the government's policy of favoring British merchant-creditors over Virginia debtors and by the futile efforts of the

---

element in that growth (*Capital and Credit in British Overseas Trade: The View from the Chesapeake, 1700–1776* [Cambridge, Mass., 1980], 16–19, 126). Price may be correct that the debts *should* be viewed in that positive light. In eighteenth-century Virginia, though, they were seen as a terrible burden. "The torment of mind I endure till the moment shall arrive when I shall not owe a shilling on earth," Thomas Jefferson told Nicholas Lewis on July 29, 1787, "is such really as to render life of little value." See Julian P. Boyd et al., eds., *The Papers of Thomas Jefferson* (Princeton, N.J., 1950–), XI, 640.

7. The significance of the Virginia gentlemen's British debts in their decision to rebel against Britain has been debated ever since the rebellion itself. Loyalists such as James Parker charged that gentlemen closed Virginia's courts in 1774, and then declared Independence in 1776, in order to escape their debts to British merchants. That charge was picked up by some of the Progressive historians. See Isaac Samuel Harrell, *Loyalism in Virginia: Chapters in the Economic History of the Revolution* (Durham, N.C., 1926), 26–29; Claude H. Van Tyne, *The Causes of the War of Independence* (1922; reprint, New York, 1951), 426. In 1962, Emory G. Evans and Thad W. Tate both argued convincingly that the loyalists and Progressives were wrong to view the Revolution in Virginia as a simple act of debt repudiation (Evans, "Planter Indebtedness and the Coming of the Revolution in Virginia," Tate, "The Coming of the Revolution in Virginia: Britain's Challenge to Virginia's Ruling Class, 1763–1776," both in *WMQ*, 3d Ser., XIX [1962], 323–343, 511–533). Since then, scholars have sought more complex connections between debt and Revolution. See Gordon S. Wood, "Rhetoric and Reality in the American Revolution," *WMQ*, 3d Ser., XXIII (1966), 3–32; Breen, *Tobacco Culture*, esp. chap. 4; Bruce A. Ragsdale, *A Planters' Republic: The Search for Economic Independence in Revolutionary Virginia* (Madison, Wis., 1996), esp. 23–29.

House of Burgesses to reduce or end the forced immigration of African and West Indian slaves to Virginia.

I

During the 1760s and 1770s, American pamphleteers often asserted that the British politicians that proposed to tax them without their consent were, in fact, trying to "enslave" them.[8] Some writers went further, charging that Parliament treated free colonists like slaves even before it thought of taxing them. In an anonymous essay appearing in the *Virginia Gazette* in March 1776, "An American" argued that Britain's manipulation of the colonists' commerce had turned them into "the slaves of Britain." Later in the essay, he extended the slavery metaphor. He reminded his readers that most slaveholders allowed their workers a few hours of leisure to raise some produce for their own consumption or for sale. Likewise, said the writer, who was apparently a Virginia slaveholder, "our masters in Britain, though they made us labour and toil for their emolument, yet did not attempt to take from us the little we had been permitted to earn for ourselves. In this respect, they were as indulgent to us as we are to our poor slaves." Virginia slaveholders had no right to take away their slaves' customary privilege of earning money for themselves in the evenings and on Sundays, An American said, and the home country that monopolized the free Virginians' trade had no right to tax them as well.[9]

The comparison An American drew between slavery and mercantilism points toward a possible solution to one of the great mysteries of the American Revolution: why free colonists objected so vehemently to parliamentary taxes that were a fraction of what their less wealthy kinsmen in England, Wales, and Scotland already paid. Their argument was partly constitutional: Parliament had no right to tax them, because they were not represented in it. But the Virginians' position was also practical: just as a master that already monopolized his slaves' daytime labor could lay no just claim to their evening hours, free colonists deserved to remain tax-free because, by submit-

8. This was especially true in the southern, slaveholding colonies. See Edmund S. Morgan, *American Slavery, American Freedom: The Ordeal of Colonial Virginia* (New York, 1975), 376; F. Nwabueze Okoye, "Chattel Slavery as the Nightmare of the American Revolutionaries," *WMQ*, 3d Ser., XXXVII (1980), 3–28; Jack P. Greene, " 'Slavery or Independence': Some Reflections on the Relationship among Liberty, Black Bondage, and Equality in Revolutionary South Carolina," in Paul Finkelman, ed., *Slavery, Revolutionary America, and the New Nation* (New York, 1989), 201.

9. Purdie's *VG*, Mar. 29, 1776. Other Virginians agreed with An American that, for white Virginians, British mercantilism was "a qualified slavery at best" (James City County, delegate instructions, Apr. 24, 1776, in *Revolutionary Virginia*, VI, 458).

ting to the Navigation Acts, they already contributed more than their fair share to the wealth of the British nation. An American's view was widely held, so any account of the origins of the American Revolution must focus not only on taxes but also on trade—on the struggle between Virginia tobacco growers and the British merchants that controlled their imports and exports.

An American's analogy usefully introduces into the scholarly discussion of the Navigation Acts the image of the enslaved worker. Historians studying mercantilism frequently use evidence derived from New England to develop conclusions that they then apply to the staple colonies. This will not do. Until the 1760s, Yankee peddlers found the foremost parliamentary restriction on their trade, the Molasses Act of 1733, easy to evade. In contrast, limits on the tobacco colonies' commerce were rigorously enforced.[10]

Parliament passed the first Navigation Act, which dictated that goods could be exported from the colonies to England only on British ships, in 1651, in the midst of the English Revolution, and was unable to enforce it. As soon as Charles II secured the English throne, however, he excluded Dutch mer-

10. Most historians agree that, before 1760, few northerners felt greatly injured by mercantilist legislation (Alfred F. Young, "George Robert Twelves Hewes [1742–1840]: A Boston Shoemaker and the Memory of the American Revolution," in *In Search of Early America: The William and Mary Quarterly, 1943–1993* [Williamsburg, Va., 1993], 252). But, after 1760, when the British government enforced existing restrictions on trade between the North American colonies and the foreign sugar islands, the new enforcement measures were fiercely resisted. See Arthur Meier Schlesinger, *The Colonial Merchants and the American Revolution, 1763–1776* (New York, 1918), 50–54; Thomas C. Barrow, *Trade and Empire: The British Customs Service in Colonial America, 1660–1775* (Cambridge, Mass., 1967), chap. 9, 10.

Practitioners of the "new economic history" have often made the important error of assessing the impact of the Navigation Acts on the North American colonies as a whole, improperly conflating those that received a net benefit with those that suffered greatly. See, for example, Robert Paul Thomas, "A Quantitative Approach to the Study of the Effects of British Imperial Policy upon Colonial Welfare: Some Preliminary Findings," *Journal of Economic History*, XXV (1965), 638; Gary M. Walton, "The Burdens of the Navigation Acts: A Reply," *Economic History Review*, 2d Ser., XXVI (1973), 687n. For a more nuanced study, see Curtis P. Nettels, "British Mercantilism and the Economic Development of the Thirteen Colonies," *Journal of Economic History*, XII (1952), 105–114.

Historians that argue that the Navigation Acts were an important cause of the American Revolution include John C. Miller, *Origins of the American Revolution* (Boston, 1943), 13–17; Ernst, *Money and Politics*, 360; Robert Johnson, "Government Regulation of Business Enterprise in Virginia, 1750–1820" (Ph.D. diss., University of Minnesota, 1958), 204. Those taking the opposing view include T. H. Breen, "An Empire of Goods: The Anglicization of Colonial America, 1690–1776," *Journal of British Studies*, XXV (1986), 470; John J. McCusker and Russell R. Menard, *The Economy of British America, 1607–1789* (Chapel Hill, N.C., 1985), 354.

chantmen from the Chesapeake trade, and during the next seven years the price of tobacco fell 75 percent. In 1663, Governor William Berkeley complained that growers earned "soe very little for their labores as it will not cloath them and their Families."[11] "The rigorous circumspection of [Virginia's] trade" lowered the price of tobacco and made "the poor people . . . very uneasy," Robert Beverley reported. In September 1663, even before Virginians learned that Parliament had adopted an additional Navigation Act (this one prohibited the shipment of foreign goods to American colonies except through British ports), nine Gloucester County servants plotted an insurrection that was discovered less than twenty-four hours before it was to commence. The Navigation Acts and the resulting depression in the tobacco market were repeatedly blamed for social unrest in subsequent decades, especially during Bacon's Rebellion (1676), the largest insurrection in Virginia history, and the 1682 plant-cutting riots. In the aftermath of Bacon's Rebellion, when the freemen of Lower Norfolk County politely requested the repeal of the Navigation Acts, they were branded "wholly mutinous." This censure, and the execution of many leading rebels, helped persuade tobacco growers that to criticize the Navigation Acts was hopeless and dangerous. A Virginia writer would state in the 1760s that, although the British merchants' monopoly of colonial trade had "ever been regarded here as oppressive in many Respects," it was "an Evil we with Patience now must bear, as we have it not in our Power to avoid or prevent it."[12]

For most of the eighteenth century, public criticism of the Navigation

11. Morgan, *American Slavery, American Freedom*, 146–148. As early as 1621, the English government had demanded that all Virginia tobacco be shipped to England, but the regulation proved unenforceable (Johnson, "Regulation of Business," 16).

Tobacco fetched about two pence per pound in 1660 and a halfpence per pound in 1667 (John C. Rainbolt, *From Prescription to Persuasion: Manipulation of [Seventeenth] Century Virginia Economy* [Port Washington, N.Y., 1974], 56). On Berkeley's complaint, see Warren M. Billings, John E. Selby, and Thad W. Tate, *Colonial Virginia: A History* (White Plains, N.Y., 1986), 79; Barrow, *Trade and Empire*, 21, 289 n. 3; Lawrence A. Harper, *The English Navigation Laws: a Seventeenth-Century Experiment in Social Engineering* (New York, 1939), 246; John Bland, "The Humble Remonstrance of John Bland of London, Merchant, on the Behalf of the Inhabitants and Planters in Virginia and Maryland," *VMHB*, I (1893), 141–155.

12. Robert Beverley, *The History and Present State of Virginia: A Selection* (Indianapolis, 1971), 32; Burk et al., *History of Virginia*, II, 134–135; Morgan, *American Slavery, American Freedom*, 246. On the effects of Bacon's Rebellion regarding the colonists' general opinion of the Navigation Acts, see ["Lower Norfolk County Grievances,"] *VMHB*, II (1894), 170; "A Virginian," Rind's *VG*, Dec. 11, 1766; Thomas Jefferson, cited in Merrill D. Peterson, *Thomas Jefferson and the New Nation: A Biography* (New York, 1970), 45. Nineteenth-century historian Charles Campbell stated that the Navigation Acts "had never been acquiesced in, but only submitted to from necessity" (*History of the Colony*, 530–531).

Acts remained quite rare. In the 1740s, the House of Burgesses petitioned the Privy Council for a "free export of their Tobacco to foreign Markets directly." The petition was denied. English clergyman Andrew Burnaby toured the colony in 1759 and learned that free Virginians considered "it a hardship not to have an unlimited trade to every part of the world." What Burnaby heard were private grumblings. Five years later, a member of the Virginia gentry did denounce the Navigation Acts publicly, but it is significant that the young Virginian that finally broached the subject was attending medical school in Edinburgh, close to the lavish country estates that Scottish merchants had purchased with their tobacco profits and far from the restraining influence of his older brothers. Even then, Arthur Lee spoke out only because he had been provoked, ironically enough, by the man whose name would become synonymous with free trade, Adam Smith. In his 1759 *Theory of Moral Sentiments*, Smith uncharitably called the founders of the American colonies "the refuse of the jails of Europe." Five years later, Lee wrote *An Essay in Vindication of the Continental Colonies of America*. In the midst of defending his American ancestors, Lee veered off in a new direction. "I cannot help lamenting the unequal condition of their descendents, the present inhabitants," he wrote. In response to Smith's avowal of sympathy for American slaves, Lee argued that they were not nearly so cruelly shackled as their owners—"their manufacturing hands tied up; their commerce confined; and their staple commodity," their tobacco, "oppressed with such intolerable exactions, that it yields to the labouring planter scarce one tenth of its original value." Lee said the Navigation Acts subjected Virginia tobacco growers "to the arbitrary impositions of the British merchants, who fix, like cankers, on their estates, and utterly consume them."[13]

Virginians like Arthur Lee knew that the only way they could ever enjoy the fruits of free trade would be to declare Independence from Britain. Of course, the empire would not let them go in peace. Living in a colony where the most valuable property lay within cannon shot of navigable rivers, where 40 percent of the population were slaves that would be likely to side with any enemy, and where family and other emotional ties to the mother country were still strong, free Virginians had no desire to go to war against Britain,

13. Andrew Burnaby, *Travels through the Middle Settlements in North-America, in the Years 1759 and 1760 . . .*, rev ed. (1775; Ithaca, N.Y., 1960), 25; William Zebina Ripley, *The Financial History of Virginia, 1609–1776* (New York, 1893), 64, 66; Adam Smith, *The Theory of Moral Sentiments* (1759), ed. D. D. Raphael and A. L. Macfie (Oxford, Eng., 1976), 206. Lee argued that the mercantilist empire treated free colonists in America "not as the fellow-subjects, but as the servants of Britain" ("An American" [Lee], *An Essay in Vindication of the Continental Colonies of America* [London, 1764], 20).

FIGURE 7. Arthur Lee. *Courtesy, Virginia Historical Society*

not even to destroy its monopoly of their trade. They did, however, feel pushed to the breaking point, and, if Britain should demand additional sacrifices from them, their loyalty could not be guaranteed.

By 1764, when Lee's *Essay in Vindication* appeared, free Virginians were even less willing than earlier to increase their contribution to the British Empire. Many of them had fallen deep into debt to British merchants, and they attributed their economic distress partly to the Navigation Acts. In a 1769 essay, Lee's brother Richard Henry described how "*Britain* from her exclusive trade to these colonies, and from the manner in which she tied up our manufacturing hands" had "involved the people here in a heavy debt, which agriculture, without arts, and a trade so confined, will probably never pay." Although "the enormous debt due the stores" was commonly attributed to "extravagance and want of industry in our people," its actual source was the simple fact that colonial commerce was "extremely fettered and confined, both in export and import," Richard Henry Lee had written two years earlier. Only "by making trade free" could Virginia "render it profitable." Another writer attributed the "great ballance" that Virginians owed British merchants to "parliamentary authority," which "prevents us from acquiring property except under such restrictions as are highly advantageous to Great Britain."[14]

Landon Carter blamed the Navigation Acts not only for the tobacco growers' debts but also for Virginia's trade deficit with Britain. In an essay he wrote in 1774, when he was dunned by a London merchant, Carter argued that the balance of trade "must be ever against such a people who can deal nowhere else but with those who have both the opportunity to take our Commodities for what they please and send theirs to us at their own price." Arthur Lee argued that more than half of Virginia's trade deficit could be attributed to the Navigation Acts. British mercantilism cost the tobacco colonies £500,000 per year, Lee estimated in a 1774 pamphlet, and it was largely the reason American colonists owed British merchants six million pounds.[15]

Although nothing in Arthur Lee's 1764 pamphlet indicated that he knew it, during this very period when free Virginians were falling deeper into debt and becoming more restive under the burden of the Navigation Acts, the Privy Council, meeting at Whitehall in London, was planning to add to the burden. Colonists were about to be called upon to sacrifice not only for the benefit of the British merchant class, as the Navigation Acts already forced them to, but for the imperial government itself. The government's

14. [Richard Henry Lee], preface, in [John Dickinson and Arthur Lee], *The Farmer's and Monitor's Letters, to the Inhabitants of the British Colonies* (Williamsburg, Va., 1769), iii; "Rusticus" [Richard Henry Lee], essay, [1766–1767?] (typescript filed at the end of 1769), in Paul P. Hoffman, ed., *The Lee Family Papers, 1742–1795* (microfilm, Charlottesville, Va., 1966); "Vindex," *Virginia Gazette, or, Norfolk Intelligencer*, Aug. 11, 1774. The published version of the Rusticus essay has not been found, but it may be roughly dated based on the appearance of a reply to it in Rind's *VG* on Feb. 19, 1767.

15. Jack P. Greene, ed., *The Diary of Colonel Landon Carter of Sabine Hall, 1752–1778* (Charlottesville, Va., 1965), II, 917; [Landon Carter], letter, Nov. 30, 1765, in Jack P. Greene, ed., "'Not to be *Governed*, or *Taxed*, but by . . . our Representatives': Four Essays in Opposition to the Stamp Act by Landon Carter," *VMHB*, LXXVI (1968), 290–291. Marylander Daniel Dulany estimated that Chesapeake tobacco would have fetched three pounds per hogshead more if growers were allowed to sell it directly to the Europeans that consumed 85 percent of it (Miller, *Origins of the Americans Revolution*, 14). That would have increased the growers' profits by about 30 percent. Although the above statements attributing Virginians' private debts and the provincial trade deficit to the Navigation Acts were written after Parliament tried to impose taxes on the American colonies, it seems safe to assume that, long before the taxes were imposed, many free Virginians blamed their debts partly on the Navigation Acts.

need was great. The Seven Years' War had nearly doubled its debt, from £72 million to more than £123 million. When peace came, British politicians listened avidly as army officers returning from America told of the fabulous wealth abounding there. Here were more than two million British subjects that—at a time when English, Welsh, and Scottish taxpayers reeled under a load of taxes and often resisted them—did not pay a penny in direct taxes. So Parliament adopted the Stamp Act (1765), Townshend duties (1767), and other revenue measures.[16]

The well-known constitutional arguments that free Americans made against parliamentary legislation rested upon a basic idea of fairness. Although 100 percent of Chesapeake tobacco had to be shipped to Britain, only 15 percent was consumed there, with the rest being reexported to the European continent. Thus by the time most tobacco reached its destination, the person that owned it and profited from its sale was not a Chesapeake tobacco grower but a British merchant. As colonists struggled against the new taxes that Parliament tried to levy on them in the 1760s, several of them argued that British mercantilism was itself "a heavy tax upon the colonies"— heavier than any of the taxes that were now being proposed. In 1766, George Mercer, who had tried unsuccessfully to enforce the Stamp Act in Virginia, told a parliamentary committee that, even if Virginians had bought the stamped paper, it would have cost them much less money than the Navigation Acts already did.[17]

16. T. H. Breen, "Narrative of Commercial Life: Consumption, Ideology, and Community on the Eve of the American Revolution," *WMQ*, 3d Ser., L (1993), 472–473. To retire the war debt, Parliament kept taxes "very high," and they were "paid unwillingly," as Royle's *VG* reported on Nov. 4, 1763. At the same time, Parliament adopted new navigation laws aimed at diverting more of the North Americans' income to sugar growers in the British Caribbean, to merchants in England and Scotland, and to the imperial treasury. Historians have shown that those new laws, especially the Sugar Act, harmed the northern colonies. See Schlesinger, *Colonial Merchants*, 52–61; John W. Tyler, *Smugglers and Patriots: Boston Merchants and the Advent of the American Revolution* (Boston, 1986), 75–92. It is important to note that those laws also harmed Virginia, which had a growing trade with the foreign sugar islands. See May 17, 1765, "Journal of a French Traveller in the Colonies, 1765," pt. I, *American Historical Review*, XXVI (1921–1922), 744; Francis Fauquier to Board of Trade, Jan. 25, 1765, duke of Richmond to Fauquier, June 12, 1766, in Reese, ed., *Papers of Francis Fauquier*, III, 1222, 1364; "The Contest," Purdie and Dixon's *VG*, Dec. 17, 1767; Robert Beverley to [——], May 8, 1765, Beverley Letterbook, LC; "Copy of a Letter," Purdie and Dixon's *VG*, July 11, 1766; "Philautos," Purdie and Dixon's *VG*, July 25, 1766; "T. S.," Rind's *VG*, Dec. 14, 1769.

17. Bailyn, *Ideological Origins*, 161–175; Ragsdale, *Planters' Republic*, 53. Vindex said the huge debt that Virginians owed to British merchants "arises from the interposition of parliamentary authority." That being so, "may it not with propriety be called a parliamen-

Indeed, the Navigation Acts unjustly favored British subjects living in England, Wales, and Scotland over their fellow subjects in America, Richard Bland claimed in 1766. "Why," Bland demanded, "is the Trade of the Colonies more circumscribed than the Trade of *Britain*?"[18] After Parliament repealed the Stamp Act, most British merchants and politicians expected free Virginians to express gratitude for its "indulgence," but many of them refused. "Is the Indulgence of Great Britain manifested," George Mason asked, "by prohibiting her Colonys from exporting to foreign Countrys such Commoditys as she does not want, and from importing such as she does not produce or manufacture and therefore can not furnish but upon extravagant Terms?" In 1769, an anonymous newspaper writer called the expected repeal of some of the Townshend duties "*a gift to blind your eyes*, whilst they continue to clog your TRADE."[19]

---

tary tax?" (*Virginia Gazette, or, Norfolk Intelligencer*, Aug. 11, 1774). Other colonies' resistance leaders—including Henry Laurens of South Carolina, Daniel Dulany of Maryland, Benjamin Franklin of Pennsylvania, and James Otis of Massachusetts—also called the Navigation Acts a tax. Laurens claimed in 1769 that the Navigation Acts subjected him to "a much greater tax than any person of equal fortune on the other side of the Atlantic" paid. See Charles A. Beard and Mary R. Beard, *The Rise of American Civilization* (New York, 1930), I, 202; John E. Crowley, *The Privileges of Independence: Neomercantilism and the American Revolution* (Baltimore, 1993), 21–23, 174n. Two years after Mercer's statement to Parliament, the members of the House of Burgesses echoed his claim that the British Empire already cost free Virginians a great deal of money. They pointed out that Virginians had "long been restrained from purchasing many of the necessaries of Life at any other than the *British Market*, they are confined in their Exports also" (Petition to the House of Lords, Apr. 16, 1768, in *Revolutionary Virginia*, I, 59).

18. "An Inquiry into the Rights of the British Colonies . . ." (ca. Mar. 14, 1766), in *Revolutionary Virginia*, I, 40–41. Bland's words were echoed eight years later by Thomson Mason. "Why should not Britons on this have as good a right to extend their trade to every corner of the globe as those on the other side of the Atlantic?" he asked in 1774 ("A British American" [Mason], "Number IX," July 28, 1774, in *Revolutionary Virginia*, I, 194). James Otis of Massachusetts asked a similar question: "Can any one tell me why trade, commerce, arts, sciences and manufactures, should not be as free for an American as for an European?" (Theodore Draper, *A Struggle for Power: The American Revolution* [New York, 1996], 338).

19. "A Virginia Planter" [George Mason], ". . . Letter to the Committee of Merchants in London . . . ," June 6, 1766, in Robert A. Rutland, ed., *The Papers of George Mason, 1725–1792* (Chapel Hill, N.C., 1970), I, 67. A year later, George Washington thanked a pair of London merchants for lobbying against the Stamp Act, but added, "I coud wish it was in my power to congratulate you with success, in having the Commercial System of these Colonies put upon a more enlargd and extensive footing than it is" (to Capel and Osgood Hanbury, July 25, 1767, in W. W. Abbot et al., eds., *The Papers of George Washington*, Colonial Series (Charlottesville, Va., 1983–), VIII, 15. For the 1769 quotation, see anonymous letter, Purdie and Dixon's *VG*, Nov. 9, 1769 (supplement).

To be sure, free Virginians did receive numerous benefits from the British Empire, including a parliamentary prohibition against tobacco planting in Britain, naval escorts for Virginia ships during wartime, and an imperial army that was ready to suppress any slave or Indian revolt. But free Virginians believed that the benefits of the imperial connection paled in comparison to the costs. They contrasted their condition not to what it would have been outside the British Empire—where few of them desired to be before 1775—but to that of the British merchants, who controlled all of the Virginians' trade but were allowed to send their own ships almost anywhere on the globe. Struggling under a burden they considered much more onerous than the one British taxpayers carried, free Virginians refused to make "double contributions" by submitting to parliamentary taxation as well.[20]

Thus the ambitious legislation that Parliament began to adopt in 1764 provoked colonial Americans to express, for the first time, their long-standing complaints against the Navigation Acts. This was an important change, but for the next decade it remained a limited one. Although free Virginians denounced the mercantilist system, they did not demand that it be dismantled. Their rhetorical restraint was based upon their understanding of British political economy. It was a commonplace in both Britain and America that "the true cause of British greatness"—of the expansion of the empire to five continents, of the tremendous wealth evident in the fashionable sections of London and other seaports, and of the consumer revolution that even reached down into the middling classes—was the colonial trade. Thanks to the diligence of British naval officers, the American colonists were a captive market for Britain's manufactured goods and captive suppliers of its raw materials. One-third of Britain's overseas trade was with its own American colonies. Both Lord Shelburne, who was viewed as one of the

---

20. Historians that have measured the costs of the Navigation Acts against the benefits say their net negative impact was minor. What matters, though, is not how painful the Navigation Acts *really* were, but how painful they *felt*, for it is perception, not reality, that informs motivation. See Miller, *Origins of the American Revolution*, 22–25; W. A. Speck, "The International and Imperial Context," in Jack P. Greene and J. R. Pole, eds., *Colonial British America: Essays in the New History of the Early Modern Era* (Baltimore, 1984), 405; Immanuel Wallerstein, *The Modern World-System*, III, *The Second Era of Great Expansion of The Capitalist World-Economy, 1730–1840s* (San Diego, 1989), 198. On the colonists' refusal to submit to parliamentary taxation, see "Virginia Resolutions on Lord North's Conciliatory Proposal," [June 10, 1775], in Boyd et al., eds., *Papers of Jefferson*, I, 172. Many stated that they were not only unwilling but unable to endure both the existing trade restrictions and the new taxes. To restrain the colonists' trade and at the same time tax them, Richard Bland claimed in 1766, would be "forcing them to make Bricks without Straw" ("An Inquiry into the Rights of the British Colonies," in *Revolutionary Virginia*, I, 41).

most pro-American of the peers, and Lord George Townshend, who was not, referred to the Navigation Acts as "that great Palladium"—guardian—of British commerce. One friend of the free colonists, William Pitt, vowed that, if Americans manufactured a hobnail or a horseshoe, he would fill "their towns with troops and their ports with ships of war."[21]

Colonists knew that a campaign against British mercantilism would serve only to alienate the powerful British merchants. Conservative Virginia gentleman Robert Beverley questioned the constitutionality of the Navigation Acts but told English merchant Samuel Athawes not to mention his views to his mercantile friends lest Beverley be drawn into "endless and irreconcilable disputes" with them. Thomson Mason, brother of George Mason and a bitter critic of the Navigation Acts, said many Americans were willing to endure them "for the sake of peace."[22]

During the final decade before the American Revolution, even as indebted Virginians' resentment of the British merchants' domination of their trade reached new heights, most growers agreed that the need to placate the merchants by acquiescing to their monopoly was more pressing than ever before. English and Scottish merchant princes were only too happy to lobby against the new parliamentary taxes that threatened to sap their American customers' buying power, but their support would evaporate in an instant if

21. "R. L——L," Rind's *VG*, Sept. 22, 1768; "A British American" [Thomson Mason], "Number VI," July 7, 1774, in *Revolutionary Virginia*, I, 178; Jack P. Greene, "The Seven Years' War and the American Revolution: The Causal Relationship Reconsidered," in Peter Marshall and Glyn Williams, eds., *The British Atlantic Empire before the American Revolution* (London, 1980), 86; Crowley, *Privileges of Independence*, 1–49; Townshend, Jan. 20, 1775, Shelburne, Dec. 15, 1775, in R. C. Simmons and P. D. G. Thomas, eds., *Proceedings and Debates of the British Parliaments respecting North America, 1754–1783* (White Plains, N.Y., 1982–), V, 274, VI, 367; Pitt, in Peter D. G. Thomas, *The Townshend Duties Crisis: The Second Phase of the American Revolution, 1767–1773* (New York, 1987), 3; Jack P. Greene, "The Origins of the New Colonial Policy, 1748–1763," in Greene and J. R. Pole, eds., *The Blackwell Encyclopedia of the American Revolution* (Cambridge, Mass., 1991), 95. It appears that Pitt's comments were widely reported in Virginia. "Lord Chatham would not tax us, but he would not permit us to 'manufacture a hobnail,'" one writer remarked ("C. D.," Purdie's *VG*, May 3, 1776).

22. Robert Beverley to Samuel Athawes, June 4, 1775, Beverley Letterbook, LC; "A British American" [Thomson Mason], "Number IX," July 28, 1774, in *Revolutionary Virginia*, I, 196. A July 1774 meeting of Fairfax County voters stated that Virginians had acquiesced in the imperial connection, both because of the "mutual Benefits" it conferred and also "to avoid Strife and Contention with our fellow-Subjects" (Rutland, ed., *Papers of George Mason*, I, 202). In 1776, the freeholders of James City County stated that in Virginia British mercantilism had been "acceptable to us, not as the extent of our right, but the probable cause of peace" with the mother country (Delegate instructions, Apr. 24, 1776, in *Revolutionary Virginia*, VI, 458).

the ministry could convince them that the Americans' "principal motive" was "to free themselves from the restrictions laid on their commerce," as the earl of Sandwich contended.[23] One American that labored to disprove that claim was Richard Henry Lee. Lee hated the Navigation Acts, and behind the closed doors of the First Continental Congress, he called them a "capital" violation of the colonists' rights. Yet he warned his fellow delegates not to denounce mercantilism openly, lest they "unite every man in Britain against us." Many representatives at the congress so loathed the Navigation Acts that they wanted to insist that Parliament modify them, even though the demand would alienate British merchants. Lee and other advocates of discretion prevailed—by one vote.[24]

Although through the end of 1774 most Virginians chose not to demand that Parliament lift the existing restrictions on their trade and manufacturing, they were less reticent about rumors that the imperial restrictions on

23. Simmons and Thomas, eds., *Proceedings and Debates*, V, 330. "Where will it end?" Lord North asked Parliament in 1774. "Will not the Americans likewise be desirous of rescinding the Act of Navigation?" See Crowley, *Privileges of Independence*, 31; [Robert Carter Nicholas], "Considerations on the Present State of Virginia Examined," in *Revolutionary Virginia*, I, 276; Ira D. Gruber, "The American Revolution as a Conspiracy: The British View," *WMQ*, 3d Ser., XXVI (1969), 360–372.

When Hillsborough claimed that "it was the Navigation Act" that Americans "were aiming to overthrow," Arthur Lee attributed his speech to "the fixd impressions of this dull arbitrary Lord; and the prejudices which he and his tools labour but too successfully to infuse into others" (to Richard Henry Lee, May 20, 1770, in Hoffman, ed., *Lee Family Papers*).

24. Joseph A. Ernst, "The Political Economy of the Chesapeake Colonies, 1760–1775: A Study in Comparative History," in Ronald Hoffman et al., eds., *The Economy of Early America: The Revolutionary Period, 1763–1790* (Charlottesville, Va., 1988), 241; Oct. 13, 1774, in L. H. Butterfield, ed., *Diary and Autobiography of John Adams* (Cambridge, Mass., 1961), II, 151; [Arthur Lee] to [———], Sept. 4–5, 1775, Arthur Lee Papers, Houghton. Although the motion to denounce the Navigation Acts failed at the First Continental Congress, a motion to approve them also failed (Page Smith, *A New Age Now Begins: A People's History of the United States* [New York, 1976], I, 442).

The reluctance of Virginia writers to demand the repeal of the Navigation Acts has led historians of the origins of the American Revolution into an important error. Scholars have assumed that, because the Virginians did not demand that Parliament abandon its mercantilist policies, they must not have felt injured by them. See Edmund S. Morgan and Helen M. Morgan, *The Stamp Act Crisis: Prologue to Revolution* (1953; rev. ed., Chapel Hill, N.C., 1995), 272–274; Crowley, *Privileges of Independence*, 19–29. They forget that it is possible to resent a law and yet be prudent enough not to demand its repeal. The evidence presented here indicates that free Virginians *did* resent the Navigation Acts, and that the taxes Parliament adopted in the 1760s were only the straw that broke the camel's back. Historians have focused on the straw and ignored the enormous burden the camel already carried.

American manufactures were about to be tightened. During the previous century, Parliament had prohibited Americans from making iron and from selling hats or woolen cloth outside their home colonies. In 1766, George Mason predicted that "Some Bungler in politics will soon, perhaps, be framing Schemes for restraining our Manufacturers" still further.[25] Three years later, George Washington, a pioneer in plantation textile production, informed Mason that one of his chief reasons for wanting to resist the Townshend duties was to avoid a dangerous precedent. "By virtue of the same power . . . which assumes the right of Taxation," Washington wrote, Parliament might "attempt at least to restrain our manufactories." In July 1774, Thomson Mason warned that Parliament might soon gratify British artisans' "secret wishes" that it prohibit Americans from "manufacturing the smallest article for your own use." He warned that the next Parliament might bar Americans from combing wool, tanning hides, even "fashioning a canoe." The Americans were right to worry. In the spring of 1774, Parliament tried to hobble colonial competition in the most important branch of Britain's export trade, textiles, by prohibiting the shipment of "Utensils" used in "Cotton and Linen Manufactures" out of Great Britain.[26] The free Virgin-

25. James Abercromby wanted to extend the colonial ban on commercial wool manufacturing to linen and to prohibit the exportation of wool manufacturing frames from Britain to America ("An Examination of the Acts of Parliament relative to the Trade and the Government of our American Colonies," [1752], in Jack P. Greene, Charles F. Mullett, and Edward C. Papenfuse, Jr., eds., *Magna Charta for America.* . . . [Philadelphia, 1986], 125–126). On Mason's suspicions, see "A Virginia Planter" [George Mason], "Letter to the Committee of Merchants in London," June 6, 1766, in Rutland, ed., *Papers of George Mason*, I, 69. John Dickinson of Pennsylvania shared these worries (Draper, *Struggle for Power*, 340). Their fears were justified. In 1766, the year that Mason wrote, Parliament demanded a report from every American governor on his colony's manufacturing and his legislature's encouragement of it (Board of Trade to American governors, Aug. 1, 1766, Hillsborough to American governors, Feb. 20, 1768, in Reese, ed., *Papers of Francis Fauquier*, III, 1379, 1532–1533).

26. Washington believed the gravest danger was to manufacturing concerns "of a public nature"—those that offered their merchandise for sale (to George Mason, Apr. 5, 1769, in Rutland, ed., *Papers of George Mason*, I, 97). The following year, a *VG* writer warned that colonists might soon "be deprived of the advantage of manufacturing any commodity for our immediate use, whenever such manufactures shall lessen the demand for those of Britain" ("Z.," Rind's *VG*, June 7, 1770). William Lee expressed the same concern (Ragsdale, *Planters' Republic*, 90). During the summer of 1774, Robert Pleasants heard that the British government had prohibited the export of rams to America—presumably in order to check the growth in wool production there (Pleasants to David and John Barclay and Company, July [11?], 1774, Pleasants Letterbook, LC). For Mason's warnings and Parliament's statute, see "A British American" [Thomson Mason], "Number VII," "Number VIII," July 14, 21, 1774, in *Revolutionary Virginia*, I, 183, 188; *The Statutes at Large, from the Thirteenth Year of*

ians' rejection of additional restrictions on their trade and manufacturing paralleled their refusal to pay parliamentary taxes. In both debates, they were saying that the status quo was acceptable to them, but just barely so.

In the summer of 1774, when Parliament insisted more forcefully than ever before that colonists submit both to the Navigation Acts and to the new taxes, free Virginians began refusing to submit to either. Initially, the only ones advocating that Virginians nullify the Navigation Acts were Thomson Mason and the participants in a July 1774 meeting of Albemarle County freeholders. The Albemarle meeting advised free Virginians to assert what Thomas Jefferson called their "natural right" to "a free trade with all parts of the world."[27] Jefferson argued that the British merchants, secure in their monopoly of the American trade, "indulged themselves in every exorbitance which their avarice could dictate." He said British merchants had "raised their commodities called for in America to the double and treble of what they sold for before such exclusive privileges were given them" and had paid colonists "much less for what we carry thither, than might be had at more convenient ports." Jefferson and Thomson Mason both argued that American colonists should simply declare the Navigation Acts void.[28]

Less than a year later, most leading Virginians were ready to demand the repeal of the Navigation Acts. The reason was that, after blood was spilled at

---

the Reign of King George the Third to the Sixteenth Year of the Reign of King George the Third, Inclusive, XII (London, 1776), 131–132. The bill quickly passed the House of Lords, and it received the royal assent on June 14 (Simmons and Thomas, eds., Proceedings and Debates, IV, 430, 475). My thanks to John M. Murrin for this reference.

27. "A Native, and Member of the House of Burgesses" [Jefferson], "A Summary View of the Rights of British America," in Boyd et al., eds., Papers of Jefferson, I, 123. The following year, when he wrote the House of Burgesses' response to Lord North's conciliatory proposal, Jefferson employed similar language, criticizing North for not offering free Virginians "a free trade with all the world" in return for their helping to fund the British government ("Virginia Resolutions on Lord North's Conciliatory Proposal," [June 10, 1775], in Papers of Jefferson, 172). It will be recalled that, in the Declaration of Independence, Jefferson castigated George III and Parliament for "cutting off our Trade with all Parts of the World." In that case, Jefferson was probably referring to the 1775 New England Restraining Act, which closed the few loopholes in the Navigation Acts that had allowed Americans to trade with some non-British ports. But it seems likely that, on one level or another, he also had in mind the basic mercantilist policy that he had attacked in 1774 and 1775.

28. Mason in fact argued that free Americans should refuse to obey any parliamentary act adopted after 1607. See [Jefferson], "Summary View of the Rights of British America," Albemarle County resolves, July 26, 1774, both in Boyd et al., eds., Papers of Jefferson, I, 118, 124; "A British American" [Thomson Mason], "Number IX," July 28, 1774, in Revolutionary Virginia, I, 198–200. Later in 1774, an anonymous essayist declared that "the Acts of Trade constitute one of the main Grievances of America" ("An Associator," Purdie and Dixon's VG, Dec. 8, 1774 [supplement]).

Lexington and Concord, the Virginians lost faith in the ability and inclination of the British merchant lobby to persuade Parliament to redress their more recent grievances. No longer reluctant to offend British businessmen, American colonists could speak openly of repealing the Navigation Acts. Thus, in June 1775, when the House of Burgesses brushed aside the North ministry's conciliatory proposal, one reason was "*because* on our agreeing to contribute our proportion towards the common defence, they do not propose to lay open to us a free trade with all the world." Leading Virginians seemed almost to be offering Parliament a deal: if it would repeal the Navigation Acts, they would contribute to the imperial revenue. In fact, they would do so cheerfully, for under this arrangement they would actually come out ahead. The "monopoly of our trade," the burgesses explained, "brings greater loss to us and benefit to [Britain] than the amount of our proportional contributions to the common defence." The burgesses' address was written by Thomas Jefferson.[29]

In early 1776, the Navigation Acts, which had long played an important but indirect role in the imperial debate, became significant in their own right. Now that Independence had become a realistic possibility, escaping Britain's monopoly of Virginia's trade became a powerful incentive to part company. In March 1776, when the conservative Landon Carter held back from Independence, fearing social disruption, Francis Lightfoot Lee tried to shift Carter's attention to the hated Navigation Acts. "I can't think we shall be injured by having a free trade to all the world," Lee told him. A newspaper writer acknowledged that a war for Independence would entail sacrifices but argued that they would be outweighed by "the advantages that we shall derive from unrestrained commerce."[30]

It will be recalled that An American, the anonymous writer in the *Virginia Gazette*, argued that, if the British government tried to tax free Americans even as it monopolized their trade, it would commit the same sort of crime as a slaveholder that made his workers keep producing for him even after

29. "Virginia Resolutions on Lord North's Conciliatory Proposal," [June 10, 1775], in Boyd et al., eds., *Papers of Jefferson*, I, 172; Dumas Malone, *Jefferson and His Time*, I, *Jefferson the Virginian* (Boston, 1948), 199; Edmund Randolph, *History of Virginia*, ed. Arthur H. Shaffer (Charlottesville, Va., 1970), 225; ["Richard Henry Lee's Draft Address to the People of Great Britain"], [June 27?, 1775], in Paul H. Smith et al., eds., *Letters of Delegates to Congress, 1774–1789* (Washington, D.C., 1976–), I, 550; Edmund Pendleton, resolutions offered in Congress [May 1775], in David John Mays, ed., *The Letters and Papers of Edmund Pendleton, 1734–1803* (Charlottesville, Va., 1967), I, 106; David John Mays, *Edmund Pendleton, 1721–1803: A Biography* (Cambridge, Mass., 1952), II, 32.

30. Francis Lightfoot Lee to Landon Carter, Mar. 19, 1776, Dearborn Collection, Houghton; "A Planter," Dixon and Hunter's *VG*, Apr. 13, 1776.

sundown and on Sundays. It is significant that An American associated free Americans' tax exemption with the few hours of leisure slaves enjoyed at dusk and on the Sabbath while equating the Navigation Acts with the *many* hours they worked for their owners during the day. The Navigation Acts were a heavier burden than taxation could ever be, and they decisively influenced free Virginians' response to the new taxes that Parliament proposed in the 1760s.[31]

The free colonists' gradual progression from quietly resenting the Navigation Acts to seeking Independence in order to escape them has been difficult for historians to follow, because, until 1775, the Virginians' reluctance to alienate British merchants prevented them from discussing imperial trade policy openly. One thing is clear: although the American Revolution in Virginia was in part the tax revolt we all learn about in grade school, it was also a class conflict pitting Virginia tobacco growers against the British merchants that, with the help of the Royal Navy, monopolized their trade.

I I

The imperial regulation of transoceanic commerce was not the only political arena where Virginia tobacco growers and British merchants clashed. Both groups also recognized the importance of legislation governing the debtor-creditor relationship, and both intensified their efforts to influence these laws in the early 1760s, when Virginia plunged into a terrible recession. Members of the House of Burgesses agonized over the economic decline not only because it hurt them materially but also because it provoked debtors to attack creditors and the gentry-dominated court system. The danger that desperate debtors posed is revealed in the letters of William Allason, a trader in Falmouth, located on the Rappahannock River opposite Fredericksburg. Allason discovered that the recession made the never-very-safe business of debt collection more perilous than ever before. "As it is sometimes Dangerous in Traveling through our wooden Country Particular[l]y at this time when the Planters are pressed for Old Ballances," he told a Glasgow tobacco firm in 1764, "we find it necessary to carry with us some defensive Weapons." He ordered a pair of pistols.[32]

Even when the debtor-creditor conflict involved only a farmer and a trader such as Allason, the gentry could be drawn into it. When the gentlemen justices of the county court awarded a creditor an execution against a

---

31. Purdie's *VG*, Mar. 29, 1776.

32. Allason to Bogle and Scott, July 29, 1764 (extract), in D. R. Anderson, ed., "The Letters of William Allason, Merchant, of Falmouth, Virginia," *Richmond College Historical Papers*, II (June 1917), 134–135.

debtor, the creditor could direct the county sheriff, who was also a gentleman, to seize the debtor's property or even the debtor himself. Sometimes debtors resisted arrest, and they seem to have done so with growing frequency during the recession of the early 1760s. Even more ominous, the recession prompted debtors to organize collective resistance. "In some Countys," Allason wrote in 1764, "the People have agreed to defend one another against the officers." Imprisoned debtors often tried to break jail, most commonly by taking a brand from the hearth and setting fire to the prison wall. "Scarcely a prison is allowed to stand," Allason wrote. In a typical case, the Glasgow firm of Speirs, Bowman, and Company had one of its debtors, Richmond Levins, jailed in Cumberland County in October 1764. Barely a week later, Levins was charged with "setting fire to and thereby attempting to burn and destroy the common g[ao]l." He was sent to Williamsburg to be tried for his life.[33]

Throughout the British colonies, whenever debtors recaptured their property from sheriffs or burned jails, they alarmed the local gentry. These attacks produced particular distress in Virginia, where gentlemen believed that the 40 percent of the population that was enslaved could be kept in check only if whites remained completely unified. During the recession, the House of Burgesses tried to relieve Virginia debtors' desperation by protecting them in various ways from their British creditors. In 1762, the assembly passed a bankruptcy law. "The Virginians," Liverpool merchant Charles Goore wrote in June 1763, "are in a bad plight and no appearance of recovery except they can get an Act passed to exclude 'em from paying their Debts." Glasgow merchants predicted that the bankruptcy law would be "greatly distressing to the Subjects of Britain, who have Debts owing them in Virginia." These and other merchants' criticisms of the law persuaded the Privy Council to veto it.[34]

A crucial facet of the relationship between debtors and creditors was

33. Allason to Alexander Walker, June 24, 1764 (extract), in Anderson, ed., "Letters of Allason," 134; Oct. 22, 31, 1764, Cumberland County court, order book, 47, 69, LVA. Levins's ultimate fate is not known.

34. Goore to William Bickerton, June 19, 1763, Glasgow merchants, petition against Virginia's 1762 bankruptcy law, June 17, 1763, C.O. 5/1368, 407, 415, P.R.O. (microfilm at Lamont); Elmer Beecher Russell, *The Review of American Colonial Legislation by the King in Council* (1915; reprint, New York, 1976), 125–127. The 1762 bankruptcy statute was patterned on a similar measure in Britain. Under its provisions, when Virginia debtors gave up all of their property, creditors would not be able to seize property they acquired in the future. Recognizing that the bankruptcy law would never get past the Privy Council, the House of Burgesses repealed it shortly after passing it. The Privy Council vetoed it anyway (Ragsdale, *Planters' Republic*, 28).

Virginia's money supply. Starting in 1755, the House of Burgesses financed Virginia's participation in the Seven Years' War by printing paper money. When Virginia currency depreciated in relation to the pound sterling, the assembly refused either to rein in the provincial money supply or to force Virginia debtors to pay their British debts in sterling. The assembly's recalcitrance intensified during the recession of the early 1760s. It was largely in response to the burgesses' prodebtor stance that British merchants persuaded Parliament to pass the Currency Act of 1764, which prohibited provincial legislatures from issuing legal tender—paper money that creditors would be legally required to accept in discharge of debts. Virginia tobacco growers resented the new burden. "We shall all be madmen," one grower said in 1770, "if we do not . . . make them lift that *heavy finger* from off our shoulders." Other Virginians also denounced the Currency Act.[35]

In 1765 and again in 1767, the House of Burgesses voted to lend out paper money that was not legal tender and thus did not violate the Currency Act. Its goal, the deeply indebted burgess Charles Carter explained in May 1765, was "to extricate our Country out of its present deplorable Circumstances." Although they were legal, both loan office proposals were thwarted by government officials that were loath to offend British merchants by approving any sort of paper money.[36]

In order to appreciate what a huge benefit Virginians had expected to

35. "C— R—," Rind's *VG*, Apr. 26, 1770; Richard Bland, "Extract of a Letter from a Gentleman in Virginia to his Friend in this City [London]," Aug. 1, 1771, Adams Family Papers (1672–1792), section 6 (microfilm, VHS); "Philautos," Purdie and Dixon's *VG*, July 25, 1766; Robert E. Brown and B. Katherine Brown, *Virginia, 1705–1786: Democracy or Aristocracy?* (East Lansing, Mich., 1964), 117; Ragsdale, *Planters' Republic*, 27; Isaac S. Harrell, "Some Neglected Phases of the Revolution in Virginia," *WMQ*, 2d Ser., V (1925), 166; Joseph Albert Ernst, "Genesis of the Currency Act of 1764: Virginia Paper Money and the Protection of British Investments," *WMQ*, 3d Ser., XXII (1965), 33–74. For criticism of the Currency Act in other colonies, see Jack P. Greene and Richard M. Jellison, "The Currency Act of 1764 in Imperial-Colonial Relations, 1764–1776," *WMQ*, 3d Ser., XVIII (1961), 517; Ernst, *Money and Politics*; Gary B. Nash, *The Urban Crucible: Social Change, Political Consciousness, and the Origins of the American Revolution* (Cambridge, Mass., 1979), 317.

36. Charles Carter to Landon Carter, May 20, 1765, in Paul P. Hoffman, ed., *The Carter Family Papers, 1659–1797, in the Sabine Hall Collection* (microfilm, Charlottesville, Va., 1967); Mays, *Edmund Pendleton*, I, 175–176; William Nelson to John Norton, Aug. 27, 1768, in Mason, ed., *Norton and Sons*, 66; Apr. 11, 1767, *JHB, 1766–1769*, 129; "Representation of the Lords of Trade, to His Majesty, on an Address of the House of Burgesses of Virginia, Praying Permission to Issue a Certain Quantity of Paper Money," enclosed in Board of Trade to Hillsborough, June 10, 1768, C.O. 5/1346, 21–23; E. James Ferguson, "Currency Finance: An Interpretation of Colonial Monetary Practices," *WMQ*, 3d Ser., X (1953), 178; Ernst, *Money and Politics*, 179, 235–236.

receive from the loan office, it is necessary to understand the impact of the colony's money shortage. Cash was in such short supply in Virginia that even well-to-do growers had to make most of their purchases on credit. Property for sale generally bore two prices: one for cash customers and a significantly higher one for those that bought on credit. The annualized interest incorporated into the credit customer's price ranged as high as 15 percent—triple the legal interest ceiling of 5 percent. At that level, when a cash customer paid a certain amount for eight hoes, a credit customer with the same amount of money received only seven hoes. It was hidden interest charges that explained why British manufactured goods could be obtained far more cheaply in northern seaports than in Virginia, William Lee told his brother. Northern merchants "deal for ready money [cash] or very short credit," and thus they could "well afford to sell for less advance [that is, with a lower markup] than in Virga. where the credit is unlimited," Lee said. Thousands of Virginia's credit customers could have become cash buyers if they could have mortgaged their property for cash at a government loan office. The loan office would have benefited even those Virginians that never passed through its doors. With more cash in circulation, a grower that was headed into town to buy something could stop off at the home of a neighbor that owed him or her a small debt, and count on collecting sufficient money to make a cash purchase. He or she would thus receive a discount of about 15 percent off the credit price.[37]

The money shortage that hurt tobacco farmers when they made purchases harmed them even more when one of their debts was called in. Debtors often lacked sufficient cash on hand to discharge their creditors' demands, and they were rarely able to sell property for cash at a decent price. Many creditors were willing to accept property in lieu of cash, but only if it was greatly undervalued. For that reason, an essayist calling himself "Philautos" declared in 1766, debtors paying with property instead of money sometimes had "to pay perhaps double what they owe." Debtors unable or unwilling to satisfy their creditors often had their property—slaves, horses, tools, and household items—seized by county sheriffs and auctioned off. Because of the general "want of cash," the tight money supply, "very few purchasers can attend" auctions, a *Virginia Gazette* essayist that called him-

---

37. William Lee to Francis Lightfoot Lee, July 20, 1771, William Lee Letterbook (typescript), Alexandria, Virginia, Public Library; *SAL*, VI, 102. The loan offices in other colonies did not simply benefit those that obtained loans from them. By putting more money in circulation, they benefited almost everyone (R. Terry Bouton, "Tying Up the Revolution: Money, Power, and the Regulation in Pennsylvania, 1765–1800" [Ph.D. diss., Duke University, 1996], 53–54).

self "Experience" explained. Thus the property often went at low prices, Experience said—"hardly one fourth of the real value of the poor debtors effects."[38] The sheriff had to keep putting more and more of the debtor's property on the block until enough money came in to pay the debt (and the sheriff's fee). If the British government had permitted the assembly to establish a loan office where Virginians could mortgage their property for cash, many more people would have been able to attend sheriffs' sales. Debtors would have received higher prices for their property and thus would not have had to forfeit so much of it.[39]

Another form of relief that the House of Burgesses tried to grant debtors would have narrowed the jurisdiction of Williamsburg's hustings court. The "borough court," as it was called, was one of the few Virginia courts that handled debt cases quickly; most of the judges were traders. Under existing law, plaintiffs (mostly creditors) could use the hustings court to sue any debtor they could catch within the limits of Williamsburg. An amendment that passed the House of Burgesses in 1770 would have allowed creditors to sue only permanent residents. Merchants protested, a Whitehall bureaucrat determined that the existing arrangement was "of Singular Utility in the recovery of Mercantile Debts," and the Privy Council vetoed the 1770 law. The veto was denounced by Arthur Lee in a newspaper essay signed "Junius Americanus." Lee called the "unlimited jurisdiction" of the hustings court "an usurpation." He attributed the Privy Council's veto to "a junto of North

38. "Philautous," Purdie and Dixon's *VG*, July 25, 1766; "Experience," Rind's *VG*, Nov. 25, 1773; William Allason to Alexander Walker (extract), June 24, 1764, in Anderson, ed., "Letters of Allason," *Richmond College Historical Papers*, II, 134; Richard L. Bushman, *King and People in Provincial Massachusetts* (Chapel Hill, N.C., 1985), 199. In 1767, George Washington warned an indebted friend that, if he were going to sell his estate, he had better do it quickly, because after the House of Burgesses had called in the colony's paper money, "every thing of consequence [will] sell worse" (to John Posey, June 24, 1767, in Abbot et al., eds., *Papers of Washington*, Colonial Series, VIII, 3).

39. The 1765 loan office proposal also had two special purposes. The first was to allow debtors to delay repayment of their debts. Virginia was in a recession in 1765; debtors were being aggressively dunned at a time when their crops and other property were worth very little. The loan office would have allowed debtors to pay off their merchant-creditors immediately by transferring the loan to the government and repaying it when the economy improved. The other special purpose was to rescue the members of the gentry that had accepted loans from assembly speaker John Robinson. Loans from the new loan office would allow Robinson's debtors to pay off their illegal loans (on some of which Robinson charged usurious interest), which would in turn make it possible for Robinson to return the money he had stolen. See Ernst, *Money and Politics*, 174, 177–178; Mays, *Edmund Pendleton*, I, chap. 11.

Britons [Scots], whom the favour of the Virginians had raised from beggary to affluence." Lee was dismayed that the Privy Council had sacrificed the interests of Virginia growers to "the tobacco merchants, or, to be more humiliating, the Scotch part of them." Addressing Lord Hillsborough, he asked, "Where, my Lord, will the humiliation of America end?" Lee wondered why Hillsborough did not "appoint a committee of Scotch store boys, to report to the Board of Trade on every bill that passes the two Houses of Assembly, before it is permitted to have the Governor's assent." A letter responding to "Junius Americanus" sarcastically sympathized with Arthur Lee's hatred of the hustings court, "as the Inconveniencies attending it have perhaps been oftener experienced in his Family than in any other"—that is, the Lees were one of the most sued families in Virginia.[40]

In 1766, Arthur Lee's deeply indebted brother Richard Henry proposed an additional debtor protection law that seemed so likely to be vetoed in London that his fellow burgesses chose not to adopt it. The bill would have repealed an existing statute that allowed creditors to prove in court that Virginians owed them money simply by swearing to their ledgers. Lee believed that the ease with which creditors proved their Virginia debts was "productive of too speedy a change in property"—out of the hands of American debtors and into those of British creditors. The system had been set up by the House of Burgesses in compliance with a law that Parliament had passed in 1732 at the behest of British merchants. If the House of Burgesses had endorsed Lee's proposal to force creditors to submit further proof of their Virginia debts, it would have courted a head-on collision with Parliament. This was too much for Lee's colleagues in the assembly, and they defeated his bill.[41]

40. Richard Jackson (legal counsel for the Board of Trade), in Ragsdale, *Planters' Republic*, 28; "Junius Americanus" [Arthur Lee], Rind's *VG*, Oct. 17, 1771 (reprinted from *Bingley's Journal*, July 20, 1771); "Andromachus," Purdie and Dixon's *VG*, Oct. 31, 1771; John Tayloe, Rind's *VG*, Feb. 27, 1772; *SAL*, VIII, 401–402; Feb. 28, 1772, *Acts of the Privy Council of England*, Colonial Series, V (London, 1912), 319; anonymous letter, Purdie and Dixon's *VG*, Dec. 26, 1771; A. G. Roeber, *Faithful Magistrates and Republican Lawyers: Creators of Virginia Legal Culture, 1680–1810* (Chapel Hill, N.C., 1981), 131–132. The claim that the Lee family had faced an extraordinary number of debt suits cannot be confirmed, since the records of the hustings court have not survived. To "produce no better Proof of the Depravity of a Set of Men than their being of this or that Country," Tazewell told Lee, "shows you to be driven to a wretched Shift indeed" (Purdie and Dixon's *VG*, Jan. 2, 1772).

41. "Rusticus" [Richard Henry Lee], in Hoffman, ed., *Lee Family Papers*, frames 713–716; Dec. 8, Dec. 12, 1766, *JHB, 1766–1769*, 56, 67–68; "A Poor Planter," Rind's *VG*, Feb. 25, 1773; Russell, *Royal Review*, 133–134; Ragsdale, *Planters' Republic*, 28–29.

III

A third area of grower-merchant conflict was the forced immigration of Africans and West Indians into Virginia. A leading opponent of African immigration was Thomas Jefferson. One reason Jefferson so passionately denounced the slave trade in his draft of the Declaration of Independence— he listed it as the twenty-eighth of twenty-eight charges, the capstone—was that it had hurt him personally. Jefferson had had a brief, unsolicited, and unsuccessful career as a slave trader. His father-in-law, John Wayles, and a partner, Richard Randolph, arranged to bring 280 Africans into Virginia on board a ship called the *Prince of Wales*. The ship entered Chesapeake Bay in September 1772, just as Virginia entered one of the worst recessions in its history. Many of the workers had to be sold on credit. In June 1773, Wayles died. He bequeathed to Jefferson eleven thousand acres of land and 135 enslaved people—but he also named him an executor, which made him partially responsible for settling the *Prince of Wales* accounts. Jefferson, his fellow executors, and Randolph failed to obtain payment from all of the people that had bought the Africans from Wayles, and thus they could not pay Wayles's debt to the Bristol merchants that had consigned the slaves to him. Jefferson later wrote that inherited debts like this one turned white Virginians like him into a "species of property annexed to certain mercantile houses in London." Thomas Jefferson thus declared himself the British merchants' slave.[42]

The *Prince of Wales* episode only intensified an antipathy toward the African trade that Jefferson had already expressed before the ship put into the Chesapeake. In April 1772, Jefferson and every other member of the House of Burgesses had voted for a resolution asking George III to abolish the Atlantic slave trade altogether. The unanimous vote culminated a five-year legislative effort to curb the immigration of Africans and West Indians into Virginia by raising the import duty. The fates of the duty increases and

42. John Wayles to Farell and Jones, Sept. 24, 1772, Thomas Jefferson to Farell and Jones, July 9, 1773, in Boyd et al., eds., *Papers of Jefferson*, XV, 653, 660; Richard Randolph to Farell and Jones, Dec. 30, 1772 (copy), claim of John Tyndale Warre, American Loyalist Claims, T. 79/30, P.R.O.; Steven Harold Hochman, "Thomas Jefferson: A Personal Financial Biography" (Ph.D. diss., University of Virginia, 1987), 67, 75. After the American Revolution, Wayles's executors were sued for the money Wayles and Randolph failed to remit to the British firm that owned the *Prince of Wales* and its human cargo. The executors persuaded the court that, at Wayles's death, the responsibility for collecting from the slave buyers devolved upon Randolph. Thus they prevailed in the suit (Herbert E. Sloan, *Principle and Interest: Thomas Jefferson and the Problem of Debt* [New York, 1995], 14, 21, 254n, 258n). For Jefferson's declaration of slavery, see "Additional questions of M. de Meusnier, and answers" [ca. January–February, 1786], in Boyd et al., eds., *Papers of Jefferson*, X, 27.

of the petition to eliminate the trade both rested with the Privy Council in London. There, the assembly faced a formidable enemy: the well-organized transatlantic slave merchants of Liverpool, Bristol, and other English ports.

In 1767 and 1769, when the House of Burgesses voted to double the duty it assessed on slaves arriving in Virginia from 10 to 20 percent, its goal was not to bring in more revenue but to bring in fewer slaves. This attempt at "preventing the farther importation of slaves, by laying heavy duties on such as should be imported" (as an anonymous essayist later described it) was the product of numerous motives, mostly economic. One was to curb the growth in the number of Virginia laborers—and thus in the size of the crop—in order to shore up the price of tobacco.[43] Another was to leave more money in the hands of free Virginians and thus ease the chronic cash shortage. In addition, Virginians that sold slaves to other growers had an obvious interest in doubling the duty on their foreign competition. Still another motive behind the slave impost legislation was to remove tobacco growers' temptation to finance the purchase of foreign slaves by going deeper into debt. The reduction of private debts had been a reason for the prohibitive duty of five pounds adopted back in 1710; the House of Burgesses acknowledged taxing enslaved immigrants "on purpose to discourage their importation till the country is out of debt."[44]

43. "An American," Purdie's VG, Mar. 29, 1776; "Associator Humanus," Purdie and Dixon's VG, July 18, 1771; Harry Piper to Dixon and Littledale, Dec. 16, 1770, Harry Piper Letterbook (#2981), UVA; Robert Pleasants to Anthony Benezet, Feb. 22, 1774, "Letters of Robert Pleasants of Curles," WMQ, 2d Ser., I (1921), 109. Although no surviving correspondence indicates that the price of tobacco was on the burgesses' minds when they adopted the 1767 and 1769 duties, one indication that it might have been is that, back in 1710, 1723, and 1728, when their predecessors had also voted for prohibitive slave tariffs, it was widely assumed that their goal was to shore up the price of their staple. The 1710 duty was imposed at the end of a decade-long boom in slave importation that had, Governor Alexander Spotswood reported, "lower'd the Price" of tobacco "to a great Degree." Richard Harris, a British merchant, claimed that the "Overgrown Planters who had Negroes in Abundance" secured the adoption of the 1723 duty in order to limit the tobacco harvest so "that their [tobacco] might sell dearer in the Markets of Europe." See Anthony S. Parent, Jr., " 'Either a Fool or a Fury': The Emergence of Paternalism in Colonial Virginia Slave Society" (Ph.D. diss., University of California, Los Angeles, 1982), 124, 135, 136; Johnson, "Regulation of Virginia Business," 27. In 1728, when the House of Burgesses again voted for a prohibitive slave import duty (only to see it vetoed by the Privy Council), Governor William Gooch said its purpose was to reduce the importation of slaves in order to raise the price of tobacco. See Parent, " 'Either a Fool or a Fury,' " 138–139; Ragsdale, Planters' Republic, 124.

44. Pauline Maier, The Old Revolutionaries: Political Lives in the Age of Samuel Adams (New York, 1980), 189. One reason South Carolina legislators voted a temporary ban on slave imports in 1787 was their expectation that, when local suppliers cornered the slave

Leading Virginians believed that cutting back on slave imports would not only serve all of these short-term economic goals but also help them transform Virginia, a staple colony that imported most of the manufactured goods it consumed, into a healthy mixed economy where farmers grew a variety of crops and purchased many of their manufactures from local artisans. One of the greatest obstacles to that economic overhaul was slavery, which soaked up much of the capital that might otherwise have gone to manufacturing projects at the same time that it degraded manual labor and thus (as a patriot committee would state in 1774) "prevent[ed] Manufacturers and other useful Emigrants from Europe from settling amongst us."[45]

Clearly, one reason to restrict the slave trade was fear. Slave insurrection plots helped persuade the House of Burgesses to adopt the 1710 and 1723 slave tariffs. The principal reason that William Byrd II proposed halting the African trade in 1736 was that he feared that "multiplying these Ethiopians amongst us" would lead to a "se[r]vile war" that would "tinge our rivers as wide as they are with blood." By the time Byrd wrote, Virginia's black population had achieved natural increase. This growth, together with the forced immigration of Africans and West Indians, propelled the black proportion of Virginia's population from less than 10 percent in 1700 to about 40 percent by 1775.[46] As the enslaved portion of Virginia's population quadrupled,

---

market, "negroes would rise in value" (Patrick S. Brady, "The Slave Trade and Sectionalism in South Carolina, 1787–1808," *JSH*, XXXVIII [1972], 605). On the effort to discourage tobacco growers from purchasing slaves on credit, see Parent, " 'Either a Fool or a Fury,' " 126. Some creditors joined their debtors in celebrating the effort to reduce the influx of foreign slaves. In the 1720s, in the midst of a boom in slave imports, creditor John Custis found it difficult "to get one's debts in," because "people will buy Nigros when at the same time they owes the money to other people" (Custis to Micajah Perry, ca. 1721, in Parent, " 'Either a Fool or a Fury,' " 141–142). In South Carolina in 1787, a proposal to suspend the slave trade received the support of many creditors. One Carolinian told "of a man refusing to pay any part of his debts, alledging his inability, and a few days afterwards he purchased 15 slaves!" (Brady, "Slave Trade and Sectionalism," *JSH*, XXXVIII [1972], 603).

45. Prince George County resolves, in *Revolutionary Virginia*, I, 151; Ragsdale, *Planters' Republic*, chap. 4. Gentlemen believed that the presence of slaves not only discouraged the immigration of poor whites but also caused those already in Virginia to shun manual labor (Ragsdale, *Planters' Republic*, 120).

46. Byrd to John Perceval, earl of Egmont, July 12, 1736, in Tinling, ed., *Correspondence of the Three William Byrds*, II, 487–488; Allan Kulikoff, "A 'Prolifick' People: Black Population Growth in the Chesapeake Colonies, 1700–1790," *Southern Studies*, XVI (1977), 391–428; Peter H. Wood, "The Changing Population of the Colonial South: An Overview by Race and Region, 1685–1790," in Wood, Gregory A. Waselkov, and M. Thomas Hatley, eds., *Powhatan's Mantle: Indians in the Colonial Southeast* (Lincoln, Nebr., 1989), 38.

whites' fears of their "intestine enemies" increased as well. "[P]erhaps the primary Cause of the Destruction of the most flourishing Government that ever existed"—Rome's—"was the Introduction of great Numbers of Slaves," George Mason wrote at the end of 1765. Scarcely a year later, Mason found justification for his fears: some of his slaves participated in an insurrection plot. Thomas Jefferson's 1781 statement, well known as an expression of the guilt that many slaveholders felt, also exposed his fears: "I tremble for my country when I reflect that God is just: that his justice cannot sleep for ever: that considering numbers, nature and natural means only, a revolution of the wheel of fortune, an exchange of situation, is among possible events."[47]

Arthur Lee estimated in 1764 that "in the colony of Virginia the slaves exceed the freemen by more than one third"—an estimate that was accurate only in a few tidewater counties—"and that two or three thousand are yearly imported. Would not this be a fearful odds, should they ever be excited to rebellion?"[48] Lee returned to the topic of slave rebellion three years later in an address to the House of Burgesses that appeared in the *Virginia Gazette* four days before the assembly ordered a committee to draft the 1767 duty increase. Slavery was bad for the economy and for the morals of whites, he argued. Furthermore, the ancient Romans had been "brought to the very brink of ruin by the insurrections of their Slaves," even though "the proportion of slaves among the antients was not so great as with us." Richard Henry

---

47. After issuing this warning, Mason cut short his discussion of the danger of slave revolt: "'Tis not the present Intention to expose our Weakness by examining this Subject too freely," he wrote. See ". . . [A] scheme for replevying goods under distress for rent," enclosed in Mason to George William Fairfax and George Washington, Dec. 23, 1765, in Rutland, ed., *Papers of George Mason*, I, 61–62, 64n; George Washington to John Posey, June 11, 1769, in Abbot et al., eds., *Papers of George Washington*, Colonial Series, VIII, 211, 215n; Herbert Aptheker, *American Negro Slave Revolts* (New York, 1943), 199. For "intestine enemies" quotation, see Peter Fontaine to his brothers, Mar. 2, 1756, in Ann Maury, trans. and comp., *Memoirs of a Huguenot Family* (New York, 1853), 347. On Jefferson's fears, see Thomas Jefferson, *Notes on the State of Virginia*, ed. William Peden (Chapel Hill, N.C., 1954), 163.

48. "An American" [Lee], *An Essay*, 40. Lee was not the only Virginia slaveholder that exaggerated the size of the enslaved population. Governor Dunmore claimed in 1772 (when 40 percent of Virginians were enslaved) that slaves outnumbered free Virginians by two to one. See Dunmore to Hillsborough, May 1, 1772, in K. G. Davies, ed., *Documents of the American Revolution, 1770–1783* (Shannon, Ireland, 1972–1981), V, 94; Robert Dinwiddie, cited in Peter H. Wood, " 'Liberty Is Sweet': African-American Freedom Struggles in the Years before White Independence," in Alfred F. Young, ed., *Beyond the American Revolution: Explorations in the History of American Radicalism* (DeKalb, Ill., 1993), 154.

For additional evidence that whites feared blacks during the pre-Revolutionary period, see Chapter 5, below.

Lee agreed with his brother that the slaves' "increase" was "dangerous." He wanted to make the prohibitive duty adopted during the Seven Years' War permanent, ending the forced immigration of slaves into Virginia once and for all.[49]

It may well be asked, If gentlemen really believed that Africans and West Indians posed such a threat, why did they not simply stop purchasing them? Why did they find it necessary to restrict importation by legislative fiat? In fact, by 1767, most gentlemen *had* stopped buying foreign slaves. Most "salt-water" slaves were sold to smallholders in the piedmont Southside, and farmers would continue buying them unless they were compelled to desist. It was apparently these younger and less wealthy southern piedmont growers that pressured the House of Burgesses to reduce the slave import duty from its prohibitive peak of 30 percent to only 10 percent at the end of the Seven Years' War. Farmers knew that reducing the duty by two-thirds would not only revive the international slave trade but also force Virginians that sold slaves to do so on more reasonable terms. In 1760, Lieutenant Governor Francis Fauquier said the legislative struggle over the slave import duty was "between the old Settlers who have bred great Quantity of Slaves, and would make a Monopoly of them by a Duty which they hope would amount to a prohibition; and the rising Generation who want Slaves, and don't care to pay the Monopolists for them at the price they have lately bore which was exceedingly high." Although Fauquier oversimplified the motives of the legislators that wanted to keep African and West Indian immigrants out of Virginia (they were worried about their safety and about several other economic factors besides the price of slaves), he was probably right about who wanted to revive slave imports in 1760. It was up-and-coming growers, mostly in the piedmont, that wanted to increase the availability of slaves and bring down the price.[50]

49. "Philanthropos" [Arthur Lee], anonymous letter, Mar. 19, 1767, in Richard K. Mac-Master, "Arthur Lee's 'Address on Slavery': An Aspect of Virginia's Struggle to End the Slave Trade, 1765–1774," *VMHB*, LXXX (1972), 156; Richard H. Lee, *Memoir of the Life of Richard Henry Lee, and His Correspondence with the Most Distinguished Men in America and Europe . . .* (Philadelphia, 1825), I, 17–18; Ragsdale, *Planters' Republic*, 126. Arthur Lee called for the abolition of slavery (Arthur Lee to [Richard Henry Lee], Mar. 20, 1765, in Hoffman, ed., *Lee Family Papers*). Robert Pleasants, who opposed the slave trade on moral grounds, believed that a powerful argument against it was that it threatened "the security of the state" (to Charles Pleasants, July 12, 1774, Pleasants Letterbook).

50. Ragsdale, *Planters' Republic*, 115, 127; Fauquier to Board of Trade, June 2, 1760, in Reese, ed., *Papers of Francis Fauquier*, I, 372; Ragsdale, *Planters' Republic*, 127. The South Carolina legislature's ban on slave importation, which lasted from 1787 to 1802, was generally sup-

Falmouth trader William Allason's description of the white Virginians' contest over the slave trade jibed with Fauquier's. "For sometime past, there has been great party work amongst them," Allason wrote in August 1760; "the Rich ones was for preventing Slaves being imported Alltogether by the Extorbitant duty of 20 [percent]. [T]he Poorer on the other hand was very Strenous for reducing the duty as much as possible." In the decade before the American Revolution, even as the House of Burgesses tried to restrict or abolish the slave trade, foreign slaves sold briskly in the piedmont Southside, where smallholders predominated.[51]

Despite the small farmers' support for the international slave trade, the House of Burgesses not only tried in 1767 and 1769 to limit the trade by doubling the duty but also adopted a petition asking the Privy Council to end it altogether. The burgesses' April 1772 vote in favor of the petition was unanimous. They said they were "sensible that some of your Majesty's Subjects in *Great-Britain*"—the slave merchants—"may reap Emoluments from this Sort of Traffic." But ending the forced immigration of Africans and West Indians into Virginia was the only way of "averting a Calamity of a most alarming Nature" that would "endanger the very Existance of your Majesty's *American* Dominions."[52]

The Privy Council vetoed the 1767 and 1769 Virginia laws doubling the slave import duty and issued instructions forbidding governors to approve any such legislation in the future. It also rejected the assembly's petition to shut down the slave trade altogether. Gentry Virginians had no doubt why their effort to end or at least reduce the forced immigration of Africans and West Indians into their province had failed. Back in 1736, when William Byrd II had pleaded with Britain to avert a "se[r]vile war" by abolishing the slave trade, he had recognized that his proposal would encounter the opposition

ported by representatives from the black-majority eastern districts—who had all the slaves they needed and hoped to jack up their price—and opposed by westerners. See Brady, "Slave Trade and Sectionalism," *JSH*, XXXVIII (1972), 601–628; Rachel N. Klein, *Unification of a Slave State: The Rise of the Planter Class in the South Carolina Backcountry, 1760–1808* (Chapel Hill, N.C., 1990), 127–128, 131–132; Joyce E. Chaplin, *An Anxious Pursuit: Agricultural Innovation and Modernity in the Lower South, 1730–1815* (Chapel Hill, N.C., 1993), 320–321.

51. William Allason to Halliday and Dunbar, Aug. 19, 1760, Allason Letterbook, LVA; Darold D. Wax, "Negro Import Duties in Colonial Virginia: A Study of British Commercial Policy and Local Public Policy," *VMHB*, LXXIX (1971), 39. Farmers also routinely violated the total ban on slave imports that the gentry included in the patriotic "association" of 1769 (Ragsdale, *Planters' Republic*, 132).

52. *Revolutionary Virginia*, I, 85–88. That same session also voted to increase the slave import duty (Ragsdale, *Planters' Republic*, 133).

of "a few ravenous traders" (the British slave merchants).[53] Later, when the House of Burgesses' 1772 petition against the slave trade was rejected, British slave shippers were once again blamed. "Such is the influence of a few African Merchants," Arthur Lee wrote in April 1773, "that our Assembly cannot obtain the King's consent to prohibit so pernicious and inhuman a trade in Virginia. This is one instance in which we feel, the galling yoke of dependance." Only an independent Virginia could ignore the slave merchants and halt African immigration. Thomas Jefferson was also appalled at the imperial government's policy of "preferring the immediate advantages of a few British corsairs"—the slave merchants—"to the lasting interests of the American states."[54]

In several ways, the assembly's unsuccessful 1772 bid to end the African trade paralleled its rejected 1769 petition for Kentucky. In both cases, the burgesses asked the Privy Council to grant them more control over a group of nonwhite Americans, Indians in the first instance and slaves in the second. Both petitions sought to change government policies that had harmed free Virginians economically: like the British government's ban on land speculation, the free importation of Africans and West Indians had increased white Virginians' debts. In both cases, gentlemen tried to prevent

53. William Byrd II to John Perceval, earl of Egmont, July 12, 1736, in Tinling, ed., *Correspondence of the Three William Byrds*, II, 488. British merchants had in fact secured the repeal of the prohibitive slave duty adopted by the House of Burgesses in 1728 (Walter E. Minchinton, "The Political Activities of Bristol Merchants with Respect to the Southern Colonies before the Revolution," *VMHB*, LXXIX [1971], 177).

54. Arthur Lee to Joseph Reed, Feb. 18, 1773, Jesse Frasier Transcript Collection (#8709), UVA; Billings, Selby, and Tate, *Colonial Virginia*, 281.

White Virginians later said the main reason they had wanted to halt the African trade was that it was immoral. Morality might have been the motivation of some. But the 1772 address denouncing the slave trade was apparently written by Richard Henry Lee, whose brother was at that very time "endeavoring to get [him] some Negroe Consignments" ([Arthur Lee] to [Richard Henry Lee], Feb. 14, 1773, Arthur Lee Papers). On Jefferson's opinion, see "A Summary View of the Rights of British America," in Boyd et al., eds., *Papers of Jefferson*, I, 130; Miller, *Origins of the American Revolution*, 18. Historians have called Jefferson's claim that George III had forced African slaves on free British colonists in America a "misrepresentation" or a case of psychological "projection." See Joseph J. Ellis, *American Sphinx: The Character of Thomas Jefferson* (New York, 1997), 33, 52; Conor Cruise O'Brien, *The Long Affair: Thomas Jefferson and the French Revolution, 1785–1800* (Chicago, 1996), 298–299; Wax, "Negro Import Duties in Colonial Virginia," *VMHB*, LXXIX (1971), 29–44. Actually, Jefferson's statement was, in a narrow sense, correct. Although it is true that thousands of Virginia smallholders willingly bought slaves in the 1760s and 1770s, it is also true that leaders such as Jefferson—who already possessed an expanding slave population—repeatedly tried during those years to prevent the further importation of slaves. They were, as Jefferson complained, prevented from doing so by the Privy Council.

smallholders from obtaining crucial elements in tobacco production—Indian land and African slaves—without paying a member of the gentry for them. Gentlemen wrote each petition as they struggled against another interest group, first Indians and then British slave merchants, over the direction of imperial policy. In both cases, the British government sided with the gentry's opponents.

In one important way, the Kentucky and the slave trade petitions differed. The burgesses that voted to abolish the African trade feared not only for their livelihoods but for their lives. Although the Continental Congress deleted from the Declaration of Independence Thomas Jefferson's denunciation of George III "for suppressing every legislative attempt to prohibit or to restrain this execrable commerce," it is clear that the conflict over this issue between Virginia's gentry class and Britain's mercantile class helped to bring about the American Revolution. In June 1788, George Mason reminded free Virginians that, after Independence, when "the interest of the African merchants" no longer prevented the legislature from abolishing the Atlantic slave trade, Virginia had acted quickly to end the trade. Mason exaggerated only a little when he stated that the British government's insistence upon keeping the slave trade open was "one of the great causes of our separation from Great-Britain."[55]

55. Jefferson, "Original Rough Draft," in Boyd et al., eds., *Papers of Jefferson*, I, 426; Mason, speech, June 17, 1788, in Rutland, ed., *Papers of George Mason*, III, 1086. On the slave trade as "the emotional climax of [Jefferson's] case against the King," see Pauline Maier, *American Scripture: Making the Declaration of Independence* (New York, 1997), 121; Garry Wills, *Inventing America: Jefferson's Declaration of Independence* (Garden City, N.Y., 1978), 71–75.

PART TWO : BOYCOTTS

1769–1774

Although this book has focused up to this point on how Indians and merchants in pursuit of their own interests inadvertently undermined relations between Virginia's leadership and the British government, it would be incorrect to portray the gentry as passively being influenced by these groups. Gentlemen responded to these challenges. As Jefferson stated in the Declaration of Independence, white men stood up to the British government "with manly Firmness." Twice in the five years before the American Revolution, free Virginians launched campaigns to pressure Parliament to repeal legislation they considered unjust—and at the same time to reduce their debts to British merchants. The effort had two distinct parts, "nonimportation" and "nonexportation." These two schemes are the subjects of the next two chapters.

Nor have we been wanting in
Attentions to our British Brethren.
—Declaration of Independence

3

NONIMPORTATION

In May 1769, leading Virginians inaugurated a boycott of many of the items that they normally imported from Britain. Their primary target was lavish clothing. Three months after the boycott began, gentlewoman Martha Jacqueline informed a London trading partner that she had become "an Associator." "I expect to be dressed in Virginia[-made] cloth very soon," she wrote, "and as I am a little incommoded with corns, in Mockasins likewise." Although Jacqueline's prediction that she would soon cast off her British-made shoes in favor of Indian moccasins appears not to have been serious, it reveals something important about the functions of attire in the genteel circles in which she moved. Jacqueline made it clear that her earlier reluctance to wear moccasins had nothing to do with comfort. In fact, if all she cared about were comfort, she might never have covered her feet with anything else. But, for members of the gentry, comfort was not the primary consideration in selecting shoes; fashion was. Jacqueline was certainly not the first Virginian to ridicule consumerism even as she indulged in it. English gentlemen and gentlewomen had begun to denounce a long list of luxury items even before some of them settled in Virginia and added tobacco to the list.[1] It was not until 1769 that Virginia gentlemen went beyond their

1. Martha Jacqueline to John Norton, Aug. 14, 1769, in Frances Norton Mason, ed., *John Norton and Sons, Merchants of London and Virginia: Being the Papers from Their Counting-House for the Years 1750 to 1795* (Richmond, Va., 1937), 103; Cary Carson, Ronald Hoffman, and Peter J. Albert, eds., *Of Consuming Interests: The Style of Life in the Eighteenth Century* (Charlottesville, Va., 1994); Richard L. Bushman, *The Refinement of America: Persons, Houses, Cities* (New York, 1992), 187; John Sekora, *Luxury: The Concept in Western Thought, Eden to Smollett* (Baltimore, 1977); Robert Micklus, "'The History of the Tuesday Club': A Mock-Jeremiad of the Colonial South," *WMQ*, 3d Ser., XL (1983), 42–61.

verbal attacks on imported extravagance and actually did something about it by leading a boycott of British merchandise.

The primary motivation for the nonimportation associations that American colonists adopted in 1769 and 1774 was to pressure Parliament to repeal laws that endangered their civil liberties, but historians have also identified numerous other motives. Merchants in America's great northern cities seem to have embraced nonimportation because they knew it "would enable them to clean out their old stock at monopoly prices."[2] Many colonists viewed nonimportation as a continuation of a century-long effort to promote domestic manufactures by favoring them over merchandise imported from Britain. They feared that their growing dependence on British luxury goods would enfeeble them or even "effeminate" them. They were attracted to nonimportation partly because it called on them to stop consuming luxuries and thus to reclaim their vigor and virility, historians say.[3]

It is unlikely that Martha Jacqueline boycotted British merchandise in order to obtain or regain virility. Her motive was more practical. "Believe me," she told her London agent, "our poor Country never stood in more

2. Even earlier, several New England towns had adopted limited nonimportation agreements in response to "hard times" (Arthur Meier Schlesinger, *The Colonial Merchants and the American Revolution, 1763–1776* [1918; reprint, New York, 1939], 106, 114). Many merchants also expected to use the 1769 and 1774 boycotts to "dispose of unsold British stock" (Joseph A. Ernst, "The Political Economy of the Chesapeake Colonies, 1760–1775: A Study in Comparative History," in Ronald Hoffman et al., eds., *The Economy of Early America: The Revolutionary Period, 1763–1790* [Charlottesville, Va., 1988], 209). Richard Champion, a pro-American merchant in Bristol, England, told a Philadelphia firm the 1774 nonimportation plan "becomes your Interest, from the very great Stock of Goods in the Country, which must otherwise become a Burthen" (Champion to Willing, Morris and Company, Sept. 30, 1774, in G. H. Guttridge, ed., *The American Correspondence of a Bristol Merchant, 1766–1776: Letters of Richard Champion* [Berkeley, 1934], 30).

3. "The resolutions of the patriots interdicting the purchase of British goods encouraged manufacturing enterprises" in Williamsburg. See Philip Alexander Bruce et al., *Virginia: Rebirth of the Old Dominion*, I (Chicago, 1929), 370; T. H. Breen, *Tobacco Culture: The Mentality of the Great Tidewater Planters on the Eve of Revolution* (Princeton, N.J., 1985), 193; Bruce A. Ragsdale, *A Planters' Republic: The Search for Economic Independence in Revolutionary Virginia* (Madison, Wis., 1996); Sara M. Evans, *Born for Liberty: A History of Women in America* (New York, 1989), 47; Michael Zuckerman, "A Different Thermidor: The Revolution beyond the American Revolution," in James A. Henretta, Michael Kammen, and Stanley N. Katz, eds., *The Transformation of Early American History: Society, Authority, and Ideology* (New York, 1991), 173, 180; Bernard Bailyn, *The Ideological Origins of the American Revolution* (Cambridge, Mass., 1967), 51; Edmund S. Morgan, "The Puritan Ethic and the American Revolution," *WMQ*, 3d Ser., XXIV (1967), 8–13; Bushman, *Refinement of America*, 188, 191–193; Breen, *Tobacco Culture*; Rhys Isaac, *The Transformation of Virginia, 1740–1790* (Chapel Hill, N.C., 1982), 247, 251.

need of an Effort to save her from ruin than now." Jacqueline said the nonimportation association would rescue indebted Virginians from the consequences of "our own Extravagances." It would give debtors what leading associator George Washington called "a pretext to live within bounds"— an honorable excuse to reduce their conspicuous consumption.[4]

The 1769 nonimportation association did not reach very far below the gentry class. Yet the popularity of the boycott idea increased dramatically after 1772, when a terrible recession struck the Chesapeake. In the summer of 1774, gentlemen drafted a nonimportation plan designed to pressure Parliament to repeal the Coercive Acts and at the same time reduce the Virginians' debts. In both 1769 and 1774, the Virginia associators vowed to boycott not only British merchandise but also African and West Indian slaves. Like the other provisions of the nonimportation plan, the assault on the slave trade was meant to serve a wide variety of goals, some related to the constitutional struggle against Parliament and others not.

The year of the first nonimportation association, 1769, also saw the earliest discussion of pressuring Parliament by reducing the quantity of tobacco that Virginians exported—an idea that had often been advocated for financial reasons. The economic conditions were not ripe for nonexportation in 1769, and the proposal languished. But, like nonimportation, nonexportation would gain many more supporters after the recession struck.

I

Although numerous Chesapeake gentlemen expressed dismay about economic decline between 1766 and 1770, small farmers actually did quite well during this period, as the price of their staple soared to enormous heights. By March 1770, one trader went so far as to say that "the principal Planters from the great Prices they have latly got for their Commodities are entirely out of Debt."[5] Many members of the gentry nonetheless sounded as if they were living through a depression, and they had several valid reasons for doing so. It will be recalled that, in May 1766, John Robinson, speaker of the House of Burgesses, died owing the provincial government more than

4. Martha Jacqueline to John Norton, Aug. 14, 1769, in Mason, ed., *Norton and Sons*, 103; George Washington to George Mason, Apr. 5, 1769, in Robert A. Rutland, ed., *The Papers of George Mason, 1725–1792* (Chapel Hill, N.C., 1970), I, 98. A Boston newspaper noted that the association in Virginia was essentially a "sumptuary law"; signers agreed to import only "the necessaries of life" and forego "mere luxuries" (*Boston Gazette*, Jan. 29, 1770, in Schlesinger, *Colonial Merchants*, 135).

5. Thomas Adams to Perkins, Buchanan, and Brown, Mar. 22, 1770, Adams Family Papers (1672–1792), section 6 (microfilm, VHS).

£100,000, and that Robinson had loaned most of this money to gentry friends. At his death the defalcation was discovered, and the House of Burgesses demanded that the administrators of his estate make it up, which of course required them to seek the money from the gentlemen (including many burgesses) to whom the speaker had lent it. Robinson's debtors in turn dunned their own debtors, and before long the credit contraction ramified throughout the gentry class.[6]

During the same years the Robinson loans were called in, the late 1760s, many gentlemen felt that their class was sinking deeper than ever into debt. They found culprits on both sides of their ledgers. Earlier in the eighteenth century, gentlemen had received substantial income from trade. They had purchased their neighbors' tobacco and supplied them with British manufactured goods and Native American land. But, by the mid-1760s, both of these sources of middleman income had dried up. The business of exchanging tobacco and other Chesapeake produce for foreign goods, and the accompanying commercial profits, were in large part siphoned off by English and Scottish storekeepers. Meanwhile, the market in Indian land was depressed by the Proclamation of 1763.[7]

One persistent difficulty that both reduced gentlemen's income and in-

6. John Mercer reported that Robinson's death "threw the whole country into a flame." His administrators threatened "all the Debtors with Suits." The threats not only scared the debtors themselves but "alarm'd the Merch[an]ts and every body else that had money due to them." Creditors feared that the Robinson suits would exhaust the defendants' estates and prevent them from discharging other debts. So, taking a cue from Robinson's administrators, "they brought and threatened to bring Suits" against the same defendants. See John Mercer to George Mercer, Dec. 22, 1767–Jan. 28, 1768, in Lois Mulkearn, ed., *George Mercer Papers Relating to the Ohio Company of Virginia* (Pittsburgh, 1954), 189–190; Joseph Albert Ernst, *Money and Politics in America, 1755–1775: A Study in the Currency Act of 1764 and the Political Economy of Revolution* (Chapel Hill, N.C., 1973), 174, 177–178; David John Mays, *Edmund Pendleton, 1721–1803: A Biography* (Cambridge, Mass., 1952), I, chap. 11.

7. Jacob M. Price, *Capital and Credit in British Overseas Trade: The View from the Chesapeake, 1700–1776* (Cambridge, Mass., 1980), 6; Price, *Perry of London: A Family and a Firm on the Seaborne Frontier, 1615–1753* (Cambridge, Mass., 1992); John E. Selby, *The Revolution in Virginia, 1775–1783* (Charlottesville, Va., 1988), 27; "A Scotchman," Pinkney's *VG*, Mar. 23, 1775; Breen, *Tobacco Culture*, 36; Francis Fauquier, "Answers to the Queries Sent to me . . . ," [Jan. 30, 1763], in George Reese, ed., *The Official Papers of Francis Fauquier, Lieutenant Governor of Virginia, 1758–1768* (Charlottesville, Va., 1980–1983), II, 1017; Darrett B. Rutman and Anita H. Rutman, *A Place in Time: Middlesex County, Virginia, 1650–1750* (New York, 1984), 232, 244; Keith Ryan Nyland, "Doctor Thomas Walker (1751–1794): Explorer, Physician, Statesman, Surveyor, and Planter of Virginia and Kentucky" (Ph.D. diss., Ohio State University, 1971), 52. Land speculation was also hampered by a geographic obstacle—the only land now available was drained by rivers that flowed west into the Mississippi instead of east into the Atlantic.

creased their expenses was Britain's monopoly of their trade. Another problem, strictly on the expenditure side, was their own habit of lavish spending, which many gentlemen considered the greatest reason for their debts. Before the eighteenth century, gentlemen tended to own the same kinds of products as middle-class people, only more of them. But by the era of the American Revolution, in what some historians have termed the "first consumer revolution," gentlemen began to purchase new sorts of items, the very possession of which set them apart from other Virginians. And yet, as soon as gentlemen staked out exclusive claim to some amenity, ambitious members of the middle rank began to purchase it. For instance, tea and the elaborate equipment with which to serve it were virtually nonexistent in the America of 1700, and they were not very common in Britain, either. By the time of the Revolution, however, tea was common in both Britain and America. Thus, Britons on both sides of the Atlantic tried to use luxury items both to maintain the floor between themselves and the next rank down and to pierce the ceiling that separated them from the rank above.[8] Many of these items were purchased by women. "Old women are remarkable for golden dreams," one man declared in an essay denouncing extravagance and a loan office proposal. The stirrings of a consumer revolution might not actually have been an important reason gentlemen fell into debt during the decades before the American Revolution. Economic historians have argued that what gentlemen called "debts" were usually productive investments. But many gentlemen were certain that the culprit was conspicuous consumption.[9]

8. Cary Carson, "The Consumer Revolution in Colonial British America: Why Demand?" in Carson, Hoffman, and Albert, eds., *Of Consuming Interests*, 483–697; T. H. Breen, " 'Baubles of Britain': The American and Consumer Revolutions of the Eighteenth Century," *Past and Present*, no. 119 (May 1988), 73–104. Some modern scholars agree that conspicuous consumption greatly contributed to the gentry's debt. See Breen, *Tobacco Culture*, 129–130; Kathleen M. Brown, *Good Wives, Nasty Wenches, and Anxious Patriarchs: Gender, Race, and Power in Colonial Virginia* (Chapel Hill, N.C., 1996), 328. On the material rivalry between the classes, see Grant McCracken, *Culture and Consumption: New Approaches to the Symbolic Character of Consumer Goods and Activities* (Bloomington, Ind., 1988), 94; Kevin M. Sweeney, "High-Style Vernacular: Lifestyles of the Colonial Elite," in Carson, Hoffman, and Albert, eds., *Of Consuming Interests*, 5, and Lois Green Carr and Lorena S. Walsh, "Changing Lifestyles and Consumer Behavior in the Colonial Chesapeake," 132.

9. "C— R—," Rind's *VG*, Mar. 3, 1768. In addition to criticizing women for their extravagant tastes, men blamed women for their own extravagance. "Here are great Variety of Ladys," young James Thompson wrote from Hanover, "amongst whom a person is not lookd upon unless the[y] Dress Genteel and make Some Figure, and the going to Balls which a person that lives here cannot avoid is expensive" (Thompson to William Preston, Nov. 12, 1767, Preston Family Papers [1727–1896], folder 535, VHS). Other gentlemen wor-

Addicted to luxuries, deriving less and less income from trade, and buried in the rubble of Robinson's debt pyramid, many gentlemen were—despite the booming tobacco market of the late 1760s—pushed to the wall. In early 1769, George Washington observed that "the public papers furnish but too many melancholy proofs" of "Estates daily selling for the discharge of Debts."[10] As noted above, debt drove some gentlemen to early graves, and it also had wider effects. In a world where every person that did not head a household was the dependent of someone that did, heads of households were touchy about anything that threatened to turn them into dependents. Debt posed just such a threat. Since "every debtor does in some measure feel the imperiousness of his creditor," as a newspaper writer said, debt made gentlemen dependent upon British merchants in the same way that their own children, wives, servants, and slaves were dependent upon them. It was mortifying.[11]

During the 1760s, gentlemen also began to fear that their debts would drive them into dependence upon a newly aggressive British government that was fully capable of rewarding its minions. A *Virginia Gazette* essayist warned that "luxury and idleness" lead to "necessity, and this leads us to a servile dependence upon power, and fits us for the chains prepared for us." One of the gentry's ideological mentors, Henry St. John, Viscount Boling-broke, had even accused British government leaders of deliberately encouraging "*luxury* and *extravagance*" because they were "the certain forerunners of *indigence, dependance,* and *servility*." Bolingbroke spoke in abstractions, but Virginia gentlemen like Richard Henry Lee faced the dangers he described every day. As the father of nine children, Lee had to be constantly on

---

ried about "the Temptations to Expence and Dissipation of Money and Time" that young men faced while attending British colleges (William Nelson to John Norton, Feb. 27, 1768, in Mason, ed., *Norton and Sons*, 39). On the argument over what caused the gentlemen's debts, see Price, *Capital and Credit*, 15–19; Breen, *Tobacco Culture*, 129.

10. Washington to Mason, Apr. 5, 1769, in Rutland, ed., *Papers of George Mason*, I, 97; Washington to John Posey, June 24, 1767, in W. W. Abbot et al., eds., *The Papers of George Washington*, Colonial Series (Charlottesville, Va., 1983–), VIII, 3. John Mercer also noticed that "the Gazettes were filled wth. Advertisements of Lands and Negroes to be sold," which he attributed to the pressure that Robinson's debtors felt from his administrators (to George Mercer, Dec. 22, 1767–Jan. 28, 1768, in Mulkearn, ed., *George Mercer Papers*, 189–190).

11. Andrew Burnaby found free Virginians "haughty and jealous of their liberties [and] impatient of restraint." He said they could "scarcely bear the thought of being controuled by any superior power" (*Travels through the Middle Settlements in North-America, in the Years 1759 and 1760 . . .*, 2d ed. [1775; Ithaca, N.Y., 1960], 240). "Maintaining authority . . . required constant vigilance against even small usurpations of power" (Brown, *Good Wives, Nasty Wenches*, 319). For more on the gentlemen's fear of debt, see "C— R—," Rind's *VG*, June 1, 1769; "A Planter," Rind's *VG*, Oct. 31, 1771.

guard for income opportunities. He solicited not only western land grants but a seat on Virginia's Executive Council, "the deputy Secretarys place," a lucrative county clerkship, and even the position of Virginia stamp distributor.[12] A career enforcing the hated Stamp Act would of course have stifled Lee's criticism of parliamentary taxation. He understood as well as any gentleman of his generation that a person in financial distress becomes easy prey for ministers in search of tools.

In addition to their own debts, many gentlemen worried about what they considered the excessive indebtedness of the free classes below them. Farmers were so deep in debt that they were unable to come up with the rental payments they owed gentlemen not only for land but for other property such as carts and even slaves. Although, during the tobacco boom of the late 1760s, the tenants' and smallholders' debts do not seem to have engendered much anxiety among the farmers themselves, "the extravagance and folly of the middle rank" troubled many members of the gentry.[13] Gentlemen were concerned not only about the money that they themselves were owed but about the debts that smallholders owed to British stores, which threatened to make the smallholders dependent upon storekeepers instead of upon gentlemen.

By the mid-1760s, the gentry's search for some means of escaping debt had become desperate. Individual gentlemen always had the option of reducing their debts by avoiding excessive expenditures on luxury items, and some did.[14] But frugality was painful. Landon Carter acknowledged in his diary that living "within bounds" required a constant struggle. "I must return again to a low and less expensive Prudence," he admonished himself in 1774. The reason that gentlemen like Carter kept straying away from "Prudence," the reason that luxuries were so difficult to forego, was that they served vital functions in gentry society. Not in the literal sense. "A Man may be as warm in a Coat that costs but Ten Shillings," George Mason pointed out in an anonymous essay of 1769, "as in one that cost Ten Pounds."[15] Yet

12. "Brutus," Rind's *VG*, June 1, 1769; Bolingbroke, in Bailyn, *Ideological Origins*, 50; Bushman, *Refinement of America*, 203; Pauline Maier, *The Old Revolutionaries: Political Lives in the Age of Samuel Adams* (New York, 1980), 167, 170, 176.

13. "C— R—" [Landon Carter], Purdie and Dixon's *VG*, Mar. 22, 1770.

14. E. G. Evans, "The Rise and Decline of the Virginia Aristocracy in the Eighteenth Century: The Nelsons," in Darrett B. Rutman, ed., *The Old Dominion: Essays for Thomas Perkins Abernethy* (Charlottesville, Va., 1964), 73.

15. May 20, 1774, in Jack P. Greene, ed., *The Diary of Colonel Landon Carter of Sabine Hall, 1752–1778* (Charlottesville, Va., 1965), II, 813. Provincial treasurer Robert Carter Nicholas also recognized that each gentleman's and gentlewoman's attempt to escape debt involved a painful personal struggle. Virginians could eliminate the colony's trade deficit, Nicholas

luxuries served functions that were essential in social terms. Every gentleman, George Washington explained in an April 1769 letter to George Mason, wished to live "genteely and hospitably." To live genteelly was to spend money on oneself. Displays of wealth were assertions of social superiority; they advertised the consumer's rank in society. To act hospitably was to spend money on others. One of the most important uses of luxury items was as presents. Gifts expressed affection—and also a certain dominance. Altogether, to reduce one's consumption of British manufactured goods was to leave unmet some of the social needs that imports normally filled. Most Virginia gentlemen found this impossible. In an observation that seems partly autobiographical, Washington explained why the typical debtor so often deviated from the "Prudence" to which Washington, like Landon Carter, aspired. "Prudence dictated economy to him," he wrote, "but his resolution was too weak to put it in practice." The indebted gentleman believed that, if he were to exchange his lavish style of living for that of the stereotypically frugal New Englander, he would be humiliated. "How can I, *says he*, who have lived in such a manner change my method?" Washington portrayed the debtor saying. "I am ashamed to do it."[16]

Nor was shame the only problem. A smallholder that stopped patronizing the Scottish stores or a gentleman that suddenly stopped placing orders with merchants in England and Scotland was, in effect, telling them that he had become a bad credit risk. Both the Virginians' social status and their credit ratings were fragile. A downward "alteration in the System of my living," Washington's typical debtor said, "will create suspicions of a decay in my fortune, and such a thought the World must not harbour."[17]

wrote in 1773, "could we but prevail with ourselves to lessen our Imports" (Purdie and Dixon's *VG*, Sept. 30, 1773). For Mason's comment, see "Atticus" [George Mason], "Number II," May 11, 1769, in Rutland, ed., *Papers of George Mason*, I, 108.

16. Washington to Mason, Apr. 5, 1769, in Rutland, ed., *Papers of George Mason*, I, 97–98; Ann Fairfax Withington, *Toward a More Perfect Union: Virtue and the Formation of American Republics* (New York, 1991), chap. 5; Morgan, "Puritan Ethic," *WMQ*, 3d Ser., XXIV (1967); Breen, *Tobacco Culture*, 187. As a result of the consumer revolution of the eighteenth century, "individuals learned to take their social identity from goods" (Carson, "Why Demand?" in Carson, Hoffman, and Albert, eds., *Of Consuming Interests*, 486n). At the intersection of gentility and hospitality, of vanity and generosity, was "the vicarious prestige men derived from their wives' and daughters' appearances" (Brown, *Good Wives, Nasty Wenches*, 294).

17. Brown, *Good Wives, Nasty Wenches*, 294; John Brewer, "Commercialization and Politics," in Neil McKendrick, John Brewer, and J. H. Plumb, *The Birth of a Consumer Society: The Commercialization of Eighteenth-Century England* (Bloomington, Ind., 1982), 212–215.

One way Virginians could embrace frugality without endangering their reputations or credit ratings would be for all of the members of a community to agree to reduce expenses at the same time. The problem was that such agreements could easily break down, owing to the social nature of extravagance. Suppose everyone in a neighborhood informally agreed to live more frugally. If even one of the covenanters slipped back into his lavish spending habits, soon someone nearby would feel too embarrassed to live simply while his neighbor spent so much. He too would backslide, and before long everyone would feel compelled to return to the old patterns of conspicuous consumption. A "very few instances of extravagance in a community," Landon Carter pointed out in an anonymous essay of 1770, "are like the *scabs of one sheep*, enough to poison and infect the whole flock." Even if gentlemen could have overcome the psychological and sociological obstacles to reducing their expenditures individually, they would have solved only part of the problem: although they could set an example of frugality, they could not make tenants and yeomen follow it.[18]

In this context, parliamentary tyranny appeared as a political curse but an economic godsend. Among the first to perceive the opportunity was George Washington. In April 1769, he told George Mason that, if Virginia boycotted British merchandise as other colonies had begun to do, the boycott would serve both a patriotic and a financial purpose. It would force Parliament to repeal the Townshend duties, and it would allow colonists to reduce their foreign purchases while avoiding the embarrassment and the threat to their credit ratings that frugality would otherwise entail. For years, numerous gentlemen had tried to make themselves live (as Landon Carter put it) "within bounds." But always in vain. Now, in the spring of 1769, a boycott of British merchandise would give consumers a respectable excuse to abandon their opulence. Washington told Mason, "A Scheme of this Sort will contribute more effectually than any other I can devise to immerge the Country from the distress it at present labours under."[19]

Even before Washington wrote him, Mason had drafted an association that called on Virginians to boycott a long list of items of British manufacture. Mason's plan soon came before the membership of the House of Burgesses. On May 17, the assembly was dissolved by Virginia governor Norborne Berkeley, Lord Botetourt, for its spirited defense of patriots in other colonies. The former burgesses then reconvened in a rump session, and Washington introduced a modified version of Mason's boycott proposal.

18. "An Associating Planter" [Landon Carter], Rind's *VG*, Dec. 13, 1770.
19. May 20, 1774, in Greene, ed., *Landon Carter Diary*, II, 813; Washington to Mason, Apr. 5, 1769, in Rutland, ed., *Papers of George Mason*, I, 97–98.

The burgesses endorsed it the next day, and the 1769 nonimportation association was born.[20]

As George Washington pointed out, gentry debtors had for years endured "the most violent struggles to refrain from" living lavishly. But the association allowed debtors to reduce their consumption without advertising their economic distress to social rivals. Nonimportation gave the "extravagant and expensive man [a] plea"—an excuse—"to retrench his Expences," Washington said. This view was widely shared. When Parliament repealed all of the Townshend duties except the one on tea, some Virginians wanted to end nonimportation. They argued that colonists that wished to continue "feeling the sweets of frugality" could do so on their own, as individuals. But Landon Carter remarked that "vanity carries its something so secretly with it, that few are able to reason on the causes of it, and without being tied down by *solemn engagement*," Virginians would inevitably return to their old "extravagance."[21]

Nonimportation did more than give gentlemen and gentlewomen an excuse for not meeting the needs they had once met with luxuries. It was an alternative method of meeting those same needs. Where once gentlemen and gentlewomen had demonstrated affection by showering each other with gifts and hospitality, the new language of community was shared sacrifice.[22] Nonimportation provided its own replacement for the thrill that normally greeted members of the gentry when they broke open packages containing the latest London fashions. New china and clothes were exciting, but so was the sense of patriotism that the boycott awakened.

Debtors that joined the association could also maintain their favorable credit ratings in the coffeehouses where British tobacco merchants gathered. Virginians that participated in nonimportation might give their British correspondents cause to question their political judgment and even their loyalty to the crown—but not their creditworthiness. The indebted boycotter,

20. It is not certainly known who drafted Virginia's 1769 nonimportation association. Robert Rutland, the editor of George Mason's papers, says Mason was not the author, but I agree with Bruce Ragsdale that he was. The rough draft that circulated in April 1769 contains two of Mason's pet ideas—a threat of nonexportation (which was omitted in the version of the association later adopted by the rump session of the House of Burgesses) and an open-ended promise to boycott any items that might be taxed in the future. Cf. editor's note and Mason to Washington, Apr. 5, 1769, in Rutland, ed., *Papers of George Mason*, I, 95n–96n, 99–100; Ragsdale, *Planters' Republic*, 73–78.

21. Washington to Mason, Apr. 5, 1769, in Rutland, ed., *Papers of George Mason*, I, 98; "An Associating Planter" [Landon Carter], Rind's *VG*, Dec. 13, 1770; Breen, *Tobacco Culture*, 191.

22. Zuckerman, "A Different Thermidor," in Henretta, Kammen, and Katz, eds., *Transformation of Early American History*, 180.

George Washington wrote, "saves his money, and he saves his credit." None of these personal benefits of nonimportation clashed with the gentlemen's sincere desire to pressure Parliament to repeal the Townshend duties and other obnoxious parliamentary legislation. John Page told John Norton, his creditor for a large sum, that he had "resolved not to send to England for any thing this Year, and have entered into the Association." "I like the Association because I think it will repeal the disagreeable Acts of Parliament, open the Eyes of the People with you, and must certainly clear us of our Debts."[23]

Still another reason that gentlemen preferred patriotic nonimportation to individual frugality is that it gave them an opening to less wealthy debtors. Although some of the merchandise that associators had to forgo were high-priced items, such as coaches and jewelry, that small farmers never imported anyway, the association also targeted several products that many small-holders *did* import. These were "the little Luxuries and Conveniencies of Life" that were just as welcome in the homes of humble freemen as costlier items were on gentry estates. During the half-century or so before the American Revolution, many common people throughout the British Empire had, for the first time, achieved the ability to purchase items that were not essential to their survival.[24] Virginia gentlemen blamed those minor luxuries for driving tenants and smallholders into debt. If small farmers boycotted some of them, they would reduce their debts in the same way that gentlemen hoped to.

The 1769 association's potential for reducing smallholders' and tenants' debts gave it appeal not only to Virginia debtors but to many creditors as well. Landon Carter informed *Virginia Gazette* readers that, among creditors, there was "a design in associating, to employ the imagined time of its continuance in getting in the debts of the colonies, said to be largely in arrears."[25] The creditors that expected to profit from the boycott included many gentlemen. They hoped that, as small farmers reduced their purchases at the English and Scottish stores, they would be left with enough money to pay their domestic debts. Carter envisioned "tenants, not (as usual) craving the compassion of their landlords, that they might, in some sort, accommo-

23. Washington to Mason, Apr. 5, 1769, in Rutland, ed., *Papers of George Mason*, I, 98; May 27, 1769, in Mason, ed., *Norton and Sons*, 94; "C— R—," Rind's *VG*, June 1, 1769.

24. "Atticus" [George Mason], "Number II," May 11, 1769, in Rutland, ed., *Papers of George Mason*, I, 108; Bushman, *Refinement of America*, 184.

25. Evidently considering himself a realist, Carter did not complain about the fact that some people had embraced nonimportation for economic as well as political purposes. But he feared that some associators, having achieved their economic ends, wanted to dissolve the agreement before the battle against parliamentary tyranny had been won (anonymous letter [Landon Carter], Rind's *VG*, Dec. 13, 1770).

date the hasty demands of the stores they were indebted to for the supply of their families, but with joyous countenances rewarding every such compassionate indulgence by a full discharge of rents and arrearages."[26]

Some of the gentry advocates of the 1769 boycott apparently hoped not only to reduce the small farmer's debt load but to cut the farmer himself down to size. The nonimportation idea appeared just when, in the social steeplechase that was conspicuous consumption, the poorest gentlemen were in danger of being overtaken by the fleetest of their social inferiors. The gentlemen were slowing down (having to cut back on the purchase of luxury items) even as many smallholders were speeding up (purchasing more consumer goods). Many gentlemen shared the concerns of Samuel Adams of Massachusetts, who worried that the increasing availability of consumer goods would erase "every Distinction between the Poor and the Rich." One way to prevent upstarts from overtaking struggling gentry consumers—temporarily, at least—would be to halt the importation of luxury items and thus freeze everyone at the current level of gentility.[27]

Nonimportation appealed not only to patriots, debtors, creditors, and gentlemen worried about yeoman parvenus but also to Virginians that wanted fundamentally to transform the provincial economy. Because the association allowed the continued importation of coarse cloth, free Virginians could adhere to it without reducing the quantity of clothing they imported, only the quality. But many Virginians reasoned that, if they were going to wear coarse woolens, they might as well be locally made. In thus trying to reform production as well as consumption, they revived a movement, as old as Virginia itself, to promote domestic manufacturing in the colony. The association adopted by the rump session of the House of Burgesses on May 18, 1769, entreated Virginians not to kill lambs born before May 1. The goal was to increase Virginia's output of woolen cloth, its number-one import.

26. "C—— R——" [Landon Carter], Purdie and Dixon's *VG*, Mar. 22, 1770. In 1787, some members of the House of Delegates advocated a "total prohibition of foreign Luxuries." They mentioned no political rationale for the boycott. Its sole purpose was to put Virginians in a position where, "having no temptation to spend their money," they would "devote it to Justice"—to paying their debts (James McClurg to James Madison, Aug. 5, 1787, in William T. Hutchinson et al., eds., *The Papers of James Madison* [Chicago and Charlottesville, Va., 1962–], X, 135).

27. The "escalation in living standards" in eighteenth-century Virginia is charted in Carr and Walsh, "Changing Lifestyles and Consumer Behavior," Sweeney, "High-Style Vernacular," Carson, "Why Demand?" all in Carson, Hoffman, and Albert, eds., *Of Consuming Interests*, 25, 59–166, 487. On Samuel Adams's comment, see Carson, "Why Demand?" 520–521. Kevin Sweeney suggests that a desire to rebuff a challenge from below may have been behind elite denunciations of competitive consumption (Sweeney, "High-Style Vernacular," 31).

Two months later, in July, a *Virginia Gazette* writer urged free Virginians to come to "a determination to import no goods we can make ourselves."[28]

The conversion to domestic textile production would require a massive application of the labor of both enslaved and free women. Soon there were encouraging signs. In March 1770, Landon Carter was able to report that "the polite and more considerate" Virginia families had begun wearing clothes made by the women they owned. Carter's own son, Robert Wormeley, a member of the Virginia House of Burgesses, wrote him three months later with a message for Winey, a Carter family slave. Burgess Carter wanted Winey to know that he had been wearing the suit of clothing she had recently made for him. Wherever he went, the suit received rave reviews. One of Carter's acquaintances was so eager to possess the suit that he had offered some imported silk garments in exchange. What made Carter's suit so desirable was that Winey, the person that made it, was a Virginian.[29]

Carter celebrated the power of the example that gentlemen like his son had set. No sooner did gentlemen "make their appearances, apparelled in Virginia growth, but, like an extinguisher to the extravagance and folly of the middle rank, the example convinced them of the possibility of providing an agreeable dress, by the labour of their own families." Carter, a Richmond County justice, cherished the memory of a court day during the previous winter. "With what pleasure must the patriotick eye have sparkled lately to have seen nearly a whole court yard warmly clad in the produce of their wives and daughters," he wrote.[30]

Promoters of the association publicly emphasized the motive that they and their audiences considered most respectable: the attempt to exert economic pressure on Parliament. In his private letter to George Mason of April 5, 1769, George Washington stated that nonimportation would reward the Virginia debtor with "private, as well as public advantages," since it would give him a plausible justification for reducing his spending. But in

28. "A Private Man," Rind's *VG*, July 6, 1769; "The Association," May 18, 1769, in *Revolutionary Virginia*, I, 76; Purdie and Dixon's *VG*, Dec. 14, 1769; Richard Lee to William Lee, Dec. 20, 1769, Lee Family Papers (1638–1867), section 123, VHS. The movement for home manufactures, like the effort to reduce debt generally, was in part an effort to reduce dependence upon the increasingly untrustworthy British government. Arthur Lee explained that, if colonists made more of their own clothes, tools, and other manufactures, then, if Britain "should refuse us redress, we might not be absolutely dependent upon her for the necessaries of life" ("The Monitor" [Arthur Lee], no. 6, in *The Farmer's and Monitor's Letters, to the Inhabitants of the British Colonies* [Williamsburg, Va., 1769], 83).

29. "C— R—" [Landon Carter], Purdie and Dixon's *VG*, Mar. 22, 1770; Ragsdale, *Planters' Republic*, 84.

30. "C— R—" [Landon Carter], Purdie and Dixon's *VG*, Mar. 22, 1770.

letters to British merchants Washington did not mention the economic purpose of nonimportation. Landon Carter wrote an article for the *Virignia Gazette* that endorsed nonimportation as an excellent strategy for "restoring to us that weighty situation of being *once more* clear of debt." But he went on to propose a preamble for the association that denounced "unconstitutional" parliamentary taxation and said nothing about debt.[31] There was nothing unusual or sinister in the associators' decision to emphasize their political motives and downplay economics, but it has unfortunately led historians that rely upon their public writings to do the same thing.

The commodities that associators agreed not to import included not only British manufactured goods and East Indian tea but human beings from Africa and the West Indies. Although the boycott of the slave trade was part of the effort to pressure British merchants to secure repeal of anti-American legislation, it was also a response to the recently announced royal repeal of the 1767 Virginia law doubling the duty on slaves imported into Virginia. The slave boycott would have affected smallholders far more heavily than the gentlemen that wrote it, since by 1769 it was piedmont smallholders that bought the majority of the slaves that arrived on Virginia's shores. As it turned out, however, smallholders chose to ignore the ban on slave imports. Between January 1769 and December 1770, white Virginians imported nearly fourteen hundred Africans.[32] Farmers violated the slave importation ban because, right up until the middle of 1772, tobacco fetched a high price, offering them the prospect of paying for newly acquired slaves in just a few years.

Of course, gentlemen in the tidewater also received good prices for their tobacco during these years, but they had reasons to oppose the international slave trade that smallholders in the piedmont did not share.[33] Fear of slaves was greater in the tidewater, where many counties had black majorities. Also, a wealthy gentleman in the tidewater that became involved in the slave trade in the 1760s was most likely to do so as a seller. For him, in sharp contrast to

31. Washington to Mason, Apr. 5, 1769, in Rutland, ed., *Papers of George Mason*, I, 97, 98; Washington to Robert Cary and Company, July 25, 1769, in Abbot et al., eds., *Papers of Washington*, Colonial Series, VIII, 229; "C— R—" [Landon Carter], Rind's *VG*, June 1, 1769; Ragsdale, *Planters' Republic*, 82.

32. Walter Minchinton, Celia King, and Peter Waite, eds., *Virginia Slave-Trade Statistics, 1698–1775* (Richmond, Va., 1984), xv.

33. To be sure, smallholders did share some of the gentry's motives for ending the trade, such as shoring up the price of tobacco, cutting the provincial trade deficit, expanding the money supply, and modernizing the economy. But those were outweighed by their desire for more slaves.

the smallholder, raising the price of domestic slaves was one more reason to ban the Atlantic trade.

Although the failure of the slave import ban was total, the results of the boycott of British merchandise were mixed—in both economic and political terms. Parliament, partly in response to the boycotts in Virginia and other provinces, repealed all of the Townshend duties except the one on tea. On the economic front, imports of such prohibited articles as carriages, mirrors, clocks, and jewelry diminished in 1769. By April 1770, a *Virginia Gazette* essayist was encouraged enough to observe that many Virginians were already "in a way of removing those incumbrances"—debts—"which their former luxury and extravagance had brought upon them." But this optimism was not borne out by the trade statistics. The association failed to reduce the importation of British goods into Virginia. In fact, the inhabitants of the Chesapeake (which included Maryland as well as Virginia) imported 60 percent more in 1770 and 1771 than they had in 1768 and 1769. They even increased their consumption of white glass, painters' colors, and other items that carried the hated Townshend duties.[34]

The boycott failed for several reasons. First, it allowed Virginians to continue purchasing most British merchandise, including cheap clothing, their biggest import. Thus the volume of their foreign purchases would not have plummeted even if every one of them had joined the association. Thousands of Virginians did not even do that. Smallholders and tenants saw no reason to stop importing those "little Luxuries and Conveniencies of Life" that had so recently appeared in their homes. With tobacco markets booming, Scottish storekeepers were more than willing to offer Virginians the treasures of India, the British Isles, Europe, and the Caribbean. "Let them have their goods reasonable at first for an encouragement," William Cuninghame and Company's chief factor advised a subordinate in October 1767. London consignment merchant John Norton stated in April 1770 that he had "shiped considerably more goods this year than I have ever done since my return to England" a decade earlier.[35]

The effort to encourage domestic manufacturing likewise produced little more than anecdotes. Large-scale conversion to Virginia-made cloth would

34. "Brutus," Rind's *VG*, Apr. 26, 1770; Ernst, "Political Economy of the Chesapeake," in Hoffman et al., eds., *Economy of Early America*, 231; Price, *Capital and Credit*, 162; Ragsdale, *Planters' Republic*, 87.

35. "Atticus" [George Mason], "Number II," May 11, 1769, in Rutland, ed., *Papers of George Mason*, I, 108; James Robison to Bennet Price, Oct. 7, 1767, in T. M. Devine, ed., *A Scottish Firm in Virginia, 1767–1777: W. Cuninghame and Co.* (Edinburgh, 1984), 2; John Norton to Robert Carter Nicholas, Apr. 21, 1770, Wilson Cary Nicholas Papers (#5533), UVA.

have required massively increasing the work loads of Virginia women. Since slaveholders were not willing to excuse the women they owned from their normal duties, and male farmers were not willing to take over any of their wives' and daughters' tasks so that they could devote more time to textile production, the time needed for domestic manufacturing could have come only from the women's leisure hours. But apparently both enslaved and free women successfully resisted the demand that they sacrifice some of their few hours of rest in order to spin more thread and weave more cloth. In fact, one married gentlewoman seems to have supported some of the slave women she brought to her marriage when they resisted her husband's effort to force them to spin large quantities of yarn. James Hill, George Washington's steward, complained to him about "a wench that is Kept for Spin[nin]g and has been all this year aspin[nin]g [only] 47 [lb.] wool and Says that Mrs Washgton orderd that she should Spin no more then 3 [lb.] a week." Hill claimed that another enslaved woman, "old Nanney," "wont Spin a thread and Says her Mistress left her only to Sew." Hill wanted Martha Washington to stop interfering in his management of the slaves. There is no record of how the conflict was resolved, but George Washington continued to import British clothing.[36]

II

At the same time that some Virginians struggled to reduce their consumption of British merchandise, others looked at the opposite side of their ledgers and proposed to halt their exports. "Nonexportation" would harm British merchants and tobacco manufacturers and persuade them to lobby against the parliamentary legislation that so alarmed free colonists. Cutting off tobacco shipments would also injure the imperial treasury, which derived substantial revenue from the tobacco sold in Britain. In addition, growers knew that, if they reduced the volume of tobacco they exported, they could drive up its price.

By the late 1760s, Virginians had been proposing export reduction schemes for more than a century. Between 1666 and 1682, Maryland and Virginia had made several efforts to reduce the tobacco crop, only to be thwarted by their inability to cooperate and by the obstruction of an imperial authority that collected £100,000 per year in tobacco duties. In the spring of 1682, when yet another such effort failed, a Virginia "Rabble made a May sport to dance from

36. Lest the impression be given that Martha Washington and the slave woman had reached complete agreement on her workload, it should be noted that the amount of wool she had spun in 1772 was less than half the quota she claimed Martha Washington had set (James Hill to George Washington, Aug. 30, 1772, in Abbot et al., eds., *Papers of Washington*, Colonial Series, IX, 85–86).

plantation to plantation to cut up Tobacco Plants," as provincial secretary of state Nicholas Spencer reported. The government suppressed the rioters, and their leader was hanged. "Rather than that plant cutting should cease," Spencer then reported, "the women have so cast off their modesty as to take up the hoes that the rabble were forced to lay down."[37] By one estimate, the 1682 tobacco-cutting riots destroyed ten thousand hogsheads' worth of tobacco on two hundred plantations and briefly shored up the price of the weed. Prices got another temporary boost from the Inspection Acts passed in Virginia in 1730 and in Maryland in 1747, which reduced export volume and improved quality. But as the population of the Chesapeake continued to grow—by 1775, more than 700,000 people lived in the two provinces—output grew, too, and the price of tobacco again stagnated. One possible remedy remained popular from the mid-seventeenth century right up until the Revolution. "If it was but possible to sink a whole Crop in Virginia, and Maryland," London merchant Lyonel Lyde told a Virginia associate in 1753, "I am perswaded the two Succeeding would amply repay the Loss, and render the Trade to flourishing for Twenty years to come."[38]

37. Edmund S. Morgan, *American Slavery, American Freedom: The Ordeal of Colonial Virginia* (New York, 1975), 192–194, 286; John C. Rainbolt, *From Prescription to Persuasion: Manipulation of [Seventeenth] Century Virginia Economy* (Port Washington, N.Y., 1974), chap. 3, 64–67, 113–119; George Louis Beer, *The Old Colonial System, 1660–1754* (1913; reprint, Gloucester, Mass., 1958), II, 116–124; Stephen Saunders Webb, *1676: The End of American Independence* (New York, 1984), 189; Spencer to Lyonel Jenkins, Aug. 12, 1682, in John Davenport Neville, comp., *Bacon's Rebellion: Abstracts of Materials in the Colonial Records Project* (n.p., n.d.), 100; Spencer to Leoline Jenkins, May 28, 1682, in J. W. Fortescue, ed., *Calendar of State Papers*, Colonial Series, XI, *America and West Indies* (London, 1898), 238, in Terri L. Snyder, "'Rich Widows are the Best Commodity This Country Affords': Gender Relations and the Rehabilitation of Patriarchy in Virginia, 1660–1700" (Ph.D. diss., University of Iowa, 1992), 292; Snyder, "Gender and the Margins of Anglo-American Radicalism in Seventeenth-Century Virginia" (paper presented at the Institute of Early American History and Culture Conference, Ann Arbor, Mich., June 3, 1995); Rainbolt, *From Prescription to Persuasion*, 119–121.

38. L. C. Gray, "The Market Surplus Problems of Colonial Tobacco," *Agricultural History*, II (1928), 1–34; Mays, *Edmund Pendleton*, I, 113; Robert Johnson, "Government Regulation of Business Enterprise in Virginia, 1750–1820" (Ph.D. diss., University of Minnesota, 1958), 27–28. The Philadelphia wholesale price index increased about 50 percent between 1733 and 1773, from 59.7 percent to 90 percent. Tobacco did not keep pace (Peter V. Bergstrom, *Markets and Merchants: Economic Diversification in Colonial Virginia, 1700–1775* [New York, 1985], 134, 149). Nor did tobacco prices keep pace with the rising cost of land and slaves (Roger Atkinson to Lyonel and Samuel Lyde, Aug. 25, 1772, Atkinson Letterbook, UVA).

For population estimates, see Peter H. Wood, "The Changing Population of the Colonial South: An Overview by Race and Region, 1685–1790," in Peter H. Wood, Gregory A. Wasel-

In 1769, some tobacco farmers proposed, for the first time, to use tobacco withholding for a political purpose. In April, George Mason, observing that the British government derived substantial revenue from Chesapeake tobacco, urged growers to halt their exports and thereby pressure Parliament to repeal the Townshend duties and other anti-American laws. Nonexportation would yield another benefit as well. If farmers and gentlemen went so far as to "desist . . . making Tobacco," Mason commented in an anonymous newspaper essay that appeared in May, "we shou'd have a Number of Spare Hands to employ in Manufactures."[39] Thus nonexportation, like nonimportation, would foster domestic manufacturing in Virginia.

Mason's nonexportation proposal won little support, but, during the next few years, some colonists in both Virginia and Maryland proposed to withhold their tobacco for the more practical and traditional purpose of driving up its price. The farmers in several Chesapeake neighborhoods formed associations aimed at creating local shortages of the weed. In the summer of 1770, after Maryland tobacco purchasers formed a buyers' cartel to drive down the price, farmers retaliated. They "appointed a meeting at Bladensburgh and signed an Association not to sell" below a certain price, Charles Carroll of Annapolis reported. "Upwards of 200 Planters signed the Association." That fall, the association movement spread into Virginia. "Numbers of the Planters on Potowmack," trader William Allason reported in October 1770, "have associated not to dispose of their Tobacco without the consent and approbation of a certain Committee of themselves who are to fix the price at which they shall have liberty to sell." A year later, in 1771, "A Planter" urged readers of the *Virginia Gazette* to organize meetings at their courthouses to set prices below which they would refuse to sell their tobacco.[40]

---

kov, and M. Thomas Hatley, eds., *Powhatan's Mantle: Indians in the Colonial Southeast* (Lincoln, Nebr., 1989), 38; J. Potter, "The Growth of Population in America, 1700–1860," in D. V. Glass and D. E. C. Eversley, eds., *Population in History: Essays in Historical Demography* (London, 1965), 638. On Lyonel Lyde's suggestion, see Lyde to Andrew Monroe, Sept. 24, 1753, *Lyonel Lyde v. Monroe's Administrator et al.* (1797), U.S. Circuit Court, Virginia District, Ended Cases (restored), LVA (hereafter cited as Ended Cases); Bogle and Scott to William Allason and Company, Jan. 31, 1765, Allason Papers, LVA.

39. "Atticus" [George Mason], "Number II," May 11, 1769, Mason to Washington, Apr. 5, 1769, in Rutland, ed., *Papers of George Mason*, I, 100, 108.

40. Charles Carroll of Annapolis to Charles Carroll of Carrollton, Aug. 12, 1770, Charles Carroll of Annapolis Papers, Maryland Historical Society, Baltimore (microfilm at Maryland Hall of Records, Annapolis); William Allason to John Gray, Oct. 23, 1770, Allason Letterbook, LVA; "A Planter," Rind's *VG*, Oct. 31, 1771; Ronald Hoffman, *A Spirit of Dissension: Economics, Politics, and the Revolution in Maryland* (Baltimore, 1973), 81. For additional evidence of farmers' attempts to "collude to keep up their tobacco," see James Robi-

Like nonimportation, tobacco withholding gained few supporters during the tobacco boom of 1766–1772. Just as free Virginians could not resist the temptation to purchase British manufactured goods at a time when store-keepers were free with their credit, those same tobacco farmers could not resist selling their tobacco at the high prices that the stores offered them during those years.

Then the bubble burst. In the fall of 1772, the Chesapeake economy fell into a deep recession. Between 1772 and 1773, tobacco lost nearly half of its value. The deterioration was greatest in the Northern Neck, where the price fell from 2.4 pence per pound (Virginia currency) as late as October 1772 to 1.5 pence per pound (Virginia currency) in June 1773—a decline of 37.5 percent.[41] By the latter date, the price of tobacco was considered "really too low for the Makers to live by it." One reason prices collapsed was that, starting in 1770, four successive bumper crops clogged European tobacco markets. Then, in June 1772, a financial panic struck Britain. Many people considered it the worst recession since the South Sea Bubble of 1720.[42] Because the

---

son to John Turner, Oct. 25, 1768, to William Henderson, Feb. 12, 1770, in Devine, ed., *Scottish Firm*, 10, 20.

41. My 1772 price was taken from Harry Piper to Dixon and Littledale, July 20, 1772, Piper Letterbook, UVA; James Robison to Francis Hay, Oct. 13, 1772, to William Cuninghame and Company, July 1, 1772, in Devine, ed., *Scottish Firm*, 62, 82. My 1773 price was taken from James Robison to William Cuninghame, June 23, 1773, to William Cuninghame and Company, June 17, 1773, in Devine, ed., *Scottish Firm*, 74, 114. On the Upper James River, the decline was less dramatic—from 2.7 to 2.16 pence per pound (Virginia currency) or 20 percent (James Robison to William Cuninghame and Company, July 1, 1772, May 15, 1773, in Devine, ed., *Scottish Firm*, 82, 110).

A price series compiled by Carville V. Earle showed an insignificant decline of only 4 percent in the mean price of a pound of tobacco from a 1772 high of 2.4 pence (Maryland currency) to a 1773 low of 2.19 pence (Maryland currency) (*The Evolution of a Tidewater Settlement System: All Hallow's Parish, Maryland, 1650–1783* [Chicago, 1975], 229). I believe the actual decline was more dramatic. It appears that Earle averaged the *high* price of *early* 1772 in with the *low* price of *late* 1772, and then compared this figure to a similarly averaged figure for 1773. Such a comparison would mask the sizable difference between the (very high) price of early 1772 and the (very low) price of late 1773. Letterbooks in both Maryland and Virginia document a significant decline in the price of tobacco during this period.

42. Charles Yates to Dixon and Littledale, Apr. 2, 1774, Yates Letterbook, UVA. On the York and Upper James Rivers the price to which tobacco fell during the recession was also considered "lower than the planter can afford to make it" (Trents, Crump, and Bates to Dobson, Daltera, and Walker, June 8, 1774, *Dobson and Daltera v. Trent, Crump, and Bates* [1798], Ended Cases). On the 1770 tobacco increase, see Jacob M. Price, "One Family's Empire: The Russell-Lee-Clerk Connection in Maryland, Britain, and India, 1707–1857,"

tobacco trade depended so heavily on credit, the credit contraction sapped demand for the weed.

At the same time that the recession dragged down the price of the Chesapeake farmers' tobacco, it also injured them in another way. The majority of tobacco farmers were debtors. Between 1766 and 1772, when tobacco demand was booming, many farmers had expanded their operations by buying land, slaves, and equipment. As Scottish factor James Robison put it, farmers had "made large purchases, expecting the good time which was then to continue." Many of those purchases were made on credit. When the financial panic struck in 1772, British merchants were dunned by their creditors, and they in turn leaned on their debtors in the Chesapeake. But few Chesapeake farmers could come up with the money to pay their debts. Tobacco was "of so little value that it [went] but a very inconsiderable way in discharging Acc[oun]ts," trader William Allason reported in January 1774.[43]

When tobacco farmers proved unable to pay their debts, they frequently were sued. By the spring of 1774, one-third of the free families in Pittsylvania County, Virginia, had lost debt suits. Between 1771 and 1774, the number of debt suits filed in Prince George's County, Maryland, doubled.[44] The debtors' tobacco crops were rarely valuable enough to satisfy the court judg-

---

MHM, LXXII (1977), 186. Michael L. Nicholls has shown that Virginia storekeepers had begun to contract their credit even before the famous recession struck in 1772 ("Competition, Credit, and Crisis: Merchant-Planter Relations in Southside Virginia," in Rosemary E. Ommer, ed., *Merchant Credit and Labour Strategies in Historical Perspective* [Fredericton, New Brunswick, 1990], 285–286). On the 1772 recession, see William Scott to George Bogle, Nov. 20, 1772, Bogle Papers, bundle 19, Mitchell Library, Glasgow, Scotland (microfilm at VHS); Leslie V. Brock, "The Colonial Currency, Prices, and Exchange Rates," in Frank Edgar Grizzard, ed., *Essays in History*, XXXIV (1992), 100; Warren M. Billings, John E. Selby, and Thad W. Tate, *Colonial Virginia: A History* (White Plains, N.Y., 1986), 321–322; Ragsdale, *Planters' Republic*, 29.

43. Robison to Cuninghame and Company, June 17, 1773, in Devine, ed., *Scottish Firm*, 115; Ragsdale, *Planters' Republic*, 168–172; Richard B. Sheridan, "The British Credit Crisis of 1772 and the American Colonies," *Journal of Economic History*, XX (1960), 176–177; Price, *Capital and Credit*, 124–139; Allason to John Elam and Son, Jan. 15, 1774, Allason Letterbook; John Backhouse to William Allason, Apr. 10, 1774, Allason Papers.

44. Nicholls, "Competition, Credit, and Crisis," in Ommer, ed., *Merchant Credit*, 288. That same spring, the Virginia General Court faced the largest docket of debt cases in its history (A. G. Roeber, *Faithful Magistrates and Republican Lawyers: Creators of Virginia Legal Culture, 1680–1810* [Chapel Hill, N.C., 1981], 155). On the increase in the number of debt suits in Virginia, see Allan Kulikoff, *Tobacco and Slaves: The Development of Southern Cultures in the Chesapeake, 1680–1800* (Chapel Hill, N.C., 1986), 130. Debt suits increased in other Maryland counties as well. Tommy R. Thompson, "Personal Indebtedness and the American Revolution in Maryland," *MHM*, LXXIII (1978), 20; Jean B. Lee, *The Price of Nationhood: The American Revolution in Charles County* (New York, 1994), 106.

ments, so instead families had to give up "Land, Negroes, Horses, Cows, Hoggs and Feather Beds or old Potts or Panns"—in short, their means of survival. In April 1774 Fredericksburg trader Charles Yates described Virginia farmers, using an expression that had originally referred to a woodcutter that was too despondent to position his wood properly. "Our folks are so much indebted to the Merchants," Yates wrote, "that they hardly care which end goes foremost."[45]

As economic prospects darkened, gentlemen not only shared the financial anxiety of the yeomanry but also worried about their ability to maintain solidarity among white Virginians. They remembered that, during the recession of the early 1760s, when courts had ordered gentry sheriffs to seize debtors' property or to imprison them, the debtors had sometimes fought back. Even during the prosperous period between 1766 and 1772, foreclosures and imprisonment for debt had continued—and so had debtor resistance. Creditors were aware that the debt collecting the deputy sheriffs did for them could be dangerous, and at least one of them agreed to a sort of combat pay. "I . . . wou'd by no means begrudge a gratuity to a Sherif, who may run a Risk by doing his Duty in securing a debt," John Gray told William Allason in 1769. The following year, an anonymous newspaper writer observed that many a jailed debtor had tried to escape by taking a brand from the prison fireplace and reducing his prison "to ashes, at the imminent risque, and sometimes the real loss of the prisoner's life." He warned of the imprisoned debtors' "desperation, which seems likely to be productive of the greatest disorders in society." He admonished members of the House of Burgesses that, if they hoped to preserve social peace in Virginia, they had better provide relief to jailed debtors. "Oppression will forever lessen the effect of authority in the hearts and minds of a free people," he wrote.[46]

In 1772, when the recession hit, social conflict—and the gentry's anxiety—intensified. In an echo of trader William Allason's letter of 1764 requesting a pair of pistols to protect him from his debtors, Bedford trader John Hook told his partner David Ross in June 1773 that he found it "very necessary to travell with Pistols." "Unless you can send me a good neat P[ai]r," Hook asked Ross, "please order them from hom[e]." Hook thought another of Ross's debt collectors also needed protection, so he suggested that Ross

<hr>

45. Charles Yates to Samuel Martin, Apr. 2, 1774, Yates Letterbook. The low price of tobacco during the recession, William Reynolds wrote, "drove the planters in a state of destraction" (to John Norton, June 7, 1773, William Reynolds Letterbook, p. 36, LC).

46. [John] Gray to [William Allason?], Sept. 6, 1769, in Allason to Robert Allason, Oct. 14, 1770, Allason Letterbook; anonymous letter, Rind's *VG*, June 7, 1770.

"accomodate Mr George wi[th] a P[ai]r" of pistols as well. Even when the creditor was an independent trader, like Hook, or a British storekeeper, gentlemen could be drawn into the debtor-creditor conflict. In November 1773, an anonymous newspaper item protested the sheriffs' lack of "humanity." The writer noted that, when a creditor won a lawsuit, the local sheriff was only too happy to seize the debtor's belongings and then sell them for a percentage of the proceeds. Sometimes, when sheriffs took debtors' property, the debtors took it back. In the spring of 1774, about the time that Jacob Hite was recapturing the slaves that Berkeley County sheriff Adam Stephen had impounded, Thomas Moody similarly "rescued" a slave that the sheriff had seized in discharge of his debt. Jailbreaks by imprisoned debtors also appear to have increased as the recession deepened. James Trabue, who owed money to Speirs and Bowman, a Scottish firm, "frequently broke prison." As noted earlier, the same gang of men that recaptured Jacob Hite's slaves and horses from the Berkeley County jail also freed Murty Handley, an imprisoned debtor. And it was probably debtors that set fire to the Dinwiddie County courthouse in July 1773.[47]

The recession encouraged several yeomen Virginians to voice criticism of the financial burdens that gentlemen imposed upon them. Landon Carter sensed the farmers' growing anger. In the fall of 1773, Carter wrote an essay denouncing government tobacco inspectors for demanding that growers pay their inspection fees in specie (hard money). Carter felt personally harmed by the gentry inspectors' demand, but he also predicted that this disease within the body politic would soon "gangrene into a civil distraction, similar to what was felt"—riots—"when the unhappy inspecting law first took place." He warned his fellow gentlemen of the "storm that we shall unhappily raise in our community by our own public indiscretion." An anonymous newspaper writer calling himself "Tillias" pointed out that government contracts for maintaining the county workhouse and prison were often quite profitable, since the contractors sold the goods produced by inmates in the workhouse and collected fees from white prisoners and from the owners of slaves. Tillias believed that, if the prison and workhouse were run by the county government itself, the resulting revenue would enable it to cut taxes. Tillias also denounced the county justices' practice of granting

47. Hook to Ross, June 10, 1773, John Hook Letterbook, LVA; "Experience," Rind's *VG*, Nov. 25, 1773; credit report on Thomas Moody, "British Mercantile Claims, 1775–1803," *Virginia Genealogist*, XXIII (1979), 63; debts owed to Charlotte County store, claim of Speirs and Bowman, T. 79/45, P.R.O.; William W. Hening, credit report on James Reid, "British Mercantile Claims, 1775–1803," *Virginia Genealogist*, XXVII (1983), 53; John Dixon, advertisement, Rind's *VG*, Oct. 28, 1773; Purdie and Dixon's *VG*, July 29, 1773.

lucrative licenses to a favored few tavernkeepers. The magistrates should set up a government-run tavern, the proceeds of which would, like the profits from the prison and workhouse, permit them to "ease the Levies." "Since we are for Amendments," Tillias wrote, "let us do it thoroughly, and leave no Stone unturned to destroy all Extortion."[48]

From the perspective of more than two centuries it is clear that these attacks and criticisms posed no real threat to the gentry's social position. But gentlemen believed that, in a colony where 40 percent of the population was enslaved, there must be no cracks in the foundation of white solidarity.[49] The gentry's anxiety about strain on the social fabric added urgency to its search for a way out of the recession.

One way to alleviate the effects of the recession was to reduce the importation of British merchandise, as many Virginians had attempted to do in 1769. By 1773, frugality was once again in vogue. According to Philip Fithian, a tutor in the Northern Neck, gentlemen had found "that their estates by even small extravagance, decline, and grow involved with debt," and they had therefore decided "to be frugal, and moderate." The largest impetus for reviving nonimportation came not from gentlemen but from provincial traders and British merchants. Traders, under tremendous pressure from their creditors and unable to collect money from their own debtors, believed that they would not be able to survive unless they reduced their foreign purchases. Early in 1774, when Virginia trader Charles Yates learned that Whitehaven merchant Samuel Martin had shipped him a large cargo of merchandise, Yates said the thought of receiving so much inventory in the midst of the economic slump "throws me into a Sweat." Yates, who lived in Fredericksburg on the Rappahannock River, knew that he would be able to sell the goods only on credit, with little prospect of early payment. So he diverted the shipment to the James River, hoping that "Money or Tobacco unmortgaged for years to come may be in greater plenty" there. Meanwhile, in Alexandria, William Allason surveyed the impact of the recession on his fellow traders and reported that it had "oblige[d] many to abridge their orders for Goods." At the same time, British merchants shipped fewer of the items that their Virginia agents and trading partners did order. During prosperous times, Scottish storekeepers in the Chesapeake could expect their Glasgow principals to ship them every item they listed in their "schemes," or

48. Landon Carter, Rind's *VG*, Nov. 11, 1773; "Tillias," Purdie and Dixon's *VG*, Nov. 25, 1773.

49. Kathleen Brown argues that there were also psychological reasons for gentlemen to fear even the tiniest resistance to their authority (*Good Wives, Nasty Wenches*, 319).

importation orders. But William Cuninghame and Company's chief factor James Robison noted in June 1773 that "the schemes for the fall have undergone very considerable amputation." The combination of the Virginia traders' frugality and the British merchants' newfound caution dramatically reduced the volume of tools, clothing, and other merchandise that was shipped from British ports to the Chesapeake. The trade was worth an average of £1,120,000 in 1771 and 1772. In 1773 its value fell to £589,000—a decline of 47 percent.[50]

The reduction in Virginia's imports began during a lull in imperial tensions. Then, on the night of December 16, 1773, Bostonians dumped East India Company tea into their harbor, and Parliament retaliated with the Coercive Acts of 1774. Throughout the thirteen colonies, the year 1774 stands out as the one during which ordinary farmers that had previously shown little interest in the imperial struggle suddenly became enthusiastic participants.[51] The most important reason farmers became involved is that the Coercive Acts seemed a much greater threat to Americans' civil liberties than any of the measures that Parliament had adopted during the previous decade. In Virginia, there was also another reason for farmers to throw themselves into the imperial struggle: the primary strategy that patriots adopted in response to the Coercive Acts—another boycott of trade with Britain—seemed likely to benefit farmers not only politically but economically as well. William Reynolds, a Virginia trader that was deep in debt to Londoner John Norton, explained to him that nonimportation would both pressure Parliament to repeal the anti-American measures and help Virginians re-

50. Philip V. Fithian to Enoch Green, Dec. 1, 1773, in Hunter Dickinson Farish, ed., *Journal and Letters of Philip Vickers Fithian, 1773–1774: A Plantation Tutor of the Old Dominion* (Williamsburg, Va., 1957), 27; Yates to Martin, Apr. 2, 1774, Yates Letterbook; William Allason to John Backhouse, July 15, 1773 (extract), to Archibald Ritchie, Oct. 13, 1773 (extract), to Alexander Knox, Nov. 25, 1773 (extract), in D. R. Anderson, ed., "The Letters of William Allason, Merchant, of Falmouth, Virginia," *Richmond College Historical Papers*, II (1917), 150, 152; John Norton to John Hatley Norton, Mar. 20, Sept. 25, 1773, in Mason, ed., *Norton and Sons*, 308, 351; William Lee to Francis Lightfoot Lee, Jan. 30, 1773, Apr. 21, 1774, Arthur Lee Papers, Houghton; James Robison to William Cuninghame, June 23, 1773, in Devine, ed., *Scottish Firm*, 74; Harry Piper to Dixon and Littledale, Jan. 13, 1773, Piper Letterbook; Price, *Capital and Credit*, 162; William Cuninghame and Company to James Robison, July 1, Aug. 21, Oct. 20, 1772, bundle P/2, Cuninghame of Lainshaw Muniments, VCRP.

51. Robert A. Gross, *The Minutemen and Their World* (New York, 1976), 10, 33; Joy Day Buel and Richard Buel, Jr., *The Way of Duty: A Woman and Her Family in Revolutionary America* (New York, 1984), 68–70; Edward Countryman, *The American Revolution* (New York, 1985), 87, 114; Marc Egnal and Joseph A. Ernst, "An Economic Interpretation of the American Revolution," *WMQ*, 3d Ser., XXIX (1972), 30; Michael Zuckerman, *Peaceable Kingdoms: New England Towns in the Eighteenth Century* (New York, 1970), 248.

THE ALTERNATIVE OF WILLIAMS·BURG.

Plate IV.

London Printed for R. Sayer & J. Bennett, N.º 53 Fleet Street as the Act directs 16 Feb. 1775.

FIGURE 8. The Alternative of Williams-burg. *A merchant is forced to sign the Continental Association. The artist's inclusion of women, children, and a black man among the mob seemed to suggest that the gentlemen's rebellion against Britain might lead their fellow subjects to rebel against them. Courtesy, Colonial Williamsburg Foundation*

duce their debts. "I shall not write for any more Cargoes (perhaps a few trifles [f]or family use) untill I have made you such Remittances as I may suppose satisfactory," Reynolds told Norton early in June 1774. "Indeed if the Association shou'd take place the 1st August next as is expected not to import any Articles whatever from Great Britain it will prevent our troubling the Merch[an]ts and enable us to pay of[f] all old Arrears." The conservative Robert Beverley also saw that nonimportation had two distinct functions, and he celebrated both of them. The boycott promised to be a "Mode of Preservation"—an effective means of parrying Parliament's assault on the Americans' civil liberties. It was also intended as a "sumptuary Law to restrain the general Expences," a strategy that might "be a Means of extricating many People from their present Distresses."[52]

The 1774 boycott was much more comprehensive than the 1769 plan. Where the earlier association had specified certain items that signers could not purchase and allowed them to import everything else, the Continental Association of 1774 banned almost everything. Although the 1774 association demanded much more of free Virginians than the 1769 measure, almost all of them complied with it. The results were impressive. Residents of the Chesapeake imported £690,000 sterling worth of European goods in 1774; in 1775, when the sweeping boycott took effect, the value of imports dropped to £2,000 sterling.[53]

A principal reason that the 1774 boycott succeeded so well was the recession that had begun two years earlier. The economic slump discouraged British merchants from selling their goods on credit, and the Virginians were unable to pay cash. Thus, by the time many farmers decided to boycott British goods, they had already been prevented from buying them by economic necessity. At the same time that the recession paved the way for nonimportation by forcing most Virginians to reduce or eliminate their foreign purchases, it also left the shelves of Virginia stores stocked with sufficient excess merchandise for free Virginians to survive a brief boycott without undue hardship. "I am told, by Men acquainted with these Things," Thomas Nelson, Jr., told a patriotic meeting in Yorktown on July 18, "that the Goods already in the Country, and those expected in the Fall, will be sufficient to supply the Wants of all Virginia for two Years."[54]

52. Washington to Mason, Apr. 5, 1769, in Rutland, ed., *Papers of George Mason*, I, 98; Reynolds to Norton, June 4, 1774, in Mason, ed., *Norton and Sons*, 371; Robert Beverley to [Samuel Athawes], Sept. 6, 1774, Beverley Letterbook, LC.

53. Price, *Capital and Credit*, 162.

54. *Revolutionary Virginia*, I, 166. The belief that Virginia stores contained two years'

Although officially the 1774 boycott was aimed at distressing British merchants and manufacturers into lobbying Parliament against the Coercive Acts, not all merchants condemned it. To be sure, Gustavus Brown Wallace reported from Glasgow in May 1775 that "the people here think it hard" that Virginians should boycott British goods "untill they get their debts paid." But other Glaswegians welcomed the nonimportation scheme. The Scottish firm of William Cuninghame and Company, which was owed tens of thousands of pounds by Virginians, expressed the hope in July 1774 that they would "be enabled to pay off part of their debt to Britain during such an agreement subsisting." Virginia trader Charles Yates also saw economic value in the boycott. He predicted in July 1774 that nonimportation would "have a happy affect, without viewing it in the intended light of expressing resentment and Indignation against the Boston Port Bill."[55]

The 1774 boycott apparently had another "happy" effect as well. Although the recession that began in 1772 had created fissures in the alliance between gentlemen and smallholders, nonimportation seemed to close the gap. Farmers apparently appreciated the gentry's aggressive effort to protect both their civil liberties from parliamentary encroachment and their farms from the auctioneer's gavel. Thus the recession that began as a dividing wedge became, through gentry leadership, a bond of union.

Although the Continental Association was both more extreme and more successful than the 1769 effort, the two were in many respects similar. The 1774 boycott revived the patriotic campaign for domestic manufacturing that had begun in 1769. "Let America but stop her *importing Hand*," provincial treasurer Robert Carter Nicholas advised in a pamphlet that appeared in

---

worth of excess inventory was sufficient to dissuade the August 1774 convention from making any exceptions to nonimportation ("A Real Associator," Purdie and Dixon's *VG*, Dec. 15, 1774). As late as the fall of 1775, George Gilmer of Albemarle County said, "what we have on hand, with what we annually make, may last untill we get into a way of making all we want." By January 1776, "all Trade whatever" had been "entirely suspended" for a year, Robert Honyman noted. But he observed that "The County does not suffer much on that account as yet, the people applying themselves to manufacturing Cotton or flax for clothing for themselves and Slaves." See "Address of George Gilmer to the Inhabitants of Albemarle," in "Papers, Military and Political, 1775–1778, of George Gilmer, M.D., of 'Pen Park,' Albemarle County, Va.," VHS, *Collections*, N.S., VI (1887), 122; Jan. 2, 1776, Honyman diary, LC; Robert Donald to Patrick Hunter, Apr. 18, 1775, *Buchanan and Millihen v. Robert Donald*, 1794, Ended Cases.

55. Gustavus Brown Wallace to Michael Wallace, May 15, 1775, Wallace Family Papers (#38–150), UVA; William Cuninghame and Company to John Turner, July 18, 1774, in T. M. Devine, *The Tobacco Lords: A Study of the Tobacco Merchants of Glasgow and Their Trading Activities, c. 1740–90* (Edinburgh, 1975), 104; Charles Yates to Samuel Martin, July 5, 1774, Yates Letterbook.

August, and "apply a proper Share of her Industry to Manufactures . . . and I have the most sanguine Expectations that she will, not only very speedily extricate herself from Debt, but find the Balance [of trade] considerably in her Favour." The document proposed by a patriotic meeting in Fairfax County on July 18 urged "Gentlemen and men of fortune" to contribute "to the Improvement of Arts and Manufactures" and to sell sheep to their neighbors "at a Moderate price, as the most certain means of speedily increasing our breed of Sheep, and Quantity of Wool."[56]

In addition to celebrating Virginia manufactures, the 1774 associators echoed the sentiments that had been expressed in 1769 in favor of items associated with Native Americans. Just as Martha Jacqueline had predicted in August 1769 that she would soon be wearing moccasins, an early proposal for a Fairfax County rifle company had the soldiers wearing "painted Hunting-Shirts and Indian Boots." For reasons that will become apparent below, numerous Virginia counties had formed independent military companies by the summer of 1775, and many of the soldiers carried "a Tommyhawk or Scalping knife," as one loyalist reported. Even many of the gentlemen attending the House of Burgesses session that June showed up with "a Tomahawk by their Sides."[57] In 1774, as in 1769, Virginians gave up East Indian tea and brewed the local herbs that Native Americans had taught them to collect. In the same essay in which he warned that Parliament might soon prohibit Americans from "fashioning a canoe," Thomson Mason said nonimportation advocates expected "hickory ashes" to "supply the place of" imported salt, as they "formerly did to the native Indians."[58]

Another common feature of the 1769 and 1774 associations was that both banned the Atlantic slave trade. It will be recalled that the 1769 association

56. [Nicholas], "Considerations on the Present State of Virginia Examined," in *Revolutionary Virginia*, I, 279, Virginia Convention, 130–131; Robert Beverley to [Samuel Athawes?], Sept. 6, 1774, Beverley Letterbook.

57. Isaac, *Transformation of Virginia*, 256, 258.

58. Boycotters in other colonies also used Indians to demonstrate the point that beauty and comfort were in the eyes of the beholder (or "socially constructed," as modern theorists put it). An anonymous essay appearing in South Carolina in 1774, probably written by Christopher Gadsen, argued that "nothing but custom makes the curl-pated beau a more agreeable sight . . . than the tawney savage with his paint and bear's grease" (Breen, "'Baubles of Britain,'" *Past and Present*, no. 119 [May 1988], 99). For Mason's comment, see "A British American" [Thomson Mason], "Number VIII," July 21, 1774, in *Revolutionary Virginia*, I, 188, 190. There was irony in the patriots' emulation of the self-reliant Indian, since by this time most Indians east of the Mississippi River had become highly dependent on European manufactured goods. Even the famous hunting shirts and tomahawks were generally made in Europe.

came on the heels of a Privy Council veto of a House of Burgesses law aimed at reducing the number of enslaved West Indians and Africans arriving on Virginia's shores. By 1774, the assembly had twice more tried to slow down the international slave trade, and both laws had been vetoed in London. So its boycott, and the later Continental Association, revived the voluntary ban on slave importations. Although in 1774, as in 1769, the ostensible reason for halting the international slave trade was to pressure British slave merchants to lobby Parliament to repeal anti-American legislation, the resolves adopted by county meetings during the summer of 1774 reveal additional motives. Only one county, Fairfax, linked its vow to halt slave purchases to the struggle against George III.[59] The most frequent complaint was that the importation of Africans and West Indians "obstructs our Population by Freemen, Manufacturers, and others, who would emigrate from Europe and settle here," as the Caroline County freeholders put it. Half of the counties that blamed West Indians and Africans for keeping Europeans out of Virginia also noted that the slave trade "occasions an annual Increase of the Balance of Trade against this Colony."[60]

The 1769 association's boycott of African and West Indian slaves had been its most conspicuous failure; forced immigration into Virginia had grown considerably in 1770 and 1771. But the 1774 slave boycott was a total success. British slave traders, discouraged not only by the nonimportation association but also by the increasingly unstable political situation in the thirteen colonies, virtually stopped sending slave ships to mainland North America. Although the prohibition of African and West Indian imports helped free Virginians reduce their debt loads, it did not accomplish another of its goals, the easing of tensions between enslaved Virginians and their owners. In fact, nonimportation helped to create the conditions for the greatest movement of black resistance that Virginia had ever known.

59. It would be unwise to import slaves, the Fairfax freeholders declared, "during our present difficulties and distress. . . . And we take this Opportunity of declaring our most earnest wishes, to see an entire Stop forever put to such a Wicked, Cruel and unnatural Trade" (resolves, in *Revolutionary Virginia*, I, 132).

60. Caroline, Culpeper, Nansemond, Prince George, Princess Anne, and Surry Counties, resolves, in *Revolutionary Virginia*, I, 116, 119, 146, 151, 154, 162.

4 NONEXPORTATION

To be successful, a Chesapeake storekeeper had to stay abreast of the tobacco growers' frame of mind. In 1773, the most sensitive students of the agrarian mood began to detect a subtle but important change.

The year got off to a terrible start. On January 8, James Robison, the chief factor for the Glasgow firm of William Cuninghame and Company, described tobacco growers in pathetic terms. Although they were "loathe to part with their tobacco" at the low prevailing price of two pence per pound, he said, "that price must go down." At first glance, the sympathy that Robison expressed seems to parallel the comment that John Hook made in April: he remarked that persuading farmers to sell their tobacco at the low prevailing price was "like dragging an Ox to the slaughter."[1] Actually, the two observations were quite different. Where Robison saw farmers as objects of pity, Hook found that many of them had made themselves into the sort of people that (like an ox) would not be pushed around. The transformation from fatalism to desperate stubbornness that Hook recorded was crucial not only to the farmers' survival but to the struggle against Britain.

For some tobacco growers, the transformation began early in 1773, when the price of their crop dipped so low that they could not bear to hand it over to the British factors and independent traders that normally bought it or accepted it in discharge of debts. Those farmers' desperation turned to hope when they realized that, if they really did refuse to part with their tobacco, they might be able to preserve it until the market improved. For most growers, however, the strategy of holding out for higher tobacco prices was

1. James Robison to William Cuninghame and Company, Jan. 8, 1773, in T. M. Devine, ed., *A Scottish Firm in Virginia, 1767–1777: W. Cuninghame and Co.* (Edinburgh, 1984), 103; John Hook to David Ross, Apr. 20, 1773, John Hook Letterbook, LVA.

fatally flawed. They were in debt to the storekeepers, and if they did not hand over their tobacco, they would be sued. Another problem was that, no matter how long they withheld their tobacco from the market, its price would never recover if other farmers continued to sell it. Tobacco withholding would not accomplish its purpose until growers found ways to stave off their creditors and to flush out the glutted European market.

They found both in the Continental Association of 1774. Signers of the association vowed not to import anything from Britain after December 1, 1774. Associators also vowed that, if their grievances were not redressed by September 10 of the following year, they would not export anything to the mother country, either. Although nonexportation failed of its sole stated purpose of pressuring Parliament to repeal the Coercive Acts, it accomplished another goal that was much more significant in the daily lives of Chesapeake tobacco farmers. It ended the tobacco glut. Between the summer of 1774 and the summer of 1775, as British and European shopkeepers stocked up on tobacco in anticipation of the imminent boycott, the price of the weed nearly doubled. Indebted tobacco farmers were able to withhold their crops while they waited for a price recovery, because many Maryland courts delayed adjudication of creditors' lawsuits and Virginia courts simply closed their doors.

The tobacco farmers' successful use of nonexportation to rescue their commodity from a devastating price slump shows that, at a critical stage in the development of the American Revolution, one large group of participants was motivated partly by economic goals. But the Chesapeake farmers did not simply repudiate their debts, as historians once claimed.[2] The story is more complex than that.

2. Charles A. Beard, *Economic Origins of Jeffersonian Democracy* (New York, 1915), 270; Isaac Samuel Harrell, *Loyalism in Virginia: Chapters in the Economic History of the Revolution* (Durham, N.C., 1926), 26–29; Robert Johnson, "Government Regulation of Business Enterprise in Virginia, 1750–1820" (Ph.D. diss., University of Minnesota, 1958), 204; Merrill Jensen, *The Articles of Confederation: An Interpretation of the Social-Constitutional History of the American Revolution, 1774–1781* (Madison, Wis., 1940), 23–24. For two refutations of the Progressive interpretation, see Thad W. Tate, "The Coming of the Revolution in Virginia: Britain's Challenge to Virginia's Ruling Class, 1763–1776," Emory G. Evans, "Planter Indebtedness and the Coming of the Revolution in Virginia," both in *WMQ*, 3d. Ser., XIX (1962), 323–343, 511–533. More recently, scholars have revealed that the indebted Virginia gentry's uneasiness about its dependence on British creditors made it more receptive to the republican values of austerity and independence. See T. H. Breen, *Tobacco Culture: The Mentality of the Great Tidewater Planters on the Eve of Revolution* (Princeton, N.J., 1985), 158–159; Rhys Isaac, *The Transformation of Virginia, 1740–1790* (Chapel Hill, N.C., 1982), 247, 251.

I

During the terrible recession that struck the Chesapeake in 1772, the fundamental problem for farmers was the low price of tobacco. Four successive bumper crops and a credit crisis that sapped demand for the weed nearly put growers in the same position as the farmer in *Macbeth* that "hanged himself on the expectation of plenty." By April 1774, trader Charles Yates wished the Chesapeake would "luckily have Flys to destroy the Plants or no Season [rain] to put them in the ground for a year or two."[3]

Starting in the spring of 1773, Chesapeake smallholders created a strategy for surviving the recession. A small number of them began refusing to deliver their tobacco to the traders and factors to whom they usually sold it. At first the farmers did not seem to know what they were going to do with their tobacco—only that they could not "think of taking the low price talked of by the Merchants," as trader Harry Piper reported from Alexandria in May 1773. By mid-June, James Robison found that the "planters are very unwilling in various parts of the colony to part with their tobacco at the prices offered."[4]

Some smallholders withheld their tobacco from buyers like Piper, Hook, and Robison because they hoped to do what many larger growers generally did—sell their crops in Britain instead of the Chesapeake. In June 1773, Piper reported that the price of tobacco remained only 1.5 pence per pound. Piper found smallholders "very unwilling to sell at that, and some threaten to Ship" their crops to Britain, hoping to find a better market there.[5] But the British price was just as low.

During 1773, it occurred to many farmers that tobacco, for all its shortcomings as a staple crop, has one great advantage: it keeps. Most of the

3. *Macbeth*, II, iii, 5–6; Charles Yates to Dixon and Littledale, Apr. 2, 1774, Yates Letterbook (#3807), UVA.

4. Harry Piper to Dixon and Littledale, May 29, 1773, Piper Letterbook (#2981), UVA; Trent, Crump, and Bates to Dobson, Daltera, and Walker, Mar. 12, 1773, in *Dobson and Daltera v. Trent, Crump, and Bates* (1798), U.S. Circuit Court, Virginia District, Ended Cases (restored), LVA (hereafter cited as Ended Cases); Alexander Hamilton to Brown and Company, May 28, 1774, in Richard K. MacMaster and David C. Skaggs, eds., "The Letterbooks of Alexander Hamilton, Piscataway Factor," pt. I, "1774," *MHM*, LXI (1966), 159. Robison reported that growers withheld their tobacco throughout his firm's purchasing area—in Fredericksburg, the lower Northern Neck, Petersburg, Amherst County, Rocky Ridge, and Richmond on the Upper James River and Cabin Point on the Lower James (to Cuninghame and Company, Jan. 8, June 17, 1773, in Devine, ed., *Scottish Firm*, 103, 114, 115).

5. Piper to Dixon and Littledale, June 21, July 17, 1773, Piper Letterbook; Robison to Cuninghame and Company, June 17, 1773, in Devine, ed., *Scottish Firm*, 114; James H. Soltow, *The Economic Role of Williamsburg* (Williamsburg, Va., 1965), 73–74.

tobacco harvested each August in the Chesapeake was not even shipped across the Atlantic until the following spring or summer.[6] In fact, tobacco could be stored for years without losing much of its value. Knowing this, many farmers decided as early as June 1773 "to keep their Tobo. over Year," as Piper observed. Their plan was to house their crops on their farms until 1774, hoping that in the interim the glutted European market would clear and their produce would once again be worth something.[7]

Although farmers initially had no specific reason to believe the price of tobacco was going to recover in 1774, they soon found one. The source of the farmers' hope was, ironically, the distress to which they and their neighbors were reduced. As the low price of tobacco was discussed on tavern porches and church lawns throughout 1773, more and more farmers declared that in 1774 they would give up tobacco production altogether and become grain farmers.[8] Dumfries trader William Carr noted early in May 1774 that the "independant Planters will neither Ship" their tobacco to Britain "nor sell" it in Virginia, "Expecting it will be much higher Next Year the intention of the Planters in general being to reduce the Quantity of Tobacco." If thousands of Chesapeake farmers switched to grain, the chief beneficiaries would be those that did not. A reduction in tobacco output would soon force up the price.[9]

6. By the time it was unloaded on the quays of France, Holland, and other destinations on the European continent (where nearly 90 percent of it ended up by 1760), tobacco had been out of the ground for more than a year (Robison to Cuninghame and Company, Jan. 8, 1773, in Devine, ed., *Scottish Firm*, 102).

7. Piper to Dixon and Littledale, June 21, 1773, Piper Letterbook; Yates to George McCall, July 10, 1773, to Samuel Martin, Aug. 19, 1773, to Dixon and Littledale, July 7, 1774, Yates Letterbook.

8. Piper to Dixon and Littledale, June 21, Sept. 26, 1773, Piper Letterbook; Yates to Fletchers and Company, Oct. 1, 1773, to Samuel Martin, Dec. 10, 1773, Yates Letterbook; Robison to Cuninghame and Company, Nov. 9, 1773, in Devine, ed., *Scottish Firm*, 126; Douglas Southall Freeman, *George Washington: A Biography*, III, *Planter and Patriot* (New York, 1951), 347.

9. Carr to Russell, May 10, 1774, Russell Papers at Coutts and Company, bundle 2, VCRP; Piper to Dixon and Littledale, Mar. 12, Apr. 27, 1774, to Samuel Martin, Apr. 28, 1774, Piper Letterbook. Throughout the Chesapeake during the summer of 1773, the crop-withholding strategy came to the attention of more and more tobacco buyers (Trent, Crump and Bates to Dobson, Daltera, and Walker, Aug. 1, 1773, in *Dobson and Daltera v. Trent, Crump, and Bates*, Ended Cases). In the spring of 1774, farmers became increasingly confident that their neighbors were going to divert laborers from tobacco to grain starting with the 1774 crop. See Henry Fleming to [——], Apr. 15, 1774, Fleming Letterbook, in *The Papers of Henry Fleming, 1772–1795* (microfilm, with an introduction by Jacob M. Price, n.d.); Yates to Gale and Fearon, [Feb.] 17, 1774, to Dixon and Littledale, Apr. 2, 1774, Yates Letterbook; Robison to Cuninghame and Company, Apr. 16, 1774, in Devine, ed., *Scottish Firm*, 139; Robert Beverley

The tobacco-withholding idea gained momentum in the spring of 1774. One captain of a tobacco ship said "he never knew the people in Virginia so backward with their Crops."[10] "I believe there never was less Tobo ready at this season of the year, both on Patuxent and Potomack," Marylander James Forbes reported at the end of February. Tobacco deliveries decreased even more drastically in the Northern Neck of Virginia, where Richard Henry Lee claimed on April 15 that the Dumfries, Colchester, and Falmouth warehouses "had not taken 10 days ago, much above one third of their usual quantity."[11]

A striking feature of the crop-withholding strategy is that it appears to have been adopted almost exclusively by smallholders. Surviving correspondence of traders and factors does not mention the names of any gentlemen that orchestrated the strategy or even employed it. The terms that traders

---

to Landon Carter, May 16, 1774, Landon Carter Papers, item 15, VHS. Maryland growers received an additional incentive to withhold their tobacco in December 1773, when the legislature renewed Maryland's tobacco inspection law, which had expired three years earlier. The reopening of the inspection warehouses was expected to regain the British merchants' respect for Maryland tobacco and bolster its price (Hamilton to Brown and Company, May 18, 1774, in MacMaster and Skaggs, eds., "Letterbooks of Alexander Hamilton," pt. I, "1774," *MHM*, LXI [1966], 156). Awaiting that outcome, hopeful Marylanders withheld their crops (Samuel Galloway to James Russell, May 8, 1774, Russell Papers, bundle 7.)

10. Charles Grahame to James Russell, May 30, 1774, Russell Papers, bundle 20; Henry Fleming to Fisher and Bragg, Apr. 27, 1774, Fleming Letterbook; Hamilton to Brown and Company, May 18, June 13, 1774, in MacMaster and Skaggs, eds., "Letterbooks of Alexander Hamilton," pt. I, "1774," *MHM*, LXI (1966), 156, 164; Yates to Gale and Fearon, [Feb.] 17, 1774, Yates Letterbook.

11. James Forbes to James Russell, Feb. 21, 1774, Russell Papers, bundle 6; Richard Henry Lee to William Lee, Apr. 15, 1774, in James Curtis Ballagh, ed., *The Letters of Richard Henry Lee* (New York, 1911–1914), I, 105; Robison to Cuninghame and Company, Apr. 16, May 28, 1774, in Devine, ed., *Scottish Firm*, 139; William Carr to James Russell, Apr. 13, 1774, Russell Papers, bundle 2. The low quantity of tobacco arriving in the warehouses was all the more surprising in light of the fact that the 1773 crop was "very large" (Robison to Cuninghame and Company, Nov. 9, 1773, in Devine, ed., *Scottish Firm*, 124).

The reduction in the amount of tobacco coming into the warehouses was blamed partly on weather conditions. See Richard Henry Lee to William Lee, Apr. 15, 1774, in Ballagh, ed., *Letters of Richard Henry Lee*, I, 105; Hamilton to Brown and Company, May 18, 1774, in MacMaster and Skaggs, eds., "Letterbooks of Alexander Hamilton," pt. I, "1774," *MHM*, LXI (1966), 156; Yates to Gale and Fearon, Mar. 9, 1774, Yates Letterbook; Robison to Cuninghame and Company, Nov. 9, 1773, in Devine, ed., *Scottish Firm*, 124. The warehouse in Fredericksburg suffered from an additional problem: a smallpox epidemic there discouraged growers from bringing their crops to town (Robison to Cuninghame and Company, Feb. 7, 1774, in Devine, ed., *Scottish Firm*, 130).

used in describing crop withholding were those—"the planters," "the people," "our folks"—that they usually applied to smallholders, not gentlemen.[12] Nor does the correspondence of consignment agents in British ports reveal that a substantial number of gentlemen abandoned their customary practice of shipping tobacco to Britain. Gentlemen might have expected the British merchants to whom they consigned their tobacco to withhold it from the market until prices improved, but few if any of them seem to have withheld it from the consignment merchants themselves. Perhaps gentlemen believed honor required them to fill the ships that their creditors sent to Virginia.

Despite the farmers' confidence that prices would rise toward the end of 1774, the decision to retain tobacco was still not easy. Stored tobacco could be ruined in a calamity such as a fire or flood. The smallest mistake in packing could lead to spoilage. Furthermore, the majority of tobacco farmers were in debt, and a debtor that refused to deliver his tobacco to his creditor ruined his chances of receiving another loan any time soon. Determined to hang on to their crops but also desperate to preserve their credit ratings, farmers searched for some pretext, some honorable excuse, for withholding their produce. On April 16, 1774, William Carr alerted James Russell, his principal in London, to a rumor that Russell's financial straits had led him into illegal activity. "As the Planters in General have an aversion against shipping the Price for Tobacco being with you so Very low they will be glad of any Excuse" not to load their crops onto Russell's ships, Carr warned.[13]

Indebted farmers also ran another, greater risk if they kept back their tobacco; they could be sued. When Maryland traders learned that many of their debtors would not "Bring their Tobacco to the Warehouses," the traders' recourse was "to sue them," Piscataway factor Alexander Hamilton reported in May 1774. Hamilton himself had "sued a great many." Because debtors feared legal action, a much smaller proportion of debtors than nondebtors withheld their crops. Traders that described the crop-withholding strategy often specified that it was the "independant" smallholders that adopted it—those that were "disengaged" from creditors. Nonetheless, many debtors did withhold their tobacco. In the Petersburg area, the reduction of

12. Harry Piper to Dixon and Littledale, May 29, June 21, 1773, Piper Letterbook; Yates to Martin, Apr. 2, 1774, Yates Letterbook.

13. Carr to Russell, Apr. 16, 1774, Russell Papers, bundle 2. For examples of those rumors about Russell, see Joshua Johnson to Wallace, Davidson, and Johnson, Jan. 10, Feb. 4, 1774, in Jacob M. Price, ed., *Joshua Johnson's Letterbook, 1771–1774: Letters from a Merchant in London to His Partners in Maryland* (Chatham, 1979), 114–115, 119; William Lee to Richard Henry Lee, Jan. 1, 1774, in Paul P. Hoffman, ed., *The Lee Family Papers, 1742–1795* (microfilm, Charlottesville, Va., 1966).

the price of tobacco to 1.8 pence per pound "determined many of the planters to keep up and suffer themselves to be sued rather than part with their crops on these terms," James Robison reported. William Carr told James Russell that Russell's debtors in the Northern Neck of Virginia "will rather be sued than ship" their tobacco to Britain at the low prevailing price.[14] The disastrous effects of being sued by a creditor were mitigated for most Chesapeake debtors by the slowness of the courts in both Maryland and Virginia. As the recession deepened, the members of county courts shielded debtors by proceeding through their dockets of debt suits even more slowly than usual. The Amherst County, Virginia, justices "resolved not to sit to do business but twice in the year, untill the Inhabitants are clear of debt," Richmond trader Robert Donald claimed in February 1773. The justices of Charles County, Maryland, apparently adopted a similar strategy. "Last Charles County March Court I expected Judgment against several people whom I had Sued the March preceding," Alexander Hamilton wrote on May 28, 1774, but the justices refused to do any business. "The Court was adjourned untill the 26th [of May] and has since been adjourned to a further time. By such things as these," Hamilton told his employers in Glasgow, "I have been prevented from making you a better remittance."[15]

Useful as that protection was to debtors, it was only temporary and did not relieve them from the enormous costs associated with a lawsuit. Thus, as more and more tobacco withholders were sued, some of them began to

14. Hamilton to Brown and Company, May 28, 1774, in MacMaster and Skaggs, eds., "Letterbooks of Alexander Hamilton," pt. I, "1774)," *MHM*, LXI (1966), 159; Carr to Russell, Mar. 30, Apr. 16, May 10, 1774, Russell Papers, bundle 2; Robison to Cuninghame and Company, June 17, 30, 1773, in Devine, ed., *Scottish Firm*, 115, 117; Piper to Dixon and Littledale, May 29, 1773, Piper Letterbook; Trent, Crump, and Bates to Dobson, Daltera, and Walker, Mar. 12, 1773, in *Dobson and Daltera v. Trent, Crump, and Bates*, Ended Cases.

15. During the recession of the early 1760s, Robert Beverley stated (with considerable exaggeration) that, in Spotsylvania County, the "Court never did business." See Beverley to Mr. Dixon, Mar. 26, 1765, in Breen, *Tobacco Culture*, 166; Henry Fleming to Fisher and Bragg, Feb. 19, 1774, Fleming Letterbook; Seymour Powell to [John Miller], June 22, 1773, Miller's claim, American Loyalist Claims, T. 79/49, P.R.O.; Calvin Brewster Coulter, Jr., "The Virginia Merchant" (Ph.D. diss., Princeton University, 1944), 238–239. For Robert Donald's comment, see Donald to Charles Steuart, Feb. 10, 1773, in Soltow, *Economic Role of Williamsburg*, 143–144. Another trader, William Allason, had made a similar accusation in 1768. "Frederick [County] Court Sitts only once in three months and then do very little Business, which I Believe owing to no other reason but that the Justices are mostly sued and take this method to prevent Judgments against themselves" (to Glen and Gregory, Oct. 12, 1768, Allason Letterbook, LVA). For Hamilton's complaint, see Hamilton to Brown and Company, May 28, 1774, in MacMaster and Skaggs, eds., "Letterbooks of Alexander Hamilton," pt. I, "1774," *MHM*, LXI (1966), 159–160.

search for more dramatic methods of surviving the recession. Many recognized that if the individuals that withheld their tobacco went one step further—if they banded together and formed a well-disciplined organization that bound its members to refuse to sell tobacco below a certain price—they could do more than wait for the price of tobacco to rise. They could *make* it rise. Some tobacco farmers might have remembered their grandparents' stories about the 1682 riots, during which farmers tried to shore up the price of tobacco by destroying the entire year's harvest in the field. And it is likely that the recession provoked many to imagine schemes such as Lyonel Lyde's proposal (mentioned above) that growers "sink a whole Crop" in order to "render the Trade flourishing for Twenty years to come."[16]

The first crop-withholding association was organized in the lower counties of the Northern Neck of Virginia, where, James Robison reported on June 17, 1773, "the planters have entered into an Association, lodged their tobacco in certain persons' hands, and have determined not to sell unless they can procure [2.16 pence per pound]. . . . This association it is said ties up 1,000 hogsheads." Members of the association held out for a price that was more than one-third higher than the 1.5 pence per pound that traders were willing to pay them. Some farmers in Bedford County went further. They too formed an "Association" and pledged not only to refuse to sell their tobacco until the price rose but "*Not to pay their Debts unless they can get such Prices for their Commodities as they have affixed.*"[17]

The crop-withholding associations that appeared in 1773 were local affairs. Organizers, realizing that crop withholding would not appreciably raise the price of tobacco until it substantially reduced the number of hogsheads that left Chesapeake wharves, worked to build a broader movement. On October 21, 1773, "A Planter" devised a way for "the Body of the Planters" to "save our Estates (that we have been toiling for all the Days of our Lives)." He published a letter in Purdie and Dixon's *Virginia Gazette* proposing that tobacco growers in every county in the province elect four men to represent them in all negotiations with the storekeepers that purchased their tobacco. He had sounded out his Louisa County neighbors on the idea, and they liked it. Farmers in Caroline and Bedford Counties also endorsed the idea of

16. Lyde to Andrew Monroe, Sept. 24, 1753, in *Lyonel Lyde v. Monroe's Administrator et al.* (1797), Ended Cases, box 16, file 5.

17. Robison to Cuninghame and Company, June 17, 1773, in Devine, ed., *Scottish Firm*, 114; anonymous letter, Purdie and Dixon's *VG*, Nov. 25, 1773. Although "Tillias" claimed to have heard that Bedford gentleman Guy Smith was interested in the idea of a crop-withholding association, no document stating the name of any association organizer has survived (Purdie and Dixon's *VG*, Nov. 25, 1773).

linking the county crop-withholding leagues into a colonywide association. "The Planters in general in this Country are willing to associate," "A Planter in Caroline" declared in the *Virginia Gazette*, "and adopt such Measures as may seem most adviseable to frustrate the ungenerous Designs of the Merchants." "Let us directly set a Price on our Tobacco," anonymous writer Tillias urged, "and bind ourselves by the most solemn Ties not to Part with it for less than the Price established by us Planters, in every County. . . . Let us BEDFORDMEN lead the Van."[18]

As of May 1774, the crop-withholding associations had failed to force traders to agree to a higher price for tobacco. There were several reasons for this failure. One appears to be the lack of powerful gentry sponsors.[19] The associations had no enforcement mechanism. And indebted members of crop-withholding associations exposed themselves to the same risks as individual debtors that withheld their tobacco—ruining their credit ratings and being sued. Crop withholding thus lacked two crucial elements: an enforcement device and protection for debtors.

Many Virginians believed that the responsibility for bringing up the price of tobacco belonged to the House of Burgesses, whose genteel membership enjoyed the benefits of preeminence in Virginia society and ought to carry out the attendant duties. "I have long expected that our great and learned Men would exert their Abilities in this very important Affair," A Planter in Caroline wrote in November 1773, "but suppose they have their Reasons why they do not. If those who are chosen to represent and redress the Grievances [of] their Constituents remain silent on this Occasion, I am at a Loss to know what Use we have for such Men." If elite Virginians did not awaken to their responsibilities, A Planter in Caroline warned, "the present Situation of the Planters may, possibly, draw more fatal Consequences." Although the Caroline County writer no doubt intended his warning as a friendly one, he was rebuked by another anonymous writer. "Never aim at introducing popular Tumults," "Philalethes" declared.[20]

---

18. "A Planter in Caroline," Purdie and Dixon's *VG*, Nov. 4, 1773; "Tillias," Purdie and Dixon's *VG*, Nov. 25, 1773. Although none of the references to tobacco-withholding associations that appear in the newspapers and correspondence of 1773 and 1774 makes any reference to the colonial struggle against Britain, it is interesting to speculate about whether the associators were encouraged by the example of the patriot associations of the 1760s.

19. Actually, it is possible that gentlemen did guide the tobacco-withholding efforts. The fact is that none of the crop withholders' names survives. But a lack of gentry support might have been a major reason for the movement's failure.

20. Purdie and Dixon's *VG*, Nov. 4, 1773; "To Tillias," letter from "Philalethes," Purdie and Dixon's *VG*, Feb. 10, 1774.

III

It was in that context of ruinously low tobacco prices, an expanding but flawed crop-withholding movement, and growing demands for gentry intervention in the economy that Chesapeake gentlemen finally decided, during the spring of 1774, to do something about the recession. The impetus came from Parliament, which, in March 1774, punished Boston for its famous tea party by adopting the Boston Port Act, which closed Boston Harbor. Leading men in both Maryland and Virginia found a strategy that, they hoped, would strike a blow against the Boston Port Act and at the same time pull the Chesapeake out of the recession. Two Virginia brothers living in London, William and Arthur Lee, wrote their friends in Virginia and Maryland and proposed that all tobacco growers do what many smallholders had already done: refuse to ship any tobacco to England or Scotland. The Lees apparently realized that a tobacco boycott would accomplish three goals. It would protest the Boston Port Act, clear out European tobacco markets, and furnish tobacco farmers with a patriotic justification—the "Excuse" that William Carr noticed them desperately seeking in April 1774—for withholding their crops while they waited for the tobacco glut to end.[21]

In addition to nonexportation, the Lee brothers proposed that Virginia and Maryland halt their importation of British manufactured goods. If the American colonies stopped their trade with Britain, William Lee wrote his Virginia brother Francis Lightfoot Lee, the trade boycott would both force Parliament to repeal the Boston Port Act and also "tend to the particular pecuniary advantage of each Colony." Although William Lee did not identify in this letter what the "pecuniary" benefits of nonexportation would be, he later predicted that the plan would double the price of tobacco.[22]

It is not clear when Arthur and William Lee's letters touting the political and pecuniary benefits of a trade cutoff reached their two brothers in the Virginia House of Burgesses. But on May 10, 1774, burgess Richard Henry Lee launched his own bold effort to remove the greatest obstacle keeping indebted farmers out of the crop-withholding movement: their fear of being

21. "Junius Americanus" [Arthur Lee?], Rind's *VG*, May 19, 1774; "A Gentleman in London to a Friend in Annapolis, Md.," Mar. 31, 1774, in Peter Force, comp., *American Archives: Consisting of a Collection of Authentick Records, State Papers, Debates, and Letters and Other Notices of Publick Affairs*, 4th Ser. (Washington, D.C., 1837–1846), I, 230–231; Carr to Russell, Apr. 16, 1774, Russell Papers, bundle 2.

22. [William Lee] to [Francis Lightfoot Lee], Apr. 2, 1774, Arthur Lee Papers, Houghton; William Lee to Francis Lightfoot Lee, July 16, 1774, in Worthington Chauncey Ford, ed., *Letters of William Lee . . . , 1766–1783* (Brooklyn, N.Y., 1891), I, 86; Philip Ludwell Lee to William Lee, July 13, 1774, Lee Family Papers (1638–1867), section 106, VHS; Richard Henry Lee to [William Lee], June 29, 1774, in Ballagh, ed., *Letters of Richard Henry Lee*, I, 120.

sued. Lee proposed that the House of Burgesses refuse to renew the law establishing the fees charged by Virginia's court officers. The effect of Lee's motion would be to close Virginia's courts, thus preventing creditors from suing debtors. That legal immunity would make it possible for indebted tobacco farmers to keep their crops out of their creditors' hands. Crop withholding would expand throughout the province and succeed both in pressuring Parliament and in raising the price of tobacco. Lee's fellow burgesses did not want to go on record in support of closing Virginia's courts, so they rejected his proposal and voted to continue the fee act renewal on its passage through the legislative mill.[23]

But the idea of closing the courts did not die. Some loyalists, like Norfolk trader James Parker, believed that the reason many Virginians wanted to halt judicial proceedings was that they wished to repudiate their debts to British merchants (like him). The "more a Man is indebted here," Parker told a British correspondent on May 17, "the stronger he is posessed with the Spirit of Patriotism."[24] Actually, the connection between debt and the movement to close the courts was subtler than that. Leading Virginians recognized that it was only by halting legal proceedings that they could permit indebted tobacco farmers to join in the nonexportation movement without fear of being sued by their creditors. Dumfries trader William Carr recognized that the courts would have to close if nonexportation were to succeed. Farmers planned, he told James Russell on May 26, "to Stop the Exportation of Tobacco and Every other Commodity to great Britain *to carry this into Execution* the Courts of Justice will be stopt."[25]

If court-closing was intended primarily as a strategy for carrying out nonexportation, nonexportation was something more than the patriotic protest movement that its supporters claimed it was. William Carr was in

23. May 10, 1774, *JHB, 1773–1776*, 85; Warren M. Billings, John E. Selby, and Thad W. Tate, *Colonial Virginia: A History* (White Plains, N.Y., 1986), 327–328. The proposal to close the courts came from the courts committee, which Lee chaired. Although it is possible that he was not the sponsor of the plan, it is highly unlikely that his committee would have proposed it without his approval.

24. James Parker to Charles Steuart, May 17, 1774, Steuart Papers, National Library of Scotland, Edinburgh (microfilm at LVA).

25. Carr to Russell, May 26, 1774, Russell Papers, bundle 2 (emphasis added); Billings, Selby, and Tate, *Colonial Virginia*, 330; George M. Curtis III, "The Role of the Courts in the Making of the Revolution in Virginia," in James Kirby Martin, ed., *The Human Dimensions of Nation Making: Essays on Colonial and Revolutionary America* (Madison, Wis., 1976), 123, 138; Paul L. Webb, Jr., "The Coercive Acts and the Coming of the Revolution in Virginia," in Richard A. Rutyna and Peter C. Stewart, eds., *Virginia in the American Revolution* (Norfolk, Va., 1983), II, 27–28.

charge of procuring tobacco from James Russell's debtors to fill the ships Russell sent to the Potomac River. In April he had warned Russell that debtors sought "any Excuse" not to sell at the low prevailing price of 1.5 pence per pound. In late May, after crop withholding had evolved into the patriotic nonexportation proposal, Carr recognized that "2/3ds of the Inhabitants would rejoice at the Proposal." It was "so Pleasant and agreable to those indebted," Carr told Russell on May 26, "that I fear it will be caried into Execution and the ships compelled to Return Empty" to England.[26] Chesapeake farmers agreed with the nonexportation idea at least in part because it would allow them to wait until the price of tobacco recovered from its terrible slump.

Nonexportation was also discussed in Maryland during May 1774. Annapolis traders Charles Wallace and John Davidson received a letter from their London partner, Joshua Johnson, stating that London tobacco merchants expected growers to "enter into resolves not to have any more goods and not to ship any more tobacco until the [Boston Port] act is repealed." In the same letter, Johnson reported that, during the previous two weeks, the price of tobacco had advanced by more than 5 percent.[27] On May 25, Anne Arundel County freeholders gathered in Annapolis and endorsed the nonimportation and nonexportation proposals that the Boston Town Meeting had drafted earlier in the month. The Marylanders made one significant addition to the Boston plan: they asked lawyers to refuse to try cases for British merchants. Debt suits had to cease if Maryland growers were to participate in nonexportation, a later meeting in Anne Arundel County explained, "as remittances can be made only from exports, after stopping the exports [to] Great Britain and the West Indies, it will be impossible for very many of the people of this province . . . to pay off their debts."[28] Only if the courts were closed could all growers participate in nonexportation.

But what would Virginia do? On May 10, the House of Burgesses had rejected Richard Henry Lee's proposal that it vote to close the courts. Two weeks later, though, the burgesses found a way to close Virginia's courts without having to vote to do so. The burgesses knew that Virginia governor John Murray, Lord Dunmore, would dissolve them, preventing them from renewing the fee act that was vital to the operation of Virginia's courts, if

26. Carr to Russell, Apr. 16, May 26, 1774, Russell Papers, bundle 2.

27. Joshua Johnson to Wallace, Davidson, and Johnson, Apr. 6, 177[4], in Price, ed., *Joshua Johnson's Letterbook*, 131–132; Baltimore Committee of Correspondence to Virginia Committee of Correspondence, May 25, 1774, in *Revolutionary Virginia*, II, 79.

28. Anne Arundel County meeting, June 4, 1774, in J. Thomas Scharf, *History of Maryland from the Earliest Period to the Present Day* (1879; reprint, Hatboro, Pa., 1967), II, 150.

they should "enter on Politics." So, on May 24, they approved a resolve calling Parliament's decision to close Boston Harbor "a hostile Invasion" and calling for "a Day of Fasting, Humiliation, and Prayer" to protest it."[29] Dunmore played his part, dissolving the assembly on May 26. The former burgesses returned to their counties with news of their dissolution, and during June the gentlemen justices of Virginia's local courts began to refuse to hear lawsuits. At the time, gentlemen attributed their decision to close the courts to the expiration of the fee act, which they said the House of Burgesses had wanted to renew. But John Burk, who interviewed several former burgesses for his Whiggish *History of Virginia*, acknowledged that the expiration of the fee act was only a "pretext" for closing the courts. The real reason was to prevent creditors from suing debtors.[30] Thus protected, indebted farmers could refuse to export any of their tobacco. Nonexportation both drove up the price of the leaf and also (as Burk noted) pressured Parliament to repeal the Boston Port Act.[31] Provincial leaders, eager for both

29. [William Lee] to [Francis Lightfoot Lee], Apr. 2, 1774, Arthur Lee Papers; *Revolutionary Virginia*, I, 94–95. The likelihood that Dunmore would dissolve the assembly if it adopted inflammatory resolves was frequently discussed in the days before he actually did. See Robert Wormeley Carter to Landon Carter, May 10, 1774, in Paul P. Hoffman, ed., *The Carter Family Papers, 1659–1797, in the Sabine Hall Collection* (microfilm, Charlottesville, Va., 1967); June 3, 1774, in Jack P. Greene, ed., *The Diary of Colonel Landon Carter of Sabine Hall, 1752–1778* (Charlottesville, Va., 1965), II, 818; "From a Member of the Virginia Assembly to His Correspondent in London," May 20, 1774, in Force, comp., *American Archives*, 4th Ser., I, 340. Edmund Pendleton acknowledged that, during May 1774, the burgesses had "expected" a "dissolution" by Dunmore if they should adopt "Spirited Resolves." Pendleton said that the assembly had initially planned to adopt "Spirited Resolves" only after renewing the fee act and other laws. But he said the assembly changed its plan and decided to adopt the "hostile Invasion" resolve before passing the fee act and other laws. See *Revolutionary Virginia*, I, 94; Edmund Pendleton to Joseph Chew, June 20, 1774, in David John Mays, ed., *The Letters and Papers of Edmund Pendleton, 1734–1803* (Charlottesville, Va., 1967), I, 93.

30. Robison to Cuninghame and Company, June 7, 1774, in Devine, ed., *Scottish Firm*, 142; Seymour Powell to John Millar, June 3, 1774, Millar's claim, T. 79/49; John Burk et al., *The History of Virginia from Its First Settlement to the Present Day* (Petersburg, Va., 1804–1816), III, 425. Burk wrote his book under the "tutelage" of Thomas Jefferson (Jack P. Greene, *Understanding the American Revolution: Issues and Actors* [Charlottesville, Va., 1995], 332). An important piece of evidence for Burk's claim that the expiration of the fee act was only a pretext for halting lawsuits is that Virginia courts continued to perform other functions that also involved fees (Frank L. Dewey, *Thomas Jefferson, Lawyer* [Charlottesville, Va., 1986], 102).

31. Many patriot leaders—including Richard Henry Lee and George Washington— claimed that Dunmore surprised them by dissolving the House of Burgesses. They said they had hoped to stay in session long enough to renew the fee act, which would have kept the

political and economic reasons to close the courts but unwilling to do so openly, had goaded Governor Dunmore into doing it for them.

I V

During the summer of 1774, nonexportation was warmly embraced by well-attended county meetings and provincial conventions in both of the Chesapeake colonies. The Virginia convention, which gathered in Williamsburg the first week of August, removed from the Boston Town Meeting's embargo plan many of the sacrifices that the plan would have required of Virginians. On May 13, Boston had urged that the thirteen colonies cut off trade both with the mother country and with the British West Indies. The Virginia association cut off trade only with Britain itself, allowing Virginia's lucrative and expanding grain trade with the British West Indies to continue.[32]

courts open. See Dewey, *Thomas Jefferson, Lawyer*, 100; Bruce A. Ragsdale, *A Planters' Republic: The Search for Economic Independence in Revolutionary Virginia* (Madison, Wis., 1996), 181; Billings, Selby, and Tate, *Colonial Virginia*, 328; Curtis, "Role of the Courts," in Martin, ed., *Human Dimensions of Nation Making*, 121–146.

However, there is ample evidence that the burgesses knew that they would be dissolved if they adopted inflammatory resolves. See "Englishman," June 30, 1774, *Virginia Gazette, or, Norfolk Intelligencer;* [John Randolph], *Considerations on the Present State of Virginia*, in *Revolutionary Virginia*, I, 214. It had happened three times during the previous decade. See John G. Kolp, "The Dynamics of Electoral Competition in Pre-Revolutionary Virginia," *WMQ*, 3d Ser., XLIX (1992), 660–661; Paul Leicester Ford, comp. and ed., *The Works of Thomas Jefferson*, Federal Edition, I (New York, 1904), 12–13; Fairfax County, resolves, July 18, 1774, *Revolutionary Virginia*, I, 129. Henry Fleming predicted that legislators would soon "support the Bostonians, in consequence of which a Dissolution of the assembly is Hourly expected" (to Fisher and Bragg, May 18, 1774, Fleming Letterbook).

Furthermore, the House of Burgesses adopted the May 24 resolve at a time when leaders throughout Maryland and Virginia discussed the necessity of closing the courts. Annapolis, Maryland, voted on May 25 to ask lawyers to boycott British creditors' suits (Scharf, *History of Maryland*, II, 144). In Virginia, Richard Henry Lee had made an unprecedented effort to kill the fee bill on May 10. At least three people in Virginia learned of court-closing proposals *before* learning of the assembly's May 24 resolve or its dissolution. See Henry Fleming to Fisher and Bragg, May 18, 1774, Fleming Letterbook; Carr to Russell, May 26, 1774, Russell Papers, bundle 2; James Parker to Charles Steuart, May 17, 1774, Steuart Papers.

32. Virginia treasurer Robert Carter Nicholas pointed out that the province could continue to receive substantial export income if it simply stopped shipping tobacco to England and Scotland while still "cultivating and raising such Articles, as she is allowed to export to other Markets"—chiefly grain for southern Europe and the West Indies. See "Considerations on the Present State of Virginia Examined," *Revolutionary Virginia*, I, 279; David Klingaman, "The Significance of Grain in the Development of the Tobacco Colonies," *Journal of Economic History*, XXIX (1969), 268–278; Klingaman, "The Development of the Coastwise Trade of Virginia in the Late Colonial Period," *VMHB*, LXXVII (1969), 26–45;

In another departure from Boston's embargo plan, the Virginia convention decided to continue exports to Britain for one more year. That would allow Virginia tobacco farmers to sell the crop that they and their slaves were about to harvest. Meanwhile, British merchants, anticipating the boycott, would stock up on tobacco and drive up its price. Then tobacco farmers would not have to wait until after the boycott to enjoy the benefits of high tobacco prices, as the Lees had proposed. The high prices would come *before* the boycott. With the large incomes that their 1774 crops would bring them, the farmers would be able substantially to reduce their debts to British merchants.[33]

The August 1774 convention called on Virginia farmers not only to stop selling tobacco on August 10, 1775, but also not even to plant a 1775 crop. James Robison noted early in 1775 that the "declaration of the Virginians to leave off the culture of tobacco joined to the non-exportation scheme, seems to have been a wise measure to revise the value of their staple." Robison said the convention's appeal to farmers to grow less tobacco "took its rise as much from the low price tobacco then bore as from the spirit of patriotism." The convention hoped that in 1775 farmers would contribute to the diversification of the Virginia economy by shifting to crops, like cotton, hemp, and flax, that would "form a proper Basis for Manufacturers." Tobacco growers could also do what many other Virginians had already done: shift to grain, which they could profitably export to southern Europe and the West Indies. "If Virginia raises Wheat instead of Tobacco," Edward Rutledge later pointed out, "they will not suffer."[34] Rutledge exaggerated, for nonexportation would

---

Paul G. E. Clemens, *The Atlantic Economy and Colonial Maryland's Eastern Shore: From Tobacco to Grain* (Ithaca, N.Y., 1980), chap. 6. It is true that the grain trade was even more important to Bostonians than to Virginia. But Bostonians were in a position to favor grain nonexportation, since the Boston Port Act had already closed their harbor.

33. Carr to Russell, June 6, 1774, Russell Papers, bundle 2; Robison to Cuninghame and Company, June 7, 1774, in Devine, ed., *Scottish Firm*, 142; Nicholas, "Considerations on the Present State of Virginia Examined," Virginia Convention, "Instructions for the Deputies Appointed to Meet in General Congress on the Part of This Colony," Aug. 6, 1774, both in *Revolutionary Virginia*, I, 238, 278–279. Some Virginians, including several of the Lee brothers, continued to favor halting exports immediately ([Arthur Lee] to Richard Henry Lee, Dec. 6, 1774, Lee Family Papers [1638–1867], section 108). In contrast to the delayed nonexportation plan, a prompt cessation of exports would have brought immediate pressure on Parliament while postponing the economic benefits of nonexportation until after it ended.

34. Robison to Cuninghame and Company, Mar. 31, 1775, in Devine, ed., *Scottish Firm*, 177, 180; Virginia Association, Aug. 6, 1774, *Revolutionary Virginia*, I, 233; ["A Speech by Francis Lightfoot Lee"], [1774?], in Hoffman, ed., *Lee Family Papers*, reel 2, frame 309; Edward Rutledge, ["Notes of Debates in the Continental Congress, 26–27 September 1774"],

disrupt the economy of the Chesapeake in the short term. For instance, Virginia courts closed their doors to domestic as well as British creditors, a policy that displeased many gentlemen. Still, most believed the long-term benefits justified the short-term cost. "Tho' almost every one must feel the Effects of such a stagnation to Trade," Bermudan Henry Tucker declared after reading the Virginia news, "a few years w[oul]d fully recompence them as they w[oul]d in that time introduce Manufactures of their own Sufficient to Supply themselves . . . and whenever Matters Came to be settled their produce (especially Tobacco, Rice and Flax seed) w[oul]d yield a greater price."[35]

The association that the Virginia convention adopted was the model for the Continental Association, adopted by the First Continental Congress on October 18. The Congress made one important change in the boycott that strengthened it as a political weapon while creating some economic hardship for Chesapeake growers: it banned the colonies' lucrative grain trade with the British West Indies. But on the question of when nonexportation should begin, the delegates from the other colonies had to yield to Virginia's desire to delay nonexportation for one year.[36]

What would have happened if Virginia had allowed nonexportation to begin immediately? That would have quickly deprived Britain of its two largest imports, tobacco and sugar. The cutoff of Britain's sugar imports would have been indirect but effective. The thirteen colonies would have stopped sending food, lumber, and other products to the British West Indies. The lumber embargo would have deprived the sugar plantations of the firewood they needed to boil down their sugarcane and the barrels they needed to ship sugar, molasses, and rum to Britain. Meanwhile, the food

---

in L. H. Butterfield, ed., *Diary and Autobiography of John Adams* (Cambridge, Mass., 1961), II, 139. Robert Beverley, who opposed nonexportation, claimed that, when he asked convention delegates why they voted to continue exports to the British West Indies, they pointed out "the Folly of depriving ourselves of a Vent for the Produce of our Lands" (to Landon Carter, Aug. 28, 1774, Landon Carter Papers, item 18, VHS).

35. Henry Tucker to St. George Tucker, July 31, 1774 (typescript), Tucker-Coleman Papers, William and Mary. There were also farmers in other colonies that believed nonexportation would enhance the value of their crops. When loyalist Samuel Seabury tried to discredit this belief, he implicitly acknowledged its prevalence ("A. W. Farmer" [Seabury], *A View of the Controversy between Great-Britain and Her Colonies* . . . [New York, 1774], 36).

36. Samuel A'Court Ashe, *History of North Carolina* (Greensboro, N.C., 1908), I, 422–423; ["Notes of Debates in the Continental Congress, 26–27 September 1774,"] in Butterfield, ed., *Diary of John Adams*, II, 137–140; Virginia Convention, "Instructions for the Deputies Appointed to Meet in General Congress on the Part of This Colony," Aug. 6, 1774, *Revolutionary Virginia*, I, 238.

embargo would have forced sugar growers either to shift their slaves into food production or watch them starve (and possibly rebel). It is just possible that an immediate blow to Britain's tobacco and sugar imports would have forced Parliament to offer the thirteen colonies a deal that they would have accepted. As it was, American exports continued until September 1775, and Britain did not feel any pinch from tobacco nonexportation until early 1776 (when the 1775 crop would normally have begun to arrive). The British West Indies were not affected by the thirteen colonies' food embargo until late in the summer of 1776, when sugar growers normally would have bought much of the mainland colonies' 1776 grain crop.[37] By then, the war had begun, and the thirteen colonies had already declared Independence.

There was one more wrinkle in the nonexportation plan. On October 20, 1774, when the Continental Association was presented to the assembled members of Congress for signing, the South Carolina delegates suddenly balked at the prohibition on rice and indigo exports to Britain. Rice, unlike tobacco, was selling well in 1774.[38] Thus, while tobacco farmers had both economic and political incentives to support nonexportation, the rice growers' only inducement was political. It was not enough. The South Carolinians could see that nonexportation imposed little hardship on their fellow colonists to the north, since most colonies carried on extensive commerce with southern Europe and the foreign West Indies and could continue to do so after the Continental Association went into effect. But Britain was the sole market for South Carolina's indigo and took the greatest part of its rice. The South Carolinians, unwilling to give up the British market, announced they would have nothing to do with the association document that had just been presented to them. They then marched out of Carpenter's Hall.[39]

37. Richard B. Sheridan, "The Crisis of Slave Subsistence in the British West Indies during and after the American Revolution," *WMQ*, 3d Ser., XXXIII (1976), 615–641; Continental Association, Oct. 20, 1774, in Julian P. Boyd et al., eds., *The Papers of Thomas Jefferson* (Princeton, 1950–), I, 151; Jean B. Lee, *The Price of Nationhood: The American Revolution in Charles County* (New York, 1994), 119–120.

38. Anne Bezanson, Robert D. Gray, and Miriam Hussey, *Prices in Colonial Pennsylvania* (Philadelphia, 1935), 422; Arthur Harrison Cole, *Wholesale Commodity Prices in the United States, 1700–1861, Statistical Supplement: Actual Wholesale Prices of Various Commodities* (Cambridge, Mass., 1938), 61–68. One South Carolinian, Christopher Gadsen, approved the rice export ban (David Ammerman, *In the Common Cause: American Response to the Coercive Acts of 1774* [Charlottesville, 1974], 83).

39. The "commodities they usually sent to the mother country were but trifling; and their real trade, would be but little affected by the association," Rutledge said. He estimated that only about 7 percent of the commodities that Philadelphia exported went to the mother country (John Drayton, *Memoirs of the American Revolution, from Its Commence-*

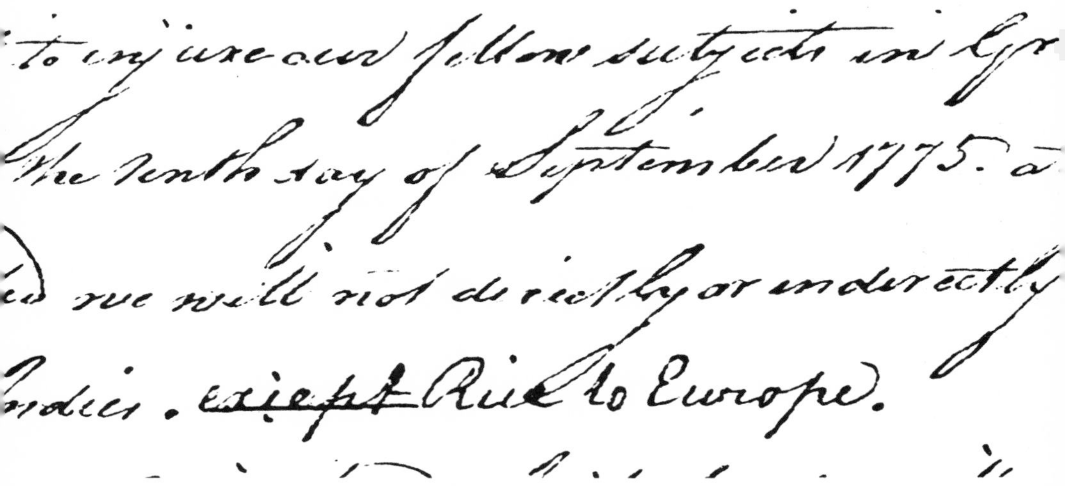
to injure our fellow subjects in Gr
the tenth day of September 1775. a
we will not directly or indirectly
Indies. except Rice to Europe.

FIGURE 9. Article 4, Continental Association. *Note the last-minute addition of the words "except Rice to Europe."* Journals of the Continental Congress, *1774, I. Courtesy, Library of Virginia, Richmond*

The walkout stunned the delegates from the other provinces. First Georgia had refused to send representatives to the Continental Congress, and now here was South Carolina refusing to sign the Continental Association. With neither Lower South colony participating in the association, it could hardly be called "Continental." Congress had no choice but to give in. Someone took up the association document and found some space left at the end of the nonexportation article. Here he hastily wrote, "except Rice to Europe," and everyone present, including the now-enthusiastic South Carolinians, signed the Continental Association.[40] Thus tobacco growers were the only

---

ment to the Year 1776, Inclusive; As Relating to the State of South-Carolina . . . (Charleston, 1821), I, 169–170. On the South Carolinians' disavowal of the association, see Ammerman, *In the Common Cause*, 82–83.

40. The South Carolinians did make one important concession: they gave up their indigo exports. The wording of the last-minute amendment that the South Carolina delegates demanded has led to some confusion among scholars. See the photocopy of the association in the pocket in Worthington Chauncey Ford, ed., *Journals of the Continental Congress, 1774–1789*, I (Washington, D.C., 1904). The last four words of the nonexportation article have often been interpreted as simply permitting the continuation of the rice trade to southern Europe. Actually, the south European rice trade could have continued even if that phrase had been left out, since nonexportation was directed only at the British Empire (Continental Association, Oct. 20, 1774, in Boyd et al., eds., *Papers of Jefferson*, I, 151). The reason Congress used the words "to Europe" was to clarify that rice growers were allowed to send their crops to Britain and Ireland (the "European" part of the British Empire) but not

significant group of American farmers whose exports would be substantially reduced. Nonexportation was a virtually painless protest strategy for farmers outside the Chesapeake—and a rewarding one for tobacco farmers, since they stood to gain by reducing their exports.

V

In part, nonexportation was just what growers said it was: a protest against the anti-American Coercive Acts that Parliament adopted in 1774. But it was also an outgrowth of a crop limitation effort that was more than a century old and of the crop-withholding strategy that tobacco farmers had adopted—for frankly economic reasons—in 1773, when the Chesapeake colonies' relations with Britain were fairly amicable. In theory, farmers could have created a Chesapeake-wide crop-withholding association without claiming to have any but economic motives. But by merging crop withholding into the Continental Association and calling it nonexportation, farmers gave crop withholding a patriotic stamp. Debtors that kept their tobacco out of their creditors' hands did less damage to their credit ratings; their British creditors might disagree with their politics, but that was better than having their creditworthiness questioned. (It will be recalled that Virginians' credit ratings were also protected by nonimportation, which allowed them to reduce their conspicuous consumption without provoking suspicion that their fortunes had decayed.) Patriotic nonexportation also accomplished the goal that some Chesapeake leaders had unsuccessfully pursued in 1773 and early 1774: it drew individual crop withholders into a movement that encompassed the entire Chesapeake. Thus united, farmers could do more than wait for tobacco prices to rise. They could also restrict the world's supply of tobacco and force the price up. Supply reduction schemes work only if they can be enforced, and nonexportation now had that advantage, too. Violators could be ostracized as "Enemies of American Liberty."[41] Just as the Navigation Acts had guaranteed the British merchants' monopoly of Chesapeake tobacco and allowed them to force the price down, the threat of ostracism strengthened nonexportation and ensured that the price of the weed would rise.

---

to the British West Indies. "Rice is the only article which the association allowed to be exported to Great Britain, after 10th September," 1775, the South Carolina Council of Safety stated (to Stephen Drayton and William Ewen, Jan. 1, 1776, in Philip M. Hamer et al., eds., *The Papers of Henry Laurens*, X [Columbia, S.C., 1985], 604). See also Robert M. Weir, "South Carolina: Slavery and the Structure of the Union," in Michael Allen Gillespie and Michael Lienesch, eds., *Ratifying the Constitution* (Lawrence, Kans., 1989), 206.

41. Continental Association, Oct. 20, 1774, in Boyd et al., eds., *Papers of Jefferson*, I, 152.

The most important advantage of the patriots' 1774 nonexportation pro-posal over the crop-withholding scheme that smallholders had begun to employ in 1773 was that it was accompanied by legal immunity for debtors. In fact, the majority of tobacco farmers actually won protection from their creditors even before September 1775. The Virginia courts closed in June 1774, more than a year before nonexportation began. Although Maryland courts did not formally close until September 1775, several county courts in Maryland deliberately stalled their determination of debtors' lawsuits. Scot-tish factor Alexander Hamilton described an incident that was perhaps typical. Just as the Charles County court began its December 1774 session, three members of the county patriot committee burst into the courtroom. The three men demanded that the justices close the court. They failed to gain that point, Hamilton reported: "Notwithstanding they gained another very material one, to have the Court adjourned untill February, which the Jus-tices have been greatly blamed for complying with." The official reason that the Charles County court delayed adjudication of debt suits was to apply pressure to the British government through the medium of British mer-chants.[42] Certainly patriotism was part of the reason. But it is important to remember that the Charles County justices had also adjourned without taking up any debt cases in February 1774—before Parliament passed any of the Coercive Acts. Hamilton's reports on the two decisions of the Charles County court to delay proceedings—first in early 1774, when relations be-tween free Marylanders and the British government were more or less cor-dial, then in the fall of the same year, after imperial relations had deterio-rated—are remarkably similar. Hamilton, in fact, conflated the February 1774 and December 1774 court delays (as well as others) when he complained in August 1775 of the "Many adjourned Courts in Charles County."[43]

42. Hamilton to Brown and Company, Dec. 23, 1774, in Richard K. MacMaster and David C. Skaggs, eds., "The Letterbooks of Alexander Hamilton, Piscataway Factor," pt. II, "1774–1775," *MHM*, LXI (1966), 321. William Fitzhugh also commented on the December 1774 adjournment of the Charles County court: "The Committee of Chas. County I am told, went to the Court whe[n] setting, and order'd them to Adjourn, forbidding them to proceed to any Business but Criminal" (to Russell, Jan. 6, 1775, Russell Papers, bundle 6).

43. Hamilton to Brown and Company, May 28, 1774, in MacMaster and Skaggs, eds., "Letterbooks of Alexander Hamilton," pt. I, "1774," *MHM*, LXI (1966), 159–160; Hamilton to Brown and Company, Aug. 20, 1775, in Richard K. MacMaster and David C. Skaggs, eds., "The Letterbooks of Alexander Hamilton, Piscataway Factor," pt. III, "1775–1776," *MHM*, LXII (1967), 151; Lee, *Price of Nationhood*, 127.

Other Maryland courts also put off trying creditors' suits against their debtors. The Maryland general court canceled its September 1774 session. The official reason was that

The closing of the courts allowed thousands of Virginia debtors that had shied away from the crop-withholding movement to join it and wait for the high prices of 1775. Before the courts closed, traders and factors that reported on crop withholding often qualified their reports by saying that it was only the "independant" farmers—those that were "disengaged" from creditors—that withheld their crops. But, starting in June 1774, these qualifications disappeared from the traders' correspondence.[44] In fact, indebted farm families were in an even stronger bargaining position than their neighbors that owed nothing. Because merchants seeking to collect their debts before exports stopped could not force their debtors to pay up, they had to be tempted with high prices for their tobacco. "I am afraid the nonexportation taking place will induce the Merchants who have outstanding Debts to allow more for Tobacco than the real value of it," Thomas Irving wrote in November 1774. Thus the Virginia smallholders' greatest source of vulnerability in their negotiations with British merchants over the price of their tobacco—their debts to those merchants—became, after June 1774, their greatest source of strength. Early in 1775, James Robison expressed his fear that, with nonexportation imminent, debtors would soon be "extorting a high price for their tobacco."[45]

In calling farmers extortionists, Robison illustrated just how much the balance of power in the trader-smallholder relationship had shifted during

---

many of the lawyers that normally practiced at the court were in Philadelphia attending the First Continental Congress (William Fitzhugh to Russell, Nov. 24, 1774, Russell Papers, bundle 6).

44. In Maryland, where most courts remained open much longer than those in Virginia, traders and factors that reported on crop withholding still sometimes qualified their remarks by saying that they referred only to the independent farmers (Hamilton to Brown and Company, Aug. 6, 1774, in MacMaster and Skaggs, eds., "Letterbooks of Alexander Hamilton," pt. II, "1774–1775," *MHM*, LXI [1966], 309). It is clear from the correspondence of traders and factors that small farmers valued economic independence—freedom from debt—as much as the gentlemen described by Breen in *Tobacco Culture*.

45. Thomas Irving to Neil Jamieson, Nov. 3, 1774, Jamieson Papers, LC; Robison to Cuninghame and Company, Nov. 16, 1774, Jan. 8, 1775, in Devine, ed., *Scottish Firm*, 166, 173; James Forbes to James Russell, Dec. 10, 1774, Russell Papers, bundle 6. On June 7, 1774, as the Virginia courts began to close, trader David Ross predicted that, because there was no "means to compell payment, planters will hold up their commodities till an agreable price shall tempt them to part with it" (Ross to John Hook, June 4, 1774, Hook Papers). Alexander Hamilton reported that the "Many adjourned Courts" in Charles County, Maryland, had "kept the business very backward." "Many who owe live in that County and they have taken advantage of the times," Hamilton said (to Brown and Company, Aug. 20, 1775, in MacMaster and Skaggs, eds., "Letterbooks of Alexander Hamilton," pt. III, "1775–1776," *MHM*, LXII (1967), 151.

1774. Others rang the change as well. In April 1774, trader Charles Yates had described Virginia farmers as "so much indebted to the Merchants that they hardly care which end goes foremost." But, in August 1775, Yates paid tribute to the rising power of the smallholders, stating, "They have as times go all in their own hands."[46]

The buyers' predictions of rising tobacco prices proved to be on the mark. By mid-April 1775, on the eve of the battle of Lexington and Concord, the Petersburg price, which had been 1.8 pence per pound in April 1774, had increased by 67 percent to 3 pence per pound. During the same period, the Northern Neck price rose from 1.5 to as much as 2.7 pence—an increase of 80 percent. Farmers could either accept the high prices offered in Virginia or try for even higher prices in Britain. James Robison found that many farmers, "expecting great prices in Europe," refused to sell their crops in the Chesapeake.[47] The high prices of 1775 finally persuaded growers to deliver their tobacco to the warehouses. They did not bring in just their 1774 crops. They also brought in tobacco that they had grown in 1773 and withheld for more than a year. Some were still hanging on to tobacco they had grown in 1772 and earlier. It all came to the warehouses in 1775. The 1775 tobacco shipment exceeded one hundred million pounds. It was the second largest export in the history of the Chesapeake.[48]

Normally, such a large supply of tobacco coming to market would have brought down the price. But, in 1775, the price not only did not fall but continued to rise, because buyers knew that tobacco shipments would end

46. Yates to Martin, Apr. 2, 1774, to Gale and Fearon, Aug. 29, 1775, Yates Letterbook. Smallholders were variously described as "saucy," "in high Spirits," and so forth (Robert Donald to Patrick Hunter, Apr. 18, 1775, *Buchanan and Milliken v. Robert Donald* [1794], Ended Cases).

47. Robison to Cuninghame and Company, Apr. 16, 1774, May 29, June 5, 1775, in Devine, ed., *Scottish Firm*, 138, 139, 195, 197; Robert Pleasants to Farell and Jones and to Dobson, Daltera, and Walker, Apr. 14, 1775, Pleasants Letterbook, LC; Yates to Martin, Apr. 18, 1775, Yates Letterbook (2.4 pence per pound); Piper to Dixon and Littledale, June 6, 1775, Piper Letterbook; Hamilton to Brown and Company, Aug. 6, Dec. 23, 1774, in MacMaster and Skaggs, eds., "Letterbooks of Alexander Hamilton," pt. II, "1774–1775," *MHM*, LXI (1966), 309, 322. Some tobacco growers did just the opposite; they abandoned their usual practice of selling their tobacco in Britain and instead sold it in Virginia. See Moses Robertson to John Norton and Sons, Aug. 1, 1775, in Frances Norton Mason, ed., *John Norton and Sons, Merchants of London and Virginia: Being the Papers from Their Counting-House for the Years 1750 to 1795* (Richmond, Va., 1937), 382; Robert Polk Thomson, "The Tobacco Export of the Upper James River Naval District, 1773–75," *WMQ*, 3d Ser., XVIII (1961), 400–401.

48. The largest was in 1771; it was a prominent reason the price of tobacco plummeted the following year (Jacob M. Price, *Capital and Credit in British Overseas Trade: The View from the Chesapeake, 1700–1776* [Cambridge, Mass., 1980], 162).

altogether in September. Thus tobacco farmers defied a basic economic law: they advanced the price of their produce even as they increased output.[49] Since price times quantity equals revenue, the surge during 1775 both in the price of Chesapeake tobacco and of the quantity shipped resulted in enormous incomes for Chesapeake tobacco farmers. And it was not only on the revenue side of their ledgers that farmers benefited in 1775. Because nonimportation began on December 1, 1774, the Chesapeake provinces imported goods worth only about two thousand pounds in 1775. Their 1775 trade surplus was thus virtually equal to the value of their exports that year. It was easily the largest in the history of the Chesapeake.[50]

The huge 1775 trade surplus enabled Chesapeake farmers, large and small, to reduce their debts to British merchants. After seeing off the last shipload of tobacco that he sent to his London principals before nonexportation began, Alexander Hamilton told them, "I am in hopes your debts will be considerably reduced by this years Remittance." The valuable 1775 exportation allowed some growers to wipe out their debts altogether. In August 1775, William Anderson informed John Norton, his creditor in London, that his 1775 remittance would "about square the yards with us."[51] Although Richard Champion probably exaggerated when he claimed in 1784 that Americans had reduced their British debt from £6 million to £2 million in 1775, the magnitude of the debt reduction was impressive. The Chesapeake farmers that withheld their crops starting in the spring of 1773 and signed the Continental Association starting late in 1774 had made a bold and successful effort to "revise the value of their staple."[52] Members of the gentry had additional cause for celebration. During the worst months of the recession, small-

49. An economist would say that the tobacco growers only *appeared* to increase sales volume and price-per-pound at the same time. When the sizable volume of tobacco shipped in the twelve months before Sept. 10, 1775, is averaged in with the volume shipped in the twelve months after that date (virtually zero), the total is rather low, and so the accompanying price increase was no surprise.

50. United States Bureau of the Census, *Historical Statistics of the United States, Colonial Times to 1957* (Washington, D.C., 1960), II, 1176–1178.

51. Hamilton to Brown and Company, Sept. 14, 1775, in MacMaster and Skaggs, eds., "Letterbooks of Alexander Hamilton," pt. III, "1775–1776," *MHM*, LXII (1967), 158; Will[iam] Anderson to John Norton and Sons, Aug. 17, 1775, John Norton and Sons Papers, CWF; Thomas Fisher to James Russell, Aug. 27, 1774, Russell Papers, bundle 6; John Dabney, credit report on Thomas Doss, "British Mercantile Claims, 1775–1803," *Virginia Genealogist*, XXV (1981), 36.

52. Richard Champion, *Considerations on the Present Situation of Great Britain and the United States of America* (rev. ed., London, 1784), 269n, in Price, *Capital and Credit*, 8; Robison to Cuninghame and Company, Mar. 31, 1775, in Devine, ed., *Scottish Firm*, 180. For a twentieth-century effort to raise prices by restricting output, see Tracy Campbell, *The Politics of Despair: Power and Resistance in the Tobacco Wars* (Lexington, Ky., 1993).

holders had begun to express deep dissatisfaction with gentry leadership. But when gentlemen took aggressive action against both Parliament and the recession by promulgating the nonexportation plan, they restored harmony between themselves and their fellow tobacco growers. Gentlemen thus transformed a source of conflict into an opportunity to demonstrate their own indispensability.

The evidence presented here casts doubt upon the Progressive historians' claim that free Virginians participated in the American Revolution in order to repudiate their debts. Indeed, a major purpose of nonexportation was to raise the price of tobacco and thus to facilitate debt repayment. Yet the story of nonexportation seems to confirm the more general Progressive notion that economic interests and conflicts helped spark the American Revolution. Chesapeake farmers might not have signed the Continental Association if tobacco had been in demand in 1774. But they could see that the gentry's Continental Association would continue and amplify the crop-withholding strategy that they had initiated a year earlier. So the farmers embraced the gentry's association, and it became one of the vehicles that carried the thirteen colonies into the American Revolution.

PART THREE :

UNINTENDED CONSEQUENCES

1775–1776

At the end of 1774, when copies of the Continental Association arrived in London, many British statesmen believed that the colonists had cut off trade with the mother country as a prelude to increasing their commercial ties with rival European empires, especially France. In the spring of 1775, members of Parliament moved to nip this prospect in the bud. They passed legislation that effectively told Americans (in the words of Sir William Draper), "If you will not trade with us, you shall not trade at all."[1] The New England Restraining Act prohibited southern as well as northern rebel colonies from engaging in even the limited foreign trade they had been permitted under the Navigation Acts. Thus the Continental Association soon led to an unintended consequence—a total suspension of overseas trade. Virginia's economic isolation in turn produced outcomes that few gentlemen could have imagined when they voted to stop trading with Britain.

The Continental Association brought other unexpected results as well. In several Maryland counties and throughout Virginia, an important, if unofficial, component of the nonexportation plan was the partial closure of the county

1. "Viator" [William Draper], *The Thoughts of a Traveller upon Our American Disputes* (London, 1774), 21.

courts. Moderates and loyalists warned that the dismantling of Virginia's governmental machinery would lead to "anarchy." In December 1774, when the patriot committee of Charles County, Maryland, demanded that the county court adjourn without trying any debt cases, the court "thought it most safe and Discreet to obey," trader William Fitzhugh reported. "The Lord grant a speedy End, to this Democratical confusion."[2] These fears were somewhat exaggerated but not entirely unjustified. Even though the county courts continued to handle criminal cases, something was lost when they stopped holding their regular monthly or quarterly meetings—something undefinable that had kept most slaves in awe of free Virginians and most smallholders in awe of the gentry. Although common Virginians' deference or intimidation did not disappear when the courts closed, it diminished enough to frighten many gentlemen.

Like the white Virginians' 1774 decision to cut off trade with Britain, the actions of insurgent slaves and smallholders in 1775 and 1776 would have results that few people could have anticipated. The resistance they mounted starting early in 1775 contributed—inadvertently but powerfully—to the movement for Independence.

2. William Fitzhugh to James Russell, January 6, 1775, Russell Papers at Coutts and Company, bundle 6, VCRP.

He has excited domestic
Insurrections amongst us.
—*Declaration of Independence*

FREE VIRGINIANS

VERSUS SLAVES AND

GOVERNOR DUNMORE

For more than six months after the battle of Lexington and Concord, the fighting between British and patriot troops was confined to the northern colonies. Then, on the morning of October 27, 1775, a squadron of British naval vessels attacked Hampton, Virginia. The Revolutionary War had come to the South. The battle of Hampton resulted partly from the actions of a "small mulatto man" named Joseph Harris. Only four months earlier, Harris had been a resident of Hampton and the property of another Hamptonian, Henry King, whom he served as a pilot on Chesapeake Bay. Harris was reportedly "well acquainted with many creeks on the *Eastern* Shore, at *York, James* River, and *Nansemond*, and many others." All in all, he was "a very useful person."[1]

Harris's knowledge gave him an opportunity to gain his freedom. On June 8, 1775, Virginia's last royal governor, Lord Dunmore, fearing an attack from the increasingly belligerent patriots, fled Williamsburg and took refuge on HMS *Fowey*. There he set about assembling a small squadron to fight the patriots. For that he needed people that knew the bay. So, when Harris

1. Howard H. Peckham, ed., *The Toll of Independence: Engagements and Battle Casualties of the American Revolution* (Chicago, 1974), 9; George Gray, deposition, Sept. 4, 1775, in *Revolutionary Virginia*, IV, 70; George Montague to Matthew Squire, July 20, 1775, in Peter Force, comp., *American Archives: Consisting of a Collection of Authentick Records, State Papers, Debates, and Letters and Other Notices of Publick Affairs . . .* , 4th Ser. (Washington, D.C., 1837–1846), II, 1692.

slipped away one night in July and presented himself to the British, he was welcomed and immediately put to work as a pilot on a schooner called the *Liberty*.

On the night of September 2, 1775, a hurricane swept through tidewater Virginia, driving the *Liberty* ashore near Hampton. On board Harris's ship when it went aground was Matthew Squire, captain of the *Liberty's* mother ship, the *Otter*. Harris obtained a canoe from a slave, and he and Squire managed to get across Hampton Roads to the *Otter*, which was anchored off Norfolk. Meanwhile, the beached *Liberty* fell into the hands of a group of rebels, who helped themselves to the sails, swivel guns, and other equipment and then set the boat ablaze. The *Liberty* "was burnt by the people thereabouts," the *Virginia Gazette* reported, "in return for [Squire's] harbouring gentlemen's negroes, and suffering his sailors to steal poultry, hogs, etc." Captain Squire was furious. He demanded that Hampton at least return the *Liberty's* stores. The rebel committee that ruled the town said it would be happy to comply with the captain's request—as soon as Squire returned Joseph Harris and other black crewmen to their former owners. This Squire refused. A patriot newspaper called Harris Squire's "Ethiopian director" and offered sarcastic praise for his "singular ATTACHMENT AND LOYALTY to his sovereign."[2]

Eventually deciding that the contest could not be resolved peacefully, Squire attacked Hampton on October 27 with several small craft. The little squadron came under deadly rifle fire and had to retreat. A British tender called the *Hawke* ventured too close to the town, and two of its crewmen were mortally wounded. The captain and Joseph Harris plunged from the tender into the chilly river and made it to another of the British boats. For the second time in as many months, Harris had escorted one of his officers to safety. Meanwhile, the *Hawke* was captured. On board were two black men, "1 white woman," and several white men, including Joseph Wilson, an indentured servant that had escaped from George Washington. The white prisoners were "treated with great humanity," a patriot newspaper reported. The black crewmen were "tried for their lives."[3]

2. Purdie's *VG*, Sept. 8, 1775; Dixon and Hunter's *VG*, Sept. 23, 1775; *Otter* muster roll, Admiralty 36/7763 (my thanks to the Public Record Office for providing a photocopy).

3. Purdie's *VG*, Nov. 3, 1775; Dixon and Hunter's *VG*, Oct. 28, 1775; Pinkney's *VG*, Nov. 2, 1775. Washington had purchased Wilson to paint Mount Vernon (Lund Washington to George Washington, Dec. 3, 1775, in W. W. Abbot et al., eds., *The Papers of George Washington*, Revolutionary War Series [Charlottesville, Va., 1985–], II, 479). The *Hawke's* black crewmen were probably sent to the West Indies to be sold (Moss Armistead, petition, May 27, 1784, Virginia Legislative Petitions [Elizabeth City County], LVA).

FIGURE 10. Attack on Hampton. *The battle of Hampton is depicted here. From Mary Tucker Magill,* History of Virginia for the Use of Schools *(Lynchburg, Va., 1890), 188. Courtesy, Virginia Historical Society*

Thomas Jefferson reported that the battle of Hampton "raised our country into perfect phrensy."[4] If Joseph Harris had not made his dash for freedom, or if Captain Squire had not needed his help, Squire and white Hamptonians might not have come to blows at that time.

Joseph Harris was but one of thousands of enslaved Virginians that found opportunity within the breach that opened between loyalist and patriot

---

4. Thomas Jefferson to John Randolph, Nov. 29, 1775, Archibald Cary to Jefferson, Oct. 31, 1775, in Julian P. Boyd et al., eds., *The Papers of Thomas Jefferson* (Princeton, N.J., 1950–), I, 249, 269; Edmund Randolph, *History of Virginia*, ed. Arthur H. Shaffer (Charlottesville, Va., 1970), 227–229. George Montague, captain of the first naval vessel on which Harris served, said Joseph Harris was free (to Matthew Squire, July 20, 1775, in Force, comp.,

whites in 1774. A majority of those that reached British lines ended up worse off than before. Many were recaptured and subjected to worse working conditions than ever, in Chiswell's Mines, which supplied rebel soldiers with lead, or on West Indies sugar plantations. Others were killed in battle, and hundreds died from disease. One casualty was Joseph Harris, who served a year in the Royal Navy and then died on July 19, 1776 (probably from disease) off Charles Island in the northern Chesapeake. In the single year 1776, however, four hundred former slaves sailed away from Virginia to freedom, and thousands more escaped later in the war.[5] One result of the slaves' struggle was political: in seeking their own freedom, black Virginians indirectly helped motivate white Virginians to declare Independence from Britain.

Although in August 1774 most white Virginians were furious at Parliament for adopting the acts they called Intolerable, they were content to express their anger by cutting off trade with Britain. It was a long way from the boycott of 1774 to the Revolution of 1776. What happened during the crucial year 1775 that turned mere boycotters into revolutionaries? White Virginians became angry when the British army invaded far-off Massachusetts, and they surmised that it might invade Virginia, too, sometime in the future. Another

---

American Archives, 4th Ser., II, 1692). This he certainly was when Montague wrote, but the captain's statement implies that Harris was already legally free before he joined the crew of the *Fowey*. Certainly there were free blacks in pre-Revolutionary Hampton, but it is not known whether Harris was one of them. Every other reference to Harris says he was a fugitive slave (Sarah Shaver Hughes, "Elizabeth City County, Virginia, 1782–1810: The Economic and Social Structure of a Tidewater County in the Early National Years" [Ph.D. diss., College of William and Mary, 1975], 32).

5. *Otter* muster book, Adm. 36/7763, July 19, 1776, *Otter* log, Adm. 51/663, VCRP; Benjamin Quarles, *The Negro in the American Revolution* (Chapel Hill, N.C., 1961); Sylvia R. Frey, "Between Slavery and Freedom: Virginia Blacks in the American Revolution," *JSH*, XLIX (1983), 375–398; Frey, *Water from the Rock: Black Resistance in a Revolutionary Age* (Princeton, N.J., 1991); Peter H. Wood, " 'The Dream Deferred': Black Freedom Struggles on the Eve of White Independence," in Gary Y. Okihiro, ed., *In Resistance: Studies in African, Caribbean, and Afro-American History* (Amherst, Mass., 1986), 166–187; Wood, " 'Liberty Is Sweet': African-American Freedom Struggles in the Years before White Independence," in Alfred F. Young, ed., *Beyond the American Revolution: Explorations in the History of American Radicalism* (DeKalb, Ill., 1993), 149–184; Robert A. Olwell, " 'Domestick Enemies': Slavery and Political Independence in South Carolina, May 1775–March 1776," *JSH*, LV (1989), 21–48; Charles W. Carey, Jr., " 'These Black Rascals': The Origins of Lord Dunmore's Ethiopian Regiment," *Virginia Social Sciences Journal*, XXXI (1996), 65–77. For earlier studies of African Americans in the Revolution, see William Tittamin, "The Negro in the American Revolution" (M.A. thesis, New York University, 1939); Herbert Aptheker, *The Negro in the American Revolution* (New York, 1940); Aptheker, *American Negro Slave Revolts* (New York, 1943); Luther P. Jackson, "Virginia Negro Soldiers and Seamen in the American Revolution," *JNH*, XXVII (1942), 247–287.

source of the white Virginians' anger was neither geographically remote nor hypothetical: they were irate at Governor Dunmore for first threatening to ally with enslaved Virginians and then, later, actually doing so.

Neither Dunmore's April 1775 threat to free Virginia's slaves nor his November 1775 proclamation offering freedom to patriots' slaves that joined his army would have carried much significance if black Virginians had remained entirely passive during the Revolutionary crisis. But slaves were not passive. Even before the governor published his proclamation, scores of them had joined his little army. Still earlier, before Dunmore even threatened to offer freedom to the slaves, black workers in different parts of Virginia had gathered to discuss how to take advantage of the growing rift among whites. And the slave resistance of 1774 and 1775 was only the culmination of a tradition of black resistance that was as old as Virginia slavery itself.[6]

I

Afro-Virginians were most often the victims, not the perpetrators, of interracial violence. But they struck back often enough to maintain a permanent undercurrent of fear in the minds of most whites in the Chesapeake. At the same time that the black proportion of the population increased, the proportion of slaves that killed whites also grew.[7]

6. Quarles, *Negro in the Revolution;* Frey, "Between Slavery and Freedom," *JSH*, XLIX (1983); Wood, " 'The Dream Deferred,' " in Okihiro, ed., *In Resistance*, 166–187; Wood, " 'Liberty Is Sweet,' " in Young, ed., *Beyond the Revolution*, 149–184.

7. Philip J. Schwarz, *Twice Condemned: Slaves and the Criminal Laws of Virginia, 1705–1865* (Baton Rouge, La., 1988), ix–x, chap. 6 (esp. 143–144); Richard Bland and William Fleming, petition, Nov. 5, 1764, James Boyd, petition, Nov. 7, 1764, *JHB, 1761–1765*, 237, 239; Daniel Hamlin, petition, Feb. 25, 1772, *JHB, 1770–1772*, 189; Thomas Patterson, petition, May 12, 1774, and public claims committee, report, May 13, 1774, *JHB, 1773–1776*, 92, 98; Augusta County Court, order book, Apr. 11, 1772, in Lyman Chalkley, ed., *Chronicles of the Scotch-Irish Settlement in Virginia, Extracted from the Original Court Records of Augusta County, 1745–1800* (Rosslyn, Va., 1912), I, 167; John Davis, *Travels of Four Years and a Half in the United States of America during 1798, 1799, 1800, 1801, and 1802* (1803; reprint, New York, 1909), 414; Eugene A. Maloney, *A History of Buckingham County* (Waynesboro, Va., 1976), 38; Herbert Clarence Bradshaw, *History of Prince Edward County, Virginia* (Richmond, Va., 1955), 33; Philip D. Morgan, "Slave Life in Piedmont Virginia, 1720–1800," in Lois Green Carr, Philip D. Morgan, and Jean B. Russo, eds., *Colonial Chesapeake Society* (Chapel Hill, N.C., 1988), 441, 455–56; Henry Lee to Richard Lee, Feb. 16, 1767, Richard Bland Lee Letterbook (part of the Custis-Lee Papers), LC; Malcolm H. Harris, *History of Louisa County, Virginia* (Richmond, Va., 1936), 20; Thaddeus W. Tate, *The Negro in Eighteenth-Century Williamsburg* (Charlottesville, Va., 1965), 101–102; David John Mays, *Edmund Pendleton, 1721–1803: A Biography* (Cambridge, Mass., 1952), I, 22, 35; Warren M. Billings, John E. Selby, and Thad W. Tate, *Colonial Virginia: A History* (White Plains, N.Y., 1986), 281;

If individual whites had nightmares about waking up amid flames or feeling the first spasms of a stomach invaded by poison, whites as a group frequently worried about large-scale servile insurrection. Slave plots seemed to be especially rife during the Seven Years' War (1754–1763). In July 1755, Charles Carter reported to Lieutenant Governor Robert Dinwiddie that enslaved workers had gathered near his son's home, possibly with a view to allying with the Native American and French soldiers that had just defeated General Edward Braddock's army near Fort Duquesne (present-day Pitts-burgh). Dinwiddie replied on July 18. "The Villany of the Negroes on any Emergency of Gov't is w[ha]t I always fear'd," he told Carter; "I greatly approve of Y[ou]r send'g the Sheriffs with proper Strength to take up those [tha]t apear'd in a Body at Y[ou]r Son's House." If the slaves were "found guilty of the Expressions mention'd," Dinwiddie said, "an Example of one or two at first may prevent those Creatures enter[in]g into Combinat[ion]s and wicked Designs." Later in the war, Richard Henry Lee told the House of Burgesses that slaves, "from the nature of their situation, can never feel an interest in our cause, because . . . they observe their masters possessed of liberty which is denied to them."[8]

White Virginians became especially alarmed about their slaves during

---

Jack P. Greene, "Society, Ideology, and Politics: An Analysis of the Political Culture of Mid-Eighteenth-Century Virginia," in Greene, Richard L. Bushman, and Michael L. Kammen, *Society, Freedom, and Conscience: The American Revolution in Virginia, Massachusetts, and New York*, ed. Richard M. Jellison (New York, 1976), 68; Gerald W. Mullin, *Flight and Rebellion: Slave Resistance in Eighteenth-Century Virginia* (New York, 1972), 58–59; Freeman H. Hart, *The Valley of Virginia in the American Revolution, 1763–1789* (Chapel Hill, N.C., 1942), 15; *SAL*, VI, 104–112.

8. Dinwiddie advised Carter to keep "Patrollers out for the Peace of Y[ou]r Co[un]ty" and instruct undersheriffs to "seize all Horses used by Negroes in the Night Time" (Dinwiddie to Charles Carter, July 18, 1755, in R. A. Brock, ed., *The Official Records of Robert Dinwiddie . . .* [Richmond, Va., 1883–1884], II, 102–103). After Braddock's defeat, Dinwiddie refused to send all available troops to fight the Indians. "I must leave a proper number in each county to protect it from the combinations of the negro slaves, who have been very audacious in the defeat on the Ohio" (W. Robert Higgins, "The Ambivalence of Freedom: Whites, Blacks, and the Coming of the Revolution in the South," in Higgins, ed., *The Revolutionary War in the South: Power, Conflict, and Leadership: Essays in Honor of John Richard Alden* [Durham, N.C., 1979], 54–55). See also Mark J. Stegmaier, "Maryland's Fear of Insurrection at the Time of Braddock's Defeat," *MHM*, LXXI (1976), 467–483; Wood, " 'Liberty Is Sweet,' " in Young, ed., *Beyond the Revolution*, 154; undated speech, in Richard Henry Lee, *Memoir of the Life of Richard Henry Lee, and His Correspondence with the Most Distinguished Men in America and Europe . . .* (Philadelphia, 1825), I, 18; Aptheker, *American Negro Slave Revolts*, 18–208; Tate, *Negro in Williamsburg*, 205–207; Theodore Allen, " '. . . They Would Have Destroyed Me': Slavery and the Origins of Racism," *Radical America*, IX (1975), 56; Schwarz, *Twice Condemned*, 171, 175; Mays, *Edmund Pendleton*, I, 119–120.

Pontiac's Rebellion. For the first time in recent memory, Indians spared the lives of blacks at the settlements they attacked; gentlemen wondered why. "As the Indians are saving and Carressing all the Negroes they take," militia lieutenant William Fleming told Governor Fauquier in July 1763, "should it be productive of an Insurrection it may be attended with the most serious Consequences." The following month, a Virginia clergyman reported that the rebel Indians had "carried a great number of women and children, as well as some men, and (for the first time too) a good many negroes, into captivity."[9]

Although the slave-Indian alliance that so frightened white Virginians never materialized, black workers continued to meet to plan insurrections after Pontiac's Rebellion. A group in Loudoun County revolted in early 1767 and killed an overseer named Dennis Dallis. Three of them were hanged. In neighboring Fairfax County that same year, a group of enslaved workers poisoned several overseers. "Some of the negroes have been taken up, four of whom were executed about three weeks ago, after which their heads were cut off, and fixed on the chimnies of the court-house," a Boston newspaper reported, "and it was expected that four more would soon meet with the same fate." Frederick County slaves also reportedly plotted a rebellion in the 1760s. In Stafford County in May 1769, some of John Knox's slaves "barbarously murdered" him. Suspicion fell on two fugitives named Phill and Winny, and Knox's brothers offered a reward of £105 for their capture and conviction. Within a month, both had been apprehended and put to death, along with one of the "house wenches," who had not initially been a suspect in her master's death. Around Christmas of the same year, the slaves on Bowler Cocke's plantation in nearby Hanover County attacked the steward, his assistant, and a neighbor, beating each severely. When a band of whites arrived to suppress the rebellion, Cocke's slaves "rushed upon them with a desperate fury, armed with clubs and staves." The whites saved themselves by shooting dead two of the rebels and nearly decapitating a third.[10]

9. William Fleming to Francis Fauquier, July 26, 1763, in George Reese, ed., *The Official Papers of Francis Fauquier, Lieutenant Governor of Virginia, 1758–1768* (Charlottesville, Va., 1980–1983), II, 998; Peter Fontaine to Moses and John Fontaine and Daniel Torin, Aug. 7, 1763, in Ann Maury, trans. and comp., *Memoirs of a Huguenot Family . . .* (New York, 1853), 372; Benjamin Johnston, advertisement, Rind's *VG*, Dec. 16, 1773. For a March 1755 effort by the South Carolina legislature to promote enmity between Indians and slaves, see Wood, " 'Liberty Is Sweet,' " in Young, ed., *Beyond the Revolution*, 154.

10. *Boston Chronicle*, Jan. 11–18, 1768; Aptheker, *American Negro Slave Revolts*, 198–199; Mar. 23, 24, 1767, Nov. 23, 1769, *JHB, 1766–1769*, 91, 93, 286; Schwarz, *Twice Condemned*, 146–147; Robert Knox and Willim Knox, advertisement, news item, both in Rind's *VG*, June 15, July 20, 1769; Rind's *VG*, Jan. 25, 1770. Although the discussion above, which documents

As Lieutenant Governor Dinwiddie had said in 1755, "any Emergency" that divided white Americans could give blacks the opportunity to launch rebellions. The American Revolution was such an emergency. "In one of our Counties lately," James Madison reported in November 1774, "a few of those unhappy wretches met together and chose a leader who was to conduct them when the English Troops should arrive." Enslaved workers in other colonies also met to discuss how to take advantage of the imperial conflict. In St. Andrew Parish, Georgia, slaves rebelled in December 1774 and killed four whites before being captured and burned alive. An account of a New York plot appeared in the *Virginia Gazette*s in mid-March, 1775; it had been discovered when a white man overheard two enslaved conspirators discussing how to obtain more gunpowder and shot.[11]

The fears that these plots induced in white Virginians were heightened by the rumor that the British government might encourage slave insurrections as a way of suppressing the patriot movement. Ever since Francis Drake's raids against Spanish ports in the Caribbean in the 1570s, Englishmen had occasionally made common cause with their enemies' slaves. In the fall of 1774, William Draper, who had just returned to London from an extended tour of America, published a pamphlet arguing that one way to put down the patriot rebellion would be to "Proclame *Freedom* to their Negroes." Arthur Lee, who was living in London, had obtained a copy of Draper's pamphlet by early December 1774, when he mentioned Draper's "proposal for emancipating your Negroes by royal Proclamation and arming them against you" to his brothers in Virginia. Lee claimed the plan "meets with approbation from ministerial People." James Madison heard in early 1775 that a slave emancipation bill had been introduced in Parliament. No such bill has been found, but Edmund Burke noted (in his March 1775 speech "On Conciliation with the Colonies") that many progovernment members favored "a general enfranchisement of [the] slaves." During the spring of 1775, many Virginians believed that those proposals were about to be implemented. According to a House of Burgesses report, British officials contem-

---

white fears, focuses on violent means by which slaves sought their freedom, it should be noted that not all slaves that struck out for freedom in the pre-Revolutionary era used violence. Several slaves that learned about the *Somerset* decision, in which Lord Mansfield had attempted to outlaw slavery in the British Isles, tried to reach England (Wood, " 'Dream Deferred,' " in Okihiro, ed., *In Resistance*, 169). Also, several enslaved Virginians tried to sue for their freedom during this period (Duncan J. MacLeod, *Slavery, Race, and the American Revolution* [London, 1974], 109–111).

11. Madison to William Bradford, Jr., Nov. 26, 1774, in William T. Hutchinson et al., eds., *The Papers of James Madison* (Chicago and Charlottesville, Va., 1962–), I, 130; Wood, " 'Liberty Is Sweet,' " in Young, ed., *Beyond the Revolution*, 161–163.

plated "a Scheme, the most diabolical," to "offer Freedom to our Slaves, and turn them against their Masters." A similar accusation was made in an anonymous letter that appeared in Alexander Purdie's *Virginia Gazette* in June. The writer alluded to recent slave plot rumors and then added: "From some hints, it was inferred that the negroes had not been without encouragement from a Gentleman of the Navy"—probably Captain Henry Colins, whose HMS *Magdalen* patrolled the Chesapeake in those months.[12]

Without waiting for British "encouragement," several groups of slaves in the James River watershed reportedly assembled to plan rebellions during the third week of April 1775 (see Figure 11). On April 15, 1775, a Prince Edward County slave named Toney was charged with insurrection and conspiracy to commit murder; he received fifteen lashes. Three days later, whites in nearby Chesterfield County were "alarm'd for an Insurrection of the Slaves," trader Robert Donald reported. Slave patrols were usually somewhat lax in Virginia, but the Chesterfield patrol was now quickly revived. "We Patrol and go armed—a dreadful enemy," Donald wrote on April 18. Three more days passed. Then "Sentence of death [was] passed upon two Negroes . . . tried at Norfolk, for being concerned in a conspiracy to raise an insurrection in that town," the *Virginia Gazette* reported. One of the Norfolk conspirators was named Emanuel, and he was the property of Matthew Phripp, the militia lieutenant for Norfolk County. The other's name was Emanuel de Antonio, and before resorting to rebellion he had tried to obtain his freedom by legal

12. Edmund S. Morgan, *American Slavery, American Freedom: The Ordeal of Colonial Virginia* (New York, 1975), 9–42; "Viator" [William Draper], *The Thoughts of a Traveller upon Our American Disputes* (London, 1774), 21; Arthur Lee to Richard Henry Lee, Dec. 6, 1774, Lee Family Papers (1638–1867), section 108, VHS; William Bradford, Jr., to James Madison, Jan. 4, 1775, in Hutchinson et al., eds., *Papers of James Madison*, I, 132; Edmund Burke, speech on conciliation with the colonies, Mar. 22, 1775, in Burke, *Speeches and Letters on American Affairs* (London, 1908), 102; House of Burgesses, address to Dunmore, June 19, 1775, *JHB, 1773–1776*, 256; anonymous letter, Purdie's *VG*, June 16, 1775; Jack P. Greene, ed., *The Diary of Colonel Landon Carter of Sabine Hall, 1752–1778* (Charlottesville, Va., 1965), II, 959; Virginia Convention, "Declaration of the Delegates," Aug. 26, 1775, in *Revolutionary Virginia*, III, 501; Frey, *Water from the Rock*, 55–56; Schwarz, *Twice Condemned*, 181–182. The rumor that the British government intended to arm enslaved Americans against their masters circulated in other colonies as well. During the critical month of April 1775, Philadelphia Quaker James Kenny reported that "a great Woman in London" had written a Philadelphian, saying several members of the House of Lords had informed her of a "secret Plan": "arms" were "to be given to all . . . the Negros to act against the Collonies." See Kenny to Humphry Marshall, Apr. 25, 1775 (typescript), Marshall Papers, William L. Clements Library, University of Michigan, Ann Arbor (my thanks to Rob Cox for bringing this document to my attention); Henry Cruger to Ralph Izard, Mar. 21, 1775, *Correspondence of Mr. Ralph Izard, of South Carolina . . .* (New York, 1844), 58.

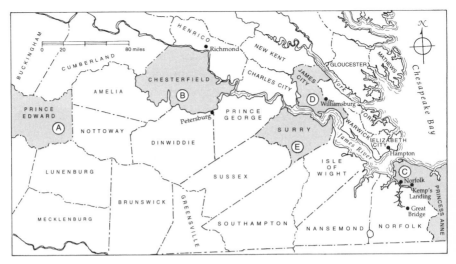

FIGURE 11. Rumors of Slave Plots in the James River Watershed, April 15–April 21, 1775. A. April 15. Prince Edward County. A slave named Toney is charged with insurrection. B. April 18. Chesterfield County. White inhabitants are "alarm'd for an Insurrection of the Slaves." C. April 21. Norfolk. Two slaves, Emanuel and Emanuel de Antonio, are convicted of leading a slave revolt. D. April 21. Williamsburg. Edmund Pendleton reports "some disturbances in the City, by the *Slaves*." E. April 21. Surry County. Dunmore and the Williamsburg town council say slaves in a nearby county (later identified as Surry) have conspired to rebel. *Drawn by Richard Stinely*

means. In March 1771, Antonio, who was owned by the trading house of James Campbell and Company, had sued the firm for his freedom. He claimed he was "a free born subject of his catholic majesty"—the king of Spain. Although in those years several enslaved Virginians secured their freedom by establishing in court an unbroken line of female ancestors extending back to an Indian woman (who could not have been legally enslaved after 1705), Emanuel de Antonio's suit was unsuccessful, and he remained a slave. The two Emanuels do not complete the list of slaves that were accused of rebellion that week. On April 21, the very day that they were sentenced to die, Edmund Pendleton reported that the free half of Williamsburg's population had been frightened by "some disturbances in the City, by the *Slaves*."[13]

13. Michael Lee Nicholls, "Aspects of the African-American Experience in Eighteenth-Century Williamsburg and Norfolk" (report prepared for CWF, October 1990), 69–70; Peter Wallenstein, "Indian Foremothers: Race, Sex, Slavery, and Freedom in Early Virginia," in Catherine Clinton and Michelle Gillespie, eds., *The Devil's Lane: Sex and Race in the Early South* (New York, 1997), 62–68; Schwarz, *Twice Condemned*, 182, 184; Robert Donald to Patrick Hunter, Apr. 18, 1775, *Buchanan and Milliken v. Robert Donald* (1794), U.S. Circuit

It is possible that the two Emanuels in Norfolk and Toney in Prince Edward County were not in touch with each other, with the Williamsburg plotters, or with those in Chesterfield County. Inevitably, though, many white Virginians believed that the alleged occurrence of four slave conspiracies in different parts of the James River watershed during the same week— the largest number in such a short time before Gabriel's conspiracy in 1800— was no coincidence. They believed that what they were facing was not just a few scattered outbreaks but a coordinated attack. "There was a suspicion" that spring "of the Negroes having formed a conspiracy," a group of Virginia traders later recalled. Edward Stabler, a Williamsburg Quaker, would note in May that "There hath been many Rumours here of the Negroes intending to Rise." Although Stabler considered the rumor of a wide-ranging slave conspiracy "without much foundation," it was real enough to terrify many of his fellow whites. An anonymous newspaper essayist stated in June that "various reports of internal insurrections" had circulated during the spring. "Whether this was general, or who were the instigators, remains as yet a secret," he said.[14]

I I

It was in this context of rising aspirations among blacks and mounting fears among whites that Governor Dunmore decided to put Virginia's major ammunition cache out of the reach of patriot militiamen. Early on Friday morning, April 21, 1775, he had a detachment from HMS *Magdalen* remove

---

Court, Virginia District, Ended Cases (restored), LVA. Although charged with insurrection, Toney of Prince Edward County was only convicted of a misdemeanor. See Dixon and Hunter's *VG*, Apr. 29, 1775 (supplement); Edmund Pendleton to George Washington, Apr. 21, 1775, in David John Mays, ed., *The Letters and Papers of Edmund Pendleton, 1734–1803* (Charlottesville, Va., 1967), I, 102. My thanks to Michael Nicholls for biographical information on Emanuel de Antonio.

14. Edward Stabler to Israel Pemberton, May 16, 1775, Pemberton Papers, XXVII, 144, Historical Society of Pennsylvania, Philadelphia; anonymous letter, Purdie's *VG*, June 16, 1775; unnamed merchants, replies to questions in Archibald Cary to James Lyle et al., June 12, 1775, C.O. 5/1353, 401, P.R.O., VCRP; Hugh Hamilton, deposition, in Committee on the Late Disturbances, report, June 14, 1775, *JHB, 1773–1776*, 234.

Were the white Virginians that suspected a connection among the various slave conspiracies in the James River watershed in April 1775 in fact correct? Certainly a conspiracy this extensive was possible. Twenty-five years later, in 1800, organizers of Gabriel's conspiracy managed to recruit clusters of supporters in counties throughout the tidewater and piedmont sections of Virginia. See Mullin, *Flight and Rebellion*, 140–163; Philip J. Schwarz, "Gabriel's Challenge: Slaves and Crime in Late Eighteenth-Century Virginia," *VMHB*, XC (1982), 283–309; Douglas R. Egerton, *Gabriel's Rebellion: The Virginia Slave Conspiracies of 1800 and 1802* (Chapel Hill, N.C., 1993).

fifteen half-barrels of gunpowder from the colonial powder magazine in the center of Williamsburg and secure them in the warship. Many white Virginians believed that the governor's timing was no coincidence—that he intentionally removed the powder amid the swirl of insurrection rumors in order to abandon whites to the fury of their slaves. Years later, Edmund Randolph, who had lived in Williamsburg in April 1775, pronounced the removal of the powder "not far removed from assassination." He said the governor "designed, by disarming the people, to weaken the means of opposing an insurrection of the slaves . . . for a protection against whom in part the magazine was at first built."[15]

In 1774, Governor Dunmore had led an attack against the Shawnee and Mingo nations that forced them to cede Kentucky and the region east of the Ohio River to Virginia. In March 1775, a patriot convention unanimously praised the governor "for his truly noble, wise and spirited Conduct on the late Expedition against our Indian Enemy." As late as April 20, despite the anti-British currents sweeping over the American colonies, Dunmore remained what Norfolk merchant James Parker pronounced him in January 1775, upon hearing that the governor had just named his new daughter "Virginia": "as popular as a Scotsman can be among weak prejudiced people." Overnight, the removal of the gunpowder turned him into a villain. By dawn on the morning the powder was removed, most of white Williamsburg gathered on the town green near the governor's palace. Many carried weapons. The people in the crowd meant to force the governor to return the gunpowder, but they agreed to stand down while the town council and provincial leaders first gave Dunmore a chance to give up the powder peacefully. A delegation met with him and surprised everyone by agreeing to let the powder stay on board the *Magdalen*. Returning to the green, the leaders persuaded the crowd to disperse.[16]

Williamsburg lapsed into "perfect tranquility." But then "a Report was spread by his Excellency's throwing out some threats respecting the Slaves." The report was true. On April 22, the day after he removed the gunpowder,

15. Randolph, *History of Virginia*, ed. Shaffer, 219; Sussex County committee, May 8, 1775, proceedings, Aug. 25, 1775, Virginia Convention, "Declaration of the Delegates," Aug. 26, 1775, in *Revolutionary Virginia*, III, 107, 488, 501; Dunmore to William Legge, Lord Dartmouth, May 1, 1775, in K. G. Davies, ed., *Documents of the American Revolution, 1770–1783* (Shannon, Ireland, 1972–1981), IX, 109; John E. Selby, *The Revolution in Virginia, 1775–1783* (Charlottesville, Va., 1988), 2.

16. Mar. 25, 1775, in *Revolutionary Virginia*, II, 376; James Parker to Charles Steuart, Jan. 27, 1775, Steuart Papers, National Library of Scotland, Edinburgh (microfilm at LVA); Selby, *Revolution in Virginia*, 1–2.

FIGURE 12. Williamsburg Gunpowder Magazine.
Courtesy, Colonial Williamsburg Foundation

Dunmore reignited the crisis. In an effort to discourage patriot violence, he gave Dr. William Pasteur, a member of the Williamsburg town council, a message for Peyton Randolph, the speaker of the House of Burgesses: If any senior British official was harmed, Dunmore "would declare freedom to the slaves and reduce the City of Wmsburg to ashes."[17]

Now it became clear what had probably prompted Speaker Randolph and other white leaders to back off so quickly from their April 21 demand that Dunmore immediately return the gunpowder. They did not want to provoke him to employ a weapon far more lethal than fifteen half-barrels of ammunition: the more than 180,000 Virginians that were enslaved. In Williamsburg, the town fathers doubled the nightly slave patrol. In Amelia County, the patriot committee, fearful "for the internal security of the county," ordered "that patrollers in every neighbourhood be constantly kept on duty."[18]

17. John Dixon, deposition, in Committee on the Late Disturbances, report, June 14, 1775, *JHB, 1773–1776*, 233; Randolph, *History of Virginia*, ed. Shaffer, 220; "Deposition of Dr. William Pasteur. In Regard to the Removal of Powder from the Williamsburg Magazine," *VMHB*, XIII (1905), 49.

18. Peter H. Wood, "The Changing Population of the Colonial South: An Overview by Race and Region, 1685–1790," in Peter H. Wood, Gregory A. Waselkov, and M. Thomas Hatley, eds., *Powhatan's Mantle: Indians in the Colonial Southeast* (Lincoln, Nebr., 1989), 38;

Dunmore's suspiciously timed removal of the gunpowder and his threat to free the slaves coincided with the decision of Massachusetts governor (and American commander in chief) Thomas Gage to send troops to Concord to seize patriot military stores—especially gunpowder. White colonists imagined a ministerial plot to disarm them, and the government had, in fact, ordered royal governors to prevent the patriots from obtaining war matériel. Although the battle of Lexington and Concord was destined to receive much more attention than the events in Virginia, it was clear at the time that in the slave provinces the government's effort to disarm the patriots carried the greatest danger.

Now white Virginians debated how best to respond. Provincial leaders in Williamsburg believed the safest strategy was to avoid antagonizing Dunmore. In the countryside, however, independent military companies mustered and prepared to march to the capital. At least seven counties that had not yet formed independent companies now hastily did so. Although the battle of Lexington and Concord was clearly one reason that so many white Virginians turned their attention to military preparedness at this time, they were also concerned about events in their own colony. The Sussex County committee said the reason it had formed an independent company was that the removal of the gunpowder had made it not only justifiable but "absolutely necessary that this county be put into the best posture of defence possible." More than six hundred members of independent companies converged on Fredericksburg by April 29 and made ready to march south to the capital. Among their goals, a Virginia historian recalled many years later, was "to seize the governor and crush at once the seeds of insurrection."[19]

The men that gathered for the march to Williamsburg no doubt expected whites in the capital to be comforted to hear that help was on the way.

Benjamin Waller and John Dixon, depositions, in Committee on the Late Disturbances, report, June 14, 1775, *JHB, 1773–1776*, 232–233; May 3, 1775, in *Revolutionary Virginia*, III, 83.

19. Sussex County committee, resolutions, in *Revolutionary Virginia*, III, 107; John Burk et al., *The History of Virginia, from Its First Settlement to the Present Day* (Petersburg, Va., 1804–1805), III, 410; Archibald Cary to James Lyle et al., June 12, 1775, C.O. 5/1353, 400; Randolph, *History of Virginia*, ed. Shaffer, 220. The counties that formed independent companies in the wake of the gunpowder removal were Mecklenburg, New Kent, Chesterfield, Louisa, Essex, Henrico, and Nansemond. See James Lyle and Robert Donald, Thomas Mitchell, Archibald Ritchie, Archibald Bryce, Andrew Sprowle, et al., depositions, in Committee on the Late Disturbances, report, June 14, 1775, *JHB, 1773–1776*, 234–237; New Kent County committee, May 3, 1775, Mecklenburg County committee, May 8, 1775, in *Revolutionary Virginia*, III, 85, 105; Mays, *Edmund Pendleton*, II, 353n; Dale E. Benson, "Wealth and Power in Virginia, 1774–1776: A Study of the Organization of Revolt" (Ph.D. diss., University of Maine, 1970), 173.

Actually, they were terrified. The moment provincial treasurer Robert Carter Nicholas and speaker Peyton Randolph learned that the independent companies had gathered, they began "writing letters over all the country to prevent those meetings," according to Norfolk trader James Parker. Randolph warned the Fredericksburg encampment that "violent measures may produce effects, which God only knows the consequences of." Randolph's fears were not unfounded. On April 28, the day after Dunmore learned that the independent companies intended to march against him, he reiterated his threat to raise the slaves. The governor drew a line in the sandy tidewater soil, telling Dr. Pasteur that "if a large Body of People came below *Ruffin's Ferry* (a place about thirty Miles from this City), that he would immediately enlarge his plan and carry it into execution." If any whites had dared to hope that Dunmore's earlier threat to free the slaves had been only the product of momentary passion, he now set them straight. During "this alarming crisis," a group of Williamsburg slave patrollers said, "even the whispering of the wind was sufficient to rouze their fears." The governor underscored that he would not strike the first blow; Pasteur reported that he "more than once did say he should not carry these Plans into Execution unless he was attacked."[20]

Fearful gentry leaders managed to persuade most of the independent volunteer companies to disband. Most, but not all. The Albemarle County volunteers voted on April 29 to march to Williamsburg "to demand satisfaction of Dunmore for the powder, and his threatening to fix his standard and call over the negroes," the company's first lieutenant noted. Apparently, the Albemarle company had second thoughts and turned back, but a company from Hanover County, led by Patrick Henry, voted on May 2 to march on.[21]

20. James Parker said Nicholas had found "it more difficult to extinguish a flame than kindle it." See Parker to Charles Steuart, Norfolk, May 6–7, 1775, Steuart Papers; Randolph and the Corporation of the City of Williamsburg to Mann Page, Jr., Lewis Willis, and Benjamin Grymes, Jr., Apr. 27, 1775, in *Revolutionary Virginia*, III, 64; William Pasteur, deposition, June 14, 1775, *JHB, 1773–1776*, 231; "Intelligence Extraordinary," Pinkney's *VG*, May 4, 1775; Dunmore to Dartmouth, May 1, 1775, in Davies, ed., *Documents of the American Revolution*, IX, 109; Frederick County committee, June 19, 1775, in *Revolutionary Virginia*, III, 209; James Madison to William Bradford, Jr., May 9, 1775, in Hutchinson et al., eds., *Papers of James Madison*, I, 145; Charles Campbell, *History of the Colony and Ancient Dominion of Virginia* (Philadelphia, 1860), 609.

21. George Gilmer notebook, Albemarle County independent company, [Apr. 29, 1775], both in *Revolutionary Virginia*, III, 52n, 69–70; Pinkney's *VG*, June 30, 1775. It has generally been believed that the Hanover men sought only the return of the gunpowder to the Williamsburg munitions depot. But Hanover's patriot committee said the men marched to Williamsburg because they had heard that white inhabitants of the capital felt "apprehension for their persons and property." See Hanover County committee, May 9, 1775, in

As Henry's group headed toward Williamsburg, "some Negroes" went to the governor's palace and "offered their Service," Attorney General John Randolph reported. The governor turned them away, but he told Randolph that if Henry's group attacked him and "Negroes on that Occasion offered their Service they would be received." On May 3, Dunmore issued a proclamation reminding free Virginians of their "internal weakness"—their vulnerability to slave and Indian uprisings. He assured colonists that he would "avail myself of any means" necessary to restore his authority. Meanwhile, he "armed his servants, together with the Shawanese hostages" that had been handed over to him at the end of the autumn 1774 Indian war, as historian John Burk later reported. For the next few days, "Parties of negroes mounted guard every night at the [governor's] palace," Burk wrote. In this context, it was natural for the Sussex County patriot committee to read Dunmore's May 3 proclamation as a threat to expose free Virginians "to the attacks of a savage invasion, or a domestick foe." Now the governor was threatening to ally with Indians as well as slaves! Dunmore's proclamation was probably interpreted in the same way by Patrick Henry, and it might have helped persuade Henry and Receiver General Richard Corbin to reach a face-saving compromise in which Corbin paid Henry for the gunpowder—which remained on board the *Magdalen*.[22]

The powder magazine incident is one of those chestnuts of Virginia history. It is significant because it was the first time since Bacon's Rebellion in 1676 that a large number of Virginians had taken up arms to attack a royal governor, and even more because it served "to widen the unhappy breach between Great Britain and her colonies," as the soldiers encamped at Fredericksburg declared. While the Hanover independent company marched toward Williamsburg in the midst of the crisis, Patrick Henry observed that "it was a fortunate circumstance, which would rouse the people from North to South."[23]

Revolutionary Virginia, III, 111; Archibald Govan et al., deposition, in Committee on the Late Disturbances, report, June 14, 1775, *JHB, 1773–1776*, 236; "A True Patriot," May 11, 1775, in *Revolutionary Virginia*, III, 117; George Dabney to William Wirt, May 14, 1805, Patrick Henry Papers, LC; Campbell, *History of the Colony*, 612.

22. John Randolph, Benjamin Waller, depositions, in Committee on the Late Disturbances, report, June 14, 1775, *JHB, 1773–1776*, 231; Dunmore, proclamation, May 3, 1775, Pinkney's *VG*, May 4, 1775; Burk et al., *History of Virginia*, III, 407, 409; Sussex County committee, resolutions, May 8, 1775, in *Revolutionary Virginia*, III, 107; "Intelligence Extraordinary," Pinkney's *VG*, May 4, 1775; Selby, *Revolution in Virginia*, 4; Randolph, *History of Virginia*, ed. Shaffer, 220.

23. Fredericksburg encampment, Apr. 29, 1775, in *Revolutionary Virginia*, III, 71; Henry,

Henry and his comrades would have been surprised at the widespread modern notion that the only reason they were angry at their governor was that he had removed the gunpowder. A group of Hanover County traders stated that the political ferment that Dunmore caused was "heightened and encreased by his threatening to enfranchise the Slaves." Benjamin Waller, a member of Williamsburg's patriot committee, informed the governor that he had forfeited "the Confidence of the People not so much for having taken the Powder as for the declaration he made of raising and freeing the Slaves." Dunmore himself boasted that his "declaration that I would arm and set free such slaves as should assist me if I was attacked has stirred up fears in them which cannot easily subside."[24]

The looming presence of an enslaved and potentially rebellious workforce guaranteed an intensely hostile white reaction not only to Dunmore's emancipation threat but also to his decision to remove the gunpowder. The editor of a South Carolina newspaper believed that the governor's odd timing—he took the ammunition at the end of a week when rumors of slave revolts had poured into Williamsburg from up and down the James River—was deliberate. "The monstrous absurdity that the Governor can deprive the people of the necessary means of defense at a time when the colony is actually threatened with an insurrection of their slaves," the *South-Carolina Gazette; And Country Journal* reported, "has worked up the passions of the people there

---

in George Dabney to William Wirt, May 14, 1805, Patrick Henry Papers; Gloucester County committee, Apr. 26, 1775, New Kent County committee, May 3, 1775, Orange County committee, May 9, 1775, Richmond County committee, May 12, 1775, Mecklenburg County committee, May 13, 1775, all in *Revolutionary Virginia*, III, 61, 85, 112, 121, 124; "Civis," "Brutus," Purdie's *VG*, May 26, 1775 (supplement), Aug. 4, 1775 (supplement). On April 20, the day before Dunmore removed the gunpowder, Robert Munford had said that he intended to ask the voters of his county to endorse a loyalist address that he had written. After learning of the gunpowder incident and Dunmore's threat to free the slaves, Munford decided not to present his loyalist petition. In fact, he ultimately became a major in the patriot army (Munford to William Byrd III, Apr. 20, 1775, in Marion Tinling, ed., *The Correspondence of the Three William Byrds of Westover, Virginia, 1684–1776* [Charlottesville, Va., 1977], II, 806, 806n).

24. Benjamin Waller, Archibald Govan et al., depositions, both in Committee on the Late Disturbances, report, June 14, 1775, *JHB, 1773–1776*, 232, 236; Dunmore to Dartmouth, June 25, 1775, in Davies, ed., *Documents of the American Revolution*, IX, 204; Mays, *Edmund Pendleton*, II, 13–14. Louisa County trader Thomas Mitchell noted "that the Governor's Declaration to give Freedom to the Slaves greatly inflamed the Minds of those who believed it," although not everyone did. See deposition, in Committee on the Late Disturbances, report, June 14, 1775, *JHB, 1773–1776*, 234; "Deposition of Dr. Pasteur," *VMHB*, XIII (1905), 50 (resolution at foot); Randolph, *History of Virginia*, ed. Shaffer, 220; Ivor Noël Hume, *1775: Another Part of the Field* (New York, 1966), 146–147.

FIGURE 13. John Murray, Fourth Earl of Dunmore.
Courtesy, Virginia Historical Society

almost to a frenzy." The Fredericksburg encampment also considered Dunmore's decision suspiciously "ill timed."[25]

The possibility must be considered that patriot writers deliberately exaggerated the likelihood of a slave insurrection in order to heap further odium upon their governor. Actually, though, the white Virginians that said they feared a slave revolt seem to have been telling the truth. James Robison, a staunch loyalist, agreed with patriots that "an insurrection . . . was dreaded" in Virginia during the spring of 1775. Although patriot writers sometimes exaggerated evidence of black resistance, they just as often withheld it. In November 1774, when James Madison told a fellow Princeton alumnus that some of his enslaved neighbors had met to discuss how to take advantage of an expected British invasion, he judged it "prudent such attempts should be concealed as well as suppressed." A year later, when editor John Pinkney printed a letter from South Carolina in his *Virginia Gazette*, he omitted part of it. "This letter goes on farther," Pinkney informed his readers, "and relates a great deal about the negroes in South Carolina; but we think it prudent to suppress the account."[26]

In the aftermath of Dunmore's removal of the gunpowder and his subsequent threat to free the slaves, some white Virginians expressed their grow-

---

25. Peter H. Wood, " 'Taking Care of Business' in Revolutionary South Carolina: Republicanism and the Slave Society," in Jeffrey J. Crow and Larry E. Tise, eds., *The Southern Experience in the American Revolution* (Chapel Hill, N.C., 1978), 282; Fredericksburg encampment, Apr. 29, 1775, in *Revolutionary Virginia*, III, 71; Gloucester County committee, Apr. 25, 1775, Henrico County committee, Apr. 26, 1775, Fredericksburg encampment, Apr. 29, 1775, New Kent County committee, May 3, 1775, Richmond County committee, May 12, 1775, Virginia Convention, "Declaration of the Delegates," Aug. 26, 1775, all in *Revolutionary Virginia*, III, 61, 62–63, 71, 84–85, 121, 501; Rawleigh Downman to Samuel Athawes, July 10, 1775, Downman Letterbook, LC.

Even Herbert Aptheker, a careful searcher for evidence of slave conspiracies, believed that there was no plot in Virginia in April 1775 (*American Negro Slave Revolts*, 204). Aptheker's conclusion was understandable given that the only evidence before him was Governor Dunmore's public claim that he had removed the powder to protect whites from a rumored slave "insurrection in a neighbouring county" (Dunmore to Williamsburg Common Hall, Apr. 21, 1775, in *Revolutionary Virginia*, III, 55). Aptheker's skepticism regarding Dunmore's claim that he removed the gunpowder in order to protect whites from a rumored slave plot was justified, for Dunmore himself acknowledged in a letter to Dartmouth, the secretary of state, that the plot was not the real reason for the removal of the powder. But apparently the governor sincerely believed the slave plot rumor himself, for he stated in the same letter to Dartmouth that whites in Williamsburg really were "apprehensive of insurrections among their slaves (some reports having prevailed to this effect)" (May 1, 1775, in Davies, ed., *Documents of the American Revolution*, IX, 107–108).

26. James Robison to William Cuninghame and Company, May 3, 1775, in T. M. Devine, ed., *A Scottish Firm in Virginia, 1767–1777: W. Cuninghame and Co.* (Edinburgh, 1984), 187.

ing rage at him in jokes about his relations with black women. There had long been talk about the governor's philandering. Now, for the first time, his sex partners were said to include blacks. In June 1775, Pinkney's *Virginia Gazette* sarcastically predicted that "The BLACK LADIES" would "be jollily entertained at the p[alace]." A year later, after Dunmore had assembled his mostly black army to battle the patriots, Purdie's *Virginia Gazette* claimed that the diminutive Dunmore and his army celebrated their landing on Gwynn's Island "with a promiscuous ball, which was opened, we hear, by a certain spruce little gentleman, with one of the black ladies." It is significant that both newspapers called the black women that joined Dunmore "ladies." This was meant ironically. White Virginians referred to adult female slaves as "women" or "wenches," but never as "ladies." In July 1776, Landon Carter of Richmond County heard a story about a patriot cannonball passing right between Dunmore's legs. Carter joked in his diary that perhaps the "shot cooled his latitudinous virility for that night at least."[27]

III

The actions that Governor Dunmore and Virginia slave rebels took in April 1775 inflamed the patriot movement not only in Virginia but in other colonies as well. Accounts of the Virginia slave plots, the taking of the gunpowder, and Dunmore's threat to ally with slave conspirators soon spread throughout the South. At the same time, the same routes carried reports of the battle of Lexington and Concord and rumors from London about an emancipation bill being proposed in Parliament. All of that news led many southerners of every race and condition to believe that the British government might soon forge some sort of alliance with enslaved Americans. Governor Dunmore's April 22 threat to "declare freedom to the slaves" was ambiguous (perhaps deliberately so). Had the governor planned to free only those slaves he could enlist in the British army—or *all* of them? Many southerners believed that Britain might adopt "an Act of Grace" by which enslaved Americans would "be all set free," as Charleston merchant Josiah

27. Pinkney's *VG*, June 1, 1775; Purdie's *VG*, May 31, 1776; July 16, 1776, in Greene, ed., *Diary of Landon Carter*, II, 1058. Still later, Adam Stephen predicted that Dunmore would participate in a rumored British invasion of Virginia "in order to add some more odiferous beauties to his Ethopian seraglios." See Stephen to Richard Henry Lee, Apr. 22, 1777, in Harry M. Ward, *Major General Adam Stephen and the Cause of American Liberty* (Charlottesville, Va., 1989), 168; Brent Tarter, "Some Thoughts Arising from Trying to Find Out Who Was Governor Dunmore's Mistress" (manuscript). On the language used to describe enslaved women, see Kathleen M. Brown, *Good Wives, Nasty Wenches, and Anxious Patriarchs: Gender, Race, and Power in Colonial Virginia* (Chapel Hill, N.C., 1996).

Smith, Jr., reported on May 18. A group of Charleston slaves had apparently contemplated a rebellion since April, and the alleged conspiracy terrified whites. The news from Virginia, Massachusetts, and London persuaded many South Carolinians that the new governor, Lord William Campbell, who was due to arrive in June, was going to free the slaves and "encourage an insurrection," as the governor himself later reported. The rumor kept white South Carolinians on tenterhooks from early May until June 19, when Governor Campbell landed without incident.[28]

In North Carolina, too, the news from London, Massachusetts, and Virginia contributed to talk that the British government might soon incite a slave revolt. In early July, when a widespread slave conspiracy was discovered in Pitt, Craven, and Beaufort Counties, whites suspected that British officials had discussed strategy with the conspirators and made certain promises to them. Allegedly, the plan was for blacks to start a rebellion on the night of July 8. They were to kill their owners and then move westward toward the backcountry, where "they were to be received with open arms by a number of Persons there appointed and armed by [the] Government for their Protection," according to Colonel John Simpson of Pitt County.[29]

Many enslaved Americans carried the rumors about British aid for black insurrection one step further: they believed that the whole purpose of the expected British invasion of the South was to liberate them. In South Carolina, a slave reported that Thomas Jeremiah, a free black fisherman and harbor pilot that hoped to link the British army with rebel slaves, told enslaved workers "the War was come to help the poor Negroes." Further south in St. Bartholomew Parish at about the same time, a black preacher named George told gatherings of slaves "That the Young King, meaning our Present One, came up with the Book, and was about to alter the World, and set the Negroes Free." George was executed. The widespread belief among

28. "Deposition of Pasteur," *VMHB*, XIII (1905), 49; Robert Beverley to William Fitzhugh, July 20, 1775, Beverley Letterbook, LC; Josiah Smith to James Poyas, May 18, 1775, to George Appleby, June 16, 1775, Josiah Smith Letterbook, Southern Historical Collection, University of North Carolina, Chapel Hill; Olwell, " 'Domestick Enemies,' " *JSH*, LV (1989); Wood, " 'Liberty Is Sweet,' " in Young, ed., *Beyond the Revolution*, 166–168; Wood, " 'Taking Care of Business,' " in Crow and Tise, eds., *Southern Experience*, 280–287; Robert M. Weir, *Colonial South Carolina: A History* (Millwood, N.Y., 1983), 200–203.

29. Wood, " 'The Dream Deferred,' " in Okihiro, ed., *In Resistance*, 175; Jeffrey J. Crow, "Slave Rebelliousness and Social Conflict in North Carolina, 1775 to 1802," *WMQ*, 3d Ser., XXXVII (1980), 83–86; Alan D. Watson, "Impulse toward Independence: Resistance and Rebellion among North Carolina Slaves, 1750–1775," *JNH*, LXIII (1978), 317–328. On the importance of the backcountry as a haven for emancipated slaves, see Wood, " 'Liberty Is Sweet,' " in Young, ed., *Beyond the Revolution*, 162.

black southerners that the British intended to free them was known to whites. John Drayton reported many years after the Revolution that Arthur Lee's assertion that the London government meant to incite an insurrection was "the more alarming; because, it was already known, [slaves] entertained ideas, that the present contest was for obliging us to give them their liberty."[30] The rumor that freeing the slaves was one of Great Britain's principal aims—perhaps even the primary one—might have been fabricated by black leaders in the hope that it would serve as a self-fulfilling prophecy. If a real slave revolt crystallized around the apocryphal story of a British army of liberation, British statesmen might indeed be drawn into an alliance with the slave rebels.

The deepest fears of white leaders, and the highest hopes of blacks, were not realized. Governor Dunmore did not proclaim a general emancipation. During the summer, however, he began assembling a small fleet to confront the patriots. The governor soon began to offer a quiet welcome to fugitive slaves such as the aforementioned Joseph Harris. Previously, fugitive slave advertisements appearing in the *Virginia Gazette*s commonly surmised that the escapee had gone to visit family. By September 1775, advertisers began to conjecture that their slaves had fled slavery altogether by joining the British.[31]

The story of one fugitive illustrated how the meaning of escape changed in the summer of 1775. On February 10, 1775, a fifteen-year-old girl (whose name is not known) was purchased by Virginia's official vintner, Andrew Estave. The teenager might have been one of the many young Virginians that were sold far away from their families as they reached adulthood. In any event, she found life with Estave so intolerable that, in her first few months as his property, she ran away three times. Each time the girl was recaptured and suffered forty lashes. The torture did not have its desired effect, so Estave suspended it and assumed that the fifteen-year-old would be thereby reconciled to her fate. She was not. Early in the summer of 1775, as Estave told

30. Frey, *Water from the Rock*, 58, 62; John Drayton, *Memoirs of the American Revolution, from Its Commencement to the Year 1776, Inclusive; As Relating to the State of South-Carolina . . .* (Charleston, S.C., 1821), I, 231; William Lee to Robert Carter Nicholas, Mar. 6, 1775, in Worthington Chauncey Ford, ed., *Letters of William Lee . . . , 1766–1783* (Brooklyn, 1891), I, 143; Henry M. Muhlenberg, in Graham Russell Hodges, ed., *The Black Loyalist Directory: African Americans in Exile after the American Revolution* (New York, 1996), xiii; James W. St. G. Walker, *The Black Loyalists: The Search for a Promised Land in Nova Scotia and Sierra Leone, 1783–1870* (New York, 1976), 4.

31. Mullin, *Flight and Rebellion*, 109, 132–133. White servants, especially convicts, also ran away and headed to the British naval squadron. See Francis Smith and James Tutt, advertisements, July 27, Nov. 2, 1775, Pinkney's *VG;* Dunmore to Dartmouth, June 25, 1775, in Davies, ed., *Documents of the American Revolution*, IX, 202–203.

readers of the *Virginia Gazette*, another of the women he owned "found my child, together with this cruel and unnatural wretch, concealed behind my barn, among the bushes, with her thumb thrust into the private parts of my poor child." Estave was summoned. "During the confusion," the fifteen-year-old escaped and fled to the governor's palace in Williamsburg, where she hoped to cast her lot with Dunmore. But the governor had himself recently fled—to the *Fowey*—and the teenager was soon returned to her master for punishment. First she suffered "eighty lashes, well laid on." Then Estave poured embers on her back. Although the teenager's escape attempt was unsuccessful, it is significant that she sought refuge in the building that until recently had symbolized the enforcement, not the evasion, of white rule.[32]

The new opportunities produced by the conflict among white Virginians inspired resistance even among those slaves that did not try to reach Dunmore. In the summer of 1775, the number of enslaved workers brought before the county courts for criminal trials reached a record level. Diarist Philip Fithian reported in June that slaves were "running off daily."[33] No doubt many white Virginians blamed the crime wave on Governor Dunmore.

In the fall of 1775, Dunmore gave white Virginians additional reasons to hate him and the government he represented. On November 14, at Kemp's Landing south of Norfolk, his outnumbered force, made up largely of former slaves, defeated three hundred members of the Princess Anne County militia, killing several militiamen and putting the rest to flight. The patriot

32. This story is based entirely on a newspaper notice that Estave published in order to justify what some of his white neighbors had called his "cruel and inhuman" treatment of the enslaved teenager (Pinkney's *VG*, July 20, 1775). We can only imagine how the story would change if we had testimony from the fifteen-year-old. Estave was colonial Virginia's official vintner. He was provided with slaves—perhaps including the fifteen-year-old he spoke of in his newspaper notice—and land by the House of Burgesses. See Bruce A. Ragsdale, *A Planters' Republic: The Search for Economic Independence in Revolutionary Virginia* (Madison, Wis., 1996), 141; Edward D. C. Campbell, Jr., "Of Vines and Wines: The Culture of the Grape in Virginia," *Virginia Cavalcade*, XXXIX (1990), 110. If the teenager had reached the governor's palace before Dunmore left, he might have been able to grant her sanctuary ("Charter of Williamsburg," in "The Building of Williamsburg," *WMQ*, 1st Ser., X [1901], 87). My thanks to Brent Tarter and John M. Hemphill, Jr., for this reference.

33. June 17, 1775, in Robert Greenhalgh Albion and Leonidas Dodson, eds., *Philip Vickers Fithian: Journal, 1775–1776: Written on the Virginia-Pennsylvania Frontier and in the Army around New York* (Princeton, N.J., 1934), 31. John Bailey's slaves Phil and Mial "received guilty verdicts in Southampton County conspiracy trials" (Schwarz, *Twice Condemned*, 181, 183, 184). On July 3, 1775, William Johnson's slave Gloster was sentenced to death for burglary "but broke out of jail and vanished" (Randolph W. Church, comp., *Virginia Legislative Petitions: Bibliography, Calendar, and Abstracts from Original Sources, 6 May 1776–21 June 1782* [Richmond, Va., 1984], 24–25).

commander, Joseph Hutchings, was captured by two of his own former slaves. Kemp's Landing persuaded Dunmore that ex-slaves could be valuable allies indeed. The governor "was so ela[ted] with this Victory," John Page, vice-chairman of the Committee of Safety, reported, that he immediately published his famous proclamation declaring "all indented Servants, Negroes, or others, (appertaining to Rebels,) free that are able and willing to bear Arms, they joining His MAJESTY's Troops." About a thousand slaves escaped their owners and joined Dunmore. Enlisted in his Ethiopian Regiment and wearing uniforms that pointed up the hypocrisy of liberty-seeking patriots by proclaiming "Liberty to Slaves," former slaves soon made up the major part of the loyalist troops. In order to glimpse the psychological impact of emancipation on the people that reached Dunmore, it may be sufficient to note the case of a man whites called Yellow Peter. He escaped one day in 1775 or 1776 and was later seen "in Governor Dunmore's regiment with a musquet on his back and a sword by his side." He had changed his name to *Captain* Peter.[34]

Although Dunmore apparently meant to limit his emancipation offer to able-bodied men, half of those that joined him and survived the war were women and children. Among them was Francis Rice's slave Mary. One night in the spring of 1776, Mary, a resident of Hampton, grabbed up her three-and-a-half-year-old daughter Phillis and made a dash for the British lines. The two got in safely, survived the war, and settled afterward in Nova Scotia.[35]

Still, for the 99 percent of slaves that did *not* escape to Dunmore, his emancipation proclamation was in many ways a disappointment. Instead of

---

34. Jan. 2, 1776, Robert Honyman diary, LC; Selby, *Revolution in Virginia*, 64; John Page to Thomas Jefferson, [Nov.] 24, 1775, in Boyd et al., eds., *Papers of Jefferson*, I, 265; Dunmore, proclamation, Nov. 7, 1775, in *Revolutionary Virginia*, IV, 334–335; Dixon and Hunter's *VG*, Dec. 2, 1775; James Jones, credit report on Edmund Taylor, "British Mercantile Claims, 1775–1803," *Virginia Genealogist*, XVI (1972), 104–105.

35. Hodges, ed., *Black Loyalist Directory* (Mary and Phillis Halstead are listed on p. 201); Quarles, *Negro in the Revolution*, 172; "*Women Embarked at* MILL POINT, *May 21, 1776, on board the* DUNLUCE," Dixon and Hunter's *VG*, August 31, 1776; Sarah Stroud, "Tracing Runaway Slaves from Norfolk County, Virginia, during the American Revolutionary War" (seminar paper, Randolph-Macon Woman's College, Fall 1995). During the American Revolution, many of the enslaved women that ran away took their children with them—an occurrence that was very rare before and after the war (Sara M. Evans, *Born for Liberty: A History of Women in America* [New York, 1989], 52). For accounts of other black Americans that joined the British and settled in Nova Scotia and Sierra Leone after the war, see Gary B. Nash, "Thomas Peters: Millwright and Deliverer," in David G. Sweet and Gary B. Nash, eds., *Struggle and Survival in Colonial America* (Berkeley, Calif., 1981), 69–85; Ellen Gibson Wilson, *The Loyal Blacks* (New York, 1976); Walker, *Black Loyalists*.

A List of Negroes that went off to Dunmore April 14th 1776.

Women	Ages	Girls	Boys	Negro Men	Ages
Pleasant	55	1		Sasser, a Sawer	60
Nancy	46	4		Tobey Do	54
Marcy	50	2		Ned	44
Judey	28	3		Peter, a house Carpenter	57
Lucy	25		6	Jacous, a Shoemaker	35
Heziah	23		3	Robin, a Sawer	25
Cate	30	2	1	Bob	30
Rachel	25		4	Charles	24
Easter	27			Glascow	21
Betise	23	1		Will	21
Jenny	42			Anthony	19
Lindah	27	2	2	George	18
Manda	25		5	Jacob	20
Dynah	26	2		Isack	16
Lidia	26	2	1		
Bey	29		3		
Bess	23	1		Total. 87.	
Jenny	30				
Josse	16			Entailed.	

Nell	25	2		Brister a Sawer	25
Pegg	18			Moses a house Servt	25

Nell & Fee Simple

Women	Girls	Boys		Men
21	25	27		16

Jno. Willoughby

making the abolition of slavery a goal of the war, Dunmore had offered freedom only to those individuals that joined British forces. Even as Dunmore's decision to fight a conventional war destroyed the hopes of many black Virginians, it emboldened whites. To them, a black regiment in the British army was frightening, and the loss of enslaved workers would be financially devastating, but neither was as daunting as an official promise of general emancipation.[36] By August 1776, patriots forced Dunmore's vastly outnumbered army to retreat to New York City.

The relief that white Virginians experienced when Dunmore chose not to dissolve the institution of slavery did not diminish their anger at him for allying with the slaves. As early as spring 1775, free subjects had begun literally to demonize their governor. In November, when he published his "Damned, infernal, Diabolical" emancipation proclamation, the process intensified. Citizens denounced Dunmore's "Diabolical scheme" and "his infernal tribe." "Our Devil of a Governor goes on at a Devil of a rate indeed," member of Congress Benjamin Harrison commented after reading the Virginia news.[37]

The deterioration in Dunmore's popularity among white Virginians was not the only political result of his proclamation. Thomas Jefferson spoke for other white Americans when he stated, in the largest and angriest complaint in the Declaration of Independence, that Dunmore's emancipation proclamation was a major cause of the American Revolution. (Although Jefferson's colleagues in Congress shortened the statement, they left it at the *end* of Jefferson's list of complaints—a case of saving the best for last.) All over Virginia, observers noted that the governor's freedom offer turned neutrals and even loyalists into patriots. "The Inhabitants of this Colony are deeply alarmed at this infernal Scheme," Philip Fithian wrote in his journal as he passed through the Virginia backcountry in late November. "It seems to quicken all in Revolution to overpower him however at every Risk." Richard Henry Lee told Catherine Macauley that "Lord Dunmores unparalleled conduct in Virginia has, a few Scotch excepted, united every Man in that large

36. Judith Bell to Alexander Speirs, Feb 16, 1776, Speirs of Elderslie Papers, Glasgow County Archives, Glasgow, Scotland.

37. House of Burgesses, address to Dunmore, June 19, 1775, *JHB, 1773–1776*, 256; Raleigh Downman to Samuel Athawes, July 10, 1775, Downman Letterbook, LC; John Hatley Norton to John Norton, [Dec. 9, 1775], in Frances Norton Mason, ed., *John Norton and Sons, Merchants of London and Virginia: Being the Papers from Their Counting-House for the Years 1750 to 1795* (Richmond, Va., 1937), 391; Thomas Nelson, Jr., to Mann Page, Jan. 4, 1776, Benjamin Harrison to Robert Carter Nicholas, Jan. 17, 1776, Francis Lightfoot Lee to Landon Carter, Feb. 12, 1776, all in Paul H. Smith et al., eds., *Letters of Delegates to Congress, 1774–1789* (Washington, D.C., 1976–), III, 30, 107, 237. For an additional reference to Dunmore as devilish, see George Washington to Richard Henry Lee, Dec. 26, 1775, in Abbot et al., eds., *Papers of Washington*, Revolutionary War Series, II, 611. A rumored British scheme to ally with Native Americans was also described as "Diabolical" and "infernal" (George Washington to John Augustine Washington, Oct. 13, 1775, Richard Henry Lee to George Washington, Nov. 13, 1775, in Abbot et al., eds., *Papers of Washington*, Revolutionary War Series, II, 161, 363).

Colony." Archibald Cary agreed. "The Proclamation from L[or]d D[un-more], has had a most extensive good consequence," he wrote; white "Men of all ranks resent the pointing a dagger to their Throats, thru the hands of their Slaves." Cary noted that, by endangering loyalists as well as patriots, Dunmore's proclamation turned many of the former into the latter.[38]

Although those patriot writers' comments on Dunmore's proclamation might have reflected some measure of wishful thinking about its impact on neutral and loyalist whites, it did convert many of them. It even pushed two members of the colony's powerful Executive Council, Robert "Councillor" Carter and William Byrd III, from the loyalist to the patriot camp. Originally, Byrd had offered to lead British troops. After Dunmore confirmed his alliance with black Virginians, Byrd and Carter both became patriots, and Colonel Byrd tendered his services to the rebels.[39]

Some of Byrd's fellow conservatives initially believed that, as soon as Dunmore's superiors in London learned about his emancipation proclamation, they would repudiate it and recall him. At the end of 1775, Landon Carter assured himself that it was "not to be doubted" that Dunmore would soon receive "some missive commission to Silence all his iniquities both male and female." (That was yet another reference to Dunmore's alleged miscegenation.)[40] But the winter of 1775–1776 came and went with no evidence that anyone at Whitehall objected to Dunmore's decision to offer freedom to the slaves. The ministry's silence implied consent. Although Dunmore was the only royal governor that made a formal offer of freedom to his colony's slaves before July 4, 1776, other British leaders informally cooperated with slaves and thereby helped motivate white Americans to declare Independence. In North Carolina in June 1776, patriot James Iredell

---

38. Nov. 28, 1775, in Albion and Dodson, eds., *Philip Vickers Fithian: Journal*, 135; Richard Henry Lee to Catherine Macauley, Nov. 29, 1775, Archibald Cary to Richard Henry Lee, Dec. 24, 1775, in Paul P. Hoffman, ed., *The Lee Family Papers, 1742–1795* (microfilm, Charlottesville, Va., 1966); Page Smith, *A New Age Now Begins: A People's History of the American Revolution* (New York, 1976), I, 704; Garry Wills, *Inventing America: Jefferson's Declaration of Independence* (Garden City, N.Y., 1978), 71, 75.

39. William Byrd III to Jeffery Amherst, July 30, 1775, in Tinling, ed., *Correspondence of the Three William Byrds*, II, 812–813; Feb. 25, 1776, in Greene, ed., *Diary of Landon Carter*, II, 989; *Revolutionary Virginia*, V, 386n–387n; Selby, *Revolution in Virginia*, 66; Thomas Jefferson to William Wirt, Sept. 29, 1816, *Reminiscences of Patrick Henry in the Letters of Thomas Jefferson to William Wirt* (Philadelphia, 1911), 29; Allan Kulikoff, *Tobacco and Slaves: The Development of Southern Cultures in the Chesapeake, 1680–1800* (Chapel Hill, N.C., 1986), 308; Jeannie Ford Dissette, "Slavery and the Coming of the Revolution in Virginia, 1774–1776" (seminar paper, University of Pennsylvania, 1972), 28–49.

40. Greene, ed., *Diary of Landon Carter*, II, 960.

said that, when royal officials encouraged enslaved Americans "to cut our throats," they "added spurs to our Patriotism."[41]

Students of the causes of the American Revolution often underestimate the contribution of enslaved Virginians, and one reason is that slaves are seldom mentioned until November 1775, when Dunmore issued his proclamation. But the governor's proclamation was only part of a process that had begun much earlier. Slaves had always resisted their condition. In 1774, they began conspiring to exploit the opportunities presented to them by the imperial crisis. The following April, as rumors of a wide-ranging insurrection plot circulated, a group of slaves knocked on the governor's door and offered to cast their lot with his. And slaves kept knocking all through the summer and into the fall. It was only after fugitive slaves had proven their skills as soldiers, sailors, and raiders that Dunmore officially offered them freedom. The slaves' insurgency played an important role in persuading Dunmore to ally with them and thus in prodding white Virginians further along the road to Independence.[42]

41. It was not just in Virginia that Dunmore's emancipation proclamation helped alienate whites from Britain. In Maryland, loyalist William Eddis observed that Dunmore's "measure of emancipating the negroes has excited an universal ferment" and would "greatly strengthen the general confederacy." Edward Rutledge of South Carolina expected that the "proclamation issued by Lord Dunmore" would tend "more effectually to work an eternal separation between Great Britain and the Colonies,—than any other expedient, which could possibly have been thought of." In Philadelphia, a play depicting Dunmore welcoming black recruits became part of the library of anti-British propaganda. In the play, *The Fall of British Tyranny*, by Philadelphia silversmith John Leacock, "Lord Kidnapper" (Dunmore) congratulates himself on raising "rebel against rebel" and says he expects his emancipation proclamation "will greatly intimidate the rebels—internal enemies are worse than open foes." See Jan. 16, 1776, in William Eddis, *Letters from America*, ed. Aubrey C. Land (Cambridge, Mass., 1969), 133; Edward Rutledge to Ralph Izard, Dec. 8, 1775, in *Correspondence of Mr. Ralph Izard*, I, 165; [John Leacock], *The Fall of British Tyranny; or, American Liberty Triumphant: The First Campaign* . . . (Philadelphia, 1776), 48; Gary B. Nash, *Forging Freedom: The Formation of Philadelphia's Black Community, 1720–1840* (Cambridge, Mass., 1988), 46; Quarles, *Negro in the Revolution*, 20, 20n; Olwell, " 'Domestick Enemies,' " *JSH*, LV (1989), 41; James Iredell, untitled essay, in Don Higginbotham, ed., *The Papers of James Iredell* (Raleigh, N.C., 1976–), I, 409; Crow, "Slave Rebelliousness," *WMQ*, 3d Ser., XXXVII (1980), 83.

42. To be sure, Dunmore's emancipation proclamation is often mentioned as a cause of the Revolution. See Burk, Jones, and Girardin, *History of Virginia*, IV, 134n; Eckenrode, *Revolution in Virginia*, 73; Dumas Malone, *Jefferson and His Time*, I, *Jefferson the Virginian* (Boston, 1948–1981), 215; Billings, Selby, and Tate, *Colonial Virginia*, 343; Clifford Dowdey, *The Great Plantation: A Profile of Berkeley Hundred and Plantation Virginia from Jamestown to Appomattox* (New York, 1957), 230–231; Campbell, *History of Virginia*, 634; John C. Miller,

When Americans think of slaves and sailing ships, they inevitably imagine the slaves crammed in the hold, enduring the indescribable Middle Passage. It is important to remember that some enslaved Americans were up on the decks of colonial vessels, and that some, like Joseph Harris, even piloted them.[43] That simple fact must, in any accurate description of Virginia in 1775 and 1776, acquire the power of metaphor, for black Virginians were not simply swept along on the political currents. Through their actions, they helped steer Virginia into the American Revolution.

"Whoever considers well the meaning of the word Rebel," an anonymous white critic of Dunmore's proclamation wrote in late November, "will discover that the author of the Proclamation is now himself in actual rebellion, having armed our slaves against us, and having excited them to an insurrection."[44] In modern terms, that author might have said that white Virginians' struggle against Dunmore and his Ethiopian Regiment was not a revolution but a counterrevolution. The war in Virginia pitted two classes, slaveowners and slaves, against each other. Thus, in that sense (as well as others), Virginia's Revolutionary experience fits the Progressive historians' interpretation of the American Revolution as a conflict over both home rule and who would rule at home.

IV

White Americans also denounced British cooperation with American Indians. The same native diplomats that indirectly advanced the Independence movement by instigating the British government to adopt an anti-

---

Origins of the American Revolution (Boston, 1943), 478; Virginius Dabney, *Virginia: The New Dominion* (Garden City, N.Y., 1971), 131; Pauline Maier, *American Scripture: Making the Declaration of Independence* (New York, 1997), 26.

Several students of the black freedom struggle have also asserted that the slaves helped push whites into the American Revolution. See Quarles, *Negro in the Revolution*, 19; Wood, " 'Liberty Is Sweet,' " in Young, ed., *Beyond the Revolution*, 171; Frey, *Water from the Rock*, 78. But they have focused on African Americans themselves and have not presented the abundant evidence that the slaves helped provoke whites to declare Independence.

For a similar argument—that enslaved Americans, through their actions, helped push Abraham Lincoln into issuing his Emancipation Proclamation—see W. E. Burghardt Du Bois, *Black Reconstruction: An Essay toward a History of the Part Which Black Folk Played in the Attempt to Reconstruct Democracy in America, 1860–1880* (New York, 1935), chap. 4; Vincent Harding, *There Is a River: The Black Struggle for Freedom in America* (New York, 1981), chap. 11.

43. W. Jeffrey Bolster, *Black Jacks: African American Seamen in the Age of Sail* (Cambridge, Mass., 1997), 2.

44. Anonymous letter, Nov. 30, 1775, in Force, comp., *American Archives*, 4th Ser., III, 1387; anonymous letter, Nov. 23, 1775, in *Revolutionary Virginia*, IV, 459–462.

expansionist land policy later helped alienate white Virginians against Britain in a more direct way. As the year 1775 opened, the Native American effort to form an anti-British coalition still had not succeeded. But as the shots fired at Lexington and Concord echoed through Indian country early that summer, the coalition builders spotted an opportunity: as the patriot rebellion spread, the imperial government was likely to need their help. An alliance with the British would give them a crucial asset that they had lacked during the late 1760s and early 1770s—a steady supply of arms and ammunition. By June, British officials were making overtures. James Wood, who toured the Ohio country as the representative of the House of Burgesses, learned that an "English Officer" had held a "Great Council" with several nations and told them "that the Virginians would take the whole Country if they did not all join together against them." By the end of his journey, Wood was convinced that "the Indians are forming a General Confederacy against the Colony."[45]

John Connolly, Dunmore's representative at Fort Pitt, might have heard about the Ohio Indians' revived effort at an antisettler league by early July, when he set out for Williamsburg to meet with the governor. Certainly Dunmore and Connolly knew about the natives' earlier coalition-building efforts, and that knowledge entered into an important decision Dunmore made at the end of the summer. At about the same time that he began to welcome the slaves that escaped to his little fleet on Chesapeake Bay, Dunmore sent Connolly to Boston. The governor wanted Commander in Chief Thomas Gage to send Connolly on to Detroit, where he would meet with representatives of the Indian nations between the Great Lakes and the Ohio River. He would ask them to join in a massive attack against the Virginia frontier. The Franco-American *habitants* that lived in Detroit and other former French settlements were also to be recruited for the attack. Then, on April 20, 1776, the first anniversary of the night Dunmore took the gunpowder from the provincial munitions depot in Williamsburg, Connolly and his red and white troops would meet Dunmore and his black and white troops at Alexandria. From that base they would march forth to conquer the Virginia patriots.

Gage approved the plan, but as Connolly and two accomplices, English-

45. James Wood, journal, July 20, 28, Wood to Peyton Randolph, August 1775, in Reuben Gold Thwaites and Louise Phelps Kellogg, eds., *The Revolution on the Upper Ohio, 1775–1777* (Madison, Wis., 1908), 44, 54, 66. Shawnee headmen later confirmed Wood's suspicion that the English officer was the official representative of the commanding officer at Fort Detroit, from whom he brought "a Belt and String of Black Wampum" (Aug. 2, 1775, *The Revolution on the Upper Ohio*, 62).

man J. F. D. Smyth and British Indian agent Alexander Cameron, headed west across Maryland, they were captured. A patriot committeeman discovered a copy of Connolly's plan hidden in the horn of his saddle. The plan showed that, in addition to allying with Indians and habitants, Connolly hoped to enlist white Virginians by offering them "a confirmation of titles to their lands."[46] Connolly and Dunmore knew that the Proclamation of 1763 had virtually shut down Virginia land speculation, and they now proposed to provide relief from the proclamation to any militia officer that would take up arms in support of the government that had promulgated it.

Although Dunmore's offer to confirm land titles showed that he had learned a great deal about white Virginians during his four years in their colony, another element in the plan that he and Connolly devised—the proposed alliance with the Ohio Indians—indicated that he had not learned enough. The revelation in November 1775 that Dunmore had encouraged Native Americans to use violence against white colonists coincided with the publication of his emancipation proclamation and helped to seal his fate in the minds of his constituents. In John Leacock's *Fall of British Tyranny*, the character "Kidnapper" (Dunmore) muses: "If we can stand our ground this winter, and burn all their towns that are accessible to our ships, and Colonel Connolly succeeds in his plan . . . we shall be able to make a descent where we please, and drive the rebels like hogs into a pen."[47]

Both Dunmore's emancipation offer to the slaves and the alliance he tried to form with the Ohio Indians were in large part dramatic responses to the rebellious activities that those two groups had already initiated. Thus the Indian and slave rebels—the fomenters of "domestic insurrections"—added fuel to the Independence movement in Virginia.

46. Wood, " 'Liberty Is Sweet,' " in Young, ed., *Beyond the Revolution*, 169.

47. Leacock, *Fall of British Tyranny*, 49. On British cooperation with Indians as a cause of white Americans' growing alienation from Britain, see Wood, " 'Liberty Is Sweet,' " in Young, ed., *Beyond the Revolution*, 169; Selby, *Revolution in Virginia*, 92; Pinkney's *VG*, Aug. 3, 1775.

Free colonists were also angry at Dunmore for emancipating and arming convict servants. See Leacock, *Fall of British Tyranny*, 45; "A British American," Dixon and Hunter's *VG*, Feb. 17, 1776.

> He has dissolved Representative
> Houses repeatedly. . . . the State
> remaining in the mean time exposed
> to all the Dangers of Invasion from
> without, and Convulsions within.
> —Declaration of Independence

6

GENTLEMEN

VERSUS FARMERS

The American Revolution is generally remembered as a supremely confident step. But for many members of the Virginia gentry, the final step along the road to revolution—the May 1776 vote to ask Congress to declare Independence—was less a display of confidence than an act of desperation. "For God's sake declare the Colonies independant at once, and save us from ruin," John Page urged Thomas Jefferson in April 1776. For gentlemen like Page, the decision for Independence was not really a decision at all; it was forced upon them by their fears.[1]

Gentry Virginians in fact had much to fear in the spring of 1776. They were in the midst of a war against a group of black and white loyalists that might, at any moment, receive support from a British invasion force. Nor were loyalists and redcoats the only problems: gentlemen were becoming increasingly concerned about smallholders and poor whites. In May, Francis Lightfoot Lee said he hoped a Virginia convention would "make such an establishment, as will put a stop to the rising disorders." In other words, the

---

1. John Page to Thomas Jefferson, Apr. 6, 1776, in Julian P. Boyd et al., eds., *The Papers of Thomas Jefferson* (Princeton, N.J., 1950–), I, 287. Charles Lee, commander in chief of patriot troops in the South, sent a similar plea to Richard Henry Lee, who would soon introduce Virginia's Independence resolve at the Continental Congress. "By the eternal God," General Lee wrote Richard Henry Lee on May 10, 1776, "if you do not declare immediately for positive independence We are all ruin'd." See Paul P. Hoffman, ed., *The Lee Family Papers, 1742–1795* (microfilm, Charlottesville, Va., 1966); Charles Lee to William Byrd III, Apr. 1, [1776], in Marion Tinling, ed., *The Correspondence of the Three William Byrds of Westover, Virginia, 1684–1776* (Charlottesville, Va., 1977), II, 818; Pauline Maier, *American Scripture: Making the Declaration of Independence* (New York, 1997), 86–88.

delegates should reestablish government in Virginia. But of course they could not create a new government until they declared Independence.[2] If poor and middling Virginians had obeyed the gentry's orders, gentlemen would have had one less reason to remove Virginia from the British Empire.

Insurgent Virginia farmers pushed the gentry toward Independence in another way as well. The colonists' boycott of British trade and the British government's retaliatory attacks on other colonial commerce virtually halted Virginia's imports and exports and led to shortages that led to riots. The only solution was to revive international trade. Another pressing reason for commercial revival was that it was only from overseas that Virginia's leaders could obtain the weapons and ammunition they needed to put a quick end to the Revolutionary War, which was itself the preeminent cause of agrarian unrest. The problem was that no foreign government would open a trade with the colonies until they declared themselves independent states.

Thus smallholders and poor whites pushed gentlemen toward Independence in two ways. First, gentlemen believed that they stood a better chance of suppressing disorder if they revived government, which they could only do by declaring Independence. Second, Independence was a prerequisite for a commercial alliance with France. Such an alliance would allow gentlemen both to satisfy the demands of the rioters and to obtain the arms and ammunition that they needed to put a quick end to the burdensome Revolutionary War.

I

As noted earlier, Virginia gentlemen believed that they could not control the 40 percent of the population that was enslaved unless they preserved unity among whites. In 1775 and 1776, white solidarity began to dissolve.

Although one reason gentlemen established independent volunteer companies in late 1774 and early 1775 was to prevent "Insurrection," many of the companies themselves soon got out of hand.[3] In the spring of 1775, when Governor Dunmore emptied the colony's largest gunpowder depot and threatened to free Virginia's slaves, independent companies mustered all over the colony. A loyalist observed that the popular clamor to confront the governor threw elites into "a terrible panic." It was only with great difficulty, Thomas Jefferson reported, that elites were able "to moderate the almost ungovernable fury of the people" and prevail upon them "to return to their

2. Lee to Carter, Apr. 9, May 21, 1776, in Paul H. Smith et al., eds., *Letters of Delegates to Congress, 1774–1789* (Washington, D.C., 1985–), III, 500–501, IV, 57.

3. Virginia Convention, Mar. 25, 1775, in *Revolutionary Virginia*, II, 375. Several counties had already established independent companies.

habitations." Patrick Henry's Hanover company had initially defied patriot leaders' urgent order to turn back. Williamsburg Quaker Edward Stabler thought Henry had been "guilty of such a rash disorderly action as I'm affraid the whole Colony will suffer for."4

At first, the independent companies had been made up entirely of gentlemen. Like gentlemen's clubs, they had chosen their officers democratically. By the summer of 1775, the independent companies consisted mostly of smallholders, yet many were still internally democratic. By that time, the companies had become far too independent, in the gentry's estimation. George Gilmer, an officer in Albemarle County, acknowledged that "many members are rather disorderly." In July 1775, a Chesterfield County company refused to submit to the county's militia officers. The gentry-run county committee denounced this "disorderly behaviour."5

Restraining the independent companies was one of the principal goals of the third Virginia Convention, which gathered in Richmond on July 17, 1775. Delegate George Mason proposed that the convention "melt down all the volunteer and independent companies into [one] great establishment" in which officers would be appointed, not elected. When delegate Francis Lightfoot Lee warned his colleagues not to create a large and expensive army, which he said would "occasion great discontent" among taxpayers, the convention tried to obtain the benefits of a regular army for the price of independent volunteer companies. It decided to hire only a thousand full-time

4. James Parker to Charles Steuart, May 6, 1775, Steuart Papers, National Library of Scotland, Edinburgh (microfilm at LVA); Jefferson to William Small, May 7, 1775, in Boyd et al., eds., *Papers of Jefferson*, I, 166n–167n (crossed out); Michael A. McDonnell, "The Politics of Mobilization in Revolutionary Virginia: Military Culture and Political and Social Relations, 1774–1783" (D.Phil. diss., Balliol College, Oxford University, 1995), 42–43, 48; Edward Stabler to Israel Pemberton, May 16, 1775, Pemberton Papers, XXVII, 144, Historical Society of Pennsylvania, Philadelphia; "Cato," Pinkney's *VG*, Oct. 19, 1775 (supplement).

5. George Gilmer to Thomas Jefferson, [July 26 or 27, 1775], in Boyd et al., eds., *Papers of Jefferson*, I, 237; Chesterfield County committee, memorial to Virginia Convention, [July 1775?], in *Revolutionary Virginia*, III, 339; William E. White, "The Independent Companies of Virginia, 1774–1775," *VMHB*, LXXXVI (1978), 160–161; John E. Selby, *The Revolution in Virginia, 1775–1783* (Charlottesville, Va., 1988), 45–49; McDonnell, "Politics of Mobilization," chap. 1. In frontier Botetourt County, the independent company undermined Virginia's solidarity with the embattled farmers of New England by pointedly refusing to march beyond the borders of the Old Dominion (Bedford County committee [June 26?], 1775, in *Revolutionary Virginia*, III, 230). The company's resolution reflected the localism that was analyzed by Albert H. Tillson, Jr., in his article, "The Militia and Popular Political Culture in the Upper Valley of Virginia, 1740–1775," *VMHB*, XCIV (1986), 285–306. Cf. *Revolutionary Virginia*, III, 231n–232n; Tillson, *Gentry and Common Folk: Political Culture on a Virginia Frontier, 1740–1789* (Lexington, Ky., 1991).

soldiers and place the chief burden of defending white Virginians on eight thousand "minutemen" that would be paid only during training sessions and military emergencies.[6]

The one thousand places in the regular army were filled quickly, for the army promised poor farmers a living wage at a time when nonexportation prevented them from selling their produce. The minuteman battalions were another matter. George Gilmer, who, as captain of an Albemarle County minuteman company, was responsible for recruiting soldiers for it, feared that, when he marched off to battle, he would look back to find no one following. "I know not from what cause, but every denomination of the people seem backward" in enlisting in the service, Gilmer said. Even men that had volunteered for the Albemarle independent companies refused to become minutemen. "[The] Convention have altered the name Volunteers to that of Minute Men, and behold! what a wondrous effect it has had. Out of near three hundred Volunteers there are how many Minute Men? So few that I am afraid to name them." All over the province, farmers refused to join the minuteman battalions. "Virginia is in the greatest confusion," Fielding Lewis wrote George Washington in November 1775; with "only one Battalion of Minute Men compleat, and little prospect of the others being so, a convention is daily expected to regulate it."[7] Gilmer learned that some smallholders

6. Mason to Martin Cockburn, July 24, 1775, in Robert A. Rutland, ed., *The Papers of George Mason, 1725–1792* (Chapel Hill, N.C., 1970), I, 241; Francis Lightfoot Lee to Landon Carter, Aug. 3, 1775, in Dale E. Benson, "Wealth and Power in Virginia, 1774–1776: A Study of the Organization of Revolt" (Ph.D. diss., University of Maine, 1970), 239n. The summer 1775 convention agreed to pay not only the soldiers in the new military establishment but also the militiamen that had participated in Dunmore's War. Earlier in the year, Adam Stephen had warned that, if the militiamen were not paid, it would "come to the Shedding of Blood" (to Richard Henry Lee, Feb. 17, 1775, in Hoffman, ed., *Lee Family Papers*).

7. Selby, *Revolution in Virginia*, 61; Jean B. Lee, *The Price of Nationhood: The American Revolution in Charles County* (New York, 1994), 163; "Address of George Gilmer to the Inhabitants of Albemarle," [Fall 1775], in "Papers, Military and Political, 1775–1778, of George Gilmer, M.D., of 'Pen Park,' Albemarle County, Va.," VHS *Collections*, N.S., VI (1887), 122; Fielding Lewis to George Washington, Nov. 14, 1775, in W. W. Abbot et al., eds., *The Papers of George Washington*, Revolutionary War Series (Charlottesville, Va., 1985–), II, 371–372; Archibald Campbell to St. George Tucker, Oct. 10, 1775, in William Bell Clark et al., eds., *Naval Documents of the American Revolution* (Washington, D.C., 1966–), II, 395; Archibald Cary to Thomas Jefferson, Oct. 31, 1775, in Boyd et al., eds., *Papers of Jefferson*, I, 249; James Freeland to John Tailyour, Oct. 20, 1775, Accomack County committee to Virginia Convention, Nov. 30, 1775, Fairfax County committee to George Mason and Charles Broadwater, Dec. 9, 1775, Virginia Convention, Jan. 10, 1776, all in *Revolutionary Virginia*, IV, 246, 498, V, 89, 372; Jan. 2, Mar. 17, 1776, Robert Honyman diary, LC. The smallholders' reluctance to become minutemen ensured that the battalions would be rife with mutiny and

not only declined to become minutemen but made "endeavors to dissuade [others] from the service." Even a gentleman, William Lyne, was accused of "endeavoring to prejudice the minute service, and exciting a mutiny."[8]

The minuteman battalions were unattractive to smallholders for precisely the same reason that they appealed to gentlemen: their purpose, celebrated by George Gilmer and lamented by common soldiers, was to replace the democracy of the independent volunteer companies with "proper subordination." Where the officers of the independent volunteer companies had been chosen by the troops they commanded, minuteman officers were selected by special district committees chosen by the county committees. Several of the district committees' appointments were considered "improper," and they provoked "many disorders."[9] Smallholders also objected to the convention's decision to exempt anyone that paid taxes on more than three slaves (or other workers) from militia duty and thus also from service as minutemen and slave patrollers. As Gilmer paraphrased the soldiers' view of the slaveholders' exemption, "It is calculated to exempt the gentlemen and to throw the whole burthen on the poor."[10]

A similar sense of emerging class consciousness was revealed in smallholders' objections to the way in which minutemen would be paid. It was

---

desertion (Leven Powell to Sarah Powell, Dec. 18, 1775 [typescript], Jan. 27, 1776, Leven Powell Papers, box 1, folder 1, William and Mary). The best sources on the minutemen are McDonnell, "Politics of Mobilization," chap. 2; McDonnell, "Popular Mobilization and Political Culture in Revolutionary Virginia: The Failure of the Minutemen and the Revolution from Below," *Journal of American History*, LXXXV (1998), 946–981.

8. Gilmer, "Address to the Inhabitants of Albemarle," VHS *Collections*, N.S., VI (1887), 123. Although a patriot subcommittee in King and Queen County found Lyne innocent of encouraging mutiny, it said he had "imprudently dropped expressions tending to injure the minute service" (King and Queen County committee, Dec. 9, 1775, in *Revolutionary Virginia*, V, 92–93).

9. Gilmer, "Address to the Inhabitants of Albemarle," VHS *Collections*, N.S., VI (1887), 122, 127; White, "Independent Companies," *VMHB*, LXXXVI (1978), 149, 151–152, 161; *SAL*, IX, 9–35, esp. 24; Benson, "Wealth and Power," 312n–313n; Cumberland County voters, petition, Dec. 22, 1775, in *Revolutionary Virginia*, V, 215; Fielding Lewis to George Washington, Nov. 14, 1775, in Abbot et al., eds., *Papers of Washington*, Revolutionary War Series, II, 372; Archibald Cary to Thomas Jefferson, Oct. 31, 1775, in Boyd et al., eds., *Papers of Jefferson*, I, 249.

10. Virginia's militia law provided a similar exemption, but only for "bona fide . . . overseer[s]" (*SAL*, VII, 93, IX, 28). It seemed to smallholders that "none" of the gentlemen of Albemarle "enter[ed] the service but as officers" (Gilmer, "Address to the Inhabitants of Albemarle," VHS *Collections*, N.S., VI [1887], 122–123). The criticism was apparently valid. Fielding Lewis acknowledged to George Washington that "young Gentlemen [were] not setting a good example by inlisting" (Nov. 14, 1775, in Abbot et al., eds., *Papers of Washington*, Revolutionary War Series, II, 372).

not that they wished to earn more; they wanted officers to earn less. Top officers in the minuteman battalions were paid eleven times as much as common soldiers. In defending these high salaries, George Gilmer did *not* suggest that officers contributed more to Virginia's defense than common soldiers did. Instead, he said that the purpose of the pay disparity was to set officers apart from common soldiers. "Without some distinction there can be no subordination," Gilmer argued, and, unless some subordinate themselves to others, "no discipline can be observed." The whole purpose of the minuteman battalions was, in fact, to obviate the need for the undisciplined independent companies. For their part, smallholders greatly favored the structure of the independent companies, where they and gentlemen had served side by side, without (in Gilmer's words) "partiality or distinction shewn." After the summer 1775 convention created the minuteman battalions, smallholders longed for the old system in which there had been "no pay at all or officers, but all marching *promiscuously* and on *equal* footing as volunteers," as Gilmer understood.[11]

The most powerful force keeping smallholders out of the minuteman battalions was its enormous demand on their time. New recruits had to leave their homes for twenty days of training; after that, minutemen had to train for another twenty-four days each year. No man that was vital to his family's productive process—and that included almost everyone below the rank of gentleman—could afford such a long absence. For minutemen, as the Accomack County committee explained, "the time of Encampment [is] Such that it must unavoidably break in upon their Whole years Business while they are only Allowed pay for the actual time of Duty."[12]

Thus the minuteman battalions, which the gentry had viewed as the solution to the problem of the disorderly independent companies, actually provoked still more dissent. The convention that gathered in Richmond in December 1775 had to yield to the smallholders' demand that it reduce dramatically the amount of time that minutemen spent in training. Fearing that the captains of the minute companies would still have trouble filling their quotas, the convention further sought to reduce its dependence on the minutemen by quadrupling the size of the regular army. The convention also required men that paid taxes on four or more workers, who had been

11. Gilmer, in McDonnell, "Politics of Mobilization," 81; Leven Powell to Sarah Powell, Dec. 5, 1775, Leven Powell Papers, VHS.

12. Accomack County committee, Nov. 30, 1775, Lunenburg County inhabitants, petition to Virginia Convention, presented May 11, 1776, both in *Revolutionary Virginia*, VI, 475; *SAL*, IX, 20; McDonnell, "Politics of Mobilization," 73–76.

exempted from all military duty by the summer 1775 convention, to serve their time on the slave patrols.[13]

Yet the virtual abolition of the minuteman battalions did not solve the problem of disorder, for gentlemen still had the regular army to worry about. On October 28, Major Alexander Spotswood of the Second Regiment "Observed with Concern" that his soldiers "Straggle into Town and are Disorderly there." On the same day, Spotswood ordered a court-martial for two camp followers, Florence Mahoney and Ann Jones, "for Rioting after sun set." A week later, Bernard Cary was court-martialed for "Spreading and Incouraging Mutiny." On December 19, regimental commander William Woodford ordered that officers make sure the chimneys of the barracks and other buildings not catch fire, lest "the confusion that hapens by Accidence might occasion mutiny amongst the men."[14]

Perhaps the gravest conflict between officers and common soldiers began in December, when the gentry-dominated convention repudiated the only gentleman that was extremely popular among the soldiers—Patrick Henry. Although Henry had been elected at the summer 1775 convention as supreme commander of the Virginia army, when the winter 1775–1776 convention persuaded the Continental Congress to take most of Virginia's full-time soldiers into continental pay, it failed to recommend that Henry remain commander in chief. Congress gave the command to William Woodford. When Henry learned of his demotion, he resigned his commission, whereupon the soldiers in his regiment "assembled in a tumultuous manner" and demanded discharges.[15] The soldiers' anger (allegedly inflamed by Henry) "begot a presenting of Pieces" at officers, as Landon Carter reported. Eventually the men stood down, but the mutiny unnerved Virginia gentlemen. It

13. *SAL*, IX, 86, 89; Selby, *Revolution in Virginia*, 78. Many smallholders were still angry that slaveholders were exempt from other military service. Petitions were sent to the next convention, which withdrew the exemption. See Lunenburg County inhabitants, petition to Virginia Convention, presented May 11, 1776, in *Revolutionary Virginia*, VI, 474–477; Chesterfield, Lunenberg, Mecklenburg, Amelia, and Caroline County freeholders, petitions, [May–June 1776], in Randolph W. Church, comp., *Virginia Legislative Petitions: Bibliography, Calendar, and Abstracts from Original Sources, 6 May 1776–21 June 1782* (Richmond, Va., 1984), 4, 9, 17, 24.

14. Oct. 28, Nov. 4, Dec. 19, 1775, in Brent Tarter, ed., "The Orderly Book of the Second Virginia Regiment, September 27, 1775–April 15, 1776," *VMHB*, LXXXV (1977), 175, 179, 309.

15. Purdie's *VG*, Mar. 1, 1776; Selby, *Revolution in Virginia*, 88–89. Henry's resignation "occasioned some disturbance in his regiment," Leven Powell told his wife Sarah (Mar. 5, 1776, in Robert C. Powell, ed., *A Biographical Sketch of Col. Leven Powell, Including His Correspondence during the Revolutionary War* [Alexandria, Va., 1877], 20).

was mid-March before Richard Henry Lee could celebrate that "The mutinous spirit of our Soldiery" was "so well subdued."[16]

Less than a month after the Henry mutiny, a rifle company from Augusta County set fire to the ferryhouse where they were stationed and committed other "Seditious and Mutinous" acts. When the court-martial that examined the Augusta men's actions returned a verdict that Lieutenant Colonel Hugh Mercer considered too lenient, he set the verdict aside, jailed two of the riflemen, and threatened to jail others. He told guards that, if any of the prisoners tried to escape, they were to "fire on the offenders With such Effect as to kill them if possible." Less than a week later, Mercer had to apologize publicly to the Augusta riflemen for his heavy-handedness. In the midst of that crisis, officers of the Virginia line selected, for the first time, a daily password that was neither a place nor a person. The watchword was "discipline." That certainly reflected the officers' most cherished goal—but not the reality on the ground. In May, a soldier in the Sixth Regiment was found guilty of "the most Henious and Dangerous of all Capitol Crimes, Mutiny," but escaped with only "slight punishment." General Charles Lee set aside the court-martial's verdict and discharged the soldier.[17]

The only certain way to suppress the disorderly behavior of the Virginia soldiers would be to end the war quickly. Victory would require guns and ammunition, but those were in such short supply that some soldiers were armed with spears, clubs, and slingshots.[18] The only way to satisfy Virginia's

16. Patrick Henry and his supporters claimed that Henry himself had talked the mutineers into laying down their weapons and then spent most of the night reconciling them to their new leaders. Landon Carter heard a different version of the story: the mutiny had been forcibly suppressed by Thomas Bullit, the army's adjutant general. "Tom Bullet collared a man or two and called out to a party well disposed who came in to his assistance and Clappt these two fellows under a close confinement," Carter said. See Mar. 12, 1776, in Jack P. Greene, ed., *The Diary of Colonel Landon Carter of Sabine Hall, 1752–1778* (Charlottesville, Va., 1965), II, 999; John Page to [Richard Henry Lee], Apr. 12, 1776, in Hoffman, ed., *Lee Family Papers*. For further evidence of insurgency within the army, see Nathaniel Cocke, advertisement, Dixon and Hunter's *VG*, Apr. 20, 1776. On the subsiding of the discontent that surrounded Henry's demotion, see Richard Henry Lee to John Page, Mar. 19, 1776, in Smith, ed., *Letters of Delegates to Congress*, III, 408n.

17. Mar. 11, 14, 17, 1776, "Orderly Book of the Company of Captain George Stubblefield, Fifth Virginia Regiment, from March 3, 1776, to July 10, 1776, Inclusive," VHS *Collections*, N.S., VI (1887), 150–154; Selby, *Revolution in Virginia*, 89; May 10, 1776, in Charles Campbell, ed., *The Orderly Book of That Portion of the American Army . . . under the Command of General Andrew Lewis . . .* (Richmond, Va., 1860), 36.

18. Charles Lee to John Hancock, Apr. 19, 1776, Andrew Lewis to Charles Lee, May 27, 1776, *The Lee Papers* (New York, 1871–1874), I, 433, II, 44; Apr. 7, 1776, in Campbell, ed.,

need for guns and ammunition would be to establish commercial ties to a European nation.[19] Would European rulers be willing to trade with the thirteen colonies while they officially remained part of the British Empire? Patriot leaders believed that they probably would not. Although Louis XVI and other monarchs were delighted at the prospect of direct trade with the British tobacco colonies, they feared that it would lead to hostilities with Britain. They were unwilling to run this risk until the Americans convinced them that their separation from Britain was permanent, and that could be demonstrated only by making it official.

Like soldiers, civilians sometimes refused to bear the unequal burdens placed on them by the war. Starting in December 1774, free Virginians had initiated nonimportation in order to exert pressure on Parliament by precipitating unemployment, and thus riots, in Britain. But, as the boycott began, Arthur Lee worried that it would also lead to social turmoil in Virginia. Lee feared that the British government would retaliate against the boycott by obstructing the flow of rum into Virginia, provoking smallholders to turn against their gentry rulers.[20] Lee's fears were not unfounded—

Orderly Book of Andrew Lewis, 17; Selby, *Revolution in Virginia*, 91; Lund Washington to George Washington, Jan. 17, 1776, in Abbot et al., eds., *Papers of George Washington*, Revolutionary War Series, III, 130. Some gentlemen believed the reason the Princess Anne County militia lost a famous skirmish to Dunmore's mostly black army at Kemp's Landing near Norfolk on Nov. 14, 1775, was that the militiamen were "less than half armed." See Richard Henry Lee to George Washington, Dec. 6, 1775, in Abbot et al., eds., *Papers of Washington*, Revolutionary War Series, II, 500; William Aylett to Richard Henry Lee, Apr. 20, 1776, in Hoffman, ed., *Lee Family Papers*.

19. Francis Lightfoot Lee to Landon Carter, Jan. 22, 1776, Benjamin Harrison to Robert Carter Nicholas, Feb. 13, 1776, Carter Braxton to Landon Carter, Apr. 14, 1776, Richard Henry Lee to Patrick Henry, Apr. 20, 1776, all in Smith, ed., *Letters of Delegates to Congress*, III, 130, 246, 522, 564; Charles Lee to Patrick Henry, May 7, 1776, *The Lee Papers*, II, 3. Leading Virginians sought a commercial treaty with France or some other European nation, not a military one. At that point, they wished to be supplied only with arms and ammunition, not with troops (Adam Stephen to Richard Henry Lee, Feb. 4, 1776, John Augustine Washington to Richard Henry Lee, Apr. 22, 1776, in Hoffman, ed., *Lee Family Papers*). One reason they were wary of military alliances was that they knew that this type of diplomacy could easily be turned against them. See Charles Lee to Patrick Henry, May 7, 1776, *The Lee Papers*, II, 2; May 2, 1776, in Greene, ed., *Diary of Landon Carter*, II, 1032; James H. Hutson, "The Partition Treaty and the Declaration of American Independence," *Journal of American History*, LVIII (1971–1972), 877–896.

20. [William Lee] to [Richard Henry Lee], Jan. 17, 1775, in Hoffman, ed., *Lee Family Papers*; Richard Henry Lee to George Washington, Sept. 26, 1775, Fielding Lewis to George Washington, Nov. 14, 1775, in Abbot et al., eds., *Papers of Washington*, Revolutionary War Series, II, 53, 373; "A British American" [Thomson Mason], "Number VIII," July 21, 1774, in

once the New England Restraining Act took effect, few vessels sailing from other countries managed to slip past the British navy ships cruising the bay.[21]

The first item to run out was salt. George Gilmer tried to persuade white Virginians that they would be healthier if they ate less salt. He argued that African Americans and Indians consumed less salted meat and salt than white Virginians, yet were healthier.[22] White Virginians were unconvinced. Salt was essential not only to their own diets but to their livestock. It was also needed to preserve meat. By November 1775, gentlemen worried that the salt shortage would lead to civil conflict. "From all parts," the Committee of Safety told the Virginia congressional delegation on November 11, the "Clamours of the people begin to be high on Acco[un]t of" the scarcity of salt, "and we greatly fear the consequences if some method cannot be fallen on to Supply their wants." On November 23, the Fairfax County committee reported that it was "apprehensive of the great Distress and Discontent that the Want of this necessary Article may occasion among the People." The next day, Lund Washington, the general's cousin, reported to him from Mount Vernon that "the people are run[nin]g mad about Salt."[23]

In early December, desperate Virginia farmers began conducting salt riots. The Hanover County committee reported that "several persons have, of their own accord, gone about in a disorderly manner to search for salt, and have taken the same." Some people questioned the heavy-handed measures that the committee employed "to preserve peace and good order, and to prevent riots and tumults." Yet they seemed to work. On December 9, the *Virginia Gazette* reported that "the disturbance in Hanover, on account of the present scarcity of salt, has subsided." Actually, the riots only shifted to

Revolutionary Virginia, I, 188; Arthur Lee to brother, Dec. 13, 1774, in Richard Henry Lee, *Life of Arthur Lee . . .* (Boston, 1829), I, 210; Boyd et al., eds., *Papers of Jefferson*, I, 150–151.

21. United States Bureau of the Census, *Historical Statistics of the United States, Colonial Times to 1957* (Washington, D.C., 1960), II, 1176–1178; Gilmer, "Address to the Inhabitants of Albemarle," VHS *Collections*, N.S., VI (1887), 118.

22. Gilmer, "Address to the Inhabitants of Albemarle," VHS *Collections*, N.S., VI (1887), 119.

23. Committee of Safety to Virginia Delegates in Congress, Nov. 11, 1775, James Freeland to John Tailyour, Oct. 20, 1775, in *Revolutionary Virginia*, IV, 246, 379; Jan. 2, 1776, Honyman diary; Nov. 26, 1775, William Cabell diary, negative photostat (accession no. 23338), LVA; Oct. 11, 1775, in Tarter, ed., "Orderly Book of the Second Virginia Regiment," *VMHB*, LXXXV (1977), 165; David John Mays, *Edmund Pendleton, 1721–1803: A Biography* (Cambridge, Mass., 1952), II, 47–50; Larry G. Bowman, "The Scarcity of Salt in Virginia during the American Revolution," *VMHB*, LXXVII (1969), 464–472; Fairfax County committee to John Hancock, Nov. 23, 1775, in *Revolutionary Virginia*, IV, 455–456; Lund Washington to George Washington, Nov. 24, 1775, in Abbot et al., eds., *Papers of Washington*, Revolutionary War Series, II, 423.

neighboring Henrico County, where "several companies of armed men" seized salt, one writer reported in mid-December. He warned that, "if a stop was not put to such marauding, some among us may be induced to make opposition [which] may produce civil discord."[24]

By the spring of 1776, numerous gentlemen feared that the salt shortage would provoke agrarian insurgency throughout Virginia. On March 19, Richard Henry Lee urged Virginia leaders to find some way to produce or procure salt, lest "the want of this Necessary . . . produce universal riot and convulsion." In April, Edmund Pendleton told Lee that "Our people will break through all restraint" if they did not obtain salt soon. Another patriot believed that the British government intentionally protracted its negotiations with the colonists, expecting that their shortages would leave them "naked, and perhaps distracted with mutual discords among ourselves."[25] Shortages not only produced internal discord but threatened to drive smallholders and poor whites into the arms of the British. John Page wondered darkly what the farmers around him would do "When to their Want of Salt there shall be added a Want of Clothes and Blankets." Page warned Thomas Jefferson that, if the shortages got much worse, smallholders and poor whites might even "give up the Authors of their Misfortunes, their Leaders" and "sacrifice them to a Reconciliation."

24. Hanover County committee, Dec. 12, 1775, in *Revolutionary Virginia*, V, 120; Dixon and Hunter's *VG*, Dec. 9, 1775; Edward Johnston to William Preston, Dec. 16, 1775, in Benson, "Wealth and Power," 302; "A Vir[g]inian," Pinkney's *VG*, Dec. 9, 1775. Eventually Virginians persuaded Congress to modify the Continental Association to permit them to import salt. But the shortage remained severe, and disturbances continued.

Shortages also led to disaffection among Virginia soldiers. Army captain Morgan Alexander found his company "very Mutinous" in December 1775, a condition he blamed on the skillful exploitation of the soldiers' hardship by a loyalist named Jonathan Dow. The "King [fo]und his soldiers better cloathing than the Country did," Dow told Alexander's men, and he "[ad]vised them to goe to the Governor." Men in Alexander's company said that "if they were not supplied with money they would Clear their Musquets and return home." One of them did, in fact, desert (Morgan Alexander, Charles Woods, Richard Partridge, depositions, [December] 1775, in *Revolutionary Virginia*, V, 181).

25. Richard Henry Lee to John Page, Mar. 19, 1776, in Smith, ed., *Letters of Delegates to Congress*, III, 408n; Edmund Pendleton to Richard Henry Lee, Apr. 20, 1776, in David John Mays, ed., *The Letters and Papers of Edmund Pendleton, 1734–1803* (Charlottesville, Va., 1967), I, 164; "To the Inhabitants of Virginia," letter from "A Planter," Dixon and Hunter's *VG*, Apr. 13, 1776. Gentlemen also expected shortages to exasperate slaves and make them more likely to rebel. One British merchant that sympathized with the rebel colonists worried about "the great number of Negroes in some of the Colonies, and the great danger which must arise from those people being in distress" (Richard Champion to Willing, Morris, and Company, Mar. 13, 1775, in G. H. Guttridge, ed., *The American Correspondence of a Bristol Merchant, 1766–1776: Letters of Richard Champion* [Berkeley, Calif., 1934], 52).

Page believed the gentry could alleviate the shortages and shore up farmers' support for the patriot cause only by "forming a commercial Alliance with France." Jefferson concurred with Page's remedy. "As to the articles of salt, blankets etc.," he told him in mid-May, "I see nothing but the measure of a foreign alliance which can promise a prospect of importing either."[26] The widespread view that Virginia should alleviate its divisive shortages by reviving its foreign trade raised the same difficult issue as the army's need for foreign arms and ammunition. Since no foreign power would trade with the thirteen colonies while they remained part of the British Empire, to call for foreign trade was to call for Independence.

II

During the winter of 1775–1776, many of the discontents brought on by the Revolutionary War came together to produce an insurrection in Loudoun County. As late as October 1775, Loudoun farmers seemed to be fully devoted to the patriot leadership. When a rumor spread that Governor Dunmore might raid Mount Vernon to take Martha Washington hostage, "the people of Loudon talkd of sendg a Guard to Conduct her up into Berkeley" County in the interior, George Washington learned from his cousin Lund. Presumably, those that meditated the rescue included some of George Washington's own tenants in Loudoun County.[27] Scarcely a month later, the mood in Loudoun had begun to sour. Early in November, farmers in several Northern Neck counties implored the Prince William County committee "to procure them Salt." Those making the "complaints and clamours" doubtless included farmers from Loudoun County on Prince William's northwestern border. In order to "quiet the minds of the people and keep peace in the Country," the committee agreed on November 14 to purchase imported salt—in violation of the Continental Association. If the committee did send salt to Loudoun County, it arrived too late to prevent a "Great disturbance for want of Salt" in Leesburg (the county seat) on November 20, diarist Nicholas Cresswell said.[28]

The most serious conflict in Loudoun and neighboring counties pitted landlords against tenants. Renters comprised about one-third of the families

---

26. Page to Jefferson, Apr. 26, 1776, Jefferson to Page, May 17, 1776, in Boyd et al., eds., *Papers of Jefferson*, I, 288, 294.

27. Lund Washington to George Washington, Oct. 5, 1775, in Abbot et al., eds., *Papers of Washington*, Revolutionary War Series, II, 116.

28. Prince William County committee to Continental Congress, Nov. 14, 177[5], in *Revolutionary Virginia*, IV, 396; Nov. 20, 1775, *The Journal of Nicholas Cresswell, 1774–1777* (London, 1925), 132.

in Loudoun—possibly the highest proportion in Virginia. One of the most prominent landlords in Fauquier County, which bordered Loudoun to the south, was Richard Henry Lee. By 1775, he had turned all of his land into rental property. The "support of a numerous family depended entirely upon these rents," he said.[29] He did not believe that the Revolutionary War should interfere with tenants' rental obligations. Although the war posed no special hardship for renters whose leases specified payment in produce, Lee's tenants, along with those of George Washington and hundreds of other landlords, were obliged to pay in cash. In September 1775, when export markets closed as a result of the rebel colonists' boycott of Britain and the government's retaliatory blockade, tenants were deprived of the income they needed to pay their rent. Their landlords nonetheless demanded payment; Lee, for one, feared that the loss of rental income would lead to his "total ruin."

During the summer of 1775, a provincial convention decided to print up £350,000 in paper money to pay for Dunmore's War against the Shawnees and Mingos and to fund the new patriot military establishment. That paper money was universally expected to depreciate.[30] Richard Henry Lee did not want to receive his rent in depreciated paper money, so he demanded that his tenants pay him in "Gold and Silver," the values of which were fixed. Lee did not really expect his tenants to hand coins to his rent collectors; he was simply trying to establish the principle that a tenant that owed him, say, ten pounds in rent would not be allowed simply to pay him ten pounds' worth of the new paper money. Instead, the tenant would have to pay Lee "as much paper money as would purchase" ten pounds' worth of metal coin.[31]

Previously, Lee's leases had not required his tenants to pay him in coin. The form of payment that he required was "current money," a fictitious money of account that had always traded at par with Virginia paper money. In fact, many of Lee's leases had been negotiated in 1765, during an earlier period of paper money inflation.[32] In the 1760s, Lee had apparently been

29. Richard Henry Lee to [Patrick Henry], [May 26, 1777], in James Curtis Ballagh, ed., *The Letters of Richard Henry Lee* (New York, 1911–1914), I, 298.

30. *SAL*, IX, 67–68; Richard Henry Lee to [Patrick Henry], [May 26, 1777], in Ballagh, ed., *Letters of Richard Henry Lee*, I, 298; William Allason to John Washington, Sept. 1, 1775, in D. R. Anderson, ed., "The Letters of William Allason, Merchant, of Falmouth, Virginia," *Richmond College Historical Papers*, II (June 1917), 168.

31. Richard Henry Lee, ". . . Reason for Desiring the Rents to Be Now Settled in Sterling," [Jan. 10, 1776], in Hoffman, ed., *Lee Family Papers*. Some parish vestries also demanded that taxpayers pay their parish levies in hard money instead of tobacco (Mecklenburg County freeholders, petition, [Spring 1776], in Church, comp., *Virginia Legislative Petitions*, 18.)

32. Thomas Ludwell Lee et al., lease to Thomas Marshall, Oct. 12, 1765, Fauquier County

forced to accept paper money from his tenants, which would help explain why he had campaigned so hard against it in the House of Burgesses. When, in the winter of 1775–1776, Lee demanded that his tenants pay him in hard money, he was seeking a concession that he had apparently failed to obtain before the war.

In 1777, Richard Henry Lee was called to account for his refusal to accept paper money at face value. In a letter to Patrick Henry, he claimed that his demand had not harmed his tenants, because, as paper money had depreciated, driving up the amount of paper that he had demanded of them, the same process of inflation had raised the prices of the commodities they produced. But Lee knew that that was not so. In the original draft of the same letter, Lee acknowledged that, after exports ceased, the price of farm produce fell to "a pittance." (He deleted that comment from the letter before sending it.)[33]

Lee's other justification for demanding specie was that paper money was not legal tender for sterling debts at the time the leases were signed. But his tenants knew the summer 1775 convention that printed the £350,000 worth of paper bills ordered that "they shall be current between all persons within this colony." Creditors were obliged to accept them in discharge of debts. Accordingly, the trickle of income that the farmers themselves received after exports ceased in September 1775 was almost all paper money. For instance, soldiers were paid in paper money. They had no recourse as the paper money began to depreciate. Richard Henry Lee might call the convention ordinance that required creditors to accept paper money "retrospective destruction" and refuse to comply with it, but most ordinary farmers had no choice.[34]

Many private employers adopted the army's practice of paying free workers in paper money. In doing so, one of them inadvertently helped to supply the Loudoun revolt with a fiery new leader. The employer was George Washington, and his conflict with his employee grew out of his attempt to protect his title to two tracts of land in the Ohio Valley. Provincial Virginia's land grant law required the recipients of land patents to make improvements on

deed book no. 2, 424; John J. McCusker, *Money and Exchange in Europe and America, 1600–1775: A Handbook* (Chapel Hill, N.C., 1978).

33. Richard Henry Lee to [Patrick Henry], [May 26, 1777], in Ballagh, ed., *Letters of Richard Henry Lee*, I, 299, 299n. After nonexportation and the British blockade began, both tobacco and wheat fetched a "very low price" (Oliver Perry Chitwood, *Richard Henry Lee: Statesman of the Revolution* [Morgantown, W.V., 1967], 137).

34. Lee, "Reason for Desiring the Rents," in Hoffman, ed., *Lee Family Papers*; Richard Henry Lee to [Patrick Henry], [May 26, 1777], to [George Wythe], Oct. 17, 1777, both in Ballagh, ed., *Letters of Richard Henry Lee*, I, 298n, 336; *SAL*, IX, 69;

their land within three years or forfeit their patents. Washington had received two large patents on the Ohio and Kanawha Rivers in December 1772; thus he had until December 1775 to make the necessary improvements. In January 1775, Washington hired James Cleveland, who had served him as an overseer since the early 1760s, to lead a crew of slaves and servants to the Ohio country to plant corn and build houses on the land. Cleveland's contract mandated that he be paid in hard money.[35] Despite the troubles he had with his white servants, some of whom ran away to the Indian towns across the Ohio, Cleveland managed to make fifteen hundred pounds' worth of improvements on the two tracts. But he had to abandon the work and return to Mount Vernon when Shawnee warriors began attacking colonists on the Ohio. When Cleveland presented his bill to Washington's cousin Lund Washington, he was paid in paper money.[36]

People like James Cleveland and the Loudoun tenants were trapped between two millstones: between landlords, like Richard Henry Lee, that demanded they pay their rent in hard money, and employers—including army officers—that paid them their wages in quickly depreciating paper money. Cleveland's anger at General Washington for placing him in this predicament apparently helped propel him to the forefront of the uprising that was just then gathering momentum in Loudoun County.[37] By mid-February 1776, Cleveland was at the "head of the Party," a mortified Lund Washington reported to his cousin. "Cleveland I am told has turn'd Polititian and is setg all Loudon to gether by the Ears."

Starting around Christmas Day 1775, the traditional date for annual rent payments, many Loudoun tenants began to follow James Cleveland's simple advice: "The Tennants shoud pay no Rents." Tenants in neighboring counties also refused to pay up, "assigning for reason that they could not sell their produce," Richard Henry Lee said.[38] Other rent collectors encountered simi-

35. Patent Book XLI, pages 69, 73, Virginia Land Office Records, LVA; George Washington to Thomas Everard, Sept. 17, 1775, in Abbot et al., eds., *Papers of Washington*, Revolutionary War Series, II, 2; *SAL*, V, 425; Benson, "Wealth and Power," 346.

36. Valentine Crawford to George Washington, June 24, 1775, Lund Washington to George Washington, Nov. 5, 1775, James Cleveland to George Washington, Nov. 16, 1775, all in Abbot et al., eds., *Papers of Washington*, Revolutionary War Series, I, 28, II, 305–306, 382; Benson, "Wealth and Power," 346.

37. Cleveland was not the revolt's only leader. To Lund Washington's surprise, the "first promoters" of the notion that landlords were not entitled to rent during nonexportation included "some of the Leadg men in Loudon" (Lund Washington to George Washington, Dec. 30, 1775, in Abbot et al., eds., *Papers of Washington*, Revolutionary War Series, II, 621).

38. Lund Washington to George Washington, Feb. 29, 1776, in Abbot et al., eds., *Papers of*

lar resistance. "From the Accounts I have from Loudon Prince William, and some other Countys," Lund Washington wrote his cousin, "there is very little hopes of Collectg money from Tenants, they say it is Cruel in the Land Holders to expect their Rents when there is no market for the produce of the Land." The tenants were willing to pay their 1775 rent in the future if exports should resume before their 1775 crops rotted. But they told Lund Washington that, "if there shoud be no market before the present Crop spoils upon there hands, it woud be the height of Injustice ever to expect to be paid for that years Rent."[39]

There was nothing new about tenants' parrying rent collectors during hard times. In two senses, however, the events in Loudoun were extraordinary. First, many of the tenants that withheld their rent mounted a united front. Second, they did not beg their landlords' indulgence (as delinquent tenants usually did) but presumed to judge when rent collection became an act of injustice. Some landlords did not harass their tenants for rent. "Perhaps if they had money I cou'd get some from them," Lund Washington wrote his cousin George in apparent resignation. Other landlords, though, directed court officers to distrain, or seize, the property of delinquent tenants. Victims of distraint would lose as much property as had to be auctioned off to pay the overdue rent—a substantial amount even in the best of times, owing to Virginia's chronic currency shortage, and even more so now that nonexportation had depressed property values. Still more property would have to be auctioned to pay cash fees to the sheriff, to attorneys, and to the county clerk.[40]

Some landlords also threatened to evict delinquent tenants. Richard Henry Lee got involved in a rent dispute with an atypical tenant, the Glasgow firm of William Cuninghame and Company. Lee had leased the firm a town lot near the Fauquier County courthouse for one of its stores. Lee and James Robison, Cuninghame's chief factor, were unable to agree on the rent, so Robison paid nothing. Although, with the closing of the courts, Robison had no recourse against the hundreds of Virginia tobacco farmers that owed money to his firm, Lee had recourse against Robison. His rental agent re-

Washington, Revolutionary War Series, III, 395–396; Richard Henry Lee to Patrick Henry, [May 26, 1777], in Ballagh, ed., *Letters of Richard Henry Lee*, I, 298.

39. Lund Washington to George Washington, Dec. 30, 1775, in Abbot et al., eds., *Papers of Washington*, Revolutionary War Series, II, 621.

40. Lund Washington to George Washington, Feb. 15, 1776, in Abbot et al., eds., *Papers of Washington*, Revolutionary War Series, III, 317; Willard F. Bliss, "The Rise of Tenancy in Virginia," *VMHB*, LVIII (1950), 433.

ported telling Robison "that he might rely you would take possession of your Tenement very shortly."[41]

In Loudoun County, the landlords' threats of property seizures and evictions were only the beginning. Property owners also persuaded the patriot committee of Loudoun County to launch an effort to intimidate the leaders of the rent strike. In December 1775, strike leaders were "cited to appear before the Committee," where they could expect to receive the same rough treatment that the committee meted out to loyalists and other enemies of the new order.[42]

The landlords' effort to crush the rent strike failed. Strike leaders, learning that they were to be hauled before the patriot committee, "said they are not at all Intimidated at it," Lund Washington reported. In fact, they threatened to "turn the Committee out of the House." Tenants also stood up to the landlords' threat to have court officers distrain their property. Washington learned that the rent strike leaders, whom he called "transgressors of the peace," had said they would "Punish the First officer that dare destrain for Rent."[43]

Even as the rent strike grew, gentlemen learned that the Loudoun families were also angry about the gentry's military policies. They complained about the eleven-to-one pay disparity between top officers and common soldiers. "The people in our County talk much of the officers wages being too high," Leven Powell of Loudoun County told his wife Sarah in early December 1775. Many Loudoun people agreed with insurgent leader James Cleveland that "the pay of officers and Soldiers shoud be the same." Better yet, officers "shoud not be paid at all," Cleveland reportedly said. They should follow the example of Cleveland's employer, George Washington, and serve for

41. Richard Parker to [Richard Henry Lee], Mar. 7, 1776, in Hoffman, ed., *Lee Family Papers*. The closing of the courts in June 1774 prevented most creditors from distraining their debtors' property, but landlords were a special case. As George Mason had explained exactly ten years earlier, when the courts had also been closed (to protest the Stamp Act), English common law gave "the Land-lord a Right to distrain upon anything on his Land for the Rent due." The landlord did not need to go to court to seize sufficient property from his tenants to pay their back rent, Mason pointed out; the law "puts his Remedy into his own Hands." See ". . . [A] Scheme for Replevying Goods under Distress for Rent," enclosed in Mason to George William Fairfax and George Washington, Dec. 23, 1765, in Rutland, ed., *Papers of George Mason*, I, 62; George Washington, lease to Francis Ballinger, [Mar. 17, 1769], in W. W. Abbot et al., eds., *The Papers of George Washington*, Colonial Series (Charlottesville, Va., 1983–), VIII, 172–173.

42. Lund Washington to George Washington, Dec. 30, 1775, in Abbot et al., eds., *Papers of Washington*, Revolutionary War Series, II, 621.

43. Ibid.

expenses only. Wealthy people like General Washington had independent sources of income and a powerful inducement to fight—protecting their property against the British army. The Loudoun tenants, by contrast, did not even own the land they worked. "There is no inducement for a poor Man to Fight," ran one of James Cleveland's slogans, "for he has nothing to defend."[44]

Angry as the soldiers were about the pay disparity, they had an even greater grievance: the gentry's prosecution of the war. The Loudoun families blamed patriot leaders for allowing the war to drag on and on. At the end of February 1776, more than a year after imports of salt and other essential commodities ceased and more than six months after the creation of the Virginia line, gentry military leaders still had not managed to force Dunmore's plucky little army from its tidewater beachhead. Soldiers were tired of waiting for the final battle that would force Dunmore to abandon the Chesapeake and allow them to return to their farms. They were also impatient to resume overseas trade. "Let us go and Fight the Battle at once, and not be Shilly Shally, in this way, until all the Poor, people are ruined," James Cleveland reportedly said.[45] Thus the rent and military grievances were intertwined. If the gentry would hurry up and defeat Dunmore, soldiers could lay down their arms and once again become grain and tobacco exporters. They could acquire the income they needed to pay their rent and other expenses.

James Cleveland was not the only Loudouner that openly challenged the patriot military establishment. When Richard Morlan of Loudoun was called to a mandatory militia muster, he declared that "he would not muster, and if fined would oppose the collection of the fine with his gun," the Loudoun County patriot committee reported. Not content with individual noncompliance, Morlan resisted "publickly" and also tried to "discourage a minute-man"—apparently a deserter—"from returning to his duty."[46]

Gentlemen anticipated that the Loudoun revolt would turn violent. "I suppose the first Battle we have in this part of the Country will be in Loudon, against General Cleveland," Lund Washington told his cousin George on the

44. Leven Powell to Sarah Powell, Dec. 5, 1775, Leven Powell Papers, VHS; Lund Washington to George Washington, Feb. 29, 1776, in Abbot et al., eds., *Papers of Washington*, Revolutionary War Series, III, 396.

45. Lund Washington to George Washington, Feb. 29, 1776, in Abbot et al., eds., *Papers of Washington*, Revolutionary War Series, III, 396. Of course, the Virginians' belief that a war that lasted more than a year was too long would seem naive to them after six more years of fighting.

46. Loudoun County committee, May 14, 1776, in *Revolutionary Virginia*, VII, 138; McDonnell, "Popular Mobilization," *Journal of American History*, LXXXV (1998).

last day of February 1776.[47] By that time, the Committee of Safety "feared" it might have to send patriot troops "to Quell" the "disturbances" in Loudoun. So the committee members made a prudent decision. They expected that any troops that would be marched to Loudoun would come from the Third Regiment of the Virginia line, which was stationed on the Potomac River. Someone pointed out that the Third Regiment included Captain Charles West's company from Loudoun County. On March 2, the Committee of Safety transferred the Loudoun company out of the Third Regiment. Later in March, the Committee of Safety ordered a minuteman company to march to Loudoun. The soldiers incurred no resistance, and, by April 2, the Committee of Safety believed that "the disturbances in Loudon are quieted." On that date it returned the Loudoun company to the Third Regiment.[48]

Still the tenants refused to pay their rent. "I really lament the torn and distracted condition of your County," Andrew Leitch told Loudoun gentleman Leven Powell on May 15. Leitch worried that some of the leaders of the Loudoun revolt might hold "principles of dissatisfaction to their native country." Those leaders, he warned Powell, "if they can talk and hold forth amongst their honest, well-meaning neighbors, shall work you more mischief in two or three church Sundays than a hundred virtuous and sensible citizens can, perhaps, eradicate in a year." Three weeks later, another of Powell's gentry friends asked him, "How goes on the spirit of Levelling?"[49]

Gentlemen knew better than to view the uprising as an isolated incident that would remain within the confines of Loudoun County. From Mount Vernon in neighboring Fairfax County, Lund Washington reported in early

47. Lund Washington said he hoped "the Consequence" of Cleveland's actions would be "the loss of his life for I woud wish every Damn'd Vilain who meddles in matters he knows nothing off, may get Hang'd" (to George Washington, Feb. 29, 1776, in Abbot et al., eds., *Papers of Washington*, Revolutionary War Series, III, 395–396).

48. Committee of Safety, Mar. 2, 20, Apr. 2, 1776, in *Revolutionary Virginia*, VI, 164, 231, 306. Initially, the Committee of Safety did not acknowledge its fear that the Loudoun Company would side with the tenants. Dale Benson points out that, on Mar. 2, when it moved the Loudoun company out of the Third Regiment, the Committee of Safety stated merely that it did so "for reasons appearing to this Committee." Only later, when it returned the Loudoun company to the Third Regiment, did the committee acknowledge that the reason it had considered it "inconvenient to have the Loudon Compy. in that regiment" was that "it was feared the 3d: Regimt. might be called on to Quell" the "disturbances" in Loudoun. See Committee of Safety, Mar. 2, Apr. 2, 1776, in *Revolutionary Virginia*, VI, 164, 306; Benson, "Wealth and Power," 348.

49. Andrew Leitch to Leven Powell, May 15, 1776, James Hendricks to Leven Powell, [June] 5, 1776, in Powell, ed., *Biographical Sketch of Leven Powell*, 85, 87.

March that "here all the talk is about the Tenants."[50] Richard Henry Lee's response to the revolt was to moderate the demands he placed on his tenants. From August 1775 through January 1776, Lee had insisted that his tenants pay him as much paper money as would equal the sterling amount in his leases. By March 1776, after the outbreak of the Loudoun revolt, Lee had agreed to accept payment in tobacco. Yet his conflict with the tenants continued, for the price at which he offered to accept their tobacco was only 1.68 pence per pound. The tenants refused to part with their crops at this price. Even when Lee's rent collector, Richard Parker, offered two pence per pound, some of the tenants, those living "at the Blue Ridge," still would not settle, Parker told Lee. "They, John Webb and one Key at their head, would not strike at any thing under" 2.4 pence per pound, Parker said. That was nearly 50 percent higher than the price at which Lee had originally offered to accept tobacco. Neither Parker nor the western tenants would budge. "I could get not a farthing from those Tenants," Parker later reported.[51]

Gentlemen believed that the only way they could prevent Loudoun's "plebian infamy" (as one gentlemen called it) from spreading to other parts of Virginia was to end the war quickly. James Cleveland had said that gentry commanders must no longer "Shilly Shally," and gentlemen were beginning to get the message. "There is no error we ought more to dread than . . . inaction," an essayist that called himself "A Planter" told *Virginia Gazette* readers in April 1776. Prolonged negotiations with Britain would lead to

50. Lund Washington to George Washington, Mar. [7, 1776], in Abbot et al., eds., *Papers of Washington*, Revolutionary War Series, III, 432.

51. Those tenants also offered to pay their rent in wheat at four and a half shillings per bushel, but Parker declined that offer (Parker to [Lee], Mar. 7, 1776, in Hoffman, ed., *Lee Family Papers*). It was not only tenants that Lee angered by refusing to accept paper money at face value. Lee's refusal was also alleged to have contributed to the depreciation of the paper money. When his policy was brought to the attention of the House of Delegates in 1777, the House refused to give Lee another term in Congress. Delegates later heard Lee in his own defense—he justified his demand for produce but said nothing of his earlier, more inflationary demand for sterling or its equivalent in paper money—and elected him to the first seat that fell vacant. See Richard Henry Lee to [Patrick Henry], [May 26, 1777], and to [George Wythe], Oct. 19, 1777, in Ballagh, ed., *Letters of Richard Henry Lee*, I, 298–299, 300, 335–337; John Banister to Theoderick Bland [incorrectly dated June 10, 1777], *The Bland Papers, Being a Selection from the Manuscripts of Colonel Theoderick Bland, Jr. . . .* , ed. Charles Campbell (Petersburg, Va., 1840), I, 57–58; James Blackwell to Richard Henry Lee, Jan. 16, 1777, Francis Lightfoot Lee and Mann Page, Jr., to the House of Delegates, June 10, 1777, both in John Carter Matthews, "Richard Henry Lee and the American Revolution" (Ph.D. diss., University of Virginia, 1939), 207, 218; Chitwood, *Richard Henry Lee*, 137–142; Herbert E. Sloan, *Principle and Interest: Thomas Jefferson and the Problem of Debt* (New York, 1995), 34–36.

"infinite dissentions among ourselves." "An enterprise that depends upon the concord and exertions of the people, will ever infallibly fail if they are long held in a state of doubtful inactivity," he wrote. If the war dragged on much longer, America would be rent by "faction and sedition." "For God's sake then," he declared, "let us waste no time in unnecessary and dangerous delays."[52]

Since the muskets, gunpowder, and lead shot that were vital to an early victory could be obtained only from Europe, the Loudoun revolt pointed gentlemen in the same direction as the disorders in the army and the salt riots: Virginia and the other rebel provinces needed to contract a commercial alliance with France or some other European nation. But first they would have to become independent states. Independence thus was increasingly considered the precondition for obtaining the salt and other supplies that were needed to prevent scarcity riots, the export income that would ease conflicts such as that between landlords and tenants, and the arms and ammunition that would allow gentlemen to meet the farmers' urgent demand (and their own urgent need) to end the war quickly.

Nor was a revival of international trade the only attraction of Independence. A formal government would stand a better chance than the extralegal conventions and committees of successfully suppressing the wave of civilian and military disorder that swept over Virginia in late 1775 and early 1776. Gentlemen favoring Independence realized by early April 1776 that the fear of disorder was a powerful tool that they could use to pull conservative gentlemen away from their attachment to Britain and into the movement for Independence.

Francis Lightfoot Lee was one of the first to recognize the political usefulness of the mounting agrarian insurgency in Virginia. Throughout early 1776, Lee maintained a steady correspondence with the conservative Landon Carter back in Virginia. Although only Lee's letters survive, they powerfully illuminate the way patriot leaders like Lee tried to persuade conservative gentlemen like Carter of the need for Independence. In March, Lee received a letter from Carter that evidently repeated the common conservative prediction that Independence would lead to anarchy. Replying on March 19, Lee at first minimized those fears. "The danger of Anarchy and confusion, I think altogether chimerical, the good behaviour of the Americans with no

52. Benson, "Wealth and Power," 343 (it is not clear where Benson found this quotation); Lund Washington to George Washington, Feb. 29, 1776, in Abbot et al., eds., *Papers of Washington*, Revolutionary War Series, III, 396; "To the Inhabitants of Virginia," letter from "A Planter," Dixon and Hunter's *VG*, Apr. 13, 1776.

Government at all proves them very capable of good Government," he told Carter. On March 30, Carter wrote back and refuted Lee's claim that ordinary Virginians had behaved well during the suspension of formal government. Possibly he reminded Lee about the December 1775 salt riots or the mutiny that followed Patrick Henry's resignation from the army. Perhaps Carter relayed information about the Loudoun tenants' revolt.[53]

Lee seized upon the information in Carter's March 30 letter and used it to turn Carter's argument against Independence on its head. "It makes me uneasy to find from yr. Letr. that licentiousness begins to prevail in Virga.," he told Carter on April 9. Lee blamed the lower-class disturbances on "the mismanagement of the Gentlemen." The problem was that the "old Government" had been "dissolved, and no new one substituted in its stead." In such a situation it was inevitable that "Anarchy must be the consequence." Then Lee came to his proposal for restoring order in Virginia. The convention that was to assemble in May 1776 should comply with an earlier suggestion from Congress and "establish such Government as wou'd best secure their peace and happiness." Lee argued that the only way Rhode Island and Connecticut had preserved "order and quiet" was by maintaining their old colonial governments. He pointed out that New Hampshire and Massachusetts had been "getting into the utmost disorder; but upon their assuming Government . . . they are restored to perfect harmony and regularity." If the May 1776 Virginia convention should fail to establish a regular government, Lee concluded, "I dread the consequences." If Virginia and the other southern colonies remained without formal governmental institutions, he warned, they would soon "have violent symptoms to encounter."[54]

Lee's April 9 letter seemed to leave open the possibility that the Virginia convention could set up a temporary government that it could dissolve upon a subsequent accommodation with Britain. But a later report from Carter describing further agrarian unrest in Virginia provided Lee the ammunition he needed to make the case for all-out Independence. Carter's letter probably reported an incident in which one of Governor Dunmore's tenders sailed up the Rappahannock River. To prevent the tender from sending a party ashore to burn the great houses along the river, a group of militiamen mustered. But, when the group asked one smallholder to lend them his firelock, the man, whom Carter identified only as "G. R.," "asked the People if they were such fools to go to protect the Gentlemen's houses on the river

53. Smith, ed., *Letters of Delegates to Congress*, III, 407. By 1783, James Cleveland was renting land from Francis Lightfoot Lee, and it is possible that he was already doing so in 1776.

54. Francis Lightfoot Lee to Carter, Apr. 9, 1776, in Smith, ed., *Letters of Delegates to Congress*, III, 500–501.

side," Carter reported in his diary; "he thought it would be the better if they were burnt down."[55]

It is even more likely that Carter told Lee about the April 1 Richmond County election, where Lee himself lost his seat in the Virginia convention. As we have seen, Lee replied that he hoped his former colleagues would "make such an establishment, as will put a stop to the rising disorders with you, and secure internal quiet for the future." It was all the more important that divisions among white patriots be suppressed, Lee argued, because soon they would have to fight British and black troops. "The violent struggle we have to go thro' this summer, the hardships we must suffer, make it necessary to cultivate the utmost harmony among ourselves," he told Carter. As he had in April, Lee argued that Virginia should follow the example of other colonies. Even the conservative middle colonies "are going fast into Independency and constituting new Governmts. convinced of the necessity of it, both for the security of internal peace and good order; and for the vigorous exertion of their whole force against the common Enemy."[56]

Carter and Lee's entire debate about Independence had centered upon the danger of agrarian insurgency. Where Carter was certain that Independence would lead to more of the refractory behavior he had already witnessed, Lee argued that Independence was actually the only way the "rising disorders" could be contained. Both men, for opposite reasons, exaggerated the danger that smallholders and tenants posed to gentlemen. But their conversation would have been very different had it not been founded upon grains of truth—the Loudoun County uprising, the salt riots, the mutiny that followed Patrick Henry's resignation, the disorders in the minuteman battalions, and the other smallholder disturbances.

Throughout 1776, other pro-Independence gentlemen joined Francis Lee in playing on their conservative brethren's fear of disorder to try to dissolve their allegiance to Britain. On April 26, John Page told Thomas Jefferson that smallholders and poor whites had pleasantly surprised him by "behaving so peaceably and honestly as they have when they were free from the Restraint of Laws." "But how long this may be the Case who can tell? . . . To prevent

55. Carter chaired the Richmond County patriot committee. He wrote in his diary that, if G. R. had been hauled before the committee, its wisest course would have been to ignore him, since people like G. R. "only want to be taken notice of, that they may have some grounds to represent to those like themselves, what persecution they endure by resisting the rich or, as they call them, the Gentlemen" (May 1, 1776, in Greene, ed., *Diary of Landon Carter*, II, 1030–1031).

56. Lee to Carter, May 21, 1776, in Smith, ed., *Letters of Delegates to Congress*, IV, 57. Lee did not know that the Virginia convention had already voted to ask Congress to declare Independence.

Disorders in each Colony a Constitution should be formed," Page wrote.[57] Jefferson actually needed no convincing on the question of Independence. No doubt Page sent him his argument linking Independence to the prevention of anarchy so that it could be passed on to the more reluctant. In the same spirit, Page sent member of Congress Richard Henry Lee a catalog of the Virginia farmers' grievances. He found "our People in some Places Discontented about Henry's Resignation." Other white Virginians were angry at the patriot leadership's military policies, especially "the removal of the Troops from their Neighbourhood." Still others were angry because they feared "being removed as the People of Norfolk and Princess [Anne] are to be into the interior Parts of the Country." Page urged Lee to come home from Philadelphia to help "prevail on the Convention to declare for Independency, and to establish a Form of Government."[58]

Lee took up this line of reasoning in an April 30 letter to provincial treasurer Robert Carter Nicholas, who opposed Independence. "Sir," Lee demanded, "do you not see the indispensable necessity of establishing a Government this Convention? How long popular commotions may be suppressed without it, and anarchy be prevented, deserves intense consideration." Lee argued that organizing a formal government would "prevent the numerous evils to be apprehended from popular rage and licence whenever they find the bonds of government removed." On December 22, 1775, Parliament had officially proclaimed the rebel colonies outside the king's protection. When Patrick Henry held back from Independence (he believed foreign alliances should come first), Lee told him that the "act of Parliament has to every legal intent and purpose dissolved our government, uncommissioned every magistrate, and placed us in the high road to Anarchy." The gentry could halt the descent into disorder only by "taking up government immediately."[59]

57. Apr. 26, 1776, in Boyd et al., eds., *Papers of Jefferson*, I, 288.

58. John Page to [Richard Henry Lee], Apr. 12, 1776, in Hoffman, ed., *Lee Family Papers*; Selby, *Revolution in Virginia*, 93. Charles Lee concentrated his forces in Williamsburg because he feared that, if the British could seize the provincial capital, they would win credibility in the eyes of enslaved Virginians and persuade thousands of them to risk trying to reach the British lines (Charles Lee to [William] Peachey and [Hugh] Mercer, Apr. 2, 1776, *The Lee Papers*, I, 369).

59. Richard Henry Lee to [Patrick Henry], Apr. 20, 1776, to Robert Carter Nicholas, Apr. 30, 1776, both in Ballagh, ed., *Letters of Richard Henry Lee*, I, 177 184; Robert E. Brown and B. Katherine Brown, *Virginia, 1705–1786: Democracy or Aristocracy?* (East Lansing, Mich., 1964), 292–293. Thomas Paine, whose pamphlet *Common Sense* alarmed many conservatives by advocating republican government, warned those same conservatives not

The Independence advocates' effort to inflame the conservative Virginia gentlemen's fears of anarchy and convert them to the cause of Independence succeeded with at least one prominent conservative. Carter Braxton resisted the impulse to Independence as long as he could. But by early May 1776, when convention delegates gathered in Williamsburg, Braxton believed they had no choice but to seize at once "the reins of government, and no longer suffer the people to live without the benefit of law." Inaction would invite "Anarchy and riot . . . and render the enjoyment of our liberties and future quiet, at least very precarious." In mid-May, Braxton reluctantly informed Landon Carter, his uncle and fellow conservative, that "The Assumption of Governt."—and, thus, a declaration of Independence—"was necessary."[60]

---

to allow the thirteen colonies to continue on with no government. "Ye that oppose independance now, ye know not what ye do; ye are opening a door to eternal tyranny, by keeping vacant the seat of government," Paine wrote (*Common Sense* [1776], ed. Isaac Kramnick [London, 1976], 99).

60. "An Address to the Convention . . . of Virginia . . . ," letter from "A Native" [Braxton], in *Revolutionary Virginia*, VI, 518; Braxton to Carter, May 17, 1776, in Smith, ed., *Letters of Delegates to Congress*, IV, 19. The fear of anarchy also led many gentlemen in other colonies to favor Independence (Richard L. Bushman, *King and People in Provincial Massachusetts* [Chapel Hill, N.C., 1985], 216); Edward Rutledge to Ralph Izard, Dec. 8, 1775, *Correspondence of Mr. Ralph Izard, of South Carolina . . .* (New York, 1844), I, 165. The constitution adopted by the South Carolina provincial congress accused the British government of working to "loosen the bands of government, and create anarchy and confusion in the Colonies" (John Drayton, *Memoirs of the American Revolution, from Its Commencement to the Year 1776, Inclusive; As Relating to the State of South-Carolina . . .* [Charleston, S.C., 1821], II, 189). Even in Maryland, where (as Ronald Hoffman has shown) for months the gentry's fear of the lower classes had prevented it from favoring separation from Britain, that same fear eventually led many gentlemen to embrace Independence as the lesser evil. Charles Carroll of Annapolis told his son that the only way to rescue Maryland from disorder was to "establish a government" (Charles Carroll, in Hoffman, *A Spirit of Dissension: Economics, Politics, and the Revolution in Maryland* [Baltimore, 1973], 150).

PART FOUR : INDEPENDENCE

1776

Whenever any Form of Government
becomes destructive of these ends,
it is the Right of the People to
alter or to abolish it.
—Declaration of Independence

7

SPIRIT OF THE PEOPLE

We have seen that smallholders and poor whites indirectly helped push gentlemen into the American Revolution. These two groups also pushed gentlemen toward Independence in a more direct and intentional way: they simply demanded it. The gentry delegates at the May 1776 Virginia convention felt tremendous pressure from ordinary Virginians to make the final break with Britain.

I

One reason that many smallholders and poor whites sought an independent government was that they expected it to be much more amenable to their influence. This expectation took a while to develop, for the first pro-Independence essays to appear in Virginia made no suggestions about what form an independent government should take. Clearly, the authors favored Independence because of British provocation (military attacks, Dunmore's emancipation proclamation, and so on) and as a matter of practical necessity. For them, the attraction of Independence was not that it would allow free Virginians to redesign their internal government. But by late 1775, as formal separation from Britain became a realistic option, more and more colonists began to imagine what a new Virginia government might look like. They quickly grasped that Virginia could not simply secede from the empire while maintaining the same government institutions that had developed during the colonial era. When Virginians discovered the internal implications of Independence, some drew back in horror. Others had just the opposite reaction.

Britain's government balanced three distinct forms: monarchy, aristocracy, and democracy. The crown represented kingship, the House of Lords embodied the aristocracy, and the House of Commons represented the common people. This structure could not be replicated in America. Because of the widespread "tenure of landed property, and the absence of *hereditary distinctions* of *rank*" in America, a *Virginia Gazette* writer explained, there was nothing like the British aristocracy. America also lacked a royal family from which to draw a hereditary king. These obvious differences were pointed out to the readers of the *Virginia Gazette* by an opponent of Independence that called himself "Hampden." He imagined independent American states trying to set up a new form of government. "Is it probable that they will establish a form on the same salutary principles as the old one; or is it practicable? If they should incline to do so, who among us has pretensions to the *throne?*"[1]

The only answer to Hampden's question was that there would *be* no throne, and no House of Lords either. The lower house of the legislature would reign supreme. Even if the government were balanced among three branches, as Britain's was, the personnel of each branch would have to be selected—directly or indirectly—by the freeholders. And Virginia, like the other American colonies, had an electorate that was much broader than Britain's; in fact, the majority of free white men could vote.[2]

The prospect of abandoning the monarchical and aristocratic elements in the British constitution worried many Virginia gentlemen. To be sure, these conservatives would have been even more opposed to giving up the democratic part of the British government—the lower house of the legislature. As much as gentlemen cherished the dominant role of the House of Commons, however, they also celebrated the fact that it was kept in check by the House of Lords and the crown.[3] George Washington recognized that the gentry

1. "Hampden," Dixon and Hunter's *VG*, Apr. 27, 1776; "E. F.," Purdie's *VG*, May 17, 1776; Thomas Paine, *Common Sense* (1776), ed. Isaac Kramnick (London, 1976), 98; "A Native" [Carter Braxton], "An Address to the Convention . . . of Virginia . . . ," in *Revolutionary Virginia*, VI, 521. "Nowhere in eighteenth-century America had the legal attributes of nobility been recognized or perpetuated" (Bernard Bailyn, *The Ideological Origins of the American Revolution* [Cambridge, Mass., 1967], 275).

2. Bailyn, *Ideological Origins*, 280–281; Richard Henry Lee to Edmund Pendleton, May 12, 1776, in Paul H. Smith et al., eds., *Letters of Delegates to Congress, 1774–1789* (Washington, D.C., 1976–), III, 667; "Viator" [William Draper], *The Thoughts of a Traveller upon Our American Disputes* (London, 1774), 7; Robert E. Brown and B. Katherine Brown, *Virginia, 1705–1786: Democracy or Aristocracy?* (East Lansing, Mich., 1964), chap. 6.

3. Even Thomas Jefferson was worried enough about the prospect of a runaway lower house of the legislature that he wanted to make the members of the upper house "independent" of the common people. In one of his famous forced choices, Jefferson said that, if he had to choose between senators that served life terms and senators that were "a mere

conservatives' discomfort with the idea of an unrestrained legislature was the last strand that bound them to the mother country. "My Countrymen I know, from their form of Government, and steady Attachment heretofore to Royalty, will come reluctantly into the Idea of Independancy," he told a Pennsylvanian in April 1776.[4]

Gentlemen used two terms to describe the type of government in which the lower house of the legislature acts without the restraining influence of a House of Lords or monarch: "simple democracy" and "republic."[5] What made this constitutional form so unacceptable, many gentlemen argued, was that it was too responsive to the will of the majority of voters. One result was that democratic and republican governments often did not have the stomach to suppress "internal . . . commotions," Landon Carter said. Another Virginian that opposed Independence recoiled at the thought of the colonial governments' being replaced by "those *wild* and *turbulent republics,* which hold out dissentions, civil war, massacre, and bloodshed, in perpetual prospect." Carter Braxton fretted that the draft constitutions that had been "recommended to the Colonies, seem to accord with the temper of the times, and are fraught with all the tumult and riot incident to simple democracy." He argued that mixed governments like Britain's were much more effective than democracies at preserving "tranquility and security." One reason that republics and democracies seemed to conservatives to be beset by disorder was that they generally lacked fixed hierarchies in which everyone knew his or her place and was stuck there. Thus they fomented social mobility and competition. "I dread whether our own internal Contentions, will not again grow from this republican form we all seem to be hurrying into,"

---

creation by and dependance on the people," he would choose the former. His preference, though, was for senators chosen by the lower house to serve nine-year terms (Jefferson to Edmund Pendleton, Aug. 26, 1776, in Julian P. Boyd et al., eds., *The Papers of Thomas Jefferson* [Princeton, N.J., 1950–], I, 503–504).

4. George Washington to Joseph Reed, Apr. 1, 1776, in W. W. Abbot et al., eds., *The Papers of George Washington*, Revolutionary War Series (Charlottesville, Va., 1985–), IV, 11; Bailyn, *Ideological Origins*, 142.

5. It is unfortunate that one interpretation of the origins of the American Revolution has acquired the name "the republican synthesis." The problem with calling the elite Americans that took their colonies out of the British Empire in 1776 "republicans" is that many of them abhorred "republics," which they defined as governments in which the lower house of the legislature reigned supreme, unhindered by a monarchy or House of Lords. Until 1776, most elite Americans, patriots as well as loyalists, considered the sobriquet "republican" an insult. See W. Paul Adams, "Republicanism in Political Rhetoric before 1776," *Political Science Quarterly*, LXXXV (1970), 397–421; Cecelia M. Kenyon, "Republicanism and Radicalism in the American Revolution: An Old-Fashioned Interpretation," *WMQ*, 3d Ser., XIX (1962), 165–166.

Carter wrote in April 1776. In a republic, he said, "everybody wants to be ahead and aims at it Neck or nothing as it is commonly said."[6]

Another reason conservative gentlemen objected to the notion of a legislature responsible only to the people was their fear that, if ordinary farmers obtained political authority, they would use it to seize the property of the rich. Such a move would be prompted not only by greed but by the widespread concern that large concentrations of wealth are hazardous to republics, since great wealth can easily purchase an inordinate amount of political power. Landon Carter knew that many republicans believed "large Possessions" exert "influence against a Commonwealth." Carter Braxton's antirepublican diatribe, written in April 1776, claimed that pure republics demanded an "equal division of property."[7]

What conservatives most disliked about legislative supremacy was the faith upon which it was founded: that common people possessed sufficient virtue to govern themselves. A conservative that criticized the constitution proposed by Richard Henry Lee in 1776 noted that what distinguished Lee's proposal from Virginia's colonial government was its placement of "the choice" of leaders "in the people." Although the critic acknowledged that popular sovereignty "seems the basis of freedom," he had little faith in the wisdom of the masses. "Nothing is so easily corrupted as an ignorant Man, as soon as he gets an Idia, that he is the cornerstone in Public Happiness," he wrote. In choosing legislators, the poor man, "activated by his circumstances," was likely to vote for any candidate that would promise to "give his poverty a good relish. And with that any lie will go down, to direct his choice," he claimed. Carter Braxton agreed. "*Public* virtue," he declared in a published address to the spring 1776 Virginia convention, "never characterised the mass of the people in any state."[8]

The underlying assumption of the antirepublican authors that opposed Independence from Britain was that, if Virginia were to leave the British

6. Apr. 9, May 29, 1776, in Jack P. Greene, ed., *The Diary of Colonel Landon Carter of Sabine Hall, 1752–1778* (Charlottesville, Va., 1965), II, 1015, 1046; "Hampden," Dixon and Hunter's *VG*, Apr. 20, 1776; [Braxton], "Address to the Convention," in *Revolutionary Virginia*, VI, 519, 521.

7. [1776], in Greene, ed., *Diary of Landon Carter*, II, 1068; [Braxton], "Address to the Convention," in *Revolutionary Virginia*, VI, 522. In the republics of "antiquity, no one supposed that a man had a natural or god-given right to the fruits of his own labor; if a given individual possessed property, he held it in privilege and as a public trust" (Paul A. Rahe, *Republics, Ancient and Modern: Classical Republicanism and the American Revolution* [Chapel Hill, N.C., 1992], 70, 71).

8. Anonymous critic of Lee's plan, in *Revolutionary Virginia*, VI, 374n; Braxton, "Address to the Convention," in *Revolutionary Virginia*, VI, 522.

Empire, the only form of government available to it would be one in which the lower house of the legislature would not be restrained by anything resembling the British monarch and House of Lords. As the link between Independence and republicanism solidified in the minds of most Virginians, some conservatives carried it one step further. They claimed that many colonists favored Independence precisely because they knew it would allow them (as Carter Braxton asserted) to establish "their darling Democracy."[9] Landon Carter did not believe the "Congress Republicans" when they claimed that necessity drove them to Independence. He thought they actually desired Independence so that they could establish republics in the newly independent states and then take advantage of the states' weakness to seize power for themselves. Although gentlemen that favored Independence of course denied the conservatives' claim that their secret motive was to establish republics in America, they often conceded one essential point: If the thirteen colonies did declare Independence, their new governments would inevitably have to be republics. "E. F.," an anonymous Independence advocate, had watched "the monarchy-men display their talents in pathetick descriptions of the tumults and distractions of republicks." Another Independence advocate acknowledged that some gentlemen believed a shift to republican government in America would lead to a "dreadful train of domestick convulsions in each republick." He quoted John Milton's *Paradise Lost*, which ridiculed the notion that, in republics, "nature breeds All monstrous, all prodigious things, / Abominable, unutterable, and worse / Than fables yet have feign'd, or *fear conceiv'd*."[10]

To Virginia smallholders, what the antirepublican theorists argued was less important than what they assumed—that, if Virginia declared Indepen-

9. Mar. 29, Apr. 13, 1776, in Greene, ed., *Diary of Landon Carter*, II, 1007, 1017. Braxton claimed that, even if Britain conceded every point of contention to the colonists, "the eastern Colonies do not mean to have a Reconciliation." Massachusetts and New Hampshire wanted to be independent so they could become democracies; Connecticut and Rhode Island saw in Independence the chance to preserve and perfect the democracy that they already enjoyed (Braxton to Landon Carter, Apr. 14, 1776, in Smith, ed., *Letters of Delegates to Congress*, III, 522; cf. [Draper], *Thoughts of a Traveller*, 7).

10. May 3, 1776, in Greene, ed., *Diary of Landon Carter*, II, 1033. Carter's argument was not new; his friend Robert Beverley had made a similar accusation back in July 1775 (Beverley, " 'A Sorrowful Spectator of These Tumultuous Times': Robert Beverley Describes the Coming of the Revolution," ed. Robert M. Calhoon, *VMHB*, LXXIII [1965], 49). For additional contributions to the republicanism controversy, see Patrick Henry to John Adams, May 20, 1776, in William Wirt Henry, *Patrick Henry: Life, Correspondence, and Speeches* (New York, 1891), I, 412–413; "E. F.," Purdie's *VG*, May 17, 1776; "A. B.," Purdie's *VG*, Apr. 12, 1776; Purdie's *VG*, Mar. 8, 1776. John Adams's model constitution, the best-received of those that circulated in the spring of 1776, was universally described as "republican."

dence, it would have to adopt a more popular form of government. As smallholders studied the gentry conservatives' arguments, they began to support Independence for the same reason that some gentlemen opposed it—because an independent Virginia would inevitably be a republic.

Smallholders learned even more about the probable internal consequences of Independence from the pamphlet *Common Sense,* which appeared in January 1776. In it, the anonymous author, Thomas Paine, criticized the same British constitution that Virginia conservatives so ardently admired. Although Paine had nothing but praise for the House of Commons, he described the other two branches of the British government as "*First*—The remains of monarchical tyranny in the person of the king" and "*Secondly*—The remains of aristocratical tyranny in the persons of the peers." Paine challenged free Americans to establish the supremacy of their legislatures by declaring Independence.[11] *Common Sense* did more than any other document to equate Independence and republicanism in the minds of the American people. This was as clear to Paine's detractors as to his supporters. Landon Carter claimed that *Common Sense* was the work of "men of Republican turns." Carter denounced the pamphlet a dozen times in his diary during the six months after it appeared.[12]

The central thesis of *Common Sense,* hinted at in its title, was that the common people possessed enough sense to govern themselves. One conservative patriot that read the pamphlet, Edmund Randolph, observed many years later that it was "pregnant with . . . proud republican theories, which flattered human nature."[13] *Common Sense* showed Americans that republicanism would follow as an inevitable consequence of Independence. Thus it led thousands of farmers to venture upon Independence as a bridge to a greater say in the internal government of Virginia.

The tremendous push that *Common Sense* gave to the smallholders' and poor whites' support for Independence was everywhere celebrated by its supporters and acknowledged by its detractors. "The opinion for independentcy seems to be gaining ground," Fielding Lewis wrote George Washington in March 1776. "Indeed most of those who have read the Pamphlet Common Sence say it's unanswerable." Washington relayed this news to Joseph Reed of Pennsylvania. "By private Letters which I have lately received from Virginia, I

11. Paine called monarchy "evil" (Paine, *Common Sense,* ed. Kramnick, 68–69, 76).

12. May 3, May 29, June 14, 1776, in Greene, ed., *Diary of Landon Carter,* II, 1033, 1046, 1050.

13. Edmund Randolph, *History of Virginia,* ed. Arthur H. Shaffer (Charlottesville, Va., 1970), 233. Landon Carter also noticed the anonymous author's unprecedented faith in the average farmer. He noted that critics of *Common Sense* were accused of denying "the Majesty of the People" (Apr. 13, 1776, in Greene, ed., *Diary of Landon Carter,* II, 1016).

find common sense is working a powerful change there in the Minds of many Men," Washington said.[14] "There is abundance talked about independency," Landon Carter stated in March 1776; "it is all from Mr. Common sense." Before January 1776, Nicholas Cresswell, an Englishman traveling in Virginia, never stated that any of the Virginians he met favored Independence. Then *Common Sense* appeared, making a "great noise" and tending "to subvert all Kingly Governments and erect an Independent Republic," Cresswell said. After that, Cresswell's journal is filled with comments such as "Nothing but Independence talked of" and "Nothing but Independence will go down."[15]

As more and more smallholders and poor whites became convinced that they would soon be living in an "Independent Republic," some of them began to make specific demands about what that republic should look like. "We ask for a full representation, free and frequent elections, and that no standing armies whatever should be kept up in times of peace," the freeholders of Buckingham County told their delegates to the spring 1776 convention.[16]

II

Smallholders predominated in another group that also had a special reason to favor Independence. These were the dissenters from the Established Church, whom Jefferson reckoned at two-thirds of white Virginians at the time of the Revolution.[17] By the end of 1775, it was obvious to evangelical Christians and other dissenters that, if Virginia declared Independence, the

14. Mar. 6, Apr. 1, 1776, in Abbot et al., eds., *Papers of Washington*, Revolutionary War Series, III, 418–419, IV, 11. After the Revolutionary War, Washington tried to persuade the Virginia House of Delegates to reward Paine for *Common Sense* and some of his other writings with a grant of land or money. Thomas Jefferson and James Madison also favored the gift (Jefferson to Madison, May 25, 1784, Washington to Madison, June 12, 1784, in William T. Hutchinson et al., eds., *The Papers of James Madison* [Chicago and Charlottesville, Va., 1962–], VIII, 43, 67).

15. Mar. 28, 1776, in Greene, ed., *Diary of Landon Carter*, II, 1006. "John Penn, a delegate who had recently returned to North Carolina, reported (according to John Adams) that he 'heard nothing praised in the Course of his Journey, but Common sense and Independence. That this was the Cry, throughout Virginia'" (John Adams to James Warren, Apr. 20, 1776, in Pauline Maier, *American Scripture: Making the Declaration of Independence* [New York, 1997], 34). On Cresswell's comments, see Jan. 19, 22, 26, *The Journal of Nicholas Cresswell, 1774–1777* (London, 1925), 136. Most historians also acknowledge the decisive impact of *Common Sense*. "Prior to January 1776, when Thomas Paine launched a furious assault on monarchy in *Common Sense*, neither republicanism nor democracy had been in good odor" among elite Americans (Rahe, *Republics, Ancient and Modern*, 575).

16. [May–June 1776?], *Revolutionary Virginia*, VII, pt. i, 112.

17. Thomas Jefferson, *Notes on the State of Virginia*, ed. William Peden (Chapel Hill, N.C.. 1954), 158.

new government would accord them more freedom than they had ever enjoyed as colonists. An independent state might even disestablish the Anglican Church.

Dissenters had several reasons to think an independent government would expand their freedom. They could see that many of the leaders of the Independence movement—the people that were likely to hold power in a new regime—were also leaders in the movement for religious toleration. Patrick Henry had attacked Anglican parsons and defended imprisoned evangelicals. Thomas Jefferson had also shown an interest in toleration. And *Common Sense* called for an American Magna Carta that would safeguard "above all things the free exercise of religion." "As to religion," Paine stated later in the pamphlet, "I hold it to be the indispensible duty of all government, to protect all conscientious professors thereof, and I know of no other business which government hath to do therewith."[18] Since everyone acknowledged that a newly independent Virginia would have to be a republic, dissenters looked to the existing republics for clues about the possible religious policies of a republican Virginia. What they found encouraged them, for both the Swiss cantons and the Dutch states were conspicuously tolerant of dissenting sects.

As encouraging as these signs were, dissenters worked right up until the moment of Independence to ensure that the new regime would grant them more religious freedom. On April 26, 1776, a letter in Purdie's *Virginia Gazette* argued that, for unity's sake, Virginia should stop forcing dissenters to pay the established clergymen's salaries. Nor should dissenters have to hire Anglican parsons to perform their wedding ceremonies. The letter was signed, "A Dissenter from the Church of England." That same week, the Charlotte County freeholders urged their convention delegates to establish a government that would "secure to us the enjoyment of our civil and religious rights and privileges." One Baptist Church in Prince William County seemed to offer patriots a deal: if they would disestablish the Anglican Church, the Prince William Baptists would "gladly unite with our Brethren of other denominations, and to the utmost of our ability promote the common cause of *Freedom*."[19]

Thus free farmers in Virginia discovered that Independence promised them both a greater role in government and broader religious toleration. All that

18. Paine, *Common Sense*, ed. Kramnick, 97, 108–109.

19. "A Dissenter from the Church of England," Purdie's *VG*, Apr. 26, 1776; Apr. 23, 1776, in *Revolutionary Virginia*, VI, 448; petition of "a Baptist Church at Occaqon, Pr. William Coun[ty]," May 19, 1776, in Rhys Isaac, *The Transformation of Virginia, 1740–1790* (Chapel Hill, N.C., 1982), 292. J. C. D. Clark notes that colonial dissenters, recognizing that the rebel-

remained was for farmers to express their support for Independence to the gentry. They did that with a vengeance in the spring of 1776.

Thomas Jefferson spent the winter of 1776 at Monticello and returned to Philadelphia the following spring convinced that 90 percent of the freeholders in the upper counties of Virginia wanted to separate from Britain. Charles Lee traveled to Virginia in April 1776 and came away convinced that almost all white Virginians supported a declaration of Independence. The "spirit of the people . . . cr[ies] out for this Declaration," Lee told Patrick Henry early in May. The "military in particular," he said, "are outrageous on the subject." Lee knew that Henry hung back from the final step toward Independence, so he wrote him, saying, "A man of your excellent discernment need not be told, how dangerous it would be in present circumstances to dally with the spirit, or disappoint the expectations of the bulk of the People." Lee's letter to Henry concluded by appealing to the gentry's fear of anarchy. If the smallholders' demand for Independence was not met, he warned, "May not despair, anarchy, and finally submission be the bitter fruits?"[20]

Small farmers clearly expressed their desire for Independence when they gathered at the county courthouses in April 1776 to elect delegates to what would turn out to be colonial Virginia's last convention. In the past, Virginia freeholders had hardly ever told their representatives how to vote on legislation. But smallholders apparently were emboldened by their success at forcing the winter 1775–1776 convention essentially to abolish the minute service and by other, smaller victories. Now many counties instructed their delegates to the spring 1776 convention to vote for Independence. "Papers it seems are every where circulating about for poor ignorant Creatures to sign, as directions to their delegate[s] to endeavour at an independency," Landon Carter told George Washington as the convention delegates gathered in Williamsburg. Even in James City County, where Robert Carter Nicholas, an opponent of Independence, was elected to the convention, a majority of the voters gathered at a tavern on April 24 to sign instructions to Nicholas and his fellow delegate William Norvell to vote for Independence. The instructions constituted a remarkable document; rarely had a majority of the voters of a Virginia county signed *anything*. By the time the great assembly con-

---

lion was against both England and the Church of England, generally supported it (*The Language of Liberty, 1660–1832: Political Discourse and Social Dynamics in the Anglo-American World* [Cambridge, 1994], esp. 379–381).

20. Charles Lee to Patrick Henry, May 7, 1776, in *The Lee Papers* (New York, 1871–1874), II, 1–3; John C. Miller, *Origins of the American Revolution* (Boston, 1943), 485, 489; Dumas Malone, *Jefferson and His Time*, I, *Jefferson, the Virginian* (Boston, 1948), 217.

vened, delegate Edmund Randolph later recalled, "the disposition of the people . . . could not be mistaken." The "now apparent spirit of the people" decisively favored Independence. The spirit seemed to be universal and enthusiastic. Several counties that had not bothered to send delegates to previous conventions now did so.[21]

If any of the delegates in Williamsburg still harbored doubts about whether the pro-Independence freeholders meant business, they could just look around them. Many of the delegates to earlier conventions were no longer present, for they had been defeated at the polls. "The election of delegates for the Convention," Edmund Randolph recalled many years later, "was now depended in very many, if not in a majority, of the counties upon their candidates pledging themselves . . . to sever . . . the colonies from Great Britain."[22] Many incumbents that refused to endorse Independence were turned out. The most stunning electoral upset was in Richmond County, where the two incumbent delegates, both of whom had won the previous seven elections, were voted out of office. The two were replaced, as one of them noted, with "determined men." One of the defeated incumbents, Robert Wormeley Carter, opposed Independence. He received only forty-five votes. The freeholders also turned out Francis Lightfoot Lee, a member of Congress that actually favored Independence. He had, in the contemptuous language of Robert Carter's father Landon, "merely kissed the arses of the people and very servilely accommodated himself to others." Apparently, one reason Lee was nonetheless defeated was that he was off in Philadelphia attending Congress and could not participate in the convention. It seems that Richmond County freeholders, recognizing that this convention would be a major event in Virginia history, wanted to make sure that they were fully represented in it. The April 1 election in Richmond County was viewed by Landon Carter (who could not resist calling it "a kind of April fool") as a blow to the old deferential relationship between the gentry and the common people. He noted that "even relations as well as tenants all Voted against" the two incumbents.[23]

A month after the election, Landon Carter sat down to analyze the results. "The old deligates were left out . . . and these new ones chose for this Very

21. Landon Carter to George Washington, May 9, 1776, in Abbot et al., eds., *Papers of Washington*, Revolutionary War Series, IV, 237; *Revolutionary Virginia*, VI, 458, 462n; Randolph, *History of Virginia*, ed. Shaffer, 250.

22. Randolph, *History of Virginia*, ed. Shaffer, 234.

23. Apr. 1, 1776, Robert Wormeley Carter diary, CWF; Apr. 1, 4, 1776, in Greene, ed., *Diary of Landon Carter*, II, 1008–1010; William Aylett to Richard Henry Lee, Apr. 20, 1776, in Paul P. Hoffman, ed., *The Lee Family Papers, 1742–1795* (microfilm, Charlottesville, Va., 1966).

FIGURE 15. Landon Carter. *Courtesy, Virginia Historical Society*

Purpose of an intire independence," Carter wrote in his diary. He said the reason the freeholders wanted to separate from Britain was that they desired an "independence in which no Gentleman should have the least share." Carter elaborated on this point a week later in a letter to George Washington. "I need only tell you of one definition that I heard of Independency," he wrote. "It was expected to be a form of Government, that by being independt of the rich men, eve[r]y man would then be able to do as he pleasd. And it was with this expectation they sent the men they did, in hopes they would plan such a form." Indeed, it is possible that Francis Lightfoot Lee lost because the delegate replacing him advocated that the government follow the dictates of public opinion. "One of the delegates I heard exclaim agst the Patrolling law, because a poor man was made to pay for keeping a rich mans Slaves in order," Landon Carter reported. The candidate's rhetoric was effective, Carter said; he "got elected by it." Carter reported that another candidate (not necessarily in Richmond County) won by criticizing "in a most seditious manner . . . the draughting the Militia by lot."[24]

The election analysis in Carter's diary entry and letter to Washington was prompted by the late-April incident (narrated above) in which the small-holder he identified as G. R. said he relished the thought of the British burning gentry mansions. Carter believed that the sentiments G. R. expressed were only an extreme version of the attitude that other Richmond County smallholders had exhibited at the election earlier in the month. In his diary, Carter combined his report on G. R. with his analysis of the election and concluded the whole with a sarcastic cheer. "Hurray for Independancy, Sedition, and Confusion," he wrote.[25]

Landon Carter was not the only gentleman that was shocked by the Richmond County election returns.[26] John Augustine Washington called the Richmond vote, which occurred on the first day of the monthlong election season, "a most unhappy beginning of the insuing general election." More unhappiness awaited the gentry throughout April, as the voter revolt spread to other counties. By April 14, Josiah Parker feared that even congressional delegates Benjamin Harrison and Carter Braxton as well as Edmund Pendleton, the chairman of the Committee of Safety and president of earlier conventions, might lose.[27]

Braxton was, in fact, defeated. He had denounced republicanism in a published address to the Virginia convention that appeared just before the election. Although the pamphlet was anonymous, voters likely discovered Braxton's conservative views. Braxton was apparently also hurt by the fact that he, like Francis Lightfoot Lee, would not be able to leave Congress to attend the convention. King William County voters wanted to be fully represented in the momentous convention that would open the following month. William Aylett, in trying to explain Braxton's defeat, found that "it had been

24. May 1, 1776, in Greene, ed., *Diary of Landon Carter*, II, 1031; Carter to Washington, May 9, 1776, in Abbot et al., eds., *Papers of Washington*, Revolutionary War Series, IV, 236–237.

25. May 1, 1776, in Greene, ed., *Diary of Landon Carter*, II, 1030–1031.

26. "We all know the determination of the Richmond Freeholders," Josiah Parker wrote Carter from Williamsburg two weeks after the election; "strange times indeed" (Apr. 14, 1776, in Paul P. Hoffman, ed., *The Carter Family Papers, 1659–1797, in the Sabine Hall Collection* [microfilm, Charlottesville, Va., 1967]).

27. John Augustine Washington to Richard Henry Lee, Apr. [15], 1776, in Hoffman, ed., *Lee Family Papers; Josiah Parker to Landon Carter, Apr. 14, 1776, in Hoffman, ed., Carter Family Papers.*

generally said among the people" that they would forfeit half of their influence in the convention if they gave one of their seats to Braxton, since "Colo Braxton being in Congress could not serve in convention." Aylett said he had "endeavour'd to convince them that it was more immediately their duty now than ever to Elect Mr Braxton." Since Lee had already lost in Richmond County, voters would badly damage the credibility of Virginia's congressional delegation if they repudiated another of its members. But, of the three candidates that sought the two King William County seats, Braxton placed third.[28]

Other, less notable incumbents, such as Thomas Blackburn, who called his county's tenants "peasants," were also turned out, and many of those that were reelected had close scares. Henry Lee (future father of Robert E. Lee) was "much push'd in P[rince] William" County, Robert Brent reported, and George Mason was "with great difficulty return'd" in Fairfax. (Probably the reason Mason nearly lost was that voters knew he was suffering from "a smart fit of the Gout" and feared he would not be present when the convention opened.)[29] William Aylett believed he would have been defeated if he had not "chang'd the Scene" through his personal "presence at the election."[30]

28. Aylett to Richard Henry Lee, Apr. 20, 1776, in Hoffman, ed., *Lee Family Papers*. Lee, in fact, lost two elections in April 1776. After his defeat in Richmond County, his supporters ran him in neighboring Lancaster, where he lost again. The April 1776 voting was something of an electoral massacre for the Carter family. In addition to Robert Wormeley Carter and his cousin Carter Braxton, both of whom actively opposed Independence, two other Carters—Charles of Corotoman and Charles of Ludlow—were also defeated. The Carters were among the wealthiest families in Virginia, and their unprecedented repudiation at the polls seemed to reflect the ascendancy of antielitism (John E. Selby, *The Revolution in Virginia, 1775–1783* [Charlottesville, Va., 1988], 94–95).

29. Thomas Blackburn, in Dale E. Benson, "Wealth and Power in Virginia, 1774–1776: A Study of the Organization of Revolt" (Ph.D. diss., University of Maine, 1970), 357; *Revolutionary Virginia*, VI, 288n; Robert Brent to Richard Henry Lee, Apr. 28, 1776, in Hoffman, ed., *Lee Family Papers*; Selby, *Revolution in Virginia*, 95. The voters' fears were justified. Mason's gout kept him out of the convention until after its May 15, 1776, vote in favor of Independence. See George Mason to George Washington, Apr. 2, 1776, to Richard Henry Lee, May 18, 1776, both in Robert A. Rutland, ed., *The Papers of George Mason, 1725–1792* (Chapel Hill, N.C., 1970), I, 267, 271; John Dalton to Virginia Delegates in Congress, May 8, 1776, in Hoffman, ed., *Lee Family Papers*.

30. Aylett to Richard Henry Lee, Apr. 20, 1776, in Hoffman, ed., *Lee Family Papers*. On election day, Aylett tried to drop out of the three-way race for the two King William County seats so that voters would be forced to choose the anti-Independence Carter Braxton as one of their two delegates. Voters would have none of it; they elected Aylett and the third candidate, Richard Squire Taylor (Virginia Convention Committee on Privileges and Elections, May 18, 1776, in Hutchinson et al., eds., *Papers of James Madison*, I, 166–167).

As gentlemen pieced together the news from the various county elections, the picture that emerged was ominous. "For many counties there have been warm contests for seats in our approaching convention," Robert Brent told Richard Henry Lee at the end of April. "Many new ones are got in." Landon Carter regretted that "inexperienced creatures" had been elected "all over the Colony." "Our Freeholders [are] all Mad, determined to have a New house altogether," Josiah Parker told Carter; "I hope for the best, tho I *fear* the Consequence." In all, nearly one-third of the incumbents that stood for reelection in April 1776 were defeated.[31]

Two days after the King William County election he nearly lost, William Aylett demonstrated that he had got the voters' message. In a letter to Richard Henry Lee, Aylett described the defeat of his former colleague Carter Braxton and then declared, "The people of this County almost unanimously cry aloud for independance." Other convention delegates got the message as well. Indeed, by early May 1776, when the delegates gathered in Williamsburg, even the most conservative gentlemen had seen their fears of a popular government eclipsed by two greater fears: they dreaded the prospect of allowing Virginia to slip into anarchy (as we have already seen), and they feared the farmers' wrath if they continued to thwart the popular demand for an independent republic. Both of those fears pointed them toward final separation from Britain. On May 15, 1776, the Virginia convention instructed Virginia's delegates in Congress to propose that the thirteen colonies declare Independence. The next day, the Union Jack that had flown over the Capitol in Williamsburg was hauled down and replaced with a Continental flag. On June 29, 1776, the convention adopted the new constitution and chose Patrick Henry as the first governor of the Commonwealth of Virginia. Accepting, Henry highlighted an important reason for the move to Independence that has since been virtually forgotten. "Government hath been necessarily assumed," he told the convention, "in Order to preserve this Common-

31. Brent to Lee, Apr. 28, 1776, in Hoffman, ed., *Lee Family Papers;* Carter to George Washington, May 9, 1776, in Abbot et al., eds., *Papers of Washington,* Revolutionary War Series, IV, 236; Parker to Carter, Apr. 14, 1776, in Hoffman, ed., *Carter Family Papers; Revolutionary Virginia,* VI, 286–290n. Seven of the ten old Northern Neck counties changed at least one of their convention delegates in the April 1776 elections. Forty-five percent of the Northern Neck delegates to the convention that opened the following month were freshmen. Where fewer than 10 percent of the convention delegates elected the previous fall had been freshmen, 38 percent of those elected in April 1776 were (Michael A. McDonnell, "The Politics of Mobilization in Revolutionary Virginia: Military Culture and Political and Social Relations, 1774–1783" [D.Phil. thesis, Balliol College, Oxford University, 1995], 95–96).

wealth from Anarchy and its attendant Ruin."[32] Thus Virginia farmers had, both by committing "disorders" that frightened the gentry and by demanding a larger role in government, powerfully influenced the transformation of Virginia into an independent state.

32. Aylett to Lee, Apr. 20, 1776, Thomas Ludwell Lee to Richard Henry Lee, May 18, 1776 (copy), in Hoffman, ed., *Lee Family Papers;* Henry, in *Revolutionary Virginia*, VII, pt. ii, 666; Randolph, *History of Virginia*, ed. Shaffer, 251.

EPILOGUE

From 1765, when the House of Burgesses took the most radical stance against the Stamp Act of any colonial legislature, to 1776, when Thomas Jefferson wrote the Declaration of Independence, Virginia was at the forefront of the American Revolution. Scholars studying the causes of the Revolution in Britain's most populous American colony have mostly focused on gentlemen—the likes of Jefferson, Washington, and Patrick Henry. Although no one can deny their importance, the thesis of this book has been that the Independence movement was also powerfully influenced by British merchants and by three groups that today would be called grassroots: Indians, farmers, and slaves. Some of the ways in which these groups helped—usually inadvertently—to sour crown-colony relations are evident in three documents produced by a unanimous House of Burgesses between 1769 and 1775. None of the three has received nearly as much attention as other Revolution texts.

As Part I demonstrated, the 1769 petition was for Kentucky. The second, adopted in 1772, was against the Atlantic slave trade. Three years later, assemblymen indicated in a formal address that free Virginians were willing to absorb some of the British Empire's American expenses—but only if Parliament granted them the same commercial rights that other British subjects enjoyed.

Today politicians as well as historians often portray the American Revolution as a tax revolt. This it certainly was, but it was also a conflict among social classes, for the British government did not act only on its own behalf. Like the modern American government, it responded to pressure from commercial interests and to a lesser extent from groups such as Native Americans. Indians and British merchants powerfully influenced the fate of the petitions that the Virginia House of Burgesses sent the Privy Council in 1769 and 1772 and of the address it adopted in 1775. Merchants organized to preserve their commercial privileges.[1] Meanwhile, significant numbers of Ohio Valley and southern Indians united to try to keep their land. Pressured by the unified merchants and fearful of the united Indians, the Privy Council refused to comply with the burgesses' two petitions or with their 1775 address. The government's refusal angered all free Virginians that depended upon international trade, that considered African immigrants a threat to Virginia's economy and security, and that hoped to make (or recover) their fortunes selling Indian land.

Nor were Indians and merchants the only interest groups that propelled the Independence movement. Part II focused upon Virginia's sizable debtor class, which included gentlemen as well as smallholders. The import and export boycotts that free Virginians endorsed in 1774 were sincere efforts to combat parliamentary tyranny, but they were also pretexts for indebted farmers and gentlemen to adopt strategies that rescued them from one of the worst recessions of the colonial era. Thus the economic origins of the American Revolution were more complex than Progressive historians recognized. Several Progressives claimed that indebted Virginia gentlemen opted for Independence simply in order to repudiate their debts.[2] The problem with this explanation is that it has gentlemen trying to lead the colony down the road to Independence starting in 1774, when they closed the courts, or even earlier. But very few members of the gentry favored Independence at this early date. In fact, the majority of gentlemen appear to have resisted separation from Britain until late 1775 or early 1776, when they came to see it as a practical necessity.[3]

The reason Independence became necessary was that, as Part III discussed, the import and export boycotts generated consequences that their

1. Historians are wrong to assume that the predominant motive for the Navigation Acts was to strengthen the British nation-state; they need to put the "merchants" back in "mercantilism."

2. William Berkeley, who was governor of Virginia in the 1660s, when Parliament first confined the tobacco trade to England, said this sort of commercial restriction put the welfare of forty English merchants above that of forty thousand Virginia colonists (John C. Rainbolt, *From Prescription to Persuasion: Manipulation of [Seventeenth] Century Virginia Economy* [Port Washington, N.Y., 1974], 28).

3. Charles A. Beard, *Economic Origins of Jeffersonian Democracy* (New York, 1915), 270; Merrill Jensen, *The Articles of Confederation: An Interpretation of the Social-Constitutional History of the American Revolution, 1774–1781* (Madison, 1940), 23–24. The "purposes of men, especially in a revolution, are so numerous, so varied, and so contradictory that their complex interaction produces results that no one intended or could even foresee" (Gordon S. Wood, "Rhetoric and Reality in the American Revolution," *WMQ*, 3rd Ser., XXIII [1966], 16).

promoters had not intended. In the fall of 1774, partly as a result of the two boycotts, white Virginians began to divide into two camps. A small band of loyalists around Governor Dunmore confronted a much larger group of patriots led by the House of Burgesses. Starting in the spring of 1775, black Virginians began offering to help the beleaguered governor in return for their freedom. That fall, when Dunmore finally grasped their outstretched hand, he infuriated white Virginians and turned many neutrals and even loyalists into patriots. Tenants and small farmers were also active in 1775 and 1776. Nonimportation led to shortages that led to riots. Although nonexportation benefited tobacco growers, it deprived grain farmers of income and helped provoke a tenants' revolt in Loudoun County early in 1776. These and other "disorders" persuaded the gentry that it had to restore formal government in Virginia.[4] Now that Dunmore's emancipation proclamation and other provocations had eliminated reconciliation with Britain as an option, the only way to restore government was to declare Independence and inaugurate a new regime.

The final chapter demonstrated that smallholders also pushed the gentry toward Independence in a more direct way. Especially after the publication of *Common Sense* in January 1776, farmers recognized that a new government would accord them much greater political influence than they had enjoyed under the old colonial regime. Thus significant numbers of people within both major groups of white Virginians—smallholders and gentlemen—came to believe that Independence would strengthen them in their continuing conflict against the other. Many gentlemen saw home rule as the only alternative to anarchy; smallholders saw it as their ticket to a greater say in who would rule at home. With the benefit of hindsight, we can say that both were probably right.

To gauge the influence of Indians, British merchants, debtors, and slaves upon the Independence movement, it is necessary to look beyond the elite patriots' public writings and speeches, for gentlemen frequently found reason to conceal that influence. For instance, through 1774 most gentlemen were determined not to give the merchant class any cause to believe that they wished to repeal the Navigation Acts. Although, behind the closed doors of the First Continental Congress, Richard Henry Lee called British mercantilism a "capital" violation of the colonists' rights, he warned his fellow delegates not to denounce it openly. To do so, he said, "would unite every man in Britain against us." George Washington, Landon Carter, and William Lee

---

4. Francis Lightfoot Lee to Landon Carter, Apr. 9, May 21, 1776, in Paul H. Smith et al., eds., *Letters of Delegates to Congress* (Washington, D.C., 1976–), III, 500–501, IV, 57.

all publicly advertised the political motives for anti-British boycotts while quietly touting the boycotts' "pecuniary" benefits.[5] Virginia gentlemen were prouder of their battle against parliamentary tyranny than of their contest against Indians for their land. Thus in September 1774, William Lee advised his brothers that, when they criticized the Quebec Act, they should focus not on its provision assigning the land north and west of the Ohio River to Quebec (the Lees' real reason for opposing it) but on its "threatened estab-lishment of Popery."[6] Likewise, the reference to slaves in the Declaration of Independence is euphemistic; George III is said to have "excited domestic Insurrections amongst us."

Although gentlemen often downplayed the impact of Indians, British merchants, and slaves upon their actions, sometimes they actually exagger-ated it. In 1775, when the House of Burgesses aired its version of why its relations with Governor Dunmore had deteriorated during the previous few months, it placed great emphasis on Dunmore's recent threat to lead a slave revolt. The burgesses gave the impression that most white Virginians had been totally loyal until the governor made his threat and that every one of them had taken it seriously.[7] Both of these assertions exaggerated the role of enslaved Virginians in turning white Virginians against their governor.

Studying the social context of the American Revolution reveals that histo-rians of its origins have erred in taking a model developed for northern colonies and applying it without modification to those below the Mason-Dixon line. Scholars say the Navigation Acts were not a burden on British colonists until about 1763, because until then they were easily and generally evaded. That is probably true for New England, but *not* for the Chesapeake,

---

5. Richard Henry Lee, in Joseph A. Ernst, "The Political Economy of the Chesapeake Colonies, 1760–1775: A Study in Comparative History," in Ronald Hoffman et al., eds., *The Economy of Early America: The Revolutionary Period, 1763–1790* (Charlottesville, Va., 1988), 241; Washington to George Mason, to Robert Cary and Company, Apr. 5, July 25, 1769, in W. W. Abbot et al., eds., *The Papers of George Washington*, Colonial Series, (Charlottesville, 1983–), VIII, 179–180, 229; "C— R—," Rind's *VG*, June 1, 1769; [William Lee] to [Francis Lightfoot Lee], Apr. 2, 1774, Arthur Lee Papers, Houghton. On the other hand, other Virginians acknowledged, and perhaps even exaggerated, the economic purpose of non-importation. John Page, Jr., and William Reynolds praised nonimportation in letters to London merchant John Norton as a strategy that would both pressure Parliament to repeal anti-American legislation and help them reduce their debts to Norton (Page to Norton, May 27, 1769, Reynolds to Norton, June 4, 1774, in Frances Norton Mason, ed., *John Norton and Sons, Merchants of London and Virginia: Being the Papers from Their Counting-House for the Years 1750 to 1795* [Richmond, Va., 1937], 94, 371).

6. William Lee to Richard Henry Lee, Sept. 10, 1774, in Worthington Chauncey Ford, ed., *Letters of William Lee, 1776–1783* (1891) (New York, 1968), I, 91–92.

7. House of Burgesses, address to Dunmore, June 19, 1775, *JHB, 1773–1776*, 256.

which could be sealed shut by one navy schooner cruising between Capes Charles and Henry. Although several students of "the Puritan ethic" have recognized the financial origins of nonimportation, they have essentially ignored nonexportation. That neglect may make sense for New England, which exported little of value to Britain, but not for the staple colonies of the South. In 1775, when New England minutemen famously rallied to the defense of their farms and families, Virginians refused to join minuteman battalions. In fact, Virginia leaders had to abandon the minuteman concept altogether.[8] Historians say Indians were the victims but not in any way the instigators of the American Revolution. That may be true of New England, but not of the South, where there were native nations numerous and thus powerful enough to scare a pence-pinching imperial bureaucracy into thwarting the will of land speculators such as George Washington and Thomas Jefferson. Of course, the most important way in which the South differed from New England was in its higher percentage of slaves. Although Boston had its Crispus Attucks, it was in the South that black Americans—inadvertently—gave Independence the most decisive push.

The four Coercive Acts that Parliament adopted in response to the Boston Tea Party applied only to Massachusetts. The alacrity with which the conservative Virginia squirearchy came to the Puritans' defense surprised many contemporaries and remains remarkable today. Historians have shown that Virginia gentlemen made common cause with Massachusetts partly out of ideological opposition to parliamentary sovereignty and partly out of fear that they could be next. Ironically, though, many of the factors that ensured Virginia would support the New Englanders did not exist in New England itself. These included powerful Indian nations, a staple economy, pervasive transatlantic debt, and a large slave population.

The distinctive social context of Virginia's American Revolution helps to explain many of its other paradoxes as well. Virginians that demanded exemption from the heavy taxes their fellow Britons paid can seem selfish, or their fears of parliamentary tyranny can seem like paranoia, until it is remembered that they already paid a "heavy tax" to Britain in the form of its costly monopoly of their trade.[9] Ignoring the relationship between Virginia farmers and British merchants—and the boom-bust business cycle that

8. Michael A. McDonnell, "Popular Mobilization and Political Culture in Revolutionary Virginia: The Failure of the Minutemen and the Revolution from Below," *Journal of American History*, LXXXV (1998), 946–981; Edmund S. Morgan, "The Puritan Ethic and the American Revolution," *WMQ*, 3d. Ser., XXIV (1967), 3–43.

9. Bernard Bailyn, *The Ideological Origins of the American Revolution* (Cambridge, Mass., 1967), 158; "Vindex," *Virginia Gazette, or, Norfolk Intelligencer*, Aug. 11, 1774.

powerfully influenced this relationship—also makes it difficult to understand why the import and export boycotts proposed in 1769 failed to arouse much interest among farmers while those offered in 1774 gained virtually unanimous support and brought Virginia's trade with Britain to an abrupt halt. Actually, the divergent fates of the 1769 and 1774 boycotts is no mystery. The initial proposals were offered during a time of rising tobacco prices and easy credit, but the 1774 plans appeared during a terrible recession.

The class context helps to explain other Revolution paradoxes as well. The white panic sparked by Governor Dunmore's seizure of the ammunition in the Williamsburg gunpowder magazine makes sense only when one recalls that Dunmore took the powder at the end of the week when more slave plot rumors had circulated than during any previous week in Virginia history. Another Revolution paradox involves the character of the founders, especially of Thomas Jefferson. Many Americans consider Jefferson a "Herald of Freedom." Others point out that he promoted the "extermination" of Indians and held slaves even as he made clear in his writings that he knew better.[10] When Jefferson is viewed in the context of the class relationships of colonial Virginia, it becomes clear that the contrasting depictions of him are both right. Jefferson sought freedom for the people with whom he identified—a coalition of smallholders and gentlemen. It is not sufficient to say, as so many writers on the American Revolution have said, that slaves and Indians were denied the fruits of Independence. To a large extent, in 1776 as in 1861, slaves and Indians—or more precisely, the Indians' land and the slaves' labor—*were* the fruits of Independence.

Allowing all of the participants in the Revolution drama their proper place on stage even helps to explain the most paradoxical figure of the nation's founding era, the gentleman revolutionary. The Introduction reported that in April 1774 a backcountry gentleman named Jacob Hite sent his son to break down the doors of a prison and then later placed weapons in the hands of his slaves. It asked why, not long afterward, Hite's peers in Virginia's ruling class, whom contemporaries sometimes called aristocrats, started a revolution. One answer to this question is that gentlemen did not know what they were getting into. The import and export boycotts that were

---

10. Dumas Malone, *Jefferson and His Time,* I, *Jefferson, the Virginian* (Boston, 1948), 215; Jefferson to George Rogers Clark, Jan. 1, 1780, in Julian P. Boyd et al., eds., *The Papers of Thomas Jefferson* (Princeton, N.J., 1950–), III, 259; Joseph J. Ellis, *American Sphinx: The Character of Thomas Jefferson* (New York, 1997), esp. 8, 144–152; Paul Finkelman, "Jefferson and Slavery: 'Treason against the Hopes of the World,' " in Peter S. Onuf, ed., *Jeffersonian Legacies* (Charlottesville, Va., 1993), 101–221; Conor Cruise O'Brien, *The Long Affair: Thomas Jefferson and the French Revolution, 1785–1800* (Chicago, 1996), chap. 7.

the cornerstones of the Continental Association of 1774 seemed like rather modest responses to parliamentary passage of the Coercive Acts and to the deepening recession. However, nonimportation, nonexportation, and other colonial resistance strategies provoked not only a punitive imperial policy but also agrarian rebellions in Virginia and Indian country. These in turn virtually forced Virginia's leaders to declare Independence. To a large extent, it was angry British statesmen and rebellious slaves, smallholders, and tenants that created the gentleman revolutionary.

Even if the Virginians' goals were never deliberately radical, their strategies sometimes seemed to be. Gentry patriots encouraged domestic manufacturing, withheld tobacco exports, and closed the courts. Slaves took advantage of the patriot-loyalist conflict to pursue their own freedom. Yet when these tactics are placed in their class context, it becomes apparent that many of them had long pedigrees. Gentlemen had promoted domestic manufacturing for more than a century. For just as long, tobacco farmers had sought ways to reduce the size of their harvest in order to obtain a higher price for it. During earlier recessions as during the crisis of 1772 to 1774, Chesapeake courts had delayed proceedings in order to shield debtors from their creditors' lawsuits. In the fall of 1774, when enslaved Virginians began to exploit divisions among whites to obtain freedom for themselves, they followed a precedent set at least as early as 1676, when slaves made a similar use of Bacon's Rebellion.

A decade and a half ago, I set out to try to answer a rather narrow political question: "Why did Virginia participate in the American Revolution?" Although I never lost my curiosity about the causes of the Revolution, I found myself growing more and more interested in the people that made it. I was intrigued to find that, despite all the differences among Indians, British merchants, smallholders, slaves, and gentlemen, they had two important traits in common. The first was a dream of freedom, and the second was a belief that they stood a better chance of achieving their goals if they banded together with others of like mind. All of these groups achieved important organizational successes in the 1760s and 1770s.

Organization was especially important to Native Americans, as Chapter 1 indicated. An uprising by one Indian nation could be suppressed by the British army at not too great an expense. But British officials knew that the cost incurred in suppressing a "*general* Indian War" would exacerbate a government fiscal crisis that was already acute. The word "general" also figured prominently in white Virginians' discussions of servile insurrection. In June 1775, when the author of an anonymous newspaper essay commented upon several recent reports of slave plots, he knew that the critical question was "whether this was general."[11]

At the same time that Anglo-Americans worried about unity among Indians and slaves, they worked to promote it among themselves. Part II showed that the signers of the 1769 nonimportation association recognized that their attempt to live more frugally required nearly unanimous support, since families that continued to indulge in conspicuous consumption would be "like the *scabs of one sheep*, enough to poison and infect the whole flock."[12] Similarly, in 1773 and 1774, tobacco farmers seeking to pull the price of their staple out of its terrible slump recognized that no effort to reduce tobacco output could work unless it was generally adopted. The sporadic "disorders" that farmers and tenants committed in 1775 and 1776 did not alarm gentlemen nearly so much as organized efforts like the salt riots and the Loudoun County tenants' revolt.

Activists of all stripes found that an effective strategy for building political unity was to urge their followers to embrace broader identities. At the First Continental Congress, Patrick Henry declared that he was "not a Virginian, but an American." He made that statement in an effort to persuade the Congress to accord votes to the colonies in proportion to their population instead of simply giving each colony one vote. Although his purpose was thus to promote the narrow interests of his populous home colony, he ironically did so by embracing a national American identity. Native American resistance leaders also advocated a broader ethnic identity, as illustrated by the Shawnee diplomat that implored his fellow Indians, "Have only the same mind, all of you who Inhabit the same Continent, and are of the same Colour."[13]

Although the ways in which the various social movements of the pre-Revolutionary era affected each other were often complex, there are certain patterns. Two of these in particular are worth noting. First, the relationship between two classes was often powerfully influenced by the actions of a third. (This argument parallels my overall thesis: that the bilateral relationship between British politicians and Virginia gentlemen was powerfully influenced by various third parties.) For example, Native Americans were

11. Lord Hillsborough to William Johnson, July 1, 1772, in E. B. O'Callaghan and B. Fernow, eds., *Documents relative to the Colonial History of the State of New-York* . . . (Albany, 1856–1887), VIII, 302 (emphasis added); anonymous letter, Purdie's *VG*, June 16, 1775.

12. "An Associating Planter," Rind's *VG*, Dec. 13, 1770.

13. Robert Douthat Meade, *Patrick Henry: Patriot in the Making* (Philadelphia, 1957), I, 325; unnamed Shawnee chief, council with Great Lakes nations and George Turnbull, Sept. 25, 1769, enclosed in Turnbull to Gage, Sept. 30, 1769, Thomas Gage Papers, William L. Clements Library, University of Michigan, Ann Arbor.

(indirectly) able to close the bluegrass region to Virginia land speculators—but not to settlers. As Chapter 1 demonstrated, the Indians' actions enabled settlers to take up land without paying speculators for it.

It is also clear that the strategies employed by grassroots groups were often appropriated—and then toned down—by elites. The small farmers' tobacco-withholding effort of 1773 became in 1774 the nonexportation clause of the Continental Association. Within weeks of the adoption of the association, black Virginians began to believe that the conflict between white loyalists and patriots would provide them an opportunity to rebel. Governor Dunmore appropriated that liberation struggle, creating a black regiment in the British army.

This work has focused on the ways in which Native Americans, British merchants, debtors (at all wealth levels), and enslaved Virginians indirectly and unintentionally helped to bring on the American Revolution. Let it conclude with a brief survey of how the Revolution affected each of those groups.

Among the worst victims of the American Revolution were Native Americans in the Mississippi Valley. Virginia's new government abandoned London's policy of conciliating the Indians and replaced it with the program that Governor Thomas Jefferson advocated for the Upper Ohio Indians in 1780. "The end proposed should be their extermination, or their removal beyond the [Great] lakes or Illinois river," Jefferson told George Rogers Clark, since "the same world will scarcely do for them and us." In the frontier region, the Revolutionary War looked less like a colonial Independence movement than a continuation of the long-standing struggle over the Indians' land. Although by 1783 that conflict had produced no clear victor, Virginia did eventually accomplish Jefferson's fundamental goal, which was, he said, to "add to the Empire of liberty an extensive and fertile Country."[14] Modern devotees of the "Empire of liberty" sometimes forget what Jefferson knew: that there could be no empire without the extermination of the Indians that blocked its path.

If the Indians' land was to be taken from them, the question remained:

14. Jan. 1, 1780, Jefferson to George Rogers Clark, Dec. 25, 1780, both in Boyd et al., eds., *Papers of Jefferson*, III, 259, IV, 237–238; Thomas Nelson, Jr., to John Page, Aug. 13, 1776, Dearborn Collection, Houghton; John E. Selby, *The Revolution in Virginia, 1775–1783* (Charlottesville, Va., 1988), 199–201; Michael N. McConnell, *A Country Between: The Upper Ohio Valley and Its Peoples, 1724–1774* (Lincoln, Nebr., 1992), 281–282; Ronald Takaki, *A Different Mirror: A History of Multicultural America* (Boston, 1993), 47, 49; Colin G. Calloway, *The American Revolution in Indian Country: Crisis and Diversity in Native American Communities* (Cambridge, 1995).

would farm families be allowed to settle Indian land free of charge, or would they have to pay speculators for it? That issue was settled by the House of Delegates in June 1779. The assembly revived many of the speculative land claims that the British government had quashed—the Loyal Company's grant, George Mason's claim to fifty thousand acres using headrights, and the Seven Years' War veterans' bounty claims. Speculators such as George Washington, who had been powerless against squatters in the late colonial years, were now able to evict them or to make them pay for their land. Western settlers forced to buy their land from an eastern firm called the Greenbrier Company (and to pay fees to government officials) claimed that so much "money [was] thus Extorted from Us" that they were unable to pay their taxes. In 1779, the House of Delegates adopted a new land law that has been celebrated as democratic but was actually little different from its colonial counterpart.[15] It is true that after the Revolution—as before—many farmers did obtain land directly from the government. But the Virginia gentry, by leading Virginia into the American Revolution, had recovered one of its largest sources of income: the sale of Indian land to yeomen farmers.

In the struggle between Virginia gentlemen and British merchants, the American Revolution produced one clear victory for the gentlemen. In 1778, the House of Delegates, no longer constrained by an imperial administration determined to protect British slave traders' profits, forever abolished the importation of foreign slaves into Virginia. Although Independence also freed Virginia tobacco growers from the restrictions of the Navigation Acts, here the impact was less clear. After the Revolution, as before, British merchants dominated the Virginia trade. A monopoly that had initially depended on the British navy now continued on the strength of British merchants' knowledge of the Virginia market, their access to the cheapest manufactured goods in the world, and their unrivaled ability to provide loans.[16] One Virginia

15. Thomas Smith to George Washington, Nov. 7, 1786, in W. W. Abbot et al., eds., *The Papers of George Washington*, Confederation Series, IV (Charlottesville, Va., 1995), 339–340; William McCay et al., petition, Virginia Legislative Petitions (Greenbrier County), LVA; Thomas Jefferson, *Notes on the State of Virginia*, ed. William Peden (Chapel Hill, N.C., 1954), 136. Thousands of Virginia's militiamen and Continental soldiers received western land grants as bounties, but most of these were bought up by speculators (Thomas Perkins Abernethy, *Western Lands and the American Revolution* [New York, 1937], 225–229, 306).

16. Jacob M. Price, "Discussion," *Journal of Economic History*, XXV (1965), 659. In the Virginia store trade, Britain did have one important rival, Philadelphia. Yet competition between the old and new buyers did not raise prices; Philadelphia merchants, especially Robert Morris, proved even more adept than their British rivals at cornering the tobacco market and driving down the price (Alan Schaffer, "Virginia's 'Critical Period,'" in Dar-

gentleman, James Madison, briefly entertained the hope that the Virginians' escape from the Navigation Acts might at least benefit them indirectly. "Notwithstanding the languor of our direct trade with Europe," Madison told Thomas Jefferson in 1784, "this Country has indirectly tasted some of the fruits of Independence. The price of our last crop of Tobacco has been on James River from 36/ to 42/6 per" hundred pounds—about double the prewar price.[17] Madison spoke too soon, however, for the high 1784 price was *not* the result of competition between British tobacco buyers and the French captains that could now legally sail their ships into Chesapeake Bay. The real reason was that Europe still suffered from the tobacco shortage that had begun with nonexportation in 1775. As soon as tobacconists finished restocking their shelves, the price of tobacco plunged to its prewar level.

Although the Virginians' escape from the British mercantile system failed to raise the price of their tobacco or make their imports cheaper, it did allow the legislature to protect Virginians in various ways from British merchants. Legislation favoring Virginia shipowners helped them claim one-third of Virginia's international trade. Even more significant was the issue of debt collection. Initially, very few Virginians had expected the closing of the courts in 1774 or even the outbreak of war the following year to allow them to write off their debts. As the war dragged on and civilian losses mounted, however, many Virginians, especially smallholders in the Southside, believed that they should not have to pay the amounts that British merchants claimed they owed. "If we are now to pay the Debts due to British Merchants," George Mason heard several growers argue, "what have we been fighting for all this while?"[18] Many debtors had died or escaped to the south or west by the 1790s, when gentlemen finally overcame popular resistance to reopening the courts to British creditors' suits. A principal reason that many voters opposed the United States Constitution was that it would force Virginia courts to try British merchants' suits.[19]

The Revolutionary War also powerfully influenced the relationship between gentlemen and small farmers. Throughout the war, Virginia courts refused

---

rett B. Rutman, ed., *The Old Dominion: Essays for Thomas Perkins Abernethy* [Charlottesville, Va., 1964], 152–170).

17. Madison to Jefferson, Aug. 20, 1784, in Boyd et al., eds., *Papers of Jefferson*, VII, 402.

18. George Mason to Patrick Henry, May 6, 1783, in Robert A. Rutland, ed., *The Papers of George Mason* (Chapel Hill, N.C., 1970), II, 771; John Dawson to James Madison, Apr. 15, 1787, in William T. Hutchinson et al., eds., *The Papers of James Madison* (Charlottesville, Va., 1962–), IX, 381.

19. Charles F. Hobson, "The Recovery of British Debts in the Federal Circuit Court of

to try creditors' suits against debtors, which prevented debtors from undermining white solidarity by attacking creditors, sheriffs, courthouses, and jails. On the other hand, most of the problems that smallholders experienced during the first year of war—shortages, lack of income, and pressure to enlist in the army—only intensified as the conflict wore on. The most severe internal struggle resulting from the war was delayed until its conclusion. Military leaders had paid soldiers and purchased supplies with an array of bonds and promissory notes. The recipients sold many of these to speculators at a fraction of their official worth. After the war, gentlemen insisted that the state rapidly pay off the bondholders at face value. (Many of them held bonds; others were determined to create a favorable investment climate.) Members of the House of Delegates also wanted Virginia to pay the full amount that Congress requisitioned in order to pay off the speculators that held federal bonds, and they were eager to tax in the paper money that had helped to finance the war. Retiring the state and national debts and the paper money required taxes that bore heavily on small farmers; by November 1784, one Virginian believed the people of his state paid "greater Taxes than any people under the sun." These high taxes drew money out of the economy, and by 1785 they—in combination with other factors—had thrown Virginia into a recession.[20] When farmers proved unable to pay their taxes and private debts, sheriffs seized their property or the farmers themselves. When the House of Delegates adopted only minor tax relief and provided no relief at all to private domestic debtors, taxpayers and debtors recaptured

---

Virginia, 1790 to 1797," *VMHB*, XCII (1984), 176–200; Myra L. Rich, "Speculations on the Significance of Debt: Virginia, 1781–1789," *VMHB*, LXXVI (1968), 301–317; Emory G. Evans, "Private Indebtedness and the Revolution in Virginia, 1776 to 1796," *WMQ*, 3d Ser., XXVIII (1971), 349–374; Allan Kulikoff, *Tobacco and Slaves: The Development of Southern Cultures in the Chesapeake, 1680–1800* (Chapel Hill, N.C., 1986), 130–131; Norman K. Risjord, *Chesapeake Politics: 1781–1800* (New York, 1978). On the other hand, voters in the northwestern section of Virginia (the area that later became West Virginia) supported the Constitution in part *because* it would guarantee British merchants' right to sue their American debtors and thus remove the British government's principal justification for maintaining forts in the territory it had ceded to the United States in 1783. These forts supplied vital arms and ammunition to Native American warriors (Risjord, *Chesapeake Politics*, 109–116, 150–151, 293–295).

20. Michael A. McDonnell, "The Politics of Mobilization in Revolutionary Virginia: Military Culture and Political and Social Relations, 1774–1783" (D.Phil. thesis, Balliol College, Oxford University, 1995); John Francis Mercer to James Madison, Nov. 12, 1784, in Hutchinson et al., eds., *Papers of James Madison*, VIII, 135; Richard Henry Lee to [James Madison], Nov. 20, 1784, in James Curtis Ballagh, ed., *The Letters of Richard Henry Lee* (New York, 1911–1914), II, 300–301. Throughout the Chesapeake, "the deflationary policy of the state governments" produced "a scarcity of money" (Risjord, *Chesapeake Politics*, 163, 175).

seized property, burned their way out of prison, and organized collective resistance. The domestic conflicts of the 1780s were considerably more intense than those of the 1760s.[21]

In the formal political arena, gentlemen were concerned during the war that uneducated and unwealthy men had begun to infiltrate the legislature. For instance, George Mason complained that many "ignorant or obscure" men had won election to the legislature. Actually, Mason need not have worried. It is true that entail and primogeniture were abolished; also, the Anglican church was disestablished, and the poll tax was repealed.[22] Yet the move toward democracy was surprisingly limited. Under the state constitution adopted in 1776, the gentry-dominated legislature chose the governor. The justices that ruled the counties served life terms and filled vacancies within their ranks. (The governor almost always appointed the men that the sitting justices had recommended—just as he had during the colonial period.) The new constitution did *not* provide for the secret ballot or eliminate the property qualification for voting.[23] In the spring of 1776, pro-Independence gentlemen had assured conservatives that their class would continue to dominate Virginia even if it became a republic. Their confidence was not misplaced.

A person comparing the lists that Norfolk gentleman Matthew Phripp made of his slaves in 1774 and 1778 would notice the disappearance during that period of a man named Emanuel. It will be recalled that he was one of two slaves executed in Norfolk in April 1775 "for being concerned in a conspiracy to raise an insurrection in that town." Emanuel was not the only enslaved worker that disappeared from Phripp's plantation during the Revolutionary

21. Thomas Jefferson to Patrick Henry, Jan. 19, 1786, in William P. Palmer, ed., *Calendar of Virginia State Papers and Other Manuscripts*, IV, *1785–1789* (Richmond, Va., 1884), 82; Risjord, *Chesapeake Politics*, 101; Edmund Randolph to James Madison, Mar. 7, 1787, John Dawson to James Madison, Apr. 15, 1787, John Dawson to James Madison, [June 12, 1787], James McClurg to James Madison, Aug. 22, 1787, James Madison to Thomas Jefferson, Sept. 6, 1787, all in Hutchinson et al., eds., *Papers of James Madison*, IX, 303, 381, X, 47, 155, 164.

22. Selby, *Revolution in Virginia*, 140–141, 147. H. James Henderson argues that one of the most significant results of the American Revolution for farmers anywhere in America was the repeal of Virginia's tax to support ministers' salaries ("Taxation and Political Culture: Massachusetts and Virginia, 1760–1800," *WMQ*, 3d Ser., XLVII [1990], 110–111). In addition, the land tax was made more progressive. See Risjord, *Chesapeake Politics*, 100; Virginia Convention, "A Constitution . . . ," June 29, 1776, in *Revolutionary Virginia*, VII, pt. ii, 653; Richard R. Beeman, *The Old Dominion and the New Nation, 1788–1801* (Lexington, Ky., 1972), 29.

23. Beeman, *Old Dominion*, 33, 35.

War. Another was named James, and we know a little of his later life. When the British army and navy evacuated New York City in 1783, about three thousand slaves went with them. Before leaving, British navy captains made a list of their formerly enslaved passengers. On board the *Danger*, anchored near Staten Island (and not far from the little island where the Statue of Liberty would rise a century later), the compilers of the list made this entry: "James Tucker, 55 years, almost worn out . . . Formerly slave to Capt. [M.] Fipps, Norfolk, Virginia; left him in 1776 with Lord Dunmore."[24] When the *Danger* cleared out of New York Harbor, bound for Nova Scotia, James Tucker was on board. Tucker might be "almost worn out," and "Black Empire Loyalists" like him faced continuing discrimination in Nova Scotia, Sierra Leone, and other British colonies where they settled. But they had wrung a larger measure of freedom from the American Revolution than any of the white colonists that had rebelled against British policies regarding taxation, territory, and trade.

It could be argued that enslaved Virginians both gained and lost more than anyone else as a result of the American Revolution. Although historians estimate that at most a thousand black fugitives joined Governor Dunmore's army (and disease killed the majority of them within a year), thousands of additional slaves escaped during the remainder of the war. Some made the long journey to British headquarters in New York City. Others joined the British armies that landed in Virginia. Thomas Jefferson estimated, probably with considerable exaggeration, that thirty thousand enslaved Virginians escaped to the British in the single year 1781.[25]

What of those that stayed behind? Between 1782 and 1806, Virginia allowed slaveowners to emancipate their slaves without legislative approval, and some did so. Between 1790 and 1810, the state's free black population more than doubled, largely as a result of emancipation. George Washington provided in his will that his slaves be freed upon the death of his widow (after he died, Martha Washington, prudently deciding not to make the slaves' freedom contingent upon her death, freed them immediately). But only a small percentage of slaves were freed, and the Revolution left the majority of enslaved Virginians worse off than before. During the war, they

---

24. Dixon and Hunter's *VG*, Apr. 29, 1775 (supplement); Graham Russell Hodges, ed., *The Black Loyalist Directory: African Americans in Exile after the American Revolution* (New York, 1996), 198; Benjamin Quarles, *The Negro in the American Revolution* (Chapel Hill, N.C., 1961), 171–172.

25. Sylvia R. Frey, *Water from the Rock: Black Resistance in a Revolutionary Age* (Princeton, N.J., 1991), 211n. Some slaves fought on the American side; they could do so only with their owners' permission (Quarles, *Negro in the American Revolution*, chap. 4, 5).

suffered disproportionate material deprivation and lost numerous relatives and friends. An important result of the war was the elimination of British restrictions on expansion west from Virginia. Some slaveholders moved to the West and Southwest (Deep South) with their slaves; others remained in Virginia with some of their slaves and sold the rest to slave traders. Most of those "sold South" never saw their families again. Perhaps a million Upper South slaves suffered this fate between the Revolutionary War and the Civil War. In the 1810s alone, almost two-thirds of Chesapeake slaves were permanently separated from close relatives.[26]

The American Revolution ended disastrously for Native Americans, yielded mixed results for enslaved Virginians, and was less revolutionary for smallholders and tenants than historians once thought. While it is thus clear that in Virginia the gentry was the war's clearest victor, this work has shown that at the *other* end of the revolutionary struggle—its inception—elite Virginians were less prominent than we have been led to believe. There were no Indians or slaves—and few small farmers—among the convention delegates that gathered in the capitol in Williamsburg on May 15, 1776, to invite twelve of Virginia's sister colonies to join in a declaration of Independence. In a sense, though, these outsiders *were* present at the capitol that spring day. When the rulers of Britain's largest American colony took it into the American Revolution, they did so partly because they were feeling pressure from below.

26. Ira Berlin, "The Revolution in Black Life," in Alfred F. Young, ed., *The American Revolution: Explorations in the History of American Radicalism* (DeKalb, Ill., 1976), 360; Allan Kulikoff, "Uprooted Peoples: Black Migrants in the Age of the American Revolution, 1790–1820," in Ira Berlin and Ronald Hoffman, eds., *Slavery and Freedom in the Age of the American Revolution* (Charlottesville, Va., 1983), 155, 159, 167.

INDEX

Consumer revolution, 54, 84n, 88n
Continental Association (1774), 105, 107, 121–122, 132, 174–175, 212. *See also* Non-exportation, Nonimportation
Corbin, Richard, 148
Cotton, 103n
County courts, xviii, 216–218; and delay of debt suits, 112; closing of, 115–119, 125–126, 131–132, 180n, 212. *See also* Sheriffs
Craven County, N.C., 153
Creeks, 16; and war against Choctaws, 17n; and Shawnee and Cherokee diplomats, 22, 27n; and Tecumseh, 31n. *See also* Southern nations
Cresap, Michael, 34n
Cresswell, Nicholas, 175, 197
Croghan, George, 14, 18, 25–26
Cumberland (Cumbria), England, 39, 41
Cumberland County, Va., 39
Cuninghame and Company. *See* William Cuninghame and Company
Currency Act (1764), 62

Daingerfield, William, 43n
Dallis, Dennis, 139
Danger (vessel), 219
Dartmouth, Lord (William Legge), 27; and American veterans, 32, 35, 37; and Quebec Act, 33
Davidson, George, 12–13
Davidson, John, 117
Debt: and free Virginians, xix, 83, 126; and Navigation Acts, 50–51; and conspicuous consumption, 81–85; as threat to patri-archy, 82–83; and gentry relations with smallholders, 83; and nonimportation, 85–90, 100, 102–103; and nonexporta-tion, 126–129
Debtors, 208, 212, 214, 216–218; and prop-erty, xiv–xv, 97–98, 217; and frontier, 30; and attacks on creditors, 60, 97–98; and attacks on sheriffs, 61; jail escapes of, 61, 97–98, 217; and arson, 98
Declaration of Independence, 3, 39, 58n, 66, 73, 75, 77, 106, 133, 158, 191, 206, 209
Delawares, xix, 5, 21, 26, 38; and Wabash

River nations, 14–15. *See also* Upper Ohio Valley nations
Detroit, 6n, 162
Dickinson, John, 57n
Dinwiddie, Robert, 138, 140; and land bounty to Seven Years' War veterans, 29n
Dinwiddie County, Va., 98
"Dissenter from the Church of England, A" (pseudonym), 198
Donald, Robert, 112, 141
Dow, Jonathan, 174n
Dragging Canoe (Cherokee), 18
Drake, Francis, 140
Draper, William, 131, 140
Drayton, John, 154
Dulany, Daniel, 51n, 53n
Dumfries, Va., 109–110
Dunkard's Bottom, 8
Dunmore, fourth earl of (John Murray), 175, 181, 185, 208; on squatters, 30; and Seven Years' War veterans, 31; and Dun-more's War, 34–35; and dissolution of House of Burgesses, 117–119; and gun-powder removal incident, 143–152, 165, 209, 211; popularity of, 144; and Shawnee hostages, 148; and African American women, 152, 159; emancipation procla-mation issued by, 156–161, 191, 208, 214; demonization of, 158
Dunmore's War (1774), 33–34, 144, 176

"E. F." (pseudonym), 195
Eddis, William, 160n
Edinburgh, Scotland, 49
Emanuel (slave), 141–143, 218
Emigration. *See* Migration
Emistisiguo (Creek), 22
English Revolution, 47
Established Church. *See* Anglican Church
Estave, Andrew, 154–155
Ethiopian Regiment, 157, 161, 186, 214
Executive Council of Virginia, xviii, 11, 29n, 33, 35, 83, 159; and preliminary land grants, 7; and Hard Labor boundary, 13
"Experience" (pseudonym), 63–64